IN ISHMAEL'S HOUSE

BOOKS BY MARTIN GILBERT

THE CHURCHILL BIOGRAPHY

OTHER BOOKS

Jerusalem Illustrated History Atlas
Sir Horace Rumbold: Portrait of a Diplomat
Jerusalem: Rebirth of a City
Jerusalem in the Twentieth Century
Exile and Return: The Struggle for Jewish Statehood
Israel: A History
Auschwitz and the Allies
The Jews of Hope: The Plight of Soviet Jewry Today
Shcharansky: Hero of Our Time
The Holocaust: The Jewish Tragedy
The Boys: Triumph over Adversity
First World War
The Battle of the Somme: The Heroism and Horror of War
Second World War
D-Day
The Day the War Ended
In Search of Churchill
Churchill and America
Empires in Conflict: A History of the Twentieth Century, 1900–1933
Descent into Barbarism: A History of the Twentieth Century, 1934–1951
Challenge to Civilization: A History of the Twentieth Century, 1952–1999
Never Again: A History of the Holocaust
The Jews in the Twentieth Century: An Illustrated History
The Story of Israel
Letters to Auntie Fori: The 5,000-Year History of the Jewish People and Their Faith
The Righteous: The Unsung Heroes of the Holocaust
Kristallnacht: Prelude to Destruction

EDITIONS OF DOCUMENTS
Britain and Germany Between the Wars
Plough My Own Furrow: The Life of Lord Allen of Hurtwood
Servant of India: Diaries of the Viceroy's Private Secretary, 1905–1910
Winston Churchill and Emery Reves: Correspondence, 1937–1964

MARTIN GILBERT
IN ISHMAEL'S HOUSE
A HISTORY OF JEWS IN MUSLIM LANDS

YALE UNIVERSITY PRESS
NEW HAVEN AND LONDON

Published by arrangement with McClelland & Stewart Ltd, Toronto, Canada

For more information about this and other Yale University Press publications,
please contact:
U.S. Office: sales.press@yale.edu   www.yalebooks.com
Europe Office: sales@yale.co.uk   www.yalebooks.co.uk

Typeset in New Baskerville by M&S, Toronto
Printed in the United States of America.

Library and Archives Canada Cataloguing in Publication

Gilbert, Martin, 1936-
    Jews under Muslim rule : a 1,400-year history / Martin Gilbert.
    ISBN 978-0-7710-3369-8
    1. Jews – Islamic Empire – History. 2. Jews – Islamic countries – History.
    3. Judaism – Relations – Islam – History.
    4. Islam – Relations – Judaism – History. I. Title.
    BP173.J8G54 2010 296.3'97 C2009-906537-1

ISBN 978-0-300-16715-3

10 9 8 7 6 5 4 3 2 1

This book is dedicated
to the 13 million Jews and the 1,300 million Muslims in the world
in the hope that they may renew
in the Twenty-First Century
the mutual tolerance, respect and partnership
that marked many periods
in their history

CONTENTS

LIST OF PHOTOGRAPHS

LIST OF MAPS

ACKNOWLEDGEMENTS

The idea for this book came from the late Israel Asper, head of the Asper Foundation of Winnipeg, Canada, who, shortly before he died, suggested it as a topic for me. The trustees of the Asper Foundation took up his idea after his death and enabled me to pursue it by making available the resources of the Foundation. Their enthusiasm, and that of Moses Levy, Executive Director, and Jeffrey Morry, Senior Program Manager, of the Asper Foundation, has been a constant support. At no point has the Asper Foundation sought editorial control.

Throughout the course of my writing, the sustained encouragement and support of Sir Ronald Cohen and Sir Harry Solomon, two special friends, has meant a great deal to me, and has considerably enhanced the book. They have been an inspiration to me in telling this much-neglected story.

The originating publisher, McClelland & Stewart of Toronto, has been supportive from the outset. I am grateful to the company and its staff, and to Doug Pepper, Susan Renouf, Marilyn Biderman, Aruna Dahanayake, Anne Holloway and Chris Bucci, for helping produce this volume to the highest standards. My Canadian literary agent and friend, Michael Levine, has been a font of encouragement. Roy Bishko made an important contribution toward the preparation of the maps. The cartographer Tim Aspden, with his usual skill and patience, has turned my rough drafts into maps of the highest quality.

I am grateful to Yale University Press, both in New Haven and London, and in particular Robert Baldock and Heather Nathan, for making the book available to the rest of the English-speaking world.

I am grateful above all to those Jews, born in Muslim lands, who have helped me with my search for material and encouraged me in my task, among them: Dr. Ada Aharoni, Lord Alliance, Mordechai Ben-Porat, Mordechai Bibi, Samuel J. Cohen, Dr. Naim E. Dangoor OBE, Ellis Douek, Bertha Fattal, Shahnaz Keypour Feinstein, Robert Khalifa, Marc Khedr, Raphael N. Luzon, Naim S. Mahlab, Jacob and Odette Masliyah, Tania Pardo, Tony Rocca, Claudia Roden, Tova Murad Sadka, Professor Victor D. Sanua, Myriam Schechter Wolf, David R. Shama, Edwin Shuker, Vivianne M. Silver, Julian Sofaer, Eli Timan, Edna Turner (Anzarut), Suzy Vidal (Sultana Latifa), Regina Waldman (Bulbil), Ovadia Yerushalmy, Levana Zamir and Aida Zelouf.

The literature on the history of Jews in Arab and Muslim lands is vast. Books and articles, academic volumes and personal memoirs, have explored every one of the fourteen countries involved. They have also explored the themes that recur throughout the story of the age-old relationship of Jews and Muslims. I have tried to do justice to this large body of published work, without which no book can be written on the subject. The bibliography in this book reflects my own indebtedness, and that of the reader.

I am also indebted to those historians without whose pioneering work this book could not have been written, in particular: Michel Abitbol, Mark R. Cohen, W.J. Fischel, S.D. Goitein, H.Z. Hirschberg, David Levering Lewis, Maurice M. Roumani, Robert Satloff and Norman A. Stillman. Important suggestions as to form and content have been made by David Matas, Allan Levine and Stanley Urman.

Many people have sent me material or put me in touch with those who could. I would like to thank in particular: Hilary E. Appell, L.L. Amior, Barbara Barnett, Daniel Behar, Emily Blanck, David Cohen, Mark Durie, Oded Eran, Dan Gillerman, Nayim Güleryüz, Danna Harman, Rabbi Aubrey Hersh, General J.F.R. Jacob, Tammy and David Kovler, Douglas Krikler, John Krivine, Rabbi N.S. Liss, Roger E. Nixon, Yoni Ozdana, Orly Rahimyan, Ken Robbins, Tony Rocca, Debra Roth, Taffy Sassoon, Rabbi Barry Schlesinger, Ruth Schweitzer, Natalie Shamash, Margaret Shannon, Morey and Barbara Shapira, Linda Shapiro, Steven Solarz, Eri Steimatzky, Judy

Stoffman, Dr. Romeo Vecht, Enid Wurtman and Ben-Dror Yemini. I am grateful to Bat Ye'or, Andrew G. Bostom and David Littman for patiently answering my queries about their work. Judy Feld Carr talked to me about her efforts to free the Jews of Syria. Professor Paul translated for me Abraham ibn Ezra's ode on the Almohad persecutions. Professor Etan Kohlberg gave me the benefit of his extensive knowledge of early Islam.

For allowing me to use photographs in their collections, I am grateful to Beth Hatefutsoth Photo Archive, the Nahum Goldman Museum of the Diaspora, Tel Aviv; the Israel Museum, Jerusalem; Ada Aharoni, Gourji C. Bekhor, Naim Dangoor and Maurice Roumani.

For helping me to sort a mass of printed and manuscript material, I am grateful to my daughter, Natalie Gilbert, and to Ela Czernecka. I was helped, as always, in the considerable task of correspondence, organisation and follow-up by Kay Thomson. Throughout the preparation and writing of this book, my wife, Esther, has been a source of encouragement and wise guidance.

A NOTE ON TRANSLITERATION AND DATING

The transliteration of both Arabic and Hebrew has changed according to various systems during my lifetime. In quotations I have adhered to the style used by the author, translator or publisher. For consistency, I have used in the main text the following transliterations of the most frequently used words and names: Mohammed (Muhammad, Mahomet, etc.), Abdullah (Abdallah), Omar (Umar), Hanukah (Chanukah) and Koran (Qur'an).

The first year of the Muslim era – the year of Mohammed's emigration from Mecca to Medina – was the year 4,382 in the Jewish calendar and AD 622 in the Christian calendar, also known as the Common Era (CE). I have used the Common Era system for all dates.

Italicised Arabic and Hebrew words and phrases are listed in the Glossary.

INTRODUCTION

'Jews: remember Khaibar'

O n 7 August 2003, Amrozi bin Nurhasin, one of the 'Bali bombers,' entered a courtroom in Bali, Indonesia. He was appearing for sentencing, having been found guilty of causing the deaths of more than two hundred people, none of them Jews. With the world's media attention focused on him, in front of the judges and the cameras, he shouted out in Arabic: 'Jews: remember Khaibar. The army of Mohammed is coming back to defeat you.'[1]

1,375 years before this outburst in court, the Prophet Mohammed, leader of the new faith of Islam, achieved one of his first military victories. It was a victory, in the year 628, against a Jewish tribe living in the oasis of Khaibar, in the Arabian Peninsula. Historical Arab sources report that between six and nine hundred Jews were killed in the battle. The few Jews who remember this defeat today, do so when recalling what is for them their distant history. But for some Muslims, the battle at Khaibar resonates with meaning even today, as Amrozi bin Nurhasin made clear.

The modern resonance of Khaibar has often echoed with hostile attitudes towards the Jewish State of Israel. The historian Gideon Kressel witnessed this first-hand in Israel in the autumn of 1989, when a group of Bedouin explained to him over breakfast, 'in a calm and friendly manner,' that Israel would soon cease to exist; it

---

[1] Quoted by Martin Chulov in: 'The Plot to Blast Bali – The Verdict,' *The Australian*, 8 August 2003. Of the 202 people killed by the Bali bombers on 12 October 2002, the largest group was Australians (88), followed by Indonesians (38) and British (24).

was because 'that is God's will – nothing can change it.' The Bedouin also told Kressel that the Battle of Khaibar was a frequent talking point among them, as a result of radio broadcasts from Egypt, Jordan and Saudi Arabia.[2] During the course of his work among the Bedouin, Kressel often heard words similar to those later used by Amrozi in the Bali courtroom: '*Khaybar-Khaybar ya Yahud, Jaysh Muhammad sa ya'ud!*' ('Khaybar-Khaybar you Jews, Mohammed's army is about to return').[3]

On 16 October 2003, two months after the sentencing in Bali, a similar hope was expressed by the Malaysian Prime Minister, Mahathir Mohamad. The Prime Minister – who in 1986 had inaugurated an 'Anti-Jews Day'[4] – told the Tenth Islamic Summit Conference that '1.3 billion Muslims cannot be defeated by a few million Jews. . . . Surely the twenty-three years' struggle of the Prophet can provide us with some guidance as to what we can and should do.'[5]

Within three years, on 25 January 2006, the same sentiment received a boost on the West Bank and in Gaza, when Palestinian Arab voters cast a majority of their votes to Hamas, the Islamic Resistance Movement.[6] (Hamas received forty-four per cent of the vote, as against forty-one per cent for their nearest rival, Fatah.) The Hamas Charter, promulgated in 1988, looks forward to the implementation of 'Allah's promise,' however long it might take. It reads: 'The Prophet, prayer and peace be upon him, said: "The Day of Judgement will not come about until Moslems fight the Jews (killing the Jews), when the Jew will hide behind stones and trees.

---

[2] Gideon M. Kressel, 'What Actually Happened at Khaybar?' in A. Paul Hare and Gideon M. Kressel, *Israel As Centre Stage: A Setting for Social and Religious Enactments*, 2001.

[3] Gideon M. Kressel, letter to the author, 20 June 2009.

[4] Barbara Crossette, 'Malaysia Tightens Secrecy on Official Documents,' *New York Times*, 8 December 1986.

[5] 'Speech by Prime Minister Mahathir Mohamad of Malaysia to the Tenth Islamic Summit Conference, Putrajaya, Malaysia, 16 October 2003': Prime Minister's Office, Malaysia.

[6] Hamas is an acronym for the Arabic words *Harakat al-Muqawama al-Islamiyya* (Islamic Resistance Movement).

The stones and trees will say, 'O Moslems, O Abdullah, there is a Jew behind me, come and kill him.'"[7]

What does this age-old schism between Jews and Muslims mean for the modern world? What did it mean during the 1,400 years in which Jews lived in many lands under Muslim rule? In the Twelfth Century, six hundred years after the death of Mohammed, the Jewish sage Maimonides, known to Muslims as Musa ibn Maymun, gave his own answer to that question. Describing the situation of the Jews after five centuries of Muslim rule, he wrote: 'No nation has ever done more harm to Israel. None has matched it in debasing and humiliating us. None has been able to reduce us as they have.'[8] He was referring to the consequences of Islam's military expansion, which occurred rapidly from the time of Mohammed in the Seventh Century onwards.

The conquests of Islam made Jews the subjects of Arab and Muslim rulers in a wide swathe of land, stretching from the Atlantic coast of Morocco to the Hindu Kush mountains of Afghanistan.[9] Being non-Muslims, these Jews held the inferior status of *dhimmi*, which, despite giving them protection to worship according to their own faith, subjected them to many vexatious and humiliating restrictions in their daily lives. The same conditions were imposed on all Christians under Muslim rule, and when Islam's conquests reached the Indian subcontinent, Hindus too were forced to accept *dhimmi* status.[10]

Yet there has also been another side to this tale of debasement and humiliation. At the end of the Twentieth Century, Bernard Lewis, a lifelong student of Jews and Islam and himself a Jew, reflected on the fourteen centuries of Jewish life under Islamic rule, eight centuries after Maimonides' damning verdict. Lewis wrote: 'The Jews were never

[7] MidEast Web Historical Documents, 'Hamas Charter, The Covenant of the Islamic Resistance Movement (Hamas) 18 August 1988.' The quotation goes on to say that there is one tree that will not call out to reveal that Jews are hiding there, the Gharkad tree, 'because it is one of the trees of the Jews.' www.mideastweb.org/hamas.htm

[8] 'Maimonides' Epistle to the Jews of Yemen,' in Norman A. Stillman, *The Jews of Arab Lands: History and Source Book*, page 241.

[9] For a map of the conquests of Islam by AD 750, and some of the towns within that area with large Jewish communities, see Map 1, page 356.

[10] Elliott A. Green, 'The Forgotten Oppression of Jews Under Islam and in the Land of Israel,' *Midstream*, September/October 2008.

free from discrimination, but only rarely subject to persecution.' He noted that the situation of Jews living under Islamic rulers was 'never as bad as in Christendom at its worst, nor ever as good as in Christendom at its best.' Lewis observed that 'there is nothing in Islamic history to parallel the Spanish expulsion and Inquisition, the Russian pogroms, or the Nazi Holocaust.' But he also commented that, on the other hand, there was nothing in the history of Jews under Islam 'to compare with the progressive emancipation and acceptance accorded to Jews in the democratic West during the last three centuries.'[11]

These two perspectives on the situation of Jews living under Muslim rule in the *Dar al-Islam* (the 'World of Islam') will be examined in this book from a historical point of view. The focus will be the Jews themselves: men and women who strived to become an integral, productive and accepted part of the countries in which they lived, and whose loyalty was to the local power, which, sadly, often turned against them. The narrative begins with the rise of Islam in the Seventh Century and continues until the present day. It includes the fateful impact of Zionism from 1897 onwards, the emergence of the State of Israel in 1948, and the experiences of Jews who were living in Arab and Muslim lands when Israel came into being; 850,000 of these Jews were forced to leave their homes and countries, driven out by persecution and hatred. The United Nations' offer of statehood to Jews and Arabs in Palestine caused a violent reaction in the Arab world, which in turn prompted a mass Jewish exodus, spread over nearly two decades. The migration was later intensified by the Arab-Israeli war of 1948-9, Israel's War of Independence, during which 726,000 Palestinian Arabs also became refugees.[12]

---

[11] Bernard Lewis, *Semites and Anti-Semites*, pages 121-22.
[12] The Palestine Conciliation Committee (supported by the United Nations) gave the figure of 711,000 Arab refugees. The figure given by UNRWA (United Nations Relief and Works Agency for Palestine Refugees in the Middle East), confirmed by the United Nations Economic Survey Mission in 1949, was 726,000. As of 30 June 2008, UNRWA gave the figure of 1,373,732 Palestinian refugees (the original refugees and their descendants) in UNRWA-administered camps and a total of 4,671,811 Palestinian Arabs registered with UNRWA as refugees (the original refugees and their descendants born outside Israel).

I am an Ashkenazi Jew with my family roots in the Russian Empire of the Tsars. I have always tried to make the story of Jews living under Muslim rule an integral part of my writings on Jewish history. In my *Atlas of the Holocaust*, I mapped the birthplaces of several thousand Jews born in the wide sweep of land from Morocco to Iraq who, because they were living in western Europe in 1939, were caught up in the destruction of the Second World War, deported to Auschwitz and murdered there.[13] In 1976, I outlined the story of Jews from Arab lands in a fifteen-map illustrated atlas, *The Jews of Arab Lands: Their History in Maps*.[14] In my letters on Jewish history to my adopted aunt in India, published as *Letters to Auntie Fori: The 5,000-Year History of the Jewish People and Their Faith*, I included seven letters about Jews of Muslim lands.[15]

This book tells the story of the Jews who lived at different times in fourteen Muslim-ruled countries. Those countries are Afghanistan, Algeria, the Bukharan Khanate in Central Asia (now Uzbekistan), Egypt, Iraq (formerly Babylonia and then Mesopotamia, and including Kurdistan), Iran (formerly Persia), Lebanon, Libya (Tripolitania and Cyrenaica), Morocco, Ottoman Turkey, Palestine (when under Muslim rule), Syria, Tunisia and Yemen, including Aden.

Three aspects of the story are interwoven, and I have given them equal weight. The first is the historical narrative, with its chronological sweep and wide range of countries, cities and personalities. The second is the documentary evidence as preserved over the centuries: the archival record of governments and institutions. The third is the human voice of those individuals whose stories make up the narrative: the actual words of participants and eyewitnesses, as preserved in letters, poems, memoirs and oral testimony. History is the collective story of myriad individuals.

With its successes and achievements, its moments of pain and

---

[13] Martin Gilbert, *Atlas of the Holocaust*, Maps 159, 226 and 245.
[14] Martin Gilbert, *The Jews of Arab Lands: Their History in Maps*. London: Board of Deputies of British Jews, 1976.
[15] Martin Gilbert, *Letters to Auntie Fori: The 5,000-Year History of the Jewish People and Their Faith*, Letters 47-50, 57, 72 and 97.

persecution, the 1,400-year story of Jews living under the rule of Islam is an integral part of the history of every Arab and Muslim nation concerned. It is also a part of the wider Jewish historical narrative, and of Jewish heritage. It is a story of communities and individuals often under stress and facing difficult restrictions. It is the story of the Jewish contribution to the welfare and well-being of Arab and Muslim countries. And it is the story of a sometimes unstable and frequently changing relationship between Jews and Muslims that held the prospect of fear and terror as well as hope and opportunity for many millions of Jews.

According to both Jewish and Muslim traditions, Jews and Arabs were descended from Abraham, whose elder son Ishmael was sent out into the desert, and whose younger son Isaac remained with his father. It was Isaac's son Jacob who was given the name Israel. According to the Book of Genesis, when Abraham died, Isaac and Ishmael together buried him in the Cave of Machpelah. The descendants of Ishmael are named in Genesis, where they are described as twelve chieftains. Isaac's son Jacob had twelve sons, the twelve tribes of Israel, who are also named. The descendants of Isaac and of Ishmael who lived a thousand years later in the lands ruled by Ishmael's descendants – in Ishmael's house – were Semites with a common ancient ancestry.

Martin Gilbert
7 March 2010

BEFORE ISLAM

'A prince of Himyar'

For more than a thousand years before Mohammed's birth in the year 570, Jews lived in what were to become – with Mohammed and his followers' conquests – Muslim lands. These lands stretched from Spain to Afghanistan, and were inhabited by Arabs, Persians, Turks, Berbers and Jews. They included the great Jewish religious academies of Sura and Pumbeditha (now Faluja in present-day Iraq), two cities that were at the centre of Jewish religious thought and ethics, and where the Babylonian Talmud was compiled more than two thousand years ago.

Across this wide swathe of land, Jewish graves of great antiquity have been found. In the Tunisian city of Carthage, Jewish gravestone inscriptions date from 813 BCE (Before the Common Era). Yemeni tradition also holds that a group of prosperous Jews arrived in Yemen from Jerusalem as early as 629 BCE, after they heard the Prophet Jeremiah predict the destruction of the Jewish Temple. It is possible that the migration of Jews to Yemen began even earlier. When Yemen was ruled by the Queen of Sheba in 900 BCE, the trading and naval networks established by King Solomon brought Jews from Judaea to Yemen, a journey of 1,400 miles.

Jerusalem, which came under Muslim rule for the first time in the year 638 CE, had formed a focal point of Jewish life for more than a millennium before the dawn of Islam. It had been the Jewish capital for more than six hundred years when it was conquered by the Babylonians in 587 BCE. The city also became the centre of a Jewish kingdom, ruled by Jewish kings, for seventy-eight years from

141 BCE to 63 BCE. Some of Jerusalem's rulers at other times, including the Romans and the Seleucid Greek Antiochus IV, turned against the Jews; others, including Alexander the Great and the Ptolemys of Egypt, allowed Jewish life to flourish.

When the King of Persia, Cyrus the Great, defeated the Babylonians in 539 BCE, he liberated the Jews of Jerusalem. Some of the 'freed slaves' – who were no longer forced to worship idols – began to rebuild their Temple, which had been destroyed forty-two years after the Prophet Jeremiah's prediction. Others went eastward to settle in Persia. Among their descendants a hundred years later were Esther and her cousin Mordecai, who forestalled an attempt by the Grand Vizier, Haman, to exterminate the entire Persian Jewish community.[1]

Similar migrations and resettlements occurred elsewhere, sending Jews to far-flung corners of those lands later conquered by Islam in the Seventh and Eighth Centuries. The Babylonian King Nabonidus brought Jewish exiles to Tayma, an oasis in modern-day Saudi Arabia, when he established his capital there a thousand years before the rise of Islam.[2] Tomb inscriptions also confirm that Jews lived in the Arabian towns of al-Hijr (Mada'in Salih) and al-Ula five hundred years before Mohammed's birth.[3] Likewise, in 312 BCE, the ruler of Egypt, Ptolemy Lagos, settled Jews in Cyrenaica – present-day Libya – as a way of strengthening his kingdom. Inscriptions in Benghazi

---

[1] Esther's tomb in the Iranian city of Hamdan is surrounded by Jewish graves, as Jews considered the area around her tomb to be holier than the main Jewish cemetery. The tomb's majestic brick dome dates back to 1602. Houman Sarshar (editor), *Esther's Children: A Portrait of Iranian Jews*, pages xviii, 23 and 25.

[2] The historian Charles C. Torrey believes that even before Nabonidus, who ruled from 555 to 539 BCE, Jewish traders had settled in the oasis towns of the Hedjaz, including the city of Yathrib (Medina). Charles C. Torrey, *The Jewish Foundation of Islam*, pages 10 and 17-18.

[3] An inscription on a sundial at al-Hijr mentions a Jew, Menasha bar Nathan Shelam, who may have been the astronomer who owned the sundial or the craftsman who carved it. The Roman general Aelius Gallus also found Jews living at al-Hijr on his way to conquer Yemen in 25 BCE. The Babylonian Talmud (late Fourth, early Fifth Century) mentions a certain Anan ben Hiyya of Hijra (Tractate Yevamot: 116a), who appears with regard to a discussion of a bill of divorce found in the Babylonian city of Sura.

and in other places across Libya show a wealthy, well-established, well-organised Jewish community living there in 146 BCE, at the start of Roman rule.[4]

In those parts of the Roman Empire that were later conquered by Arabs and brought under Muslim rule, including the whole of North Africa, as well as Syria and Egypt, Jews lived and often flourished as farmers and traders. But living as part of the *Pax Romana* did not preclude further migrations for the Jews. In 25 BCE, King Herod was installed by the Romans as the ruler of the province of Judaea, which had its capital in Jerusalem. Herod, the son of a convert to Judaism, sent a Jewish military force to establish Roman control in Yemen. The expedition was a failure, but some of the soldiers remained and settled there to form the southernmost Jewish community of Roman times.

A notable Jew who also travelled out of Judaea was Rabbi Akiva, the Jewish scholar and leader, who journeyed with others from Jerusalem to Carthage in order to teach there among the many renowned rabbis. The Jews did not always migrate from Judaea by choice in Roman times. When the Romans destroyed Jerusalem and the Temple in 70 CE – following a failed Jewish revolt – they expelled an estimated thirty thousand Jews from their ancient homeland. These deportees were sent to North Africa.

The Roman-Jewish historian Josephus recounted that a similar fate was handed to Jews held captive after Bar Kokhba's failed Jewish revolt in 136 CE. According to Josephus, twelve boatloads of Jewish captives were deported from Judaea to Cyrenaica, where half a million Jews were already living at that time. He wrote that most of the Cyrenaican Jews lived in farming villages, while those living by the sea were often sailors, and many others were potters, stonemasons, weavers and merchants.[5] The new arrivals in Cyrenaica were among as many as a million Jews who were forced to leave Judaea, renamed

---

[4] Maurice M. Roumani, *The Jews of Libya*, page 2.
[5] Josephus, quoted in Maurice M. Roumani, *The Jews of Libya*, page 2. Yosef Ben Matityahu – Joseph, son of Matthias – was known as Titus Flavius Josephus after he became a Roman citizen.

'Syria Palaestina' by the Romans in 132 CE – its coins engraved with the words 'Judaea Capta.'

In 115 CE the Jews of Cyrenaica had revolted against the Romans, with similar results. Josephus recalled that, after the revolt was crushed, the Roman Governor Catullus murdered 'all the wealthier Jews to the number of three thousand, and confiscated all their possessions.'[6] It was in response to this violent repression that many Cyrenaican Jews fled deep into the Sahara and lived there among the Berber tribes, some of whom they later converted to Judaism. Ironically, it was a Cyrenaican Jew, Mark – the St. Mark of the Gospels – who converted to Christianity and founded the Coptic Church, introducing Christianity to Africa.

Among the many new homelands for Jews who migrated in this period, Persia, known today as Iran, was one of the most significant. In 226 CE, King Shahpur I founded the Sasanian Empire there. Jews are reported to have held high-ranking positions in the empire's society and government. During the four hundred years of Sasanian rule, Persian Jews were among those who wrote the Babylonian Talmud, a crucial repository of Jewish theology and law to this day.[7]

Displaced Jews also enlarged the Yemeni Jewish community, particularly after Bar Kokhba's revolt prompted the first significant Jewish migration from Judaea to Yemen. Jews were consummate traders, and Yemen was then famous throughout the Graeco-Roman world for its prosperous trade, especially in spices.[8] Dominating the southern end of the Red Sea, Yemen was a focal point for both seaborne trade and the overland routes from southwestern Arabia. The first written evidence of a Jewish presence in Yemen dates to the Third Century CE. The Jews' proficiency in trade had led them to the northern extremity of the Red Sea as well – to the twin islands of Tiran and Sanapir in the Straits of Tiran, which were for many years Jewish islands.[9]

---

[6] Josephus, *The Jewish War* (Penguin Books edition), page 408.
[7] Houman Sarshar (editor), *Esther's Children: A Portrait of Iranian Jews*, pages xviii-xix.
[8] Itzhak Ben-Zvi, *The Exiled and the Redeemed*, page 23.
[9] Bernard Lewis, *The Middle East*, pages 44-45.

In the Fifth Century, Yemen adopted Judaism as its religion. King Ab Karib As'ad, the ruler of the Himyarite kingdom, introduced the change after converting to Judaism himself under the influence of Jews at his court. Many south Arabian converts to Judaism followed; Jewish rule in Yemen lasted almost a hundred years.

The most famous Hebrew King of Yemen, Yusuf Asar, came to the throne in 515 CE. He was a religious man known to the Arabs as Dhu Nuwas ('the man with the hanging locks'), and his rule in Yemen has been described as heralding a 'Golden Age' for local Jews and Arabs alike.[10] But his reign was not lacking in outward violence and conflict. Citing the persecution of Jews in Christian Byzantium, Dhu Nuwas attacked the Christian stronghold of Najran and massacred all those who would not renounce Christianity. Then, only ten years after ascending to the throne, Dhu Nuwas was defeated by Christians from Ethiopia, allies of the Christian empire of Byzantium. Yemen, along with the Jewish islands of Tiran and Sanapir, fell under Byzantine rule.

Within the Roman Empire in the years before Islam, hundreds of thousands of Jews made their way, by ship and overland, to new homes as far west as Spain and North Africa, as far north as the Swiss Alps, as far east as the shores of the Black and Caspian Seas, and as far south as Yemen. In their new homelands – known as the Diaspora or *galut* (exile) – these Jews built up communities where, during the three hundred years before the spread of Christianity, and the five hundred years before the rise of Islam, they maintained their faith, customs and traditions. Although they adopted local languages in their daily life and work, they preserved Hebrew as the language of literacy and prayer. They settled across a vast geographic region, and yet they retained a strong bond of connection through their religion: the belief in one God, the laws and ethical code of the Torah, and the devotion to prayer, self-help, family and community.

---

[10] David Levering Lewis, *God's Crucible*, page 25.

Jews also maintained strong ties to their ancient Judaean home-land. Yemeni Jews made great efforts to return to Judaea when bur-ying their dead, sometimes embarking on a journey across the deserts of Arabia that would take at least sixty days by caravan. In the Jewish cemetery at Beth Shearim, in the Jezreel Valley, four burial chambers were discovered in 1936 with wooden, stone and lead sarcophagi that had been brought there from Yemen. The cemetery had been in use until the late Fourth Century. On one sarcophagus was an inscription in the southern Arabian alphabet that read: 'A prince of Himyar.'[11]

Starting in 325, Judaea – as part of 'Palaestina' – was ruled for nearly three hundred years by the Christian emperors of Byzantium, whose capital was eight hundred miles away in Constantinople. The Jews of Jerusalem decided to join forces with the Persians in 614 to besiege Jerusalem and free it from Christian rule. When the Persian Army defeated the Byzantines they handed Jerusalem back to the Jews. It remained under Jewish rule for fifteen years. But in 629, Jerusalem was retaken by the Byzantine Emperor Heraclius, an Armenian Christian, and again the Jews were banished.

During his nine-year rule over Jerusalem, Heraclius carried out a campaign of vengeance against the Jews. He decreed the forcible conversion of Jews to Christianity in all the European and Asian territories of the Byzantine Empire, and in 632 – the year of Mohammed's death – he extended that conversion decree to North Africa. It was not until Arab Muslims conquered Jerusalem in 638 that the Jews were allowed to return to the city and to practise their faith. At that time, Heraclius was about to begin the Jews' forcible conversion in North Africa. But as the historian H.Z. Hirschberg writes, it was precisely at this moment that 'Arab tribes sallied forth from the desert with the slogan "There is no God but Allah, and Mohammed is the Messenger of Allah," which welded them into one people and a militant religious community.' This formidable

----

[11] Itzhak Ben-Zvi, *The Exiled and the Redeemed*, page 24.

military force 'swept Heraclius and his army from most of the areas in Asia, invaded Egypt and set their eyes on the fertile places of North Africa and Spain.'[12]

Help was at hand for the Jews persecuted in Christian lands.

---

[12] H.Z. (J.W.) Hirschberg, *A History of the Jews in North Africa,* page 59.

THE PROPHET MOHAMMED AND THE JEWS

'We will allow you to remain in this land as long as it pleases us.'

Mohammed, the founder of Islam, was born in the Arabian city of Mecca in 570. His first biographer, Ibn Ishak, wrote that at the time of Mohammed's birth, a Jew from the Arabian oasis of Yathrib stood on the roof of a house and 'called forth the Jewish people.' When a crowd gathered around the man and asked him, 'Woe to you. What is the matter?' he told them: 'This night the star has risen, under which the apostle is born.'[1]

The idea of an apostle was not new to Arabia. At the time of Mohammed's birth, some of the Arab tribes living in and around the central oases of the Arabian Peninsula were monotheistic, as a result of both Jewish and Christian influence. Other Arab tribes worshipped multiple gods, such as the moon goddess al-Lat, the fertility goddess al'Uzza and the goddess of fate Manat. Mecca was the centre for this idolatry; once Mohammed had founded his monotheistic faith and made some forty converts, he encountered opposition from the merchants of Mecca, whose livelihood depended on the city's pagan rites and sites.[2]

---

[1] Ibn Ishak, 'Sirat Rasul Allah,' published as *The Life of Mohammed, Apostle of Allah*, Alfred Guillaume (translator), pages 17-18. Mohammed ibn Ishak ibn Yasar, a compiler of oral recollections about the Prophet Mohammed, was born in Medina in 704 and died in Baghdad in either 761 or 767. He wrote 'Sirat Rasul Allah' a century and a half after Mohammed's birth.

[2] Mecca's pagan sites were dominated by the *Ka'bah*, a shrine housing the 'great black meteor.' According to Islamic tradition, following Mohammed's return to Mecca in 630, Allah gave Adam a bright, pure white stone to bring to Earth from Paradise. This stone was called *al-Hajar-ul-Aswad*, 'the Black Stone,' and was also

The merchants of Mecca plotted to kill Mohammed, and his own Quraysh tribe – which dominated Mecca – turned against him. In 622, Mohammed left the city and travelled with his followers – the Companions, or Believers – to Yathrib, where the local Arabs had been receptive to his monotheistic message because of their contact with Jews. In Yathrib, Mohammed raised the banner of his own religious beliefs. For this reason, Yathrib became known as Medina: *Madinat al-Nabi*, 'the City of the Prophet.'[3] Mohammed's journey from Mecca to Medina was the *hijra* – a journey to escape danger – and marks the first year of the Islamic calendar.

For more than five hundred years before Mohammed's journey to Medina, the Arab tribes of the Arabian Peninsula had known the Jews well. Throughout Arabia, Jews were respected for being skilled craftsmen, metal workers and jewellers, as well as for the quality of the dates grown on their plantations. A generation before Mohammed, one of the best-known poets of the peninsula was Samuel ben Adiya, a Jew known as the 'King of Tayma,' who wrote some of the finest heroic Arabic battle poetry.

As Mohammed was growing up, Jewish tribes were living in all the major Arabian towns, including Tayma, Medina and Khaibar. Twenty Jewish tribes lived in the peninsula, three of them in Medina.[4] In the words of the Jewish historian H.Z. Hirschberg, Jewish tribes had 'lived for generations' in the region where Mohammed began his preaching. Hirschberg points out that two of the leading Arab tribes at Medina, the Banu al-Aws and the Banu Khazraj, were at one time vassals of the Jewish tribes.[5]

Among the Jews of Medina were the Banu (or children of) Nadir, the Banu Qaynuqa and the Banu Qurayzah.[6] The Nadir and Qaynuqa

---

known as 'the Happiest Stone' – because it alone had been chosen of all the stones in Paradise.

[3] Also known as *al-Madinah al-Munawwarah*: 'The enlightened city' or 'the radiant city.'

[4] See Map 2, page 357.

[5] H.Z. (J.W.) Hirschberg, 'Arabia,' *Encyclopaedia Judaica*, Volume 3, columns 232-6.

[6] The Jewish Qurayzah tribe is not to be confused with Mohammed's Arab tribe, the Quraysh, who were then idol worshippers.

believed they were of Jewish priestly origin, the descendants of Aaron, although their origins are unclear. They were either descendants of exiles who fled Judaea after the revolt against Rome in 70 CE, or a pagan Arab tribe that had converted to Judaism several centuries before Mohammed, or a mixture of both exiles and converts. By the Seventh Century, the Nadir spoke a dialect of Arabic and had adopted Arabic names.

Settling in Medina, Mohammed preached his beliefs to all the local religious groups, including pagan Arab tribes like the Banu al-Aws and the Banu Khazraj. He told them that God was one and that he, Mohammed, was God's Prophet. He rejected the already five-hundred-year-old Christian doctrine of the Trinity – the Father, the Son and the Holy Ghost – stating that 'Unbelievers are those who say, "Allah is the Messiah, the son of Mary." . . . Unbelievers are those who say, "Allah is one of three." There is but one God. If they do not desist from so saying, those of them that disbelieve shall be sternly punished.'[7]

In contrast, Mohammed's preaching revealed that he believed in the same attributes of God as did the Jews. The one God – *al-Ilah* (*Allah*) – was the true God, the creator of the world, the God of justice and mercy, before whom every human being bore personal responsibility. Mohammed, like the Jews, also considered Abraham the founder of monotheism. He saw Moses as a predecessor; the Koran – the record of Mohammed's teachings and the holy book of Islam – quoted Moses more than a hundred times.[8]

Mohammed even adopted the Jewish traditions of praying in the direction of Jerusalem, of common Friday midday worship in preparation for the Sabbath day, and of fasting on the tenth day of each new year. In the latter case, the Jewish Day of Atonement (Yom Kippur)

---

[7] Koran 5:72-73.

[8] In the Koran, verse 20 of Sura Five states: 'Call to mind when Moses said to his people, "O my people, recall the favour that Allah bestowed upon you when he appointed Prophets among you and made you Kings, and gave you that which He had not given to any other of the peoples."' The Sura then quotes what it describes as the words of Moses: '"O my people, enter the Holy Land which Allah has ordained for you, and do not turn back, for in that case you will turn back losers."'

provided the model for the Muslim fast of Ashura. The word *Ashura* is reminiscent of the Hebrew word *asor* – ten – and quite early on, Ashura was fixed on the tenth day of the Muslim calendar, following the Jewish example of observing Yom Kippur ten days after the Jewish New Year.[9] Similarly, although Mohammed and his followers had prayed only twice a day in Mecca, they followed the Jewish example in Medina by introducing a third prayer at midday.[10]

Mohammed's views on modesty, on charity, on communal self-help and on strict dietary laws – essential in a desert climate – were similar to Jewish practices.[11] He adopted the Jewish ritual of circumcision, which for Jews represented the entry of every male child into the Covenant of Abraham. Because of these similarities in beliefs and lifestyle, Mohammed did not envisage a problem in winning over Jews to his prophetic vision. The word *Islam* is Arabic for 'submission' – denoting the submission of the believer to God. The Jews had already submitted to one God. *Muslim*, the active participle of the word *Islam*, is a person who has submitted, as the Jews already had done.

In response to the rejection of Islam by many of Medina's Arab tribes, Mohammed drew up a military pact to help win allies for his new faith. According to Muslim tradition the articles of the pact concerning Jews proposed a firm alliance: 'Jews who follow us shall be given aid and equality; they shall not be oppressed, nor shall aid be given to others against them.' The Jews were considered to be of 'one community with the Believers (but they shall have their own religion as Believers have theirs). There shall be mutual aid between Jews and Believers, in the face of any who war against those who subscribe to this document, and mutual consultations and advice.' Mutual aid would be given 'by the Believers and Jews against any who attack Medina. If the Jews are called upon by the Believers to make peace,

---

[9] For Shiite Muslims, the tenth day of Muharram carries a different meaning: according to Shiite tradition, Mohammed's grandson Husayn and members of his entourage fell in battle on this day in the year 680. Ashura is thus a day of mourning for all Shiite Muslims.

[10] Carl Brockelmann, *History of the Islamic Peoples*, pages 21-2.

[11] The Jewish and Muslim laws for slaughtering meat – *kashrut* and *halal* – are almost identical.

they must comply; and if the Believers are called upon by the Jews to
make peace, they must agree, except in the case of a holy war.'[12]

Whatever the truth about this much-quoted pact, the Jewish
tribes of Medina put up a strong resistance to Islam. One of
Mohammed's leading opponents, Ka'b ibn-Ashraf, a poet of mixed
Arab-Jewish descent, embraced his mother's Judaism and composed
verses against Islam, encouraging Mohammed's own Quraysh tribe
to fight against him. Such opposition from the Jews grew further in
624, when Mohammed's followers defeated a larger Quraysh force at
the oasis of Wadi Badr, twenty miles south of Mecca. This was where
caravans transporting goods from Gaza for Quraysh merchants made
their final water stop before reaching Medina.

The battle at Badr prompted Ka'b to travel to Mecca and write
even more verses against Islam, urging the Quraysh to avenge their
dead. It also led the Jewish Qaynuqa tribe to join forces with the
Arab Quraysh tribe. Mohammed decided to speak to the Jews face-
to-face. Visiting them in their section of Medina, he urged the Jews
to accept him as a Prophet – a messenger of God and a bearer of
prophetic warnings within the Jewish tradition. The Koran mentions
his efforts in Sura Five – one of its 114 suras, or chapters – which
addresses the Jews directly: 'People of the Book, there has come to
you Our Messenger' – Mohammed – 'who makes things clear to you
after a break in the succession of Prophets, lest you should say:
"There has come to us no bearer of glad tidings and no warner."
Now there has come to you a bearer of glad tidings and a warner.'[13]

For the Jews of Medina, however, as for most Jews, the era of
prophets, with their warnings, exhortations and visions, was long
over. The last Hebrew prophet, Malachi, had died a thousand years
earlier. According to Jewish tradition, the seal of prophecy was only
to be renewed with the return of the Jews to Zion. 'O Mohammed' –
the Jews are reported to have told him – 'you seem to think that
we are your people. Do not deceive yourself because you have

---

[12] Ibn Ishak, 'Sirat Rasul Allah,' published as *The Life of Mohammed, Apostle of Allah,*
Alfred Guillaume (translator), pages 76-7.
[13] Koran 5:19, Muhammad Zafrulla Khan (translator), *The Quran,* page 102.

encountered a people' – at Badr – 'who have no knowledge of war and got the better of them; for my God if we fight you, you will find that we are real men!'[14]

Internal Koranic evidence shows that the Jews of Medina were steeped in rabbinical tradition. While celebrating him as an unlearned person, the *hadith* acknowledges that Mohammed was confounded by the learned questions of these Jews. He is said to have answered them with the words, 'You have concealed what you were ordered to make plain,' thus rebuking the Jews for failing to share their religious revelation with him.[15] The Koran presents Jews as having fallen into divine disfavour on account of their disobedience. It states that Jews have blasphemed twice in their history, the second time being when they told Mohammed, 'We do believe in that which has been sent down to us.' The Koran notes: 'Thus they incurred wrath upon wrath, and for such disbelievers there is humiliating chastisement.'[16]

A few days after Mohammed was rebuffed by the Jews, there was an incident in the Qaynuqa market, where, according to Muslim tradition, a Jewish goldsmith was said to have played a trick on a Muslim woman by pinning the back of her skirt to her upper garments, so that when she stood up she exposed herself. Fighting broke out. A Jew and a Muslim were killed. Mohammed, in his official capacity as a judge of disputes, was called in to arbitrate. The Jews refused to accept his arbitration and barricaded themselves in their fortress. The Qaynuqa, hoping to rally Mohammed's Arab opponents against him, called for support but found themselves alone, without allies.

Mohammed acted quickly, attacking the Qaynuqa stronghold, besieging it and demanding that the Jews surrender. This they did.

---

[14] Ibn Ishak, 'Sirat Rasul Allah,' published as *The Life of Mohammed, Apostle of Allah,* Alfred Guillaume (translator), page 309.

[15] Albert Hourani, *A History of the Arab Peoples,* page 18.

[16] Koran 2:92. Muhammad Zafrulla Khan (translator), *The Quran,* pages 16-7. According to the Koran, the first instance of the Jews' blasphemy occurred when Moses brought the Tablets of the Law – the Ten Commandments – down from Mount Sinai to find the Jews worshipping a golden calf: 'Moses came to you with manifest signs, yet you took the calf for worship in his absence, because you were transgressors.'

It was Mohammed's first victory over the Jews. A former Arab ally of
the Jews, Abdallah ibn Ubayy, a member of the Khazraj tribe and a
recent convert to Islam, interceded with Mohammed on the Jews'
behalf. The Prophet agreed to save their lives, but he insisted on
expelling the Qaynuqa from Medina. While the two other Jewish
tribes remained in the city, all the Qaynuqa lands and part of their
possessions were taken by the Muslims. The Qaynuqa themselves
took refuge with another Jewish tribe in the Wadi al-Qura.

In the face of such unexpected opposition, Mohammed redoubled
his efforts to provide security for his new faith. He was distressed by
the hostile verses of the poet Ka'b ibn-Ashraf, who, according to later
Muslim tradition, had sought to inflame the Nadir Jewish tribe against
Mohammed. Ka'b had earlier returned to Medina, where he continued to write inflammatory verses. On Mohammed's orders he was
assassinated there in 625. The Nadir Jewish leaders went to Mohammed
to protest at the murder of one of their prominent men. Mohammed
responded that although he allowed dissident thoughts and opinions,
he would not allow seditious and treasonable action in violation of his
pact with the Jews.

The Nadir were not intimidated. Later that year, under the leadership of Huyayy ibn Akhtab, they allied themselves with the Bedouin
chief Abu Bara, another of Mohammed's opponents. At the Battle of
Uhud, sixty-five Muslims and twenty-two Meccans were killed. Shortly
after the battle, Mohammed won Abu Bara's allegiance, and in 626 he
visited the Jewish Nadir to negotiate a truce with them. According to
Muslim tradition, the Nadir were determined to avenge the death of
Ka'b ibn-Ashraf, and they planned to kill Mohammed by dropping a
heavy boulder onto his head from a rooftop. Mohammed was warned
of their plan, however, and did not venture into the Nadir quarter.

The Nadir refused to negotiate with Mohammed, preferring to
seek an alliance with his veteran opponent Ibn Ubayy. But when the
Jews retreated to their fortress, Ibn Ubayy, who realised he had
underestimated Mohammed's strength after the Battle of Uhud,
decided not to go to their aid. Mohammed then besieged the Nadir

fortress and began cutting down their date palms, on which their livelihood depended. This occurred on the Sabbath, a day of piety and prayer on which the Jews – peace-loving artisans and agricultur-alists – could not fight. For the Muslims, who ridiculed the institu-tion of the Jewish Sabbath, this refusal to fight was a sign of weak-ness. The Jews begged Mohammed to spare their lives. He agreed, but on the condition that they, like the Qaynuqa before them, leave Medina at once. He allowed them to take only those goods that could be carried on their camels.

Some Nadir Jews took refuge a hundred miles northwest of Medina in the oasis of Khaibar, where a mainly Jewish community lived. Others continued northward for a further five hundred miles, travelling as far as Palestine – their Holy Land and the ancestral home from which they had come more than 1,600 years earlier.

The expulsion of the Nadir from Medina was Mohammed's sec-ond victory against the Jews. Sura Fifty-Nine of the Koran is believed by many commentators to justify, and ascribe to Allah, the expulsion of the Nadir: 'He it is who turned out the disbelievers from their homes at the time of the first banishment. You did not think that they would go forth and they thought that their fortresses would protect them against Allah. But Allah came upon them whence they did not expect and cast terror into their hearts. . . .' Had it not been 'that Allah had decreed exile for them, He would surely have chastised them in this life also. In the Hereafter they will certainly undergo the chastisement of the Fire. That is because they opposed Allah and His Messenger; and who so opposes Allah will find that Allah is severe in retribution.'

Confronted with such an implacable enemy, the Nadir had no reason to resist further; Mohammed had deprived them of their live-lihood. Jewish Biblical ethics forbid the cutting down of fruit trees even in wartime.[17] Muslim tradition is emphatic in suggesting the contrary. Sura Fifty-Nine continues: 'Whatever palm-trees you cut down or left them standing on their roots was by Allah's command,

---

[17] 'When thou shalt besiege a city a long time, in making war against it to take it, thou shalt not destroy the trees therof by forcing an axe against them, and thou shalt not cut them down (for the tree of the field is man's life). . . .' Deuteronomy 20:19.

that He might disgrace the transgressors. Whatever Allah has given to His Messenger as spoils from them, is of His grace. You urged neither horse nor camel for it; but Allah grants power to His Messengers over whomsoever He pleases.'[18]

The exiled Nadir Jews, led by Huyayy ibn Akhtab, were driven to seek out Abu Sufyan, a prominent member of Mohammed's pagan Quraysh tribe. Abu Sufyan was then leading a Meccan alliance of Arab tribesmen who had also turned against Mohammed. A Koranic verse – 'whomever God has cursed you will find none to support him'[19] – is interpreted as referring to the conversation that occurred when Abu Sufyan asked the Jews their view on Mohammed's religious claims. 'You, O Jews,' he said, 'are the people of the first scripture and know the nature of our dispute with Mohammed. Is our religion better or is his?' To this, the Jews replied that the pagan religion of the Quraysh was definitely better; Mohammed and his followers were outraged when they heard that Huyayy and his group had defended what to them was idol worship.[20]

Not long after Mohammed expelled the Nadir, he discovered another threat to Islam from a Jewish tribe of Medina. The head of Medina's Qurayzah Jews, Ka'b ibn Asad, was pressed into joining the alliance of Mohammed's enemies led by the pagan Arab Quraysh. The news reached Mohammed's closest ally, Omar ibn al-Khattab – later the second Rashidun Caliph – who told his leader that the Jews were forming a Meccan alliance against him.[21]

---

[18] Koran 59:6. Muhammad Zafrulla Khan (translator), *The Quran*, page 555.
[19] Koran 4:51. Muhammad Zafrulla Khan (translator), *The Quran*, page 68.
[20] M.J. de Goeje et al. (editors), *Tabari's History of the Prophets and Kings*, first series, page 1464. Compiled in the Ninth Century.
[21] The title 'Caliph' or deputy (*Khalifa* in Arabic) is a shortened form of 'Caliph of God' (*Khalifat Allah*). Following the Prophet Mohammed's death in 632, 'Caliph' became the title of the ruler of the Muslim dynasties. The five Caliphates after Mohammed were the Rashidun (Medina, 632–661), whose conquests extended from Afghanistan to Tunisia; the Umayyad (Damascus, 661–750, and al-Andalus – Cordova – 756–1031); the Abbasid (Baghdad, 750–1258); the Fatimid (Cairo, 909–1171); and the Ottoman (Istanbul, 1517–1924). The Ottoman Caliphate was abolished by the Turkish leader Mustafa Kemal (Atatürk) on 3 March 1924.

Fearing that his men would be outnumbered by this alliance, Mohammed tried to sow dissent between the Qurayzah and his Arab adversaries. Within three weeks he was successful. The Jews, anticipating treachery by the Quraysh, took some of the tribe hostage to prevent it abandoning the alliance. But at this point, the soldiers of the Meccan alliance were finding it hard to feed their horses and camels. A fierce desert storm added to their distress. Abu Sufyan decided to disband the alliance altogether, addressing his troops with the defeatist words: 'O Quraysh, we are not in a permanent camp; the horses and camels are dying; the Bani Qurayzah have broken their word to us and we have heard disquieting reports of them. You can see the violence of the wind, which leaves us neither cooking pots, nor fire, nor tents to count on. Be off, for I am going!'[22]

The Qurayzah were left to face Mohammed's army alone, although the head of the exiled Nadir Jews, Huyayy ibn Akhtab, had travelled more than a hundred miles from Khaibar to join them. Accusing the Qurayzah of aiding his enemies, Mohammed sent his forces to surround and besiege the Jews. For twenty-five days the Jews held out. But as the siege continued, starvation loomed. Huyayy and Ka'b put three possibilities before their people. They could accept that by his extraordinary successes Mohammed was a true prophet, and convert to Islam. They could kill their own womenfolk and children and then attack the Muslim army; if they were killed they would not have to worry about a cruel fate for their dependents. Or they could try to trick Mohammed by attacking him on the Sabbath, when he would be taken unawares.

For religious and ethical reasons, the Jews found each of these possibilities unimaginable. Instead, they asked Mohammed if they could leave Medina on the same terms he had earlier granted the Nadir. They would allow the Muslims to confiscate their land and their property, but asked that each Jewish family take one camel-load of possessions with them. Mohammed refused. The Jewish fighters then offered

---

[22] Ibn Ishak, 'Sirat Rasul Allah,' published as *The Life of Mohammed*, Alfred Guillaume (translator), page 460.

to leave without any of their belongings, just with their families. Again Mohammed refused. He wanted them to surrender without any conditions, and to accept whatever he might decide for their fate. The Jews were left with no choice, and were taken prisoner.

In Medina, the men and women were separated and put into different courtyards, the men with their hands tied behind their backs. An Arab tribe, the Aws, with whom the Jews had earlier been allied, asked Mohammed for leniency towards the Jews. He declined their request and then appointed a leading member of the Aws tribe, Sa'd ibn Mu'adh, as an arbitrator. This was a subterfuge on the part of Mohammed, because he knew what Sa'd's judgement would be. Sa'd had been wounded and humiliated in battle; his verdict was predictably severe. The Jewish men were to be put to death, the women and children sold into slavery, and the possessions of the Jews divided as spoils among the Muslims.

When he heard of Sa'd's judgement, Mohammed exclaimed: 'You have judged according to the very sentence of Allah above the Seven Heavens!' Mohammed then gave orders for the judgement to be carried out.[23] Henceforth, Muslims considered this judgement a divine revelation. The Koran states: 'As for those who blaspheme, neither their wealth nor their progeny shall avail them one jot with God. These shall be fuel for the Fire.'[24]

On the following day, seven hundred Jewish men were taken to the market at Medina. Trenches were dug in the market square and the men, tied together in groups, were beheaded. Their headless bodies were then buried in the trenches while Mohammed watched. Only a few men were spared at the request of individual Muslims. One Jewish woman was among those executed; Aisha, Mohammed's wife, was with her after hearing an unseen voice call out her name. 'Good heavens,' Aisha cried, 'what is the matter?' 'I am to be killed,' the woman replied. 'What for?' Aisha asked. 'Because of something I did,' the woman answered. During the siege she had dropped a

---

[23] Ibn Ishak, 'Sirat Rasul Allah,' published as *The Life of Mohammed*, Alfred Guillaume (translator), page 464.
[24] Koran 3:10. Muhammad Zafrulla Khan (translator), *The Quran*, page 52.

heavy stone on one of the Muslims. Aisha commented: 'She was taken away and beheaded.'[25]

After the Jewish men and this one Jewish woman had been killed, all Jewish males who had not yet reached puberty, and all the remaining women and girls, were sold into slavery. Some were given as gifts to Mohammed's companions. The property of the Jews, including their weapons, was distributed among the conquerors. According to Mohammed's biographer Ibn Ishak, Mohammed chose as his wife one of the Jewish women, Rayhana, whose husband had been among those executed. Thus ended Mohammed's third victory over the Jews.[26]

The brutal removal of those whom Mohammed defeated became a model for future Muslim rulers. A leading Muslim jurist, Abu Yusuf (who died in 798, and who was an adviser to the Abbasid Caliph Harun al-Rashid) wrote in his commentaries on *jihad* – holy war – that whenever Muslims 'besiege an enemy stronghold, establish a treaty with the besieged who agree to surrender on certain conditions that will be decided by a delegate, and this man decides that their soldiers are to be executed and their women and children taken prisoner, this decision is lawful.' He went on to explain: 'This was the decision of Sa'd ibn Mu'adh in connection with the Banu Qurayzah.'[27]

Abu Yusuf added that it was up to the *Imam* – the religious head of the community – to decide what treatment was to be meted out. 'If the imam esteems that the execution of the fighting men and the enslavement of their women and children is better for Islam and its followers, then he will act thus, emulating the example of Sa'd ibn Mu'adh.'[28]

---

[25] Ibn Ishak, 'Sirat Rasul Allah,' published as *The Life of Mohammed*, Alfred Guillaume (translator), page 464-5.

[26] This account of the defeat of the Qurayzah is taken from Muslim sources, published and annotated in Andrew G. Bostom (editor), *The Legacy of Jihad: Islamic Holy War and the Fate of Non-Muslims*, pages 17-19.

[27] *Jihad* (struggle), from 'striving in the way of Allah' (*al-jihad fi sabil Allah*). A person engaged in *jihad* is called a *mujahid* (plural *mujahidun*).

[28] Abu Yusuf Ya'qub, *Le Livre de l'impôt foncier*. Translated in Bat Ye'or, *The Dhimmi*, pages 171-2.

Three centuries later, another leading Muslim jurist, al-Mawardi, from Baghdad (who died in 1058), wrote of the slaughter of the Qurayzah that Mohammed 'was not permitted' to forgive in a case of God's injunction; he could only forgive transgressions 'in matters concerning his own person.'[29] Indeed, for later Muslim scholars, the punishment of the Qurayzah Jews had not been decided by Mohammed's personal wishes; it was Sa'd ibn Mu'adh, the arbitrator chosen by Mohammed, whose adjudication it had been that the Qurayzah men were put to death, the women and children sold into slavery, and their possessions divided as spoils among the Muslims.

Following the defeat of the Qurayzah Jews in 628, Mohammed and his seven hundred followers reached an agreement with the Arab Quraysh tribe for a ten-year truce and the right to worship in what was then pagan-ruled Mecca, though only for three days over the following year. Thus freed from the enmity of the Quraysh, Mohammed was able to attack the largest of all the Jewish communities in the peninsula – and the Quraysh's last potential Jewish ally against him. This was the Jewish community of Khaibar, a fertile oasis where Jews maintained a substantial irrigation system and lived off its produce.

Mohammed's forces reached the oasis, unobserved, a few weeks later. Under cover of darkness, Mohammed first sent a 'commando' to assassinate the leaders of the Medinian Jews who had taken refuge there, and who were the most likely to oppose him. Then, in the morning, Mohammed's forces attacked the Jewish farmers who came out of the city to work their fields. The Jews were carrying the spades and baskets of their trade; the Muslims were armed with swords. After burning down the Jews' date palm groves – their main source of livelihood in Khaibar – Mohammed laid siege to the oasis. Then one by one, over the course of a month, each of the Jews' seven separate compounds was forced to surrender.

---

[29] M.J. Kister, 'The Massacre of Banu Qurayza: A Re-examination of a Tradition,' *Jerusalem Studies in Arabic and Islam*, issue 8, page 69.

With the conclusion of this battle, Mohammed dispelled any chance of a Jewish-Quraysh coalition against his forces. Under the terms of Khaibar's surrender, some Jews were allowed to remain and to tend what remained of their date palms and gardens. They were also granted permission to continue practising their faith. But in return for their continued residence at Khaibar, the Jews had to give fifty per cent of their harvest to the Muslims. The land itself would henceforth belong to the Muslim community. Mohammed even selected another wife, Safiyya, a leading woman of the Khaibar Jews, from among the enslaved Jewish captives.

The consequences of the Khaibar battle were extremely far-reaching. Based on Mohammed's actions there and at previous battles, Sura Fifty-Nine of the Koran states: 'Whatever Allah has bestowed on His Messenger as spoils from the people of the townships is for Allah and for the Messenger and for the near of kin and the orphans and the needy and the wayfarer, that it may not circulate only among those of you who are rich.'[30] Islam demanded an equitable distribution of the spoils of conquest – but only among Muslims.

The terms imposed on Khaibar's Jews set the precedent in Islamic case law (Sharia Law) for the subsequent treatment of all non-Muslims under Muslim rule. The relevant Sharia regulations aimed to keep non-Muslims, who are referred to as *dhimmis*, in a state of subjugation and fealty similar to the Khaibar Jews. Many millions of non-Muslims were to be affected by these rules in the coming centuries, as Mohammed's followers continued building their empire across a vast geographic area.

For some Muslims who looked back on this episode, like Amrozi in Bali 1,375 years later, the Battle of Khaibar symbolised the defeat of their Jewish infidel enemies and the beginning of the sanctioned humiliation of Jews under the *dhimma* practice. For non-Muslims, Khaibar symbolised the onset of regularised discrimination that lasted for centuries.

---

[30] Koran 59:7, Muhammad Zafrulla Khan (translator), *The Quran*, page 555. The word 'townships' is explained by some commentators as referring to the Jewish compounds at Khaibar. Khaibar itself is not mentioned in the Koran.

A central, repressive aspect of the *dhimmi* condition, the *jizya* poll tax, was clearly understood by Muslim tradition to have begun with the Jews of Khaibar. The tax originated when the Jews were forced to hand over fifty per cent of their harvest. It was elaborated upon in the early Twelfth Century by Caliph al-Amir bi-Ahkam Illah of Egypt, who ruled from 1101 to 1130. The Caliph believed that the 'prior degradation of the infidels before the life to come – where it is their lot, is considered an act of piety.' Such degradation, which included the *jizya* poll tax, was 'a divinely ordained obligation' that was based on the words from the Koran: 'until they pay the tax willingly and make their submission.'[31]

Caliph al-Amir described the *jizya* tax as a means of discrimination and humiliation, not merely a source of income. He insisted that his provincial governors 'must not exempt from the *jizya* a single *dhimmi*, even if he be a distinguished member of his community; they must not, moreover, allow any of them to send the amount by a third party, even if the former is one of the personalities or leaders of their community.' The payment of the tax by a Muslim on behalf of a *dhimmi* 'will not be tolerated.' It had to be 'exacted from him directly in order to vilify and humiliate him, so that Islam and its people may be exalted and the race of infidels brought low. The *jizya* is to be imposed on all of them in full, without exception.'

The Jews of Khaibar were explicitly mentioned as the example to follow. Caliph al-Amir explained that the traditions were 'in agreement' that Mohammed had resolved to expel the Khaibaris 'just as he had done' to other Jewish tribes. But after the Khaibaris had conveyed to Mohammed that 'they were the only ones who knew how to irrigate the palm groves properly and till the soil of the region, the Prophet let them remain as tenants; he accorded them half of the harvest, and this condition was expressly stipulated.' The Caliph then quoted Mohammed: 'We will allow you to remain in this land as long as it pleases us.' Thus, al-Amir explained, Mohammed placed the Khaibari Jews 'in a state of abasement; they

---

[31] Koran 9:29, Muhammad Zafrulla Khan (translator), *The Quran*, page 176.

remained in the land, working on these conditions; and they were neither given any privileges, nor distinction, that might exempt them from the *jizya* and make an exception between them and the other *dhimmis.*'[32]

In 629, Mohammed established his complete authority over the Jews of the central Arabian Peninsula. He began by laying siege to the Jewish villages of the Wadi al-Qura, in which the Qurayzah and other Jews had found refuge after leaving Medina. They resisted his attack for two days – and lost eleven of their own fighters – but eventually surrendered, accepting the terms that had earlier been imposed on the Jews of Khaibar.

Mohammed then concluded a treaty with a Jewish tribe in the Mu'ta oasis, allowing them to preserve their religion on payment of an annual *jizya* tax. In return Mohammed undertook to protect them from attacks by the marauding Bedouin tribes of the desert. He hoped thereby to obtain loyalty from Jews by allowing them protection under the *dhimmi* status. As a result, some of the Jews reduced to *dhimmi* status by his conquests were among the early converts to Islam.

Islam spread rapidly during Mohammed's lifetime. In 630, eight years after he left Mecca with forty followers, Mohammed returned with ten thousand fighters and took the city without a battle. Mecca was henceforth the centre for worship of the one God of Islam. Rebuffed by the Jews, Mohammed decreed that the Muslim faithful no longer pray towards Jerusalem but towards Mecca. This 'reversal of custom,' writes one Christian scholar of Islam, Sir Percy Sykes, was 'a politic stroke; for, although it laid Mohammed open to a charge of inconsistency, it must have gratified the people of Arabia by reserving to Mecca its pre-eminence in the ceremonial of the new faith.'[33]

When Mohammed died in 632, at the age of sixty-two, most of the Arabian Peninsula had been conquered for Islam. Muslim forces

---

[32] Ibn Naqqash (died 1362), quoted in Bat Ye'or, *The Dhimmi*, pages 188-9.
[33] Lieutenant-Colonel P.M. Sykes, *A History of Persia*, Volume Two, page 15.

had already ventured outside of Arabia in 630 to conquer the Persian Gulf territory of Bahrain.[34] Within a hundred and twenty years of Mohammed's death the empire of Islam stretched as far west as the Atlantic coast of Spain and North Africa, as far east as the Oxus and Indus rivers, and as far south as the Gulf of Aden. Across this wide range of territories, Muslim rule brought with it *dhimmi* status for all Christians and Jews who refused to convert.[35] The conquerors were Mohammed's successors, the first of whom, Abu Bakr, Mohammed's first father-in-law, styled his role 'Caliph' – *Khalifat Rasul Allah* ('Successor to the Messenger of God').[36]

Mohammed's successors were guided in their attitude to the Jews by the clear divisions their prophet had already drawn between Islam and Judaism. These included the Koran's three specific curses against the Jews. The first curse recalled the Jews' rebellion against Moses in the wilderness.[37] The second curse was said to have been made both by King David and by Jesus against the Jews: 'They disobeyed and were given to transgression. They did not try to restrain one another from the iniquity which they committed. Evil indeed was that which they used to do.'[38] The third curse was for the Jews' refusal to accept

---

[34] Arabic sources tell of a Jewish community in the capital, Hajar, that refused to accept conversion to Islam. Walter Joseph Fischel, 'Bahrein,' *Encyclopaedia Judaica*, Volume 4, columns 101-2. Five centuries later, the Jewish traveller Benjamin of Tudela found five hundred Jews on the Persian Gulf island of Qais, and five thousand Jews in the town of al-Qatifa, on the Arabian side of the Gulf. A. Asher (editor and translator), *The Itinerary of Rabbi Benjamin of Tudela*, pages 137-8.

[35] For the conquests of Islam by 750, and some of the towns within that area with large Jewish communities, see Map 1, page 356.

[36] Many thought that Mohammed's cousin and son-in-law, Ali ibn Abi Talib, one of the very first Muslims, had been designated the successor to Mohammed. But at thirty-three, Ali was thought by some to be too young. Shia Muslims believe that Ali and his descendants – the Imams – have special spiritual and political rule over the community, and that Ali was Mohammed's rightful successor. Shiites reject the legitimacy of the first three Rashidun Caliphs. (The word *rashidun* means 'rightly guided.')

[37] 'Thus they were smitten with abasement and penury, and they incurred the wrath of Allah because they rejected the signs of Allah and would slay the prophets unjustly, and this had resulted from their persisting in rebellion and transgression.' Koran 2:61. Muhammad Zafrulla Khan (translator), *The Quran*, page 12.

[38] Koran 5:82. Muhammad Zafrulla Khan (translator), *The Quran*, page 111.

Mohammed's teaching: 'O ye who have been given the Book, believe in that which we have now sent down, fulfilling that which is with you, before we destroy your leaders and turn them on their backs or cast them aside as we cast aside the people of the Sabbath.'[39]

There is also a charge made against the Jews in the Koran, for which they are said to deserve punishment: 'Their uttering against Mary a grievous calumny; and their saying: we did kill the Messiah, Jesus son of Mary, the messenger of Allah; whereas they slew him not, nor did they compass his death upon the Cross, but he was made to appear to them as one crucified to death . . .'[40] Mohammed also asserted that the Jews had distorted their Bible in saying that Abraham attempted to sacrifice his son Isaac to God on Mount Moriah in Jerusalem. In Islamic tradition it was not Isaac but Abraham's other son, Ishmael – from whom the Arabs claimed descent – whom Abraham had offered to sacrifice to God. This had happened not in Jerusalem but on the Black Stone of Ka'bah in Mecca.

In distancing Islam from Judaism, Mohammed disregarded the three pilgrim festivals celebrated by the Jews: Pesach (Passover), Shavuot (Pentecost) and Succoth (the Festival of Booths). Taken together, these three festivals commemorated the Jews' Exodus from Egypt and their journey through the Sinai desert to Canaan, the Promised Land. The term 'pilgrim festival' derived from pilgrimages that were made to the Temple of Jerusalem before it was destroyed by the Romans. In place of these festivals, Mohammed gave the existing Arabian pilgrimage to Mecca an Islamic character: the *hajj*, which Muslims were – and still are – obliged to undertake at least once in their lives, however far from Mecca they might live.

Mohammed had not expected to be so emphatically rejected by the Jews of Medina. Why had they refused to countenance him as a Hebrew prophet? Why had they reneged on his pact with them to defend Medina 'against all enemies'? Why had so few been willing to

---

[39] Koran 4:44-46. Muhammad Zafrulla Khan (translator), *The Quran*, page 12.
[40] Koran 4:156 and 157. Muhammad Zafrulla Khan (translator), *The Quran*, pages 95-6.

convert to Islam? Why had they joined forces against him, when they could have been his allies in a series of victorious battles?

Throughout the centuries to follow, Muslims had to decide in their relations with the Jews whether to see them as a cursed people, or as a people protected by Islam. Mohammed's example gave them ample reason to take either view. Although he had protected Jews living under *dhimmi* status and granted them religious freedom, he had also subjugated them and punished them severely. His attitude also hardened towards the end of his life; his dying wish was that 'two religions shall not remain together in the peninsula of the Arabs.'[41] The Jews of Khaibar lost the right to cultivate their former lands in obedience to that very wish.

In the fourteen centuries since Mohammed's death, Jews in Muslim lands have faced both cursing and protection. When cursed, they suffered; when protected, they flourished. The history of those years shows how intertwined that suffering and protection could be.

---

[41] 'I will expel the Jews and Christians from the Arabian peninsula (*Jazirat al-'Arab*) and will not leave any but Muslims.' (Quoted in *Sahih Muslim*, a collection of traditions of the Prophet regarded as the second most trusted collection after *Sahih al-Bukhari*). The second Caliph, Omar, drove the Khaibari Jews out of Arabia altogether in 640. According to the Twelfth-Century Caliph al-Amir, he did so with the words, 'If Allah prolongs my life, I shall certainly chase all Jews and Christians from Arabia and will leave only Muslims.' Today there are no Jews living in the Kingdom of Saudi Arabia. (Edict of Caliph al-Amir bi Akham Allah, quoted by Ibn Naqqash [died 1362]: Bat Ye'or, *The Dhimmi*, pages 188-9.)

PROTECTION OR PERSECUTION?

'Infidels are unjust'

During the two centuries following the death of Mohammed, Muslim rulers developed conflicting approaches towards their Jewish subjects. The difference in their approaches revealed an internal struggle within Islam, one that swung rulers between the two extremes of protection and intolerance – a struggle that has defined the Muslim-Jewish relationship to this day. This was typified by the beneficence of Caliph Omar ibn al-Kattab (634-644) and the malevolence of Caliph Ja'far al-Mutawakkil two hundred years later.

In 638, under the direction of the second Caliph, Omar ibn al-Khattab, Mohammed's second father-in-law, the forces of Islam drew near to Jerusalem. The city was then under the rule of Christian Byzantium. Following the victory of the Byzantines over the Persians ten years earlier, Jews had not been allowed to live in Jerusalem, or at least not to spend the night there. On his way to Jerusalem from the north, Omar conquered several Byzantine-ruled cities, including Homs, Damascus and Tiberias. In Homs, the Jews openly aided the Muslim conqueror in the hope of being freed from Christian oppression. Jewish soldiers fought in the Muslim ranks as volunteers, while other Jews acted as guides or provided food and provisions for the Muslim armies.[1]

When a Christian deputation from Jerusalem travelled to see Omar in the Hauran – today's Golan Heights – a treaty was drawn

---

[1] Christian sects (like the Copts) who were persecuted by Byzantine Christian rulers also helped the Muslims against Byzantium.

up, under which the Christian citizens of Jerusalem were guaranteed security of life and property. The safety of churches was also assured. But all non-Muslim citizens were required to pay a head tax, the *jizya*, and anyone who rejected allegiance to the Muslims was given the option to leave the city. After the treaty had been drawn up, Omar made his way to Jerusalem. Upon arrival he received the keys to the city from the Christian Patriarch. For the first time, Muslims were the masters of Jerusalem.

The Jews asked Omar for permission for two hundred Jewish families to live in the city. Because the Christian patriarch vehemently opposed this, Omar fixed the number at seventy families. These Jews were assigned a quarter southwest of the Temple Mount, in the same area as the Jewish Quarter of the Old City today.[2] This quarter lay near the site of the Temple built by Solomon and later rebuilt by King Herod – prior to its destruction by the Romans – where a magnificent Byzantine church stood at the southern edge. The seventy Jewish families were permitted to build a religious college and a synagogue, and to pray at the surviving western retaining wall of Herod's Temple enclosure.[3] It was at about this time that the Talmudic academy at Tiberias moved south to Jerusalem.

Omar's concessions at Jerusalem led the Jews to regard him as sympathetic to Jewish needs. According to one tradition, the Caliph's humane attitude towards non-Muslims inspired Jews to grant him the epithet *al-Faruq* ('he who can distinguish truth from falsehood').[4] He was even praised as a 'friend of Israel' in a Midrash – a compilation of Jewish teachings based on the Hebrew Bible.[5] Other Jewish

---

[2] Simhah Assaf, *British Journal of the Palestine Exploration Society*, issue VII, from page 22.

[3] Ben-Zion Dinaburg (Benzion Dinur), *Zion* (Jewish Historical Quarterly), issue III, 1929, from page 54. That wall, still a focal point of Jewish prayer, is known as the Western (or Wailing) Wall.

[4] Eliezer Bashan (Sternberg), 'Omar ibn al-Khattab,' *Encyclopaedia Judaica*, Volume 12, column 1382. Faruq is a popular Arabic boy's name meaning 'wise.'

[5] Midrash *Nistarot de-Rav Shimon bar Yohai* is a revelation given to Rabbi Shimon bar Yochai (who died in the mid–Second Century CE) during his time hiding in a cave while being sought by Romans. The revelation is regarded by some as an insight into 'future' Muslim history, although many scholars point out that it pre-dates Islam by four centuries, and is almost certainly not from so ancient an

sources lent further credence to this image. They related that when Omar conquered Babylonia, he allowed the leader of the Jewish community there, Bustanai ben Haninai, to retain his role as the Exilarch – 'Head of the Captivity.'[6] After conquering Persia, Omar gave Bustanai a wife, Izdundad, the daughter of Chosroes II, the King of Persia.[7] Although the Jews of Khaibar were expelled to Tayma and Jericho under Omar's caliphate, he is said to have saved them from penury by reimbursing them with half the value of their land.[8]

Yet Omar drew the same distinctions between Jews and Muslims as had Mohammed. One of the men who entered Jerusalem with him in 638 was a Jewish convert to Islam, Ka'b al-Ahbar.[9] At Omar's request, Ka'b pointed out the rock where the Jewish Temple had been built by Solomon, King of the Israelites, more than 1,500 years earlier. When Ka'b tried to persuade Omar to build the Mosque of Omar north of the holy rock, rather than directly on the spot where the Temple had stood, he was accused of Judaising tendencies. 'You wish to resemble Judaism' – Omar is said to have told Ka'b – 'but we Muslims have been commanded to pray only in the direction of the Ka'bah' – that is, towards Mecca.[10]

Omar ibn al-Khattab died in 644, after ten years as Caliph, and before a decision was made to build the dome that bears his name. After Omar's death, Ka'b stayed on at the court of the third Caliph, Othman (644–656), where his dispute with Muslim religious scholar Abu Dharr, and the latter's rebukes of Ka'ab's advice to the Caliph,

---

era. It states that a King will arise who will 'fix the breaches in the Temple area, will fight a war with the enemy and will destroy its armies.' This has been taken as referring to Caliph Omar.

[6] Those appointed Exilarch were believed to be descended from the biblical King David.

[7] Simhah Assaf, 'Bustanai ben Haninai,' *Encyclopaedia Judaica*, Volume 4, column 1537. Omar himself married the King's other daughter.

[8] Caliph Omar ibn al-Khattab was not the Omar who authored the Covenant of Omar, which codified the status of *dhimmi*. That was almost certainly issued some eighty years after Omar ibn al-Khattab's death by another Caliph of a separate dynasty, Omar ibn Abdul Azziz.

[9] The designation 'al-Ahbar' denotes a non-Muslim scholar.

[10] Shlomo D. Goitein, 'Jerusalem in the Arab Period,' Lee I. Levine (editor), *The Jerusalem Cathedra*, page 172.

contributed to Ka'ab's portrayal by early Muslim writers as 'the proto-type of Jewish opportunism.'[11]

In 670 the first Umayyad Caliph, Mu'awiya ibn Abi Sufyan, ordered the construction of Omar's planned 'Dome of the Rock' on the Temple Mount. Mu'awiya wanted the Dome to be higher and more impressive than any of the Christian churches in the city. It took twenty-one years before the imposing hexagonal structure was completed.

Although sometimes called 'the Mosque of Omar,' the Dome of the Rock – *Qubbat as-Sakhrah* – is not in fact a mosque, but a shrine built on a small outcrop of rock where Solomon's Temple once stood. It was to this rock that Jews believe Abraham brought Isaac to be sacrificed, and it was also where they believe Jacob dreamed of a ladder ascending to heaven. Later Muslim tradition spoke of Mohammed ascending to heaven from the same rock on his horse Buraq – whose hoof print is shown to visitors to this day – although there is no record of Mohammed having visited Jerusalem.

Caliph Abd al-Malik, the fourth successor to Abi Sufyan, completed the Dome in 691. He appointed Jewish families to be guardians of the Temple Mount – known to the Muslims as *Haram al-Sharif* ('The Noble Sanctuary') – and charged them with maintaining its cleanliness and with making glass vessels for the lights and kindling them. He also decreed that these particular Jews should be exempt from the *jizya* tax. Like Omar before him, Abd al-Malik thus made concessions to the Jews, allowing certain Jews to hold positions of authority under his rule. A Jew named Sumeir was in charge of minting the Caliph's coins in Damascus, while another Jew, in 698, was the administrator of the North African city of Bizerta.

Abd al-Malik followed his completion of the Dome by beginning the *al-Aqsa* ('The Farthest') Mosque on the Noble Sanctuary. This was built on the site of a small house of prayer built by Omar – itself

---

[11] H.Z. Hirschberg, 'Ka'b al'Ahbar,' *Encyclopaedia Judaica*, Volume 10, column 488. Ka'b was asked by Othman if a ruler is permitted to take money from the treasury when he is in need, and then to pay it back later. When Ka'b said it was permitted, Abu Dharr rebuked Ka'b with the words: 'You son of Jews want to teach us.'

erected on the site of an earlier Byzantine church – and was completed in 705 by Abd al-Malik's son and successor, Caliph al-Walid. The mosque, destroyed by an earthquake in 746, was rebuilt eight years later by the Abbasid Caliph al-Mansur.

It was the al-Aqsa Mosque and the Dome of the Rock that gave Jerusalem its importance to Muslims, although they continued to pray facing Mecca, more than one thousand miles to the south. Muslims believed that Mohammed was transported from the Grand Mosque in Mecca to al-Aqsa during the 'Night Journey.' In the words of the Koran: 'Worthy of praise is He who took his servant by night from the Sacred Mosque to the Distant Mosque, the precincts of which We have blessed, that We might show him some of Our Signs.'[12] In contrast, the importance of Jerusalem for Jews derived from the site of their two destroyed Temples, towards which the Jews still pray daily. Jerusalem, not mentioned in the Koran, is mentioned 654 times in the Hebrew Bible.

The treatment of Jews in Muslim lands evolved significantly under the eighth Umayyad Caliph, Omar Abd al-Azziz, who formally codified the rules for the *dhimmi* status. Abd al-Azziz, who reigned from 717 to 720, was a devout Muslim and a popular ruler who shunned the luxury that had become characteristic of Umayyad lifestyle. He redistributed to the people many estates that had been seized by Ummayad officials, left his palace in Damascus for a simpler home and wore plain linen clothes instead of the sumptuous royal robes.

Guided by a deep and sincere piety, Abd al-Azziz laid out rules that were aimed specifically at setting the Muslim and non-Muslim communities clearly apart. He did this in a pact known as the Covenant of Omar, which almost certainly dated from this period, and which formally categorised non-Muslims as *ahl al-dhimma* – 'the People of the Pact.' At the core of the Covenant was a promise to protect Jews and Christians – People of the Book – based on three essential benefits: security of life and property, freedom of religion and internal communal autonomy. Each benefit was guaranteed provided certain

---

[12] Koran 17:2. Muhammad Zafrulla Khan (translator), *The Quran*, pages 95-6.

conditions were met. First and foremost among these conditions, *dhimmis* had to pay the *jizya* tax to the local ruler and accept the condition of *ahl al-dhimma.*

In addition to codifying existing rules, Abd al-Azziz formulated new ones. Several of these were identical to laws against the Jews that were already in place in Christian Byzantium, but they were nonetheless new in the Muslim world. There could be no building of new synagogues or churches. *Dhimmis* could not ride horses, but only donkeys; they could not use saddles, but only ride sidesaddle. Further, they could not employ a Muslim. Jews and Christians alike had to wear special hats, cloaks and shoes to mark them out from Muslims.[13] They were even obliged to carry signs on their clothing or to wear types and colours of clothing that would indicate they were not Muslims, while at the same time avoid clothing that had any association with Mohammed and Islam. Most notably, green clothing was forbidden.[14]

Although the implementation of these laws varied over time, their basic principles remained constant in the lives of all *dhimmis* living under Muslim rule henceforth. A *dhimmi* could not – and cannot to this day – serve in a Muslim court as a witness in a legal case involving a Muslim. The reason for this was set out in Ali ibn Abi Bakr al-Marghinani's Thirteenth-Century commentary to Muslim law. Al-Marghinani explained that because 'infidels are unjust, it is requisite to be slow in believing anything they may advance.' This he showed by quoting the Koran: 'When an unjust person tells you anything be slow in believing him.' Al-Marghinani added that 'a *dhimmi*

---

[13] Eliezer Bashan (Sternberg), 'Omar, Covenant of,' *Encyclopaedia Judaica*, Volume 12, column 1378-82. For a detailed study of the Covenant of Omar, see Mark R. Cohen, 'What Was the Pact of 'Umar? A Literary-Historical Study,' *Jerusalem Studies in Arabic and Islam*, Number 23, (1999), pages 100-157.

[14] The colour green has a special place in Islam. It is used in the decoration of mosques, the bindings of Korans, the silken covers for the graves of Sufi saints, and in the flags of various Muslim countries. There is a Muslim tradition that green was Mohammed's favourite colour and that he wore a green cloak and turban. The Koran (Sura 76:21) relates that the inhabitants of paradise will be given 'green garments of fine silk and heavy brockade.'

may be suspected of inventing falsehoods against a Mussulman[15] from the hatred he bears him on account of the superiority of the Mussulman over him.'[16]

Other aspects of *dhimmi* existence were that Jews – and also Christians – were not to be given Muslim names, were not to prevent anyone from converting to Islam, and were not to be allowed tombs that were higher than those of Muslims. Men could enter public bathhouses only when they wore a special sign around their neck distinguishing them from Muslims, while women could not bathe with Muslim women and had to use separate bathhouses instead. Sexual relations with a Muslim woman were forbidden, as was cursing the Prophet in public – an offence punishable by death.

The property of a *dhimmi* who died was to belong to the Muslim authorities – not to the *dhimmi*'s community – until the heirs could prove their right to it under Islamic (Sharia) law. If there was no heir, the property would be transferred to the Muslim authority. The leader of the *dhimmi* communities – Jewish or Christian – acted as the official contact with the ruling Muslim authority, responsible for the collection of the *jizya* tax and for the loyalty of the community. In 1031, in Babylonia, this duty was the responsibility of the Christian Catholicos and the Jewish Exilarch.[17]

Under the *dhimmi* rules as they evolved, neither Jews nor Christians could carry guns, build new places of worship or repair old ones without permission, or build any place of worship that was higher than a mosque. A non-Muslim could not inherit anything from a Muslim. A non-Muslim man could not marry a Muslim woman, although a Muslim man could marry a Christian or a Jewish woman. This was justified as Mohammed had taken one Jewish wife – Rayhana – after his defeat of the Qurayzah, and a second – Safiyya – after the Battle of

---

[15] A Nineteenth-Century word for Muslim.

[16] Ali ibn Abi Bakr Marghinani, *The Hedaya, or Guide – A Commentary on the Mussulman Laws* (Charles Hamilton, translator), Volume Two, 1982, pages 362-3.

[17] Eliezer Bashan (Sternberg), 'Omar, Covenant of,' *Encyclopaedia Judaica*, Volume 12, column 1379. 'Catholicos' was the title given in the Syrian Church to the head bishop of an autonomous region under the Patriarch of Antioch.

Khaibar. Conversion by a Muslim to either Christianity or Judaism was strictly forbidden. Converts to Islam were welcomed.[18]

The Covenant of Omar had an enormous impact on everyday life in the Muslim world, imposing restrictions, promising security and defining relationships for Jews and other *dhimmis* in their contact with their Muslim neighbours and rulers. This omnipresence has been the subject of considerable debate.

Writing in 1962, the Jewish scholar Shlomo Goitein confessed: 'There is no subject in Islamic social history on which the present writer had to modify his views so radically while passing from literary to documentary sources, i.e. from the study of Muslim books to that of the records of the Cairo Geniza,[19] as the *jizya*.' Although the *jizya* tax was plainly discriminatory, Goitein noted how it might appear to modern observers that the tax 'did not constitute a heavy imposition, since it was on a sliding scale, approximately one, two and four dinars, and thus adjusted to the financial capacity of the taxpayer.' Nevertheless, he concluded that this impression was 'entirely fallacious, for it did not take into consideration the immense extent of poverty and privation experienced by the masses, and in particular, their persistent lack of cash, which turned "the season of the tax" into one of horror, dread and misery.'[20]

Another leading scholar, Professor Mark R. Cohen, painted a broader and more positive image of the *dhimmi* laws. He observed that *dhimmis* – unlike their Jewish counterparts in the Christian world – were not excluded from the life of Muslim society. The Covenant of Omar compelled them to distinguish themselves from Muslims, but its intention was 'not so much to exclude as to reinforce' the hierarchical

---

[18] A succinct description of *dhimmi* status can be found in Albert Hourani, *A History of the Arab Peoples*, pages 117-9.

[19] The Genizah (from the Hebrew word *ganoz*, to put aside), a store of Jewish sacred books and other written documents. The Cairo Genizah, found in 1854 in the Ben Ezra Synagogue in Fustat, is the source of more than 140,000 Jewish documents, many in fragments, from the Ninth to the Nineteenth Centuries.

[20] S.D. Goitein, 'Evidence on the Muslim Poll tax from Non-Muslim Sources,' *Journal of the Economic History of the Orient*, 1963, issue six, pages 278-9.

distinction between Muslims and non-Muslims. Non-Muslims would simply remain 'in their place.' They were not to commit an act that might challenge the superior rank of Muslims or of Islam. Yet they occupied 'a definite slot in Islamic society – a low rank but a rank, nevertheless. Like Hinduism, Islam recognized and accepted difference as a natural concomitant of the hierarchical order.'[21]

The hierarchy in Muslim society was founded on Islam's distinction between insiders and outsiders: the division of the world into the Domain of War (*Dar al-Harb*) and the Domain of Islam (*Dar al-Islam*). The Domain of War lay outside the Domain of Islam; Muslims were instructed to wage *jihad* (holy war) against unbelievers of this domain and force them to choose between Islam and the sword.[22] Ranked above those unbelievers, however, were the non-Muslims of the Domain of Islam: the *ahl al-dhimma* or Protected People. This group was given the option of paying tribute in return for protection and the relatively free exercise of religion. 'Marginal though they were,' Professor Cohen observed, the Jews and Christians of this domain 'occupied a recognized, fixed, safeguarded niche within . . . the Islamic social order.'[23]

Other historians reached a different conclusion. A leading scholar of Islamic history, Albert Hourani, pointed to how *dhimmis* themselves experienced the restrictions imposed on them. He wrote that between the Muslim ruler and his non-Muslim subjects, 'the relationship was not strengthened by a moral bond.' At the best of times, 'even if it was a peaceful and stable relationship, there was a sense in which Christians and Jews lay outside the community; they could not give the ruler the strong and positive allegiance which would come from an identity of beliefs and purposes.'[24] The historian

---

[21] Mark R. Cohen, *Under Crescent and Cross, The Jews in the Middle Ages*, pages 111-2.
[22] A non-Muslim native of the Domain of War could enter Islamic territory – on business, for example – under a guarantee of safe conduct. Such a person was classified as a *musta'min* and received an *aman*, a safe conduct or pledge of security, by which he entered Muslim territory protected by the sanctions of the law in his life and property, but only for a limited period.
[23] Mark R. Cohen, *Under Crescent and Cross, The Jews in the Middle Ages*, pages 111-2.
[24] Albert Hourani, *A History of the Arab Peoples*, page 141.

Bat Ye'or also pointed to the dramatic change in demography over the six centuries after Mohammed, during which 'the Arab-Muslim minority developed into a dominant majority, resorting to oppression in order to reduce the numerous indigenous populations to tolerated religious minorities.'[25]

The exclusion and persecution of non-Muslims depended on the severity or leniency of individual Muslim rulers. Certain rulers initiated periods of religious intolerance and of campaigns to conquer new territory for Islam. At such times, *dhimmi* restrictions were applied with a greater rigour and were even distorted to harsher effect. Synagogues and churches were occasionally destroyed by Muslim authorities who claimed that it had been forbidden to build them in the first place, since they had not been in existence in the pre-Muslim period; it did not matter that no such regulation was described in the Covenant of Omar.

In Baghdad, four Abbasid Caliphs were particularly strict in their interpretation of the *dhimmi* laws: Harun al-Rashid (786–809), Abdullah al-Ma'mun (813–833), Ja'far al-Muqtadir (908–932) and, especially, Ja'far al-Mutawakkil (847–861). In two decrees, one in 850 and the other in 854, al-Mutawakkil ordered Christians and Jews to fix wooden images of devils to their houses, level their graves with the ground, wear yellow ('honey-coloured') outer garments and ride only on mules and donkeys – not horses – with wooden saddles marked by two pomegranate-like balls.[26] He also forbade Jewish children from learning Arabic.[27]

Al-Mutawakkil was a striking example of how far Muslim rulers could stray from the beneficent actions of Caliph Omar ibn al-Khattab two centuries earlier. Yet his rule was, at the same time, an example

---

[25] Bat Ye'or, 'Islam and the Dhimmis,' *The Jerusalem Quarterly*, Number 42, Spring 1987, pages 83-88 (A Rejoinder to Mark R. Cohen, 'Islam and the Jews: Myth, Counter-Myth, History,' *The Jerusalem Quarterly*, Number 38, Spring 1986, pages 125-137). For a documented analysis of this subject, see Bat Ye'or, *The Decline of Eastern Christianity under Islam: From Jihad to Dhimmitude: Seventh–Twentieth Century*, pages 221-240.

[26] Philip K. Hitti, *History of the Arabs*, page 353.

[27] Lieutenant-Colonel P.M. Sykes, *A History of Persia*, Volume Two, page 82.

of something very different as well: how the most severe rulers made rare exceptions for a minority of *dhimmis*. Nearly all Muslim rulers employed the services of Jews with expert knowledge, among them physicians, administrators and clerks. Al-Mutawakkil was no exception. From 850 to 861 he employed a Jew named Ubaidallah ben Yahya as his Vizier, the highest-ranking official in the kingdom.[28] Later, Yahya's son served as Vizier to Caliph al-Muqtadir.

The first of the four Abbasid Caliphs of Baghdad, Harun al-Rashid, employed Jewish physicians who were intimately involved with food preparation at his court. Jews were consulted about food at most Islamic courts because of their knowledge of what made up a balanced, wise diet. But in the words of the Egyptian-born Jewish cookery writer Claudia Roden, Harun's reign was a time when 'cookery became a high art,' and in writings of this period, expert physicians were 'depicted sitting at the table with the caliphs advising them on what food was good for the body and spirit.'[29]

Easy access to such expertise was an important concern for Muslim rulers. Caliph al-Muqtadir, who came to the throne in 908, promulgated an edict to allow Jews and Christians to serve in two official functions: physicians and bankers. Later Caliphs showed a similar concern for safeguarding Jewish expertise, working around *dhimmi* laws by claiming that certain Jews were employed to carry out orders (*tanfidh*) without any personal initiative (*tafwid*). In these

---

[28] *Vizier* (Persian) and *wazir* (Arabic) mean 'burden-bearer' and 'helper': the Vizier was a high-ranking political and sometimes religious adviser, often the senior Minister, of a Muslim Caliph or Sultan.

[29] Claudia Roden, *The Book of Jewish Food*, page 185. Among the Jews for whom medicine and food were closely connected was Isaac ben Solomon ha-Israeli, an ophthalmologist who died in the Tunisian city of Kairouan in 932. He was the author of works on fevers, urine and urine analysis, and medical ethics. He also wrote a widely read treatise on the connection between diet and health, the *Kitab al-Aghdhiya* ('Book of Foods'), in which he stressed that food had to be 'really delectable' if the body and the mood were to benefit from it. Seven hundred years after his death, his book was still being used in the medical schools of Italy. It was printed (in Latin) in Padua in 1487 as *Liber Dietetarium Universalium*. Ron Barkai, 'Jewish Medical Treatises in the Middle Ages,' in Natalia Berger (editor), *Jews and Medicine: Religion, Culture, Science*, pages 51-2, and Claudia Roden, *The Book of Jewish Food*, page 189.

circumstances, rulers who adopted a strict approach to the *dhimmi* rules also exhibited a split attitude to the laws' victims – causing suffering for the masses at the same time as granting great privilege and opportunity to a few.

At the start of the Eleventh Century, one Caliph revealed again – in unusually bold fashion – how perilous life could be for *dhimmis* under Muslim rule. In Egypt in 1008, almost four hundred years after Muslim conquerors first arrived, Caliph al-Hakim bi-Amr Allah (996–1021) broke with his tolerant predecessors in the Fatimid dynasty by ordering the destruction of all synagogues and churches throughout the Fatimid Empire, including in Jerusalem. He then gave his 'protected' Jewish and Christian subjects the choice of conversion to Islam or departure from the countries under his rule.[30] His cruel persecution of *dhimmis* was almost certainly the result of mental illness. He showed a similar commitment to terrorising his Muslim subjects. Then, a year before his death, he changed his mind suddenly, allowing Jews and Christians to return to their religion and rebuild their destroyed buildings.

Al-Hakim's change of mind came too late for the Jews of Jerusalem, who did not find it easy to rebuild what had earlier been destroyed.[31] But it served as a reminder to all Jews that although the *dhimmi* laws made room for both persecution and protection, their effect was decided by the temperament, religious zeal and personal caprice of Muslim rulers.

---

[30] Eliezer Bashan (Sternberg), 'Omar, Covenant of,' *Encyclopaedia Judaica*, Volume 12, columns 1379-80. One of the Caliph's edicts also forced Jews to wear on their clothing the head of a calf, in mockery of the golden calf of the Israelites' wanderings in the desert.

[31] Shlomo D. Goitein, 'Jerusalem in the Arab Period,' Lee I. Levine (editor), *The Jerusalem Cathedra*, page 185.

4

THE FIRST FOUR HUNDRED YEARS
UNDER ISLAM

'Do not consider that killing them is treachery'

I slam unleashed a tremendous sense of devotion and destiny among its followers, propelling them out of the Arabian Peninsula and onward across vast swathes of territory.[1] As the forces of Islam advanced, Jews were sometimes among those who resisted Muslim conquest. A Jewish Berber Queen named Daha al-Kahina helped to lead a failed revolt in Cyrenaica and Tripolitania (present-day Libya) from 688 to 693, after Muslims conquered those regions from the Byzantines in 642.[2] Elsewhere, Jews welcomed the armies of Islam as they swept through Christian-ruled lands. In 641, three years after the conquest of Jerusalem, Muslim forces reached the Mediterranean port city of Caesarea, the capital of the Byzantine province of Palaestina Prima. Caesarea only fell to the Muslims when one of its forty thousand Jews showed the Muslim army how to enter the city through a concealed water channel under its strongly fortified walls.[3]

Jews often welcomed Muslim conquerors in order to be free of Christian persecution, and in many places Muslim rule provided Jews with the refuge they sought. This was true in southern Spain in the Eighth Century, where a Muslim army drove out oppressive Christian rulers and established a centre of government in the city of Cordova. Some sources state that the Muslims immediately entrusted

---

[1] See Map 1, page 356.
[2] H.Z. Hirschberg, 'The Problem of Judaized Berbers,' *Journal of African History*, No. 4, 1963, pages 331-9. Daha al-Kahina was the leader of a Berber tribe that had converted to Judaism some five hundred years earlier.
[3] Hugh Kennedy, *The Great Arab Conquests*, page 89.

the defence of Cordova to the city's Jewish inhabitants.[4] In other Christian cities in Spain, including Merida, Ecija, Jaén, Toledo and Cuenca, Jews showed a preference for Muslim rule by helping their Muslim conquerors achieve victory. In return, as a sign of trust from the Muslims, Jews were settled in sparsely populated regions of Malaga, Granada, Almeria and Alicante, and in cities where they would help to counter majority-Catholic populations.[5]

Muslim conquests in southern Spain – *al Andalus* (Andalucia) – heralded the beginning of a 'Golden Age' for Spanish Jews. Under the rule of Abd al-Rahman (756–788), Jews benefited from the Koranic verse, 'Let not a people's enmity towards you incite you to act contrary to justice' – a principle that al-Rahman himself preached at Friday prayers.[6] Jews were thus freed from persecution and were able to participate in society and government. Jewish traders brought in flax, pearls, dyes and medicines from Egypt. They took part in the importation of slaves for the Muslim army.[7] In the words of historian David Levering Lewis, 'Andalucian Jews possessed unique assets for their Muslim conquerors,' contributing 'more than loyalty, wealth and numbers to the amirate; they showed the Muslims how to run it.'[8]

The prosperity of Jews in Spain was not mirrored everywhere in the Muslim world. The Jews of Jerusalem – and the city of Jerusalem itself – witnessed a decline in prosperity from 750 onward, when the Muslim Abbasid dynasty defeated the Umayyads and began ruling Jerusalem from Baghdad, 550 miles away. When Jerusalem was later conquered by Egyptian Muslims in 878, the city's Jews were persecuted by their rulers, who enforced the *dhimmi* laws with extreme rigour. A contemporary Muslim writer, al-Jahiz, even noted that 'the hearts of Muslims are hardened toward the Jews but inclined toward the Christians.'[9] As

---

[4] Haim Beinart, 'Córdoba (Cordova, also Corduba),' *Encyclopaedia Judaica*, Volume 5, columns 963-6.

[5] These cities were Murcia, Pamplona, Guadalajara, Salamanca and Saragossa. For all of these places, see Map 4, page 359.

[6] Koran 5:8. Muhammad Zafrulla Khan (translator), *The Quran*, page 84.

[7] David Levering Lewis, *God's Crucible*, pages 204, 207 and 271.

[8] David Levering Lewis, *God's Crucible*, page 203.

[9] Quoted in Bernard Lewis, *The Jews of Islam*, pages 55-60.

David Levering Lewis wrote of Spain, no matter how benign Muslim rule might have been, 'Muslim tolerance was based more on condescension than on generosity.' In considering themselves uniquely trusted with God's final revelation, Muslim conquerors saw their Jewish subjects as a people 'stunted by failure of theological understanding.'[10]

In the absence of active persecution, Jews were able to flourish in many places under Muslim rule. Jewish intellectual life in particular benefited from the religious freedom ensured by *dhimmi* status. In Palestine, at Tiberias on the Sea of Galilee, the early centuries of Muslim rule saw the formulation of the scientific text of the Hebrew Bible, as well as the creation and perfection of Hebrew vocalisation and punctuation. The same benefits appeared in Jewish financial life as well. When the Moroccan city of Fez became the capital of a Muslim kingdom in 808, King Idris II invited a large number of Jews into the city, gave them a Quarter of their own, the *al-Funduq al-Yahud* – the Jewish Market – and guaranteed to protect them for a substantial payment in gold.[11] The Jews paid this *jizya* tax, received protection and did well as merchants and traders.

In Cordova, two centuries after Muslim rule began, Jewish craftsmen and traders continued to prosper under the benign rule of Abd al-Rahman III (912–961). Arab naval power had begun to assert itself in the region, overcoming Byzantine attempts to hold it in check, and Jewish traders were deeply involved in the maritime commerce of the Mediterranean. Silk from Spain, gold from the west coast of Africa, and metals and olive oil from all the Mediterranean hinterlands were traded at major ports, including Venice and Amalfi.[12] Jewish merchants also gained from being able to cross the frontier between Muslim and Christian lands, from one Jewish community to another.

Cordova, the capital city of the Umayyad caliphate, became a vibrant centre of Jewish life and culture – a focal point in the world of Jewish *Sepharad* (Spain) with its traditions, its liturgies and its evolving

[10] David Levering Lewis, *God's Crucible*, page 203.

[11] David Corcos, 'Fez,' *Encyclopaedia Judaica*, Volume 6, columns 1255-8.

[12] Albert Hourani, *A History of the Arab Peoples*, pages 45-6.

Judaeo-Spanish language, Ladino. Jewish philosophers, scholars and poets made their way from all over the lands of Islam to live and work in Cordova. The Jewish poet Dunash ben Labrat and the Jewish philosopher Solomon ibn Gabirol were among the many new arrivals who thrived there.[13] The Cordovan-born, Twelfth-Century Jewish historian and philosopher Abraham ibn Daud (Avraham ben David ha-Levi) commented in his *Sefer ha-Kabbalah* ('Book of Tradition') that the situation was 'good for Israel in Spain.'[14]

When Jewish communities were able to flourish, as they did in Spain, they contributed enormously to the wellbeing of Muslim societies. Rulers often recognised this value in their Jewish subjects by showing respect for Jewish religious leaders; it was faith and the synagogue that formed the centre of Jewish communal life and organisation. In Babylon, under Abbasid rule, honour was shown by the Caliph to the head of the Jewish community, the Exilarch. Equally respected were the heads of the Jewish religious academies, two in Babylonia and one in Palestine, which appointed judges to the Jewish religious courts.

Muslim rulers frequently adopted this benign approach in order to exploit their Jewish subjects' knowledge and expertise. After the Muslim conquest of Egypt – where Jews had gained respect as metal engravers and goldsmiths – the new rulers allowed existing Jewish mint masters to continue in their roles, minting the new Islamic coinage. Yet their decision was a calculated one, since working with hot metals in the heat of Egypt was unpleasant labour that Muslims avoided. In the words of Daniel M. Friedenberg, a historian of Jewish minters, Caliphs even preferred employing Jews for this work because 'it was easier to punish them for irregularities or confiscate their wealth than it would have been with influential Moslems.'[15]

Cooperation between Jews and Muslims was not always so cynical; it had substantive roots as well. The protection and religious

---

[13] Solomon ibn Gabirol's Arabic name was Abu Ayyub Suleiman ibn Yahya ibn Jabirul.
[14] Quoted in David Levering Lewis, *God's Crucible*, page 349.
[15] Daniel M. Friedenberg, *Jewish Minters & Medalists*, page 5.

freedom promised by *dhimmi* status could foster greater closeness between Jews and Muslims – never more strikingly than in the mingling of their separate cultures. In North Africa, between the Eighth and Tenth Centuries, signs of such closeness appeared under the rule of a Muslim sect called the Ibadis, which was tolerant of all Jews living in its substantial empire.[16] Rabbi Judah ibn Quraysh was among those Jewish subjects. A pioneer linguist, he advocated the usefulness of non-Hebrew languages in Jewish life, and penned a treatise that mentioned how other languages, especially Aramaic and Arabic, were essential for an understanding of the Hebrew Bible.[17]

Cultural influence flowed in both directions. In the early days of Islam, Jewish converts made a significant contribution to the new faith. Several Jews from Yemen, having embraced Islam, were asked by Muslims to share their rich Jewish oral traditions to help interpret obscure passages in the Koran. As a result, a large body of Jewish lore known as *Isra'iliyyat* became an integral part of the religious literature of Islam.[18] The Yemeni Jews were followed by countless other converts over the centuries. In fact, conversion to Islam became a feature of Jewish life under Muslim rule for many generations, whether it was encouraged by Muslim rulers, forced upon *dhimmi* populations, or undertaken willingly.

It was against this background of cooperation and interaction that individual Jews made great strides in the first four hundred years under Islam. Government officials, doctors, linguists and many others reached surprising heights of power and respect in Muslim societies. Their stories and achievements give an insight into what was possible for Jews in privileged positions in Muslim lands.

---

[16] The Ibadis asserted their authority in Tripolitania (Libya), Tiaret (central Algeria), Djerba, Jarid, the Mzab Oasis, Jebel Nafush, Tlemcen and Sijilmassa (on the edge of the Sahara, south-east of Fez): see Maps 10, 11 and 12, pages 365 and 366.

[17] Joshua Blau, 'Ibn Quraysh, Judah (second half of the ninth century),' *Encyclopaedia Judaica*, Volume 8, columns 1193-4. The rabbi's treatise was addressed to the Jews of Fez, who had – to his great dismay – decided to abolish the reciting of the Targum (the Bible in Aramaic translation) in their synagogue service.

[18] Itzhak Ben-Zvi, *The Exiled and the Redeemed*, page 26.

One such Jew was Yaqub ibn Killis, who in about 950 became a government supplier to Abu al-Misk Kafur, the Muslim ruler of Egypt.[19] Ibn Killis served as Kafur's collector of government taxes from agricultural districts, and quickly became an expert in agriculture. One Arab writer noted how ibn Killis was always ready with reliable information 'on the state or extent of crops in the districts, or on the internal or external affairs of the villages.' Kafur later promoted ibn Killis to be his economic and political adviser. In this new role, ibn Killis rose to a status so senior that other advisers could not incur the slightest expenditure without his personal orders. Even the court chamberlains 'stood up to do him honour.'[20]

Like other successful Jews, ibn Killis still faced restrictions and perils along with his prosperity. In an effort to become Vizier – the most senior administrative post in Egypt, and one from which Jews were excluded – he declared himself a Muslim, learned the Koran and entered a mosque for the first time. But the enmity of the existing Vizier, Ibn al-Furat, was decisive, and the post was not given to him. When Kafur died in 968, Ibn al-Furat had ibn Killis arrested and imposed a heavy fine on him. The once-powerful Jew was forced to borrow money from his brother. After buying his own freedom, ibn Killis fled from Egypt to the Maghreb.[21]

In Tunisia, ibn Killis achieved the success that had been taken from him in Egypt, by joining the fourth Fatimid Caliph, Ma'add al-Mu'izz, then ruler of northern Africa. Because al-Mu'izz put no restrictions on how high a *dhimmi* could rise in the service of the Caliph,

---

[19] Kafur had been the black Ethiopian slave and eunuch of Muhammad bin Tughj, founder of the Ikhshidid dynasty in Egypt. Bin Tughj freed him from slavery, made him tutor to his children and gave him command of the Egyptian military expedition to Syria (945). Kafur was effective ruler of Egypt from 946 until his death twenty-two years later.

[20] Quoted in Walter J. Fischel, *Jews in the Economic and Political Life of Medieval Islam,* pages 47-68.

[21] His brother, Abu Ibrahim Sahl, was later one of several leading Jews who were executed in 1004 by the sixth Fatimid Caliph, Mansur Abu Ali, surnamed al-Hakim bi-Amr Allah (Ruler by God's Command). Al-Hakim was one of the founders of the Druze religious sect, half of whom live today in Syria, and some six per cent in Israel, where Druze men serve in the Israeli Army.

ibn Killis returned to Judaism and for five years helped al-Mu'izz prepare for his conquest of Egypt. He seems even to have encouraged the move; in the words of Stanley Lane-Poole, a British historian of Egypt, 'his representations confirmed the Fatmid Caliph's resolve.'[22] Then, in 973, after the conquest, ibn Killis took charge of Egypt's finances, helping to lay the economic and political foundations of the sound and efficient Fatimid administration. The German orientalist C.H. Becker has ascribed to ibn Killis's administrative and economic skills the great prosperity of the Nile Valley in this period.[23]

Al-Mu'izz's son, the fifth Fatimid Caliph, Abu Mansur Nizar al-Aziz, made ibn Killis his Vizier in 976 – rewarding an ambition that ibn Killis had been denied nine years earlier. In this high position, ibn Killis reorganised the Fatimid administrative structure and was consulted on foreign policy and strategy. He also supervised the workings of the administration in all lands conquered by the Fatimids: northern Africa and Egypt, then Palestine (hitherto under the rule of a Bedouin tribe) in 982, Damascus a year later, and finally the Muslim holy cities of Mecca and Medina.

One of ibn Killis's most remarkable achievements came in 988, when he established the al-Azhar University in Cairo, which became the most important centre of learning in the Islamic world.[24] He also founded a public library in Cairo that contained an estimated 200,000 volumes. Except for a short period in which he was out of power, ibn Killis remained at the helm of Egypt's political life until his death in 991. When ibn Killis was on his deathbed the Caliph, deeply distressed, went to see his Jewish counsellor. The Caliph lamented: 'O Yaqub. How I wish that you were for sale so that I might buy you with my kingdom, or that you could be ransomed,

---

[22] Stanley Lane-Poole, *History of Egypt*, page 101, and Walter J. Fischel, *Jews in the Economic and Political Life of Medieval Islam*, pages 47-68.

[23] C.H. Becker, 'Ibn Killis, Fatimid vizier,' *Encyclopaedia of Islam*, Volume Two, pages 398-9.

[24] It was here, 1,021 years after al-Azhar was founded, that United States President Barack Obama made his appeal to the Muslim world for dialogue and understanding between Islam and the United States.

that I might ransom you.'[25] He later attended ibn Killis's funeral and laid his former adviser into the grave with his own hands – an extraordinary honour for a Muslim ruler to show to a Jew.

The success of Yaqub ibn Killis was echoed in the achievements of many other Jews in this period. During the reign of Caliph al-Aziz (975–996), Jewish talent was rewarded after the conquest of Damascus in 983, when a Jew was appointed governor in Syria. Such openness in the Caliph's government prompted Muslims to complain they were being pushed out of important posts; as a result, al-'Aziz ordered his Christian and Jewish officials to appoint more Muslims to their offices.

A century after ibn Killis, another Jewish government official, Abu al-Munajja Solomon ben Shaya, followed a similar path. As an administrator of several districts in Egypt, Solomon ben Shaya achieved fame with an irrigation canal he constructed between 1113 and 1118, bringing water into a parched agricultural landscape. So respected was he that local people gave him the Arabic title *Sani al-Dawla* ('The Noble of the State'). But, like others before him, Solomon ben Shaya was confronted with hostility and resentment. Defamatory tales about him were brought to a jealous Vizier, who exiled him to Alexandria where he was imprisoned without trial. Solomon ben Shaya managed to escape, however, and was reinstated soon afterward. He is described in documents that survive in the Cairo Genizah as a benefactor of the Jews.[26]

Prominent Jews also thrived in Muslim Spain, under the protective and benign rule of Caliph Abd al-Rahman III. One leading Jewish scholar, Moses ben Hanoch, found safety and prosperity there after a dramatic and dangerous incident at sea. In 972, while touring the Mediterranean with two fellow scholars from the Babylonian academy of Sura, Moses ben Hanoch was captured by Arab pirates – a not uncommon occurrence in the Tenth Century, when pirates based

---

[25] Walter J. Fischel, *Jews in the Economic and Political Life of Medieval Islam*, pages 47-68.
[26] Eliyahu Ashtor, 'Abu al-Munajja Solomon ben Shaya,' *Encyclopaedia Judaica*, Volume 2, column 180. According to an Arab author, Solomon ben Shaya's descendants, mostly converts to Islam, served as court physicians to the rulers of Egypt.

in Algeria roamed throughout the region.[27] The three scholars were ransomed to Jewish communities in different countries; Moses ben Hanoch, with his young son Enoch, was sent to Cordova.

After his arrival in Cordova, Moses ben Hanoch was elected by the local Jewish community as its rabbi.[28] He then founded a Talmudic academy, which marked the beginning of Talmudic learning in Spain. His work at the academy made local Jews independent of the religious authority of distant Babylonia, and – because of the hostility between the caliphates of Cordova and Baghdad – helped to protect the continuity of Jewish life in southern Spain.

The Jewish community of Cordova was at that time headed by a physician and diplomat named Hasdai Ibn Shaprut, who himself achieved favour and creative prominence. A personal physician to the Caliph, he was held in high regard by Jews and Muslims alike. The Caliph rewarded his service with the management of the kingdom's Department of Customs, which gave Ibn Shaprut authority over the taxation of ships coming from all Mediterranean ports. The Caliph also gave him the authority to settle disputes within the Jewish community, and to defend the Jewish community from its Muslim adversaries.

On one occasion Ibn Shaprut rescued a Jewish man who had been set upon by robbers ordered to attack him by a Muslim tax collector. On other occasions he persuaded the Caliph to give official appointments to members of the Jewish community. He also wrote a letter to the Byzantine Emperor Constantine VII and his Empress, urging them to grant more freedom to the Jews in their Christian domains.[29] It was not without reason that Jews gave Ibn Shaprut the title *nasi* (prince).[30]

---

[27] The two other scholars were Shemariah and Hushief, who were ransomed, respectively, to Egypt and North Africa. To avoid falling into the hands of their captors, Moses ben Hanoch's wife had asked her husband whether those who were drowned in the sea could look forward to resurrection when the Messiah came. When he answered, in the words of the Psalms, 'The Lord saith . . . I will bring them again from the depths of the sea,' she cast herself into the waters and was drowned.
[28] 'Exilarch,' '1,000 years ago Sepharad Ransoms a Babylonian Rabbi,' *The Scribe*, Issue 6, Volume 1, July-August 1972.
[29] Joan Comay, *The Diaspora Story*, page 175.
[30] Eliyahu Ashtor, *The Jews of Moslem Spain*, pages 159-64.

In 958, Ibn Shaprut mediated between the warring Christian kings of Leon and Navarre. As the caliphate's chief diplomatic adviser, fluent in the colloquial Latin of Christian diplomacy, he managed to bring the two kings to Cordova to sign a treaty in front of the Caliph. These linguistic skills had been seen seven years earlier, after Constantine VII sent the Caliph a copy of Dioscorides' *De Materia Medica*, an illuminated Byzantine manuscript written more than four hundred years earlier.[31] Working with a Byzantine monk from Constantinople, and with several Arab physicians, Ibn Shaprut supervised the translation of this pioneering work of botanical and medical science from the original Greek into Arabic. By translating this and other Greek and Latin medical books for the Caliph, he ensured that previously unknown medical remedies were made available in the correct idiomatic usage of Arabic Spain. Henceforth, Cordova and Palermo (which was then also under Muslim rule) became the leading medical centres of the early medieval world.[32]

The benign rule of Muslim Spain – and the fortunes of many Jews – fell into turmoil in the early Eleventh Century, when the caliphate that had ruled Spain from Granada collapsed. In place of the caliphate, a number of warring principalities emerged, each under different Arab and Berber rulers. Yet from 1030 to 1056, one of these principalities, the Berber kingdom of Granada, had as its vizier a Jew, Samuel ibn Nagrela.[33] For twenty-six years, Samuel ibn Nagrela not only administered this Muslim realm, he led its army into battle against the rival Muslim kingdom of Seville. That a Jew could head a Muslim army gave great pride to the Jews, who never doubted ibn Nagrela's Jewish devotion; indeed, he gave money to establish Talmudic academies,

---

[31] For the story of another copy of this codex, see page 78, note 9.

[32] David Levering Lewis, *God's Crucible*, page 331, and Jane S. Gerber, *The Jews of Spain*, page 49.

[33] He was known to the Jews of Granada as Samuel ha-Nagid, after he was granted by them the title *Nagid* ('Governor'), which acknowledged his status as a community leader. It was said that Samuel ha-Nagid's skill as an Arabic calligraphist originally led to his appointment as the personal secretary to the previous Vizier. David Goldstein (editor), *Hebrew Poets from Spain*, page 31.

endowed poor Jewish students with scholarships and carried out philanthropy among Jews throughout the Muslim world, including the
supply of olive oil to synagogues in distant Jerusalem.[34]

The 'Golden Age' of the Jewish communities in Muslim Spain
was ultimately shattered in 1066, when Samuel ibn Nagrela, was
assassinated along with his son, Joseph. Their murder had been
prompted by the revelation that Joseph wanted to set up a Sephardi-
Jewish principality in Almeria. Soon afterwards there was a savage
attack by local Muslims on the Jewish population of Granada, in
which an estimated five thousand Jews were murdered. This number
was equal to, and possibly more than, the number of Jews killed by
Christian soldiers in the Rhineland thirty years later, at the start of
the First Crusade.

The historian Andrew Bostom has suggested that the massacre of
the Jews of Granada was in part incited by the bitter ode of Abu
Ishaq, a noted Muslim jurist and poet[35]:

> Bring them down to their places and
> Return them to the most abject station.
> They used to roam around us in tatters
> Covered with contempt, humiliation and scorn.
> They used to rummage amongst the dung heaps for a bit of
>   filthy rag
> To serve as a shroud for a man to be buried in. . . .
>
> Do not consider that killing them is treachery.
> Nay, it would be treachery to leave them scoffing.

Many aspects of Jewish life under Muslim rule during this period are
revealed in documents that survive in the Cairo Genizah. Records of

---

[34] Joan Comay, *The Diaspora Story*, pages 176 and 185.
[35] Andrew G. Bostom (editor), *The Legacy of Jihad: Islamic Holy War and the Fate of
Non-Muslims*, page 58.

Jewish philanthropy show the long-standing interdependence of the Jewish world. Several hundred documents relate to donations given to poor Jews in Cairo, many of whom had migrated from as far away as Hebron, Acre, Aleppo and even as far distant as Malatya in Asia Minor. The archive also provides glimpses of Jewish business, political and cultural life. Lists of Jewish professions include bankers, rabbis, scribes, teachers, dyers, flax workers, olive oil dealers, cooks, gravediggers and servants.[36] Records document the creation of the post of *Ra'is al-Yahud* (Chief of the Jews) in 1065, a position that served as a conduit between the Jewish and Muslim authorities of Egypt. A Hebrew poem survives from Cairo, written in 1077 in honour of the Caliph al-Mustansir and the Viceroy Badr al-Jamali; the financial accounts survive of a large house in Cairo owned and lived in by both Jews and Muslims in 1234.

The letters sent between Jewish communities throughout the lands of Islam give witness to the vast size and reach of the Diaspora. These letters passed through cities like Kairouan in Tunisia – a crossroads that linked Babylonia, Palestine and Egypt with Italy, Sicily, Spain and Africa south of the Sahara. They were carried by travellers like the Radhanites, Jewish traders who used Kairouan as one of their western centres as they journeyed across Europe and Central Asia both overland and by sea.[37] Among the goods carried by the Radhanites were furs, beaver skins, swords, slave girls and eunuchs, as well as spices, incense and perfumes brought from China that were much prized in Babylonia and throughout the Mediterranean.[38]

---

[36] S.D. Goitein, *A Mediterranean Society*, pages 421, 423, 425, 435 and 512.

[37] One of the gates in Kairouan was known as the *Bab al-Radhana* – the Gate of the Radhanites.

[38] For Tenth-Century Jewish trade routes, see Map 3, page 358. The Radhanites travelled the two hundred miles from Kairouan across the Mediterranean to Sicily. They also went north to the Christian Kingdom of the Franks, whose capital was at Aix-la-Chapelle (Aachen), and east to Khazaria, between the Black and Caspian Seas, where one Khazar king converted to Judaism. From the Babylonian port of Ubullah, near present-day Basra, the Radhanites even travelled by ship to India and China, which they otherwise reached overland through Central Asia. Their name is believed to derive from a Persian word meaning 'knowing the way.' They

A letter in the Cairo Genizah written by a Jewish merchant stated that he would send his goods '*fi 'id al-goyim*' – on the festival of the Gentiles – probably a reference to a caravan taking Muslim pilgrims on the *hajj*. Another letter in the Genizah was written by a Babylonian rabbi who stopped in Kairouan on his way to Spain. Many other letters contained religious questions that were addressed to well-known rabbis. One letter, sent in 1015, asked if religious instructions transmitted by letter – rather than orally – could be valid.[39] In the early Eleventh Century, these questions were often sent eastward many hundreds of miles to Rabbi Hai ben Sherira, the Gaon (head) of the religious academy of Pumbeditha in present-day Iraq.[40]

Rabbi Hai ben Sherira's correspondence reveals the situation of the Jewish minority among the Muslim majority. In one letter, he acknowledged that Jewish children could be taught Arabic writing and arithmetic, but insisted that the language of prayer remain either Hebrew or Aramaic. He also forbade synagogue cantors to sing in Arabic, even at social gatherings. In another letter, he warned that the law preventing a Jew being robbed by a Muslim did not exist in every Muslim town, and that not every Muslim obeyed the law where it did exist. Where there was no such law prohibiting robbery, Rabbi Hai wrote that all Muslims 'must be regarded as extortionists and thieves.'[41]

Despite the wealth of information that has survived from the Diaspora in the Eleventh Century, little is known about the Jews of Jerusalem at that time. What is certain is that the majority of the city's Jews suffered throughout this period, as Jerusalem witnessed natural disasters including plague and, in 1033, an earthquake. Documents in the Cairo Genizah also show that the burden of the

---

were noted for their versatility in languages, being fluent in Arabic, Greek, Persian, French, Spanish and Slavonic.

[39] H.Z. (J.W.) Hirschberg, *A History of the Jews in North Africa*, page 257.

[40] The distance overland from Kairouan to Pumbeditha, through Cairo and Damascus, is more than 2,500 miles.

[41] H.Z. (J.W.) Hirschberg, *A History of the Jews in North Africa*, page 239.

jizya tax fell heavily on the poor Jews of the city. A Jewish visitor from North Africa, arriving among the Jews of Jerusalem in the mid–Eleventh Century, wrote of how 'meat is scarce and their cotton garments are worn out.'[42] Professor Goitein has observed how only one hundred Jews in the city possessed a regular income in 1047, because in that year the community paid a collective *jizya* tax of one hundred dinars, when the minimum *jizya* payment for each non-Muslim was one dinar. Those Jews who did not pay – and they were the majority – were 'Mourners of Zion,' recipients of charity who were exempt from payment of the poll tax.[43]

Most of the Jewish community in Jerusalem survived on money sent from the Diaspora, or brought to the city during the annual Jewish pilgrim festivals.[44] Solomon ben Judah, who arrived in Jerusalem from Fez, and who served as cantor in the early Eleventh Century, wrote several pleas for financial support to the Jewish communities in Egypt, Damascus, Aleppo and Tyre. He mentioned in a private letter that he had accepted a minimal salary as cantor, stating, 'the Jerusalemites did not give me anything worth a *perutah*, because they do not have anything.'[45] From cantor, Solomon ben Judah rose to become the head of Jerusalem's Jewish religious academy. Many of his Hebrew and Arabic letters survive to this day. One of his poems expressed a yearning for the redemption of Jerusalem.[46]

A thousand years had passed since Jerusalem was last under Jewish rule. Another nine hundred were to pass before Jews were to rule it again. As was the case everywhere under Muslim rule, Jews in Jerusalem were dependent for their prosperity on the extent of

---

[42] Eliyahu Ashtor and Haïm Z'ew Hirschberg, 'Jerusalem, Arab Period,' *Encyclopaedia Judaica*, Volume 9, column 1411.

[43] Shlomo D, Goitein, 'Jerusalem in the Arab Period,' Lee I. Levine (editor), *The Jerusalem Cathedra*, page 189.

[44] Eliyahu Ashtor and Haïm Z'ew Hirschberg, 'Jerusalem, Arab Period,' *Encyclopaedia Judaica*, Volume 9, column 1411.

[45] A *perutah* was the coin of the smallest value in Talmudic times.

[46] Eliezer Bashan (Sternberg), 'Solomon ben Judah (d. 1051),' *Encyclopaedia Judaica*, Volume 15, columns 122-4.

tolerance shown to them by their rulers, and on the goodwill or ill will of their Muslim neighbours. Although the first four centuries of Islam saw the success of individual Jews in every part of the lands of Islam – the *umma* – these years did not relieve the looming and ever-present threat of discrimination and persecution.

5

JEWS AND MUSLIMS IN THE AGE OF THE CRUSADES

'Great and small testify against us'

At the end of the Eleventh Century, Christian rulers in Europe considered it a religious imperative to recapture Jerusalem and the Holy Land, and to restore to Christian rule the many other lands that had been conquered by Islam in the preceding five centuries. The resulting wars of Christians against Muslims – the Crusades – were fought for almost two hundred years. Occasionally the Crusaders forced the armies of Islam to make considerable retreats from areas previously ruled without hindrance. When the Crusaders marched through Christian and Muslim lands, in Europe or the Levant, Jews were murdered in their path.

On 6 June 1099, at the climax of the First Crusade, Jerusalem itself lay open to Christian reconquest. Upon arriving from northern Europe, the Crusaders began their siege of the Holy City. For thirty-eight days, Muslim soldiers held the walls. In the northeastern sector, Jews and Muslims joined together to keep the battlements secure. But on July 15, after four hundred years of Muslim rule, the walls of Jerusalem were breached. The Crusaders swept through the city, massacring Muslims and Jews alike. Many Jews sought sanctuary in the synagogues, but the Crusaders set these on fire. Those Jews who were trapped inside were burned alive. Other Jews were seized and taken to Europe, where they were sold as slaves. Still others were taken to the coastal city of Ashkelon, where their Christian captors ransomed them to the Jewish community of Egypt. Jerusalem was then resettled by European Christians and

Arab converts to Christianity; Muslims and Jews were refused permission to live in the city.[1]

The First Crusade heralded a period of extreme tumult and religious intolerance, and yet within the confines of the Muslim world, great Jewish thinkers, scholars and poets continued to live and work. Many Jews held positions of considerable influence at Muslim courts, and under all but the most fanatical caliphates, Jews were highly prized in Muslim societies as doctors, linguists and writers. A number of Jewish scholars in the Tenth and Eleventh Centuries made great contributions to Jewish culture, including Yehouda ben David Hayouj, who, living in Morocco, laid the foundations of the study of Hebrew grammar.

One renowned Jewish poet of this period was Yehuda ben Samuel ibn Abbas al-Maghribi, known best as Judah Halevi. His work survives to this day in the synagogue services of both the Sephardi and Ashkenazi High Holy Days. Born in Muslim Spain in about 1070, Halevi became a physician as well as a poet. His most influential work, *Sefer Ha-Kuzari*, was a 'Book of Responses to Allegations Against the Downtrodden Faith.' Halevi's poem *Yedidi Hashachachta* ('My friend, have you forgotten?') also became significant, notably in the Babylonian and Moroccan traditions, as a poem for the seventh day of Passover that is filled with both yearning for redemption and longing for Zion.[2]

---

[1] Encyclopaedia Hebraica, 'Jerusalem, Crusader Period,' *Encyclopaedia Judaica*, Volume 9, column 1415.

[2] Another leading Jewish poet was Isaac ibn Ezra, who lived during the Twelfth Century. He was the grandson of one of the most respected and widely travelled Jewish poets, grammarians and philosophers, Abraham ibn Ezra. Isaac served for some years as the court poet in Baghdad. In one of his poems, he confessed that he had become a Muslim some years earlier, much to his grandfather's distress, but that he remained in his heart a loyal Jew and continued to keep the commandments. Born in Tudela, Abraham ibn Ezra visited Morocco, Algeria, Tunis, Egypt, Italy and France. He also lived in London for three years (1158–61), where he wrote two books. J.H. Steinschneider, 'Ibn Ezra, Isaac (12th century),' *Encyclopaedia Judaica*, Volume 8, column 1170.

The greatest Jewish scholar of the Middle Ages was Maimonides.
Known as Musa ibn Maymun in Arabic and as Rabbi Moshe ben
Maimon in Hebrew, Maimonides was commonly referred to by Jews
with his Hebrew acronym, the Rambam. He was conversant with
Arab thought and culture, spoke and wrote in Arabic, and held posi-
tions close to power in Muslim society.

In 1159, having fled the ferocious persecution of Jews by the
Almohads in Muslim Spain, Maimonides settled for five years in Fez.[3]
There he was forced to convert to Islam under an obligation introduced for all Jews living in the city. Later he was arrested by Muslim
authorities on the charge of relapsing into Judaism – an accusation
that he escaped only because a Muslim friend attested to his good
Muslim character. In his *Epistle on Martyrdom*, Maimonides justified
this formal conversion to Islam as an acceptable alternative to torture and death under the rule of fanatical Muslim rulers. He advised
his fellow Jews: 'Utter the formula' – of conversion – 'and live.'[4]

After leaving Fez, Maimonides settled in Egypt under the more
tolerant rule of the Shiite Fatimids, where he was allowed to practise
Judaism once again. It was here that he wrote his much-quoted *Epistle
to the Jews of Yemen*. The head of the Yemeni Jews had appealed to
Maimonides for advice on how to face the threat of persecution and
forced conversions under Muslim rule. In his response, Maimonides
told the Jews that 'on account of our sins God has cast us into the
midst of this people, the nation of Ishmael, who persecute us severely,
and who devise ways to harm us and to debase us. This is as the
Exalted had warned us: "Even our enemies themselves being judges."'[5]
Maimonides went on to note: 'We have done as our sages of blessed
memory instructed us, bearing the lies and absurdities of Ishmael. We
listen but we remain silent.' In spite of this silence, 'we are not spared

---

[3] See pages 64-8 for the story of the Almohads.
[4] Sherwin B. Nuland, *Maimonides*, page 85. Maimonides was echoing Deuteronomy
31:19: 'I call heaven and earth to record this day against you, that I have set before
you life and death, blessing and cursing: therefore choose life, that both thou and
thy seed may live.'
[5] Deuteronomy 32:31.

from the ferocity of their wickedness, and their outburst at any time. On the contrary, the more we suffer and choose to conciliate them, the more they choose to act belligerently towards us.'[6]

It was in his letter to the Jews of Yemen that Maimonides wrote, 'No nation has ever done more harm to Israel. None has matched it in debasing and humiliating us. None has been able to reduce us as they have.' For Maimonides, who knew about the Crusader attacks on the Jews of Europe, these words about Islam were a considered historical judgment. His own family had witnessed the persecution of Jews in Muslim Spain – then under the oppressive rule of the Almohads – and had also faced death threats in Fez. His teacher in Fez, Judah ibn Sussan, had been martyred in 1165 after refusing conversion to Islam.

In Muslim-ruled Cairo, however, Maimonides had found an environment that encouraged his learning and creativity. That he saw the authorities in Egypt as different in nature was clear when he urged them to help alleviate the Yemeni Jews' political and economic disabilities.[7] Maimonides served as Chief Rabbi of the Jewish community in Cairo, and after losing his family fortune – following the death of his brother David, a successful merchant, in a shipwreck on the way to India – Maimonides turned to practicing medicine as a livelihood. His fame as a physician was such that Saladin, as Sultan of Egypt, appointed him court physician. Saladin's two previous court physicians were both Jews: one was the Grand Rabbi of Egypt, Hibet Allah ibn al Jami; the other was Abdul-Ma'ali al Yahudi, Maimonides' brother-in-law.[8]

Among Maimonides' contributions to good health was his emphasis on a clean environment. 'City air is stagnant, turbid and thick,' he wrote, 'the natural result of its big buildings, narrow streets and refuse

---

[6] 'Maimonides' Epistle to the Jews of Yemen,' in Norman A. Stillman, *The Jews of Arab Lands: History and Source Book*, page 241.

[7] Maimonides also predicted that the inequalities imposed on the Jews would end with the coming of the Messiah, which he believed would take place in the year 1216 – the year 4976 in the Jewish calendar.

[8] Harry Friedenwald, *The Jews and Medicine: Essays*, pages 197-8. Abdul-Ma'ali al Yahudi was married to Maimonides' sister. Maimonides' wife was Abdul-Ma'ali al Yahudi's sister.

of its inhabitants. . . . The concern for clean air is the foremost rule in preserving the health of one's body and soul.'[9] In his writings on food and diet, Maimonides advocated a 'shared convivial meal' as a way to conquer anxiety and tension and also to overcome 'suspicion between ethnic groups.' His other medical writings included a treatise on sex and aphrodisiacs, *Fi 'l-Jima'* ('On Sexual Intercourse'), which concentrated heavily on nutrition – a branch of medicine in which Maimonides was a pioneer. The treatise was commissioned by Sultan Omar, the nephew of Saladin, and was written in Arabic and intended for a non-Jewish reader. But Maimonides' draft, which survives, was written in Judaeo-Arabic – Arabic words written in Hebrew characters – then the written vernacular of medieval Egyptian Jews.[10]

Maimonides also acted as physician to Saladin's eldest son, Sultan al-Malik al-Afdal, who ruled for only two years, and who suffered from depression and melancholia. Maimonides' advice to him – translated into Latin as *Regimen Sanitatis* – became one of his most widely used medical writings. In addition to his advice on personal hygiene, diet, sexual hygiene and the effects of heat and cold, it included a discussion of the strength that philosophy and ethics could give to an individual's attitude towards the problems met with in life. These two disciplines, Maimonides asserted, taught the real value of life's realities and pressures.[11]

Maimonides described his life and work in Muslim Egypt in a letter he wrote to his friend, disciple and translator, Rabbi Samuel ibn Tibbon. First he explained his duties as court physician: 'I live in Fustat and the Sultan resides in Cairo; these two places are two Sabbath limits distant from each other. My duties to the Sultan are very heavy. I am obliged to visit him every day, early in the morning, and when he, any of his children or any one of his concubines are

---

[9] Frank Heynick, *Jews and Medicine: An Epic Saga*, page 111. The filth and stench of medieval Cairo was notorious; Maimonides' baby daughter may well have died of a miasmic illness emanating from the Nile.

[10] Cairo Genizah manuscript, Cambridge University Library, T-S Ar.44.79.

[11] Harry Friedenwald, *The Jews and Medicine: Essays*, pages 210-11. *Regimen Sanitatis* was to become the first medical book published in Florence (in 1477). Between 1501 and 1535 it was published in Pavia, Venice, Augsburg and Lyon.

indisposed, I cannot leave Cairo but must stay during most of the day in the palace. . . . Hence, as a rule, every day, in the morning I go to Cairo. Even if nothing unusual happens there, I do not return to Fustat until the afternoon.'

Returning to Fustat, Maimonides would find other patients awaiting him: 'I am famished, but I find the antechambers filled with people, both Jews and Gentiles, nobles and common people, judges and policemen, friends and enemies – a mixed multitude who await the time of my return. I dismount from my animal, wash my hands, go forth to my patients and entreat them to bear with me while I partake of some light refreshment, the only meal I eat in twenty-four hours. Then I go to attend to my patients and write prescriptions and directions for their ailments. Patients go in and out until nightfall, and sometimes even, as the Torah is my faith, until two hours or more into the night. I converse with them and prescribe for them even while lying down from sheer fatigue.'

Maimonides also described his not-inconsiderable religious life: 'When night falls, I am so exhausted that I can hardly speak. In consequence of this, no Israelite can converse with or befriend me' – on religious or community matters – 'except on the Sabbath. On that day, the whole congregation, or at least the majority, comes to me after the morning service, when I instruct them as to their proceedings during the whole week. We study a little together until noon, when they depart. Some of them return and read with me following the afternoon service until evening prayers.'[12]

In recognition of his importance to Egypt's Jewish community, Maimonides was declared *Ra'is al-Yahud*, 'Head of the Jews.' The holder of this post was chosen by the Jewish notables of Fustat and was recognised by the Muslim authorities as the official representative of the Jewish community. Maimonides held the position twice: in the years 1171–2 and from 1196 until 1204.[13]

---

[12] Quoted in *Letters of Moses Maimonides*, pages xii–xiv. The letter was written in 1199.
[13] Cairo Genizah manuscript, Cambridge University Library, T-S J2.78. A draft proclamation declaring Maimonides *Ra'is al-Yahud* is in the Cambridge University Genizah manuscripts.

On 13 December 1204, while dictating to a scribe the last chapter of a book on his aphorisms, Maimonides died. He was sixty-six years old. Muslims as well as Jews mourned his passing.[14]

During the first period of Crusader rule in Jerusalem, which lasted eighty-eight years, Jewish communities in the Holy Land did not fare well. In 1119, Jews were expelled from their homes in Hebron, a city twenty miles south of Jerusalem, after Christian clerics decided to take over the Tombs of the Patriarchs – Abraham, Isaac and Jacob. A large number of those expelled Jews found sanctuary in Muslim-ruled Egypt.[15] It was not until some time towards the end of Crusader rule that Jews were allowed to resume trading inside Jerusalem. The Jewish traveller Benjamin of Tudela wrote of how he met a few Jewish dyers working in the city when visited Jerusalem in 1170.[16]

The situation in the Holy Land improved considerably seventeen years after Benjamin's visit. Saladin, the Muslim warrior, and a Kurd, reached the walls of Jerusalem and laid siege to the city for five months. When the Christians surrendered and Muslim rule was restored in 1187, Saladin encouraged the Jews to return to their former homes. Some Jews came from Ashkelon, others from as far as Yemen, and others from North Africa. Between 1209 and 1211, three hundred rabbis also reached the Holy Land from England, northern France and Provence. They settled in Jerusalem, Ramla and Acre, intent on reviving the Jewish communities there after the Crusader persecutions.

Then came a period of joint Muslim-Christian rule over Jerusalem, from 1229 to 1244, followed by a prolonged economic decline after it was conquered by the Khwarizm Turks, a Tatar tribe from Central Asia. The Tatars were driven out after six years, when Jerusalem became part of the Muslim Mamluk kingdom of Egypt. Although the city remained in decline economically, Jews continued to settle there. This was partly a result of efforts made by individuals

---

[14] Sherwin B. Nuland, *Maimonides*, page 152.
[15] S.D. Goitein, *A Mediterranean Society*, page 447.
[16] A. Asher (editor and translator), *The Itinerary of Rabbi Benjamin of Tudela*, pages 75-7.

like Nahmanides (Rabbi Moses ben Nahman), a Spanish rabbi and scholar known by his Hebrew acronym as the Ramban. After arriving in Jerusalem, Nahmanides helped to organise the local Jewish community, founding a religious academy and establishing a synagogue in a derelict house. He later moved to the coastal city of Acre, another town ruled by the Mamluks, where he served briefly as the spiritual leader of the Jewish community until his death in 1270.[17]

In the year of Nahmanides' death, an Italian-Jewish merchant, Jacob d'Ancona, arrived at the port of Acre en route from Italy to India and China. His comments about what he saw provide a valuable insight into the relationship between Jews and Muslims after the first Crusades. In his diary, Jacob wrote of Acre that 'between the Jew and the Mahometan there is more love than between the Jew and the Christian, for the Mahometan declares himself to be the son of Abraham our ancestor and reveres our teacher Moses.'

Continuing on his journey, Jacob d'Ancona reached the Babylonian city of Basra, where he observed the long-standing divisions between Jews and Muslims. 'They wear dark-coloured garments,' he wrote of the Jews, 'a vermilion cap bound around with silk cloth which is striped, and on their feet are permitted only dark shoes, by which to distinguish them from others.'[18] Yet Jacob also noted the diversity of Jewish economic life in Basra, stating that there were 'not only traders among the Jews, but also tailors, workers in wood, leather and iron, makers of shoes and saddles as well as many apothecaries and physicians.' He also observed significant prosperity among the Jewish population. 'Many Jews act as agents,' he wrote, 'and by that acquire great wealth, as also in exchanging gold and silver of different countries, in which they make great profits.'

This familiar picture of cooperation and segregation, of protection and exclusion, continued to characterise Jewish life in the lands conquered by Islam as it had before the Crusades. Outside the Holy Land, many Jewish communities under Muslim rule

---

[17] Joseph Kaplan, 'Nahmanides,' *Encyclopaedia Judaica*, Volume 12, columns 774-7.
[18] Jacob d'Ancona, *The City of Light*, pages 49-50.

remained untouched by the advance of the Crusaders. After more than a thousand years of resettlement and migration, these communities were spread widely across the Muslim-ruled regions that make up the modern-day Middle East.

In Afghanistan, Jews lived in the towns of Balkh and Ghazni during the Eleventh and Twelfth Centuries.[19] One Ghazni ruler, Sultan Mahmud (998–1030), assigned a Jew named Isaac to administer his lead mines and melt ore for him. Another Afghan Jewish community lived in Firoz Koh, in the central mountain district. The town and its inhabitants – both Muslims and Jews – were later wiped out during the Mongol invasion of Afghanistan in 1222, but some twenty tablets with Hebrew writing were discovered there in the 1920s. Jews also lived under Muslim rule in the Afghan cities of Kabul and Kandahar. A tombstone near Kabul, dated 1365, was erected in memory of a Jewish man named Moses ben Ephraim Bezalel, apparently a senior official.[20]

A large number of Jewish communities lived under Muslim rule in Kurdistan (the northern region of modern-day Iraq). On a visit there in 1170, Benjamin of Tudela came across more than a hundred Jewish communities.[21] It is known that many of the Jews of Kurdistan lived at times in poverty. It is therefore unsurprising that two messianic movements – which often arose from economic distress – emerged among the Jews there in the Twelfth Century.[22] Yet there is evidence that the Jews of Kurdistan also prospered. There were no Jewish bankers, since that role was reserved for Muslim

[19] See Map 18, page 372.
[20] W.J. Fischel, 'Afghanistan,' *Encyclopaedia Judaica*, Volume 2, columns 326-7.
[21] Thirty-eight of those hundred communities claimed descent from the tribe of Benjamin. The traveller also estimated that the town of Amadiya had a Jewish population of about two thousand, all of whom spoke biblical Aramaic as their daily language, including a number of biblical scholars. Abraham Ben-Jacob, 'Kurdistan,' *Encyclopaedia Judaica*, Volume 10, column 1297. Curiously, there were 1,820 Jews in Amadiya in 1933, all of whom later left for Israel.
[22] One movement was headed by Menahem ben Solomon ibn Ruhi, the other by David Alroy. Some scholars think these two men were one and the same. Abraham Ben-Jacob, 'Kurdistan,' *Encyclopaedia Judaica*, Volume 10, column 1297.

landowners, but Jewish tradesmen ranged from shopkeepers to peddlers, while Jewish craftsmen included weavers, dyers, gold and silversmiths, tanners and cobblers, as well as unskilled labourers. In rural areas, Jewish farmers owned orchards, vineyards, flocks of sheep and herds of cattle. They cultivated wheat, barley, rice, sesame, lentils and tobacco.[23]

One of the most prominent of all Jewish communities lived in the Babylonian city of Baghdad. Visiting the city shortly before 1170, Benjamin of Tudela noted that it was home to 'about one thousand Jews, who enjoy peace, comfort and much honour under the government of the great king.' Among them were 'very wise men and presidents of the colleges, whose occupation is the study of the Mosaic Law.' Benjamin also mentioned the city's two rabbinical schools and twenty-eight synagogues, the chief one richly ornamented with marble, gold and silver. He praised the Caliph for being versed in the Torah and able to speak and write in Hebrew – highlighting further the acceptance afforded to the Jews in Baghdad.

The head of Baghdad's Jewish community, the Exilarch, played an integral role in the city's political life. Each Thursday, as Benjamin observed, 'when the Exilarch goes to pay a visit to the great Caliph, horsemen – non-Jews as well as Jews – escort him, and heralds proclaim in advance: "Make way before our lord, the son of David, as is due unto him."' Benjamin described the pomp of this procession in great detail, noting that the Exilarch 'is mounted on a horse, and is attired in robes of silk and embroidery, with a large turban on his head, and from the turban is suspended a large white cloth adorned with a chain upon which the seal of Mohammed is engraved. Then he appears before the Caliph and kisses his hand, and the Caliph rises and places him on a throne which Mohammed had ordered to be made in honour of him.' All the Muslim princes attending the Caliph's court were commanded to stand up and salute the Exilarch, 'respectfully under penalty of one hundred stripes.'[24]

---

[23] Abraham Ben-Yaacob, 'Kurdistan.' *Encyclopaedia Judaica,* Volume 10, column 1297.
[24] A. Asher (editor and translator), *The Itinerary of Rabbi Benjamin of Tudela,* pages 100-2.

The integration of Jews in Baghdad society had developed over four centuries of Jewish-Muslim coexistence. When the city was founded by the Abbasid Caliph Abu Ja'far al-Mansur in 762, Jews had assisted in its construction. They were then given their own quarter, the Dar al-Yahud, where the Exilarch set up his residence. By the end of the Ninth Century, the two Jewish religious academies of Sura and Pumbeditha were moved to Baghdad, which then became the source of rabbinical judgments that were highly regarded throughout the Jewish world. By the end of the Tenth Century two leading Jewish families, Netira and Aaron, were powerful influences in the royal court and strong supporters of the welfare of the Jewish community. During the reign of Caliph al-Muqtafi (902–908) and his successors, the Jewish community in Baghdad flourished; its leader, the Exilarch Daniel ben Hasdai, was respected by both the Jews and the royal court alike.

Life under Muslim rule could prove beneficial for some Jews, but it still held the prospect of persecution as well as protection. In the Twelfth Century a new period of Islamic persecution had begun under the rule of the Almohads (*al-Mowahhidun*, 'Unitarians').[25] Originating among the Berber tribes of the High Atlas Mountains on the edge of the Sahara, the Almohads launched a Muslim religious movement designed to restore by force the 'pure faith' of Islam. The movement spread throughout North Africa – the Maghreb – and into Muslim Spain. Led by Muhammad ibn Tumart, who died in 1130, the Almohads were initially tolerant towards non-Muslims. But as they extended their control under Ibn Tumart's successor, Abd al-Mu'min, they began to demand that Jews and Christians accept conversion to Islam, or else face death.

Many Jews from Muslim Spain and North Africa fled for safety to the more tolerant Muslim rulers in Egypt and Palestine. And as the Almohads imposed their rule throughout Muslim Spain, Spanish Jews also fled to the Christian regions of both Spain and

---

[25] 'The People of Unity' or 'The Unitarians,' from *tawhid* – *unity* (of God).

southern France. Other Jews, like Maimonides and his family, sought refuge in the Moroccan city of Fez, where the Almohads had not initially demanded conversion to Islam. But when the Moroccan town of Sijilmassa was captured by the Almohads in 1146, the Jews living there were given the same stark choice: conversion to Islam or death. As many as 150 Jews chose death rather than become Muslims. Others, led by their religious leader, Joseph ben Amram, converted to Islam. An identical choice was given to the Jews of neighbouring Dar'a. From the chief Moroccan city, Marrakech, Jews were expelled altogether.

The Jewish poet Abraham ibn Ezra wrote an elegy on the destruction of the Jewish communities of Andalucia and the Maghreb, voicing a cry of pain that echoed throughout the tormented world of the Jews under Muslim rule:

> Woe, misfortune from heaven, has befallen Andalucia,
> And a great mourning overtaken the Maghreb.
> Therefore am I helpless;
> My eyes overflow with weeping. . . .
>
> The houses of prayer and praise
> have been transformed into houses of impiety.
> For a fierce and foreign people
> has torn asunder the faithful creed of God. . . .
>
> How has the city of Cordova become utterly forsaken,
> reduced to an ocean of ruins!
> Its sages and magnates perished through hunger and thirst;
> No Jew, no single one, survives in Jaén nor Almeria. . . .
>
> How was the Maghreb helplessly devastated?
> Woe misfortune from heaven has befallen Andalucia;
> My eyes overflow with weeping. . . .

Woe I cry as a woman in distress,
for the congregation of Sijilmassa;
City of scholars and sages,
Whose brilliance was engulfed by darkness.[26]

Under the Almohad ruler Sultan Abu Yaqub (who died in 1184), spurious conversions to Islam were common. But under Sultan Yaqub's successor, Yaqub al-Mansur (1184–1199), severe restrictions were imposed on Jewish converts. They could not marry Muslims; they could not possess slaves; they could not act as guardians; they could not wear Muslim headdress; and they could not engage in large-scale trading, hitherto a Jewish speciality. Realising that most of the Jewish converts were not sincere in their conversion to Islam, al-Mansur devised a particularly visible and degrading costume for all Jewish men who claimed to have converted: a long blue tunic with absurdly large, wide sleeves that reached to a person's feet, and a blue skull cap in the shape of a donkey's saddle that fell below the ears. Jewish converts were also made to wear a piece of yellow cloth sewn onto their outer garment.[27]

Among those who witnessed the plight of Jews under Sultan al-Mansur was the Jewish philosopher Ibn 'Aqnin. From his hometown of Barcelona, where he was born in 1150, Ibn 'Aqnin saw first-hand the forced conversions that followed the Almohad conquest of Spain. He moved to Fez, where he wrote a lament for the fate of those who – like himself – had submitted to Islam but found they were still not free from persecution. Referring to the situation during the reign of al-Mansur, Ibn 'Aqnin declared that, 'however much we appear to obey their instructions to embrace their religion and forsake our own, they burden our yoke and render our travail more arduous.'

Ibn 'Aqnin also wrote of how the Jews who abandoned their faith and wore Muslim clothes were still 'subjected to the same vexations

---

[26] Abraham ibn Ezra, translated by Professor Paul Fenton from the text in H.Z. Hirschberg, *A History of the Jews in North Africa*, Volume I, Jerusalem, 1965, pages 90-1 (in Hebrew).

[27] David Corcos, 'Almohads,' *Encyclopaedia Judaica*, Volume 2, columns 662-3.

as those who have remained faithful to their creed.' Even the descendants of Jewish converts fared badly, Ibn Aqnin wrote, for 'the conversion of their fathers and grandfathers a hundred years ago has been of no advantage to them.' He continued: 'If we were to consider the persecutions that have befallen us in recent years, we would not find anything comparable recorded by our ancestors in their annals. We are made the object of inquisitions; great and small testify against us and judgments are pronounced, the least of which render lawful the spilling of our blood, the confiscation of our property, the dishonour of our wives.'

There were brief glimmers of light whenever Muslim nobles intervened on behalf of the Jews, which occurred 'two or three times,' when, as Ibn Aqnin recalled, 'the nobles pleaded in our favour while the common folk testified against us, and the custom of the land would not allow the testimony of the vulgar to supersede that of the gentry.' But Ibn Aqnin also wrote of how the situation grew even worse when a second decree 'annulled our right to inheritance and to the custody of our children, placing them in the hands of the Muslims.' This transfer of Jewish children to Muslim custodians enabled authorities to take advantage of a particular Islamic theological position – *fitra* – that maintained that all males were born Muslims, and that they became Jews or Christians only because of the education received from their non-Muslim parents. In the words of Ibn Aqnin, it was believed that Muslims who took children from Jewish or Christian parents would 'obtain considerable reward from Allah.'

Jews were also 'prohibited to practice commerce, which is our livelihood,' Ibn Aqnin wrote. 'Then we were obliged to dismiss our servants and were forbidden to employ others.' Moreover, the clothes prescribed for converts made Jewish men 'resemble the inferior status of women' and 'were intended by their length to make us unsightly, whereas their colour was to make us loathsome.' The 'ugly bonnets' that Jewish men wore on their heads were supposed to 'differentiate us from them . . . in order that they might treat us with disparagement and humiliation.' Unfortunately, such distinctive clothing had the added effect of making Jews vulnerable to attack. Ibn Aqnin noted how the clothing 'allows our blood to be spilled with impunity. For whenever we travel on the wayside from town to town, we are waylaid by robbers and brigands and are murdered secretly at night or killed in broad daylight.'

Ibn Aqnin sought to explain the purpose of the Muslim decrees – what he called 'the persecution of Ishmael.' His answer was clear: 'whether they require us to renounce our religion in public or in private is only to annihilate the faith of Israel.' For that reason, he felt that the Jew was 'bound to accept death rather than commit the slightest sin.' Referring to those who – like him – had converted to Islam, he wrote: 'Since we have remained sinful, having taken pity on ourselves, and profaned the Name of the Lord, though not will-fully . . . these terrible calamities have befallen us.'[28]

Soon after Ibn Aqnin's death in 1220, al-Mansur's son and even-tual successor, Abu Mohammed Abd Allah al-Adil (1224–1227) – 'The Just' – allowed the Jews to return to normal robes and turbans, with yellow as their distinguishing mark. Jews were also allowed to return to Marrakech. But by that time the Almohads' power was already in decline. Following their defeat in battle by rival Muslim warriors in Spain in 1212, the Almohads were gradually replaced by a number of independent Muslim kingdoms. Jewish life and worship continued henceforth without the threat of conversion, or the extreme humiliations of exaggerated *dhimmi* rules.

Muslim rule in Spain ended after the conquest of Cordova in 1236 by King Ferdinand III of Castile, and the conquest of Granada in 1492 by Ferdinand II of Aragon and his Queen Isabella. For the Jews of Spain, the indignities of *dhimmi* status under Islam were replaced by the cruelties of Christian persecution and expulsion.

In Baghdad, the true complexity of Muslim-Jewish relations emerged after the pagan Mongols conquered the city in 1258,

---

[28] Ibn Aqnin, 'Tibb an-nufus' ('Therapy of the Soul'), Judaeo-Arabic manuscript, 1273, Bodleian Library, Oxford: quoted in Bat Yeo'r, *The Dhimmi*, pages 346-7 and 349-51.

bringing Muslim rule there to a temporary but bloody end. While the Muslims of Baghdad were ill-treated by the Mongols, the Jews were not: *dhimmi* status was abolished and neither Christians nor Jews were forced to wear distinguishing clothes or pay the *jizya* tax. In 1289 the Mongol emperor Arghun Khan appointed his Jewish physician, Sa'd ad-Daula, to be Vizier throughout the Mongol Empire. The appointment of a Jew to such a senior post roused extreme anger in the Muslim population of Baghdad. Sa'd al-Daula was accused by the Muslims of having 'impounded the wealth of Islam, raised the condition of the Jews, and brought Islam into disrepute.'[29] He was also accused of plotting to murder Arghun with poison – a frequent accusation levelled against Jews, without any basis in fact. As Arghun lay dying, Sa'd ad-Daula was murdered by a Muslim mob; his death was followed by a widespread massacre of Jews throughout Persia and Babylonia, as well as the looting of Jewish homes and workshops.[30]

During the same period, however, another Jew faced a similar danger but with different results. In 1280 the Jewish philosopher Sa'd ben Mansur ibn Kammuna wrote a compendium of inter-faith polemics, in which he examined the strengths and weaknesses of Judaism, Christianity and Islam. In the book, he rebutted arguments against Judaism and improved what he considered was a weak case then being made for Christianity. His longest chapter, on Islam, was not entirely favourable. Yet when a Muslim mob, incited by a Friday sermon against his book, tried to kill ibn Kammuna, high Muslim officials smuggled him out of Baghdad in a cask.[31]

Muslim rule eventually returned to Baghdad when the Mongol Emperor Ghazzan (1295–1304) converted to Islam. This momentous change signified a return to favour for the majority of the Mongols' subjects, but for the Jews it meant a return to *dhimmi* status,

---

[29] Ghazi al-Wasiti (alive in 1292), quoted in R. Gottheil, 'An Answer to the Dhimmis,' *Journal of the American Oriental Society*, New York, issue 41, 1921.
[30] Walter J. Fischel, *Jews in the Economic and Political Life of Medieval Islam*, page 117.
[31] Moshe Perlmann, 'Ibn Kammuna, S'ad Ibn Mansur (c.1215-1285),' *Encyclopaedia Judaica*, Volume 8, columns 1186-7.

and with it the *jizya* tax and distinctive clothing. During a number of hostile Muslim attacks, churches and synagogues were destroyed throughout Ghazzan's Empire. Under his successor, Uljaytu Khan (1305–1316), Jews were forbidden to make their annual pilgrimage to the Tomb of the Prophet Ezekiel. This tomb, located in Kifl, a hundred miles south of Baghdad, was entrusted to the care of a Muslim. Soon the site was covered over by a mosque, from whose minaret the faithful of Islam were called forth to prayer.[32]

A Jewish physician, Rashid ad-Daula, was able to achieve political success despite these adverse conditions. He was appointed Vizier in 1299, after converting to Islam and changing his name to Rashid ad-Din. In deference to his origins, he employed many Jews and Jewish converts. But his Jewish origins ultimately proved to be his undoing. In 1318, when he was seventy years old, Rashid's enemies at court accused him of poisoning Uljaytu Khan. He was then executed, together with his son, Ibrahim. Rashid's head was sent from Baghdad to Tabriz, where it was dragged through the town while a proclamation was read, declaring: 'This is the head of the Jew who dishonoured the word of God, may God's curse be upon him.' As a convert to Islam, Rashid ad-Din was buried in the Muslim cemetery in Tabriz. But a century later, the ruler of Tabriz ordered his bones exhumed and reinterred in the local Jewish cemetery.[33]

A similar slide into uncertainty occurred for Jews living in Egypt, the former refuge for those seeking an escape from persecution. The Mamluks, who ruled Egypt from 1250 to 1516, enforced *dhimmi* regulations with rigour. They laid particular emphasis on the rules that imposed distinctive dress and forbade the riding of horses. Because the employment of Jews in skilled administrative positions gave rise to jealousy, a law was instituted in 1290 forbidding Jews to serve as public officials. Then, eleven years later, synagogues were closed down throughout the Mamluk Empire; they remained shut for nine years, until 1310. The buildings were only spared from

---

[32] Today, Ezekiel's tomb is a holy place for both Muslims and Jews. Above the tomb is a Hebrew inscription dating back to late medieval times.

[33] Walter J. Fischel, *Jews in the Economic and Political Life of Medieval Islam*, page 122-4.

demolition because the Jews were able to prove – by judicious use of bribery – that these synagogues predated the Muslim era.

The mid–Fourteenth Century saw an upsurge in Mamluk fanaticism. In 1327 the synagogue in Aleppo was turned into a mosque with the approval of the Mamluk Sultan in Cairo.[34] In 1354, throughout the Mamluk dominions, some of the more onerous of the *dhimmi* restrictions were extended to Jewish converts to Islam. Converts were not allowed to serve as government officials or to work as physicians in the Muslim community. They were also forced to cut off all contact with relatives who had not converted to Islam. In addition, Jewish converts to Islam were placed under strict supervision, in order to ensure that they carried out their obligatory five daily visits to the mosque.[35]

The varied nature of Jewish life under Islam allowed Jews to prosper in some places, while their brethren elsewhere suffered. In the Persian city of Shiraz, for example, the Fourteenth-Century Jewish poet Maulana Shahin became famous and admired in this period for his Judaeo-Persian verses.[36] The interaction between Jewish and Muslim cultures continued throughout Muslim lands, where Jewish poets frequently took Arabic poetic forms and used them in their work; Judah Halevi was a master of this craft. The *qasida*, a type of epic poem, was used and embellished by both Arabs and Jews. The *muwashshah* song form, or ode, was developed by both Arabic and Jewish poets and musicians. One of the first poets to model the strophic form of the *muwashshah* was a Spanish-born Jew, Ibrahim ibn Sahl al-Andalusi al-Isra'ili. The linguist Dr. Shmuel Moreh has observed that 'Arab poets tend to explain Ibn Sahl's delicacy, lyricism, tenderness and emotional depths – unequalled

---

[34] The building still functioned as a mosque in the first decade of the Twenty-First Century, more than six hundred and eighty years later. Rabbi David Sutton, *Aleppo, City of Scholars*, page 14.

[35] Eliezer Bashan (Sternberg), 'Omar, Covenant of,' *Encyclopaedia Judaica*, Volume 12, columns 1380-81.

[36] Judaeo-Persian or Jidi (also spelled Dzhidi) was the language spoken by Jews living in Persia (Iran). It uses Persian (Farsi) grammar and structure, but is written in the Hebrew alphabet and contains many words borrowed from Hebrew.

by his successors – on the basis of his humility inspired by his Jewish origins and his love.'[37]

Jewish and Muslim intellectual life remained closely inter-linked, so that both Hebrew and Arabic were used as the languages of scholarship and study. In Yemen, between 1484 and 1493, the scholar Daud Lawani (David Levi) wrote a commentary called the *Adequate Summary* of the Pentateuch – the five books of Moses – in both Arabic and Hebrew.[38] The work of Muslim musicologist, math-ematician and scientist Ibn Abi al-Salt (born in Andalucia in 1068, died in Tunisia in 1134) much influenced the Jews of Muslim Spain. Some of his work survives in Hebrew translations made in the Fourteenth Century by a Jewish musicologist, Nathan ben Solomon.

The two extremes of exclusion and cooperation defined the Muslim-Jewish relationship, inspiring a range of conflicting loyal-ties among Jewish communities living under Muslim rule. Although Jews and Muslims had both suffered at the hands of Christian Crusaders, Jews are known to have come to the aid of Christians persecuted by Muslim rulers. In Cairo in 1343, during a massacre of Christian Copts, the Jews lent the Christians their own discrimi-natory garments, with the result that the Copts were able to leave their houses in safety, 'protected' as Jews.[39] At other times, however, when Jews were forced to choose between Islam and Christianity, they sometimes chose Islam, fighting as companions-in-arms with Muslim soldiers against the Christians. In 1431 they formed an integral part of the army of Muhammed IX, Sultan of Granada, when he was defeated at the Battle of Higueruela by the army of the King of Castile.[40]

---

[37] Shmuel Moreh, 'Ibrahim ibn Sahl al-Andalusi al-Isra'ili (Abu Ishaq, 1208–1260?),' *Encyclopaedia Judaica*, Volume 8, columns 1213-4.

[38] Yehuda Ratzaby, 'Lawani, Daud (Levi, David),' *Encyclopaedia Judaica*, Volume 10, columns 1484-5. Some scholars have identified Daud Lawani with Daud al-Lawani, a Yemeni Jewish poet who lived in the city of Sanaa.

[39] Bat Ye'or, *The Dhimmi*, page 88.

[40] There is a painting of these Jewish soldiers in action in the Gallery of Battles at the Royal Monastery of San Lorenzo de El Escorial, in Spain.

Caught between Muslim and Christian rulers, the Jews walked a fine line between acceptance and rejection, not always protected by Islam even as a protected people, but always striving to make their contribution to Muslim societies in whose midst they had been living for so many centuries.

6

THE OTTOMAN SULTANS AND OTHER MUSLIM RULERS, 1324–1699

'Here you will be free of your enemies, here you will find rest . . .'
'Every new tyrant exacted the last possible penny'

The Ottoman Turks arrived in Asia Minor from Persia at the end of the Thirteenth Century, fleeing the Mongols under the guidance of their leader, Ertugrul. It was Ertugrul's son, Osman, who established the Osmanli dynasty – known to Europeans as the Ottomans – and began the Ottoman conquest of Asia Minor in 1299.

In the vast Muslim empire built by the Ottomans from Algiers to the Caspian Sea, Jews were subjected to *dhimmi* regulations, but they became an accepted and integral part of society. Jewish money-lenders, tax collectors and bankers were crucial to the success of the central and provincial administrations. Jewish craftsmen and dealers were active in gold and silver work. In Tunis and Algiers, Jews served as the conduit for trade with the Christian countries across the Mediterranean, as the Radhanites had done five hundred years earlier. In Baghdad, Jewish merchants were the principal traders in the city.

Under the tolerant rule of the Ottomans, Jews were not only allowed to engage in commerce, but also to build synagogues, own property and establish their own religious courts.[1] These benefits were much preferred over the conditions endured by Jews in Christian lands. As a result, when the Ottomans conquered Byzantine cities,

---

[1] In Bursa, the synagogue Etz Hayyim ('The Tree of Life') was built in the outward form of a mosque. Aryeh Shmuelevitz, 'Bursa,' *Encyclopaedia Judaica*, Volume 4, column 1531.

their forces were supported by the small, impoverished Jewish communities that had been persecuted under Christian rule. According to one tradition, when the Ottomans attacked the Byzantine city of Bursa in Asia Minor in 1324, the five-hundred-year-old Jewish community there actively helped them to capture the city. As a reward, and in order to revive the city, Sultan Orhan – the son of Sultan Osman I – brought Jewish artisans and moneychangers to Bursa from Damascus. Bursa then became the first Ottoman capital city.[2]

Jews helped the Ottomans to take Gallipoli (1354), Ankara (1360) and Adrianople (1361). Into each of these towns the Jews were encouraged to settle, whether from the Ottomans' newly conquered regions of Bosnia and Serbia, or from Christian lands to the north. Adrianople – known to the Ottomans as Edirne – became a vibrant and prosperous centre of Jewish religion and culture. Its rabbinical college received students from Russia, Poland and Hungary.

Among the Jews who came to Edirne from Christian Europe in the Fourteenth Century was Rabbi Isaac Tzarfati, who was made Chief Rabbi of the Ottoman dominions. In a letter to the Jews of Swabia, the Rhineland, Styria, Moravia, northern France and Hungary, Rabbi Tzarfati recounted the news he had heard from two recent arrivals in Turkey, Rabbi Zalman and Rabbi David Cohen, about the most recent persecution of Jews in Christian lands. Rabbi Tzarfati wrote to inform the Jews 'about how agreeable is this country' – Ottoman Turkey. 'Here I found rest and happiness; Turkey can also become for you the land of peace.' He also compared Ottoman and Christian rule: 'Here the Jew is not compelled to wear a yellow hat as a badge of shame, as is the case in Germany, where even great wealth and fortune are a curse for a Jew because he therewith arouses jealousy among Christians . . .' The rabbi finished with an exhortation: 'Arise my brethren, gird up your loins, collect your

---

[2] According to another tradition, the town's Jewish and Greek Christian inhabitants fled as the Turks approached. The Greeks were not allowed back; the Jews were invited to return, which they did. Stanford J. Shaw, *The Jews of the Ottoman Empire and the Turkish Republic*, page 26.

forces, and come to us. Here you will be free of your enemies, here you will find rest. . . .'[3]

Rabbi Tzarfati knew about the terrible kinds of persecution and hostility faced by Jews in Christian lands. First among these was the Blood Libel, the accusation that Jews were murdering Christian children to use their blood at Passover.[4] Then there were accusations that the Jews were spreaders of disease and plague, the poisoners of wells from which Christians drew their water, and also that the Jews had killed Jesus – that they were 'Christ killers.' The latter was a particularly venomous charge that arose most frequently when the dates of Easter and Passover coincided, as they often did. In Prague, more than three thousand Jews were killed by a Christian mob in 1389. Three times in the Fifteenth Century, the Jewish Quarter in Prague was looted. In addition, the threat of mob attacks was coupled with a fear of mass expulsions from cities and countries – a fear that was realised in Hungary in 1376 and France in 1394.

The Ottoman Empire became – as Rabbi Tzarfati had promised – a secure haven for thousands of Jews who sought a refuge from such persecution and expulsion.[5] In 1430 the Ottomans conquered the Christian city of Salonika, on the northern shore of the Aegean Sea. Forty years later, a large community of Jewish refugees arrived there after fleeing Christian persecution in Bavaria. Settling in Salonika, they formed an Ashkenazi community alongside the city's ancient Romaniot (Greek-speaking) Jewish community, which dated back to pre-Roman times.

The expulsion of the Jews from Christian Spain in 1492, and from Christian Portugal five years later, forced yet more Jews to seek refuge in Muslim lands. At least 100,000 Jews were expelled from their homes in Spain. These expulsions were Christendom's most

[3] Israel Zinberg, *A History of Jewish Literature, Volume Four, The Jewish Center of Culture in the Ottoman Empire*, pages 5-6.

[4] The Five Books of Moses (the Torah) are emphatic: 'And ye shall eat no manner of blood.' Leviticus 7:26.

[5] For towns in the Ottoman Empire that took in Jewish refugees from Christian Europe, see Map 5, page 360.

cruel anti-Jewish action since the Crusaders had swept across Europe on their way to the Holy Land, massacring Jews in their path. Now, in the wide domains ruled by the Ottoman Turks, Jewish refugees found new homes and a security that had been denied them under Christian rule in Europe. Those who left Spain for Morocco found a protective system already in place; in Fez and other cities, separate Jewish Quarters had been established by the local Muslim rulers to protect the Jews from 'popular disturbances.'[6]

The Jews who reached the Ottoman Empire in this period belonged to a different Jewish tradition to the Romaniot Jews. The refugees from Spain brought a different language – Ladino, a medieval form of Spanish written in the Hebrew alphabet – and a different religious liturgy. They also brought a form of Jewish religious discourse, Kabbalah, which found its new and revitalised centre in the Galilee hill town of Safed. There, Jerusalem-born, Cairo-educated Isaac Luria – the son of a Sephardi (Spanish origin) mother and an Ashkenazi (northern European) father – brought to a Muslim-ruled land the most mystical of Jewish thinking.

Jewish refugees also made unique contributions to Ottoman society. Those from Spain brought printed books and the knowledge of how to produce them.[7] The Soncino family, originally from Italy, established a Hebrew printing press in Salonika in 1527, and a second press two years later in the new Ottoman capital, Istanbul. A member of the family, Gershom Soncino, used his philanthropic efforts to help the victims of the Spanish and Portuguese expulsions. His son Eliezer started a printing press in another Muslim city, Cairo.[8]

Moses Hamon, the personal physician to Sultan Suleiman – 'the Magnificent' – came from a family of physicians who had been expelled from Spain in 1492. Moses Hamon wrote several books on medicine, including an important one on dentistry that is today in the Istanbul University Library. He also owned a thousand-year-old

---

[6] Albert Hourani, *A History of the Arab Peoples*, page 123.
[7] Bernard Lewis, *The Middle East*, page 9.
[8] Abraham Meir Habermann, 'Soncino, family . . . ,' *Encyclopaedia Judaica*, Volume 15, columns 140-2.

illuminated Byzantine manuscript, *De Materia Medica*.[9] His father, Joseph Hamon the Elder, had been court physician to two Ottoman Sultans, Bayazid II and Selim I, and had accompanied Selim I as his doctor on the Turkish military incursions into Egypt in 1516–17. He also used his position at court to help his fellow Jews in times of danger. When Moses Hamon succeeded his father as court physician, he served Selim I and then – after Selim's death in 1520 – Suleiman the Magnificent, whom he accompanied on a military expedition against Persia.[10]

As the Ottoman Empire continued expanding, more and more Jewish communities were granted a reprieve from Christian persecution. In 1453 the Ottomans conquered the Christian Byzantine capital of Constantinople (known to the Turks as Istanbul), providing a new centre for the empire. Thus, a significant turning point in Ottoman history was no less significant for the Jews. As in Bursa and Adrianople, the Jews of Constantinople welcomed their liberation from the long night of Christian overlordship; the first breach in Constantinople's walls was made into one of the Jewish Quarters of the city.

––––––––––

[9] Simon Marcus, 'Hamon, family . . . ,' *Encyclopaedia Judaica*, Volume 7, column 1248. Moses Hamon's was the oldest known copy of Dioscorides' *De Materia Medica*, an illuminated Byzantine manuscript produced in about 512 for Anicia Juliana, the daughter of a former Emperor of the Western Empire. The parchment codex comprises 491 folios (almost a thousand pages) and almost four hundred colour-plate illustrations, each occupying a full page, facing a description of the plant's pharmacological properties. A supplemental text describes more than forty Mediterranean birds. As it passed through the hands of various owners, the manuscript was amended with the names of plants in Greek, Arabic, Turkish (after Constantinople fell to the Turks in 1453) and Hebrew (when it was owned by Moses Hamon). In 1569 the Emperor Maximilian II acquired the codex for the Imperial Library in Vienna, where it still resides, a rare treasure.

[10] Muslims valued Jewish medical knowledge throughout the ages, knowing of the Jews' imperative to do their utmost to save life. Indeed, the hiring of Jewish physicians by Muslim rulers became a trend that persisted into modern times. When Saddam Hussein needed a doctor for urgent treatment on his sinuses in 1979, it was an Egyptian-born British Jew, Ellis Douek, whom he asked to be flown into Iraq to operate on him.

From the first days of Ottoman rule in Istanbul, Sultan Mehmet II encouraged Jews to settle in the city and to govern themselves within their own *millet* – a religion-based community. Only three days after the conquest, Mehmet II sent messages to the Jews of Salonika, Adrianople and Bursa requesting them to come and help re-populate the city. He offered the newcomers free property, a substantial exemption in their taxes for some time and permission to build synagogues – overriding the age-old prohibition for *dhimmis* to build new places of worship.

In a proclamation issued to all Jews, Mehmet II echoed the books of Genesis and Ezra in the Hebrew Bible. He declared: 'Who among you of all my people that is with me, may his God be with him, let him ascend to Istanbul the site of my imperial throne. Let him dwell in the best of the land, each beneath his vine and his fig tree, with silver and with gold, with wealth and with cattle. Let him dwell in the land, trade in it, and take possession of it.'[11] The call was answered: by the year 1478, Constantinople had 1,647 Jewish households – about ten thousand people – constituting up to ten per cent of the city's total population.

The benefits of Ottoman rule were also evident for Jews in Libya. The Jewish community in Libya had seen nine hundred years of religious and economic freedom under Muslim rule, but was cast into danger in 1510 with the occupation of the Mediterranean port city of Tripoli by Christians from Spain. According to Libyan-Jewish tradition, eight hundred Jewish families fled into the hinterland, to the towns of Tarhuna and Gharyan, in order to avoid the perils of the Spanish Inquisition. It was not until the arrival of the Ottomans in 1551 that calm was restored, and the Jews were allowed to return to Tripoli.

Under Suleiman the Magnificent (1520–66), Ottoman and Muslim rule was further extended to Belgrade, Rhodes, Cyprus

---

[11] Stanford J. Shaw, *The Jews of the Ottoman Empire and the Turkish Republic*, pages 26-9. The quotation echoes Genesis 3:6-7 and Ezra 7:12-13.

and much of Hungary, including its capital, Buda. In all of these lands, the arrival of the Ottomans was a relief to local Jewish communities, hitherto persecuted under Christian rule. In the very years that Jews were being compelled to deny or hide their religion in Spain by the forces of the Inquisition, their brethren in the Ottoman Empire were being allowed to exercise their religious rights freely.[12]

Several thousand Jewish refugees from Christian persecution made their way to Ottoman-ruled Salonika. The Jewish poet Samuel Usque described that city as 'a mother in Israel': the Jews banished from Christian Europe had 'met in it and have received a loving welcome, as if it were our venerable mother Jerusalem.'[13] Salonika had a larger Jewish population than Istanbul – twenty thousand Jews in all – and became a centre of Jewish learning. There were thirty separate Jewish congregations and synagogues in the city. Under the Ottomans, who respected the local rabbis and their concerns, Jewish religious life blossomed. In 1551, Sultan Suleiman I granted permission to Salonika's Rabbi Samuel de Medina to rebuild synagogues there that had been destroyed in a catastrophic fire.[14]

The Island of Rhodes was another Ottoman possession that welcomed Jews and in which Jews flourished. Jews owned vineyards on the island, others were active in the manufacture of perfume, others in the textile trade. To encourage the immigration of Jews to Rhodes – to join the much older Romaniot Jewish community there – the Sultan gave the Jews exemption from taxation for one hundred years, and the right for their funeral processions to pass through Muslim streets.[15]

In Ottoman-ruled Palestine, Judaism thrived in the hill city of

---

[12] See Map 5, page 360.

[13] Abraham Danon, *Revue des Etudes Juives (R.E.J.)*, volume XL, page 207 (Salonika). It was not Islam that was to destroy this ancient and vibrant community, but Nazi Germany, which deported 43,850 Jews from Salonika (ninety per cent of the total Jewish population of the city) to their deaths in Auschwitz in March 1943.

[14] Fifteen years later, in 1566, Rabbi Moses Almoslino led a delegation to Istanbul to secure a reduction in the *jizya* tax. He was to make two further such journeys to achieve this purpose. Morris S. Goodblatt, *Jewish Life in Turkey in the XVIth Century*, pages 16-17 and 27.

[15] Marc D, Angel, *The Jews of Rhodes*, pages 21 and 42-44.

Safed – a Jewish Holy City – where many Jews went to live during Suleiman's reign. Under unobtrusive Muslim rule, the city became a centre of Jewish religious observance and mysticism. Safed's spiritual leaders in the mid–Sixteenth Century were Rabbi Isaac Luria, 'The Lion of the Kabbalah,' and Joseph Caro, whose *Shulhan Arukh* ('The Set Table') became a blueprint for Jewish conduct. A third Jewish scholar in Safed, Solomon ha-Levi Alkabetz, wrote one of the most moving hymns in the Hebrew liturgy, *Lekha Dodi*, which welcomes each Sabbath with the joy that one welcomes a bride:

> Come my beloved, to meet the Bride,
> The Sabbath presence bids her welcome.[16]

In Istanbul, at the seat of the Empire, Jews even gained influential positions in Suleiman's Imperial Court. A document in the Topkapi Palace archives in Istanbul, dated 1527, mentions 'Abraham the Jew' among the silversmiths in the Sultan's service. Abraham specialised in laying gold and silver leaves under the Sultan's precious stones in order to accentuate their brilliance.[17] Two other Jews at the court held particular influence with Suleiman: his physician, Moses Hamon, and his adviser, Don Joseph Nasi. Because of their importance to him, the Sultan took a positive interest in the welfare of his Jewish subjects, sometimes intervening to rescue Jewish lives and property in Christian lands.

In 1561 the ageing Suleiman granted to Don Joseph Nasi a Jewish principality. It consisted of Tiberias – a lakeside city visible from Safed – and seven villages near the Sea of Galilee. It was said that the Sultan ensured this grant would be valid in perpetuity by having it countersigned by his heir apparent, the future Selim II, and Selim's son, the future Murad III. But the creation of this Jewish homeland met with practical stumbling blocks. The historian Cecil Roth has

---

[16] Many versions exist in English of this refrain. This version is from *The Complete Artscroll Siddur*, page 317.
[17] Miriam Russo-Katz, 'Jewellery,' in Esther Juhasz (editor), *Sephardi Jews in the Ottoman Empire: Aspects of Material Culture*, page 174.

recounted how the Arab labourers who rebuilt the walls of Tiberias
went on strike after a local Bedouin sheikh spread the rumour that
'when Tiberias was rebuilt, Islam would fall.' Work resumed only
after Don Joseph's agent, Joseph ben Ardut, a Jew, gathered an Arab
military force in Damascus to break the strike.[18] The walls were completed in the winter of 1564–5, during the festival of Hanukah, when
the ancient triumph of the Maccabees over the Seleucid Greeks is
celebrated – a time of national pride for Jews.

In the reign of Selim II (1566–1574), Don Joseph Nasi was promoted to the Dukedom of Naxos. He continued to make the ancient
city of Tiberias available to Jewish refugees, many of whom arrived
from Christian countries hundreds of miles away.

Just as Ottoman rule provided a refuge for Jews fleeing Christian
persecution, it also gave Jews an alternative to the discrimination
they suffered in Muslim lands outside the Ottoman Empire. In the
central Asian Khanate of Bukhara, established at the end of the
Sixteenth Century, the devoutly Muslim Khan insisted on a strict
adherence to *dhimmi* rules.[19] He restricted the Jews of the Khanate to
residence in a special quarter, and would not allow Jews to buy homes
from Muslims even in that restricted area. Jews also had to wear a
special sign to distinguish them from Muslims, and the payment of
the *jizya* tax was accompanied by a humiliating slap in the face.

In Libya in 1589, the Ottomans were driven out of Tripoli by a
Muslim religious leader, Yahya ibn Yahya, who claimed to be the
Mahdi – the person who, according to Shiite doctrine, will come
before the end of days and convert the world to Islam. Ibn Yahya
ordered so many forcible conversions that it was to take two hundred
years before the Jewish community recovered. Many Jews, forced by
ibn Yahya to pull the heavy cannon for his army, were killed when
the Ottomans finally defeated ibn Yahya in battle.[20]

---

[18] Two of the strike's ringleaders were arrested and severely punished. Cecil Roth,
The House of Nasi: The Duke of Naxos, pages 109-115.
[19] See Map 18, page 372.
[20] Renzo De Felice, *Jews in an Arab Land: Libya, 1835-1970*, page 5.

Another cruel interruption of Jewish life occurred in 1625, when a Muslim warlord from Nablus, Mohammed ibn Farrukh, purchased the governorship of Jerusalem. He imprisoned the city's Jewish leaders and demanded 12,500 gold florins in ransom. In order to find the money, the Jewish community had to send emissaries throughout Christian Europe. Fortunately for them, ibn Farrukh was deposed in the following year.[21]

The Jews of Yemen were placed in similar peril five years later, after the Zaydis – the Muslim tribe that had long ruled Yemen – reconquered their patrimony from the Ottomans. One of the Zaydis' first decrees was to expel all the Jews from the capital, Sanaa, and from all towns in central Yemen. The expelled Jews were deported to the town of Mawza, located in an intensely hot and inhospitable region to the south. Their homes in Sanaa were then looted and given to the local Arabs. Meanwhile, a fifth of the Jews exiled in Mawza died from disease and starvation; it was a full year before the survivors were allowed back to the towns from which they had been deported. The reason for their return was not Muslim sympathy, but rather an economic imperative: the Jews of Yemen constituted a majority of the country's craftsmen and artisans.[22]

When the Jews finally returned to Sanaa, their homes were not returned to them. They were forced to build a special quarter for themselves outside the city boundary, and in a strict application of the *dhimmi* rules, they were forbidden to build their houses higher than the Muslims' houses nearby. The Jews also found that most of their religious artifacts had been destroyed. Itzhak Ben-Zvi, while President of Israel, wrote: 'Shabazi's (and other poets') mournful elegies on this calamity are recited to this day by the Jews of Yemen, whose long history in the country is an uninterrupted record of physical suffering and civil degradation.'[23]

Shabazi – Rabbi Shalom ben Yosef Shabazi – was among the many Jews expelled from Yemen in 1630. He was ten years old. He

---

[21] Teddy Kollek and Moshe Pearlman, *Jerusalem: A History of Forty Centuries*, page 217.
[22] See Map 19, page 373.
[23] Itzhak Ben-Zvi, *The Exiled and the Redeemed*, page 28.

became a poet, a writer, a rabbi and a community leader, and helped the Jews of Yemen survive terrible persecutions. His poetic lamentation, which recalled the expulsion to Mawza, was written for recitation during the ninth day of the Hebrew month of Av – the annual day of mourning for the destruction of the Temple.[24] A remarkable number of his poems, 550 in all, survive to this day.[25] Shabazi wrote in Hebrew, Aramaic and Arabic; his other works included a treatise on astrology and a kabbalistic commentary on the Torah. He died at the age of a hundred and one in 1720. His grave in Taizz is revered today by Jews and Muslims alike.

The Jewish community also faced perils in Persia, where problems began for the Jews at the start of the Sixteenth Century. The first Safavid ruler of Persia, Shah Ismail I (1502–1524), established Shiite Islam as the State religion, allowing the clerical hierarchy almost unlimited control and influence over all aspects of public life. The profound influence of the Shiite clerical elite continued without interruption until 1722, and then resumed from 1795 to 1925: a total of 350 years of Shiite theocracy, renewed later under the Ayatollah Khomeini in 1979.

The Shiite clerics emphasised the notion of the ritual uncleanliness (*najas*) of *dhimmis* – of Jews in particular, but also Christians and Zoroastrians – and made this the cornerstone of Muslim relations with non-Muslims.[26] The nature of this discrimination was apparent to European visitors to Persia during the reign of Ismail I. The Portuguese traveller Tome Pires observed that the Sultan 'never spares the life of any Jew.'[27] Another European traveller, Raphael de Mans, noted the 'great hatred' that Ismail bore against the Jews.[28]

When Abbas I became Shah of Persia in 1588, Jews were, however, at first much favoured. Jewish soldiers fought in the Shah's

---

[24] I am grateful to the Yizhak Ben-Zvi Institute in Jerusalem for these details about Shabazi.

[25] These poems were published for the first time in 1970, 250 years after Shabazi's death, by the Ben-Zvi Institute in Jerusalem.

[26] W.J. Fischel, 'The Jews in Medieval Iran,' *Irano-Judaica*, page 266.

[27] Tome Pires, *Suma Oriental (1512-1515)*, page 27.

[28] Quoted in W.J. Fischel, 'The Jews in Medieval Iran,' *Irano-Judaica*, page 266.

army during his military campaign against the Georgians in the Caucasus; in appreciation of their help, he allowed them to establish a new community, Farahabad – 'City of Joy' – on the shore of the Caspian Sea.[29] He was also the first Muslim ruler of Persia to show an interest in the Hebrew Bible. But towards the end of his forty-year reign, Shah Abbas fell under the influence of Jewish converts to Islam. In order to stress the sincerity of their own conversion, these converts spoke constantly to him against the Jews. As a result, distinguishing headgear was made compulsory for Jews in Persia, and Hebrew books, in particular kabbalistic books, were banned after the Shah was persuaded that they were used to perform magic against him. Worse was to come when the Jews of Isfahan were ordered to convert to Islam and live as *anusim* – forced ones – for seven years.

When Shah Safi ascended to the throne of Persia in 1629, the Jews of Isfahan were allowed to return to Judaism. But his successor, Abbas II, who became Shah in 1642, ordered the Jews of Persia to convert to Islam once again. The Persian Jews challenged this decree, explaining in open protests and petitions that the *Dar al-Yahud* ('House of Judah') had been living in Persia since ancient times, that they had always fulfilled their obligations to the State, and that they had always paid their *jizya* taxes promptly. It was to no avail; synagogues were closed and the Jews were forcibly converted to Islam.

Yet the act of conversion was not enough: Jews had to proclaim in public the Muslim confession of faith, receive Muslim religious instruction, swear on oath that they would break with their Jewish past and have their new Muslim names formally registered. They were also given the collective name *Jadid al-Islam* – New Muslims.[30] As New Muslims, many of these converts gave the appearance of practicing Islam while secretly adhering to Judaism, just like the converts to Christianity – the Marranos – had done in Spain after the forcible conversions there under the Inquisition.

---

[29] See Map 17, page 371.

[30] W.J. Fischel, 'Abbas I,' *Encyclopaedia Judaica*, Volume 2, columns 38-9.

The Jewish community in Baghdad faced similar intolerance when, in 1514, the Ottoman Turks were driven from the city by the Persian Shah Ismail I. The city's thriving Jewish community did not suffer at first, but when Ismail was succeeded by his son Tahmasp I – a fanatical Shiite and hater of non-Muslims – the Jews became daily victims of Muslim violence and humiliation. The return of the Ottomans to Baghdad in 1534 restored peace and calm to the Jewish community; once more Baghdadi Jews became prominent in the city's trade with India. But when the Persians returned in 1623, persecutions and humiliations were renewed. Not surprisingly, the Jews supported a successful attempt by the Ottoman Sultan Murad IV to restore Ottoman rule to the city. As a result of Murad's victory, the Jews declared the day of his conquest – 16 Tevet 5399 in the Jewish calendar – as a *yom nes*, a 'day of miracle.'

From the Tenth Century onward, Jewish 'court bankers' had become a feature at many Muslim courts. During Muslim rule in Spain in the Tenth and Eleventh Centuries, Jews in Cordova had been active in financial administration. In Egypt, under the Fatimid Caliph al-Mustansir in the early Eleventh Century, two Jewish brothers, Abu Sa'd al-Tustari and Abu Nasr Hesed ben Sahl al-Tustari, were influential in the Egyptian financial administration. Peril, however, always lay on a Jewish banker's path, in Muslim as well as in Christian lands. In 1517, the final year of the Mamluk period in Cairo, the Arab chronicler Ibn Iyas reported that the Sultan, Tuman Bey II, had extorted a massive sum – more than half a million dinars – from a wealthy Jewish moneychanger named Samuel.[31]

The Jews of the Muslim world constituted many scattered communities, often cut off from each other by the boundaries of conflicting empires and warring dynasties. When those empires expanded their territories, the Jews within their borders gained a greater connection and cohesion. The rise of the Ottoman Empire – with its

---

[31] Dr. Hermann Kellenbenz, 'Bankers and Banking,' *Encyclopaedia Judaica*, Volume 4, column 167.

wide reach – was beneficial to the Jewish Diaspora in precisely that way, allowing a great number of Jews to connect with each other under a single – and protective – ruler.

In 1547 the Ottoman Turks conquered large swathes of the Arabian Peninsula and established their rule over Yemen. This gave the Yemeni Jews an opportunity to make contact with the kabbalist Jewish centre in Safed, in Galilee, 1,400 miles to the north. The Ottomans also conquered Libya, driving out Spanish Christian forces. This allowed the Jewish communities there to renew their contacts with Jews as far west as Morocco. Some leading members of the Libyan Jewish community, who had been deported to Naples by the Spaniards, were permitted to return to Tripoli, where they resumed their communal duties and revived their commercial enterprises.[32]

In the Sixteenth Century a group of Jews travelled westward from Kurdistan to Ottoman-ruled Palestine, a journey of six hundred miles. They settled in Safed, among the kabbalists. In Kurdistan itself, where Jewish communities looked south to Baghdad for religious and legal judgments, local rabbis and kabbalists gained prominence at the beginning of the century. Among the rabbinical dynasties there were members of the Barazani, Mizrahi, Duga and Hariri families. Kurdish religious and secular poetry flourished, some written in Hebrew, some in Aramaic – the language of Second Temple Palestine 1,600 years earlier. The leading Jewish poets in Kurdistan included Rabbi Samuel ben Nethanel ha-Levi, the head of a rabbinical academy in Mosul in the Seventeenth Century, and his daughter, Asenath.[33]

But no matter how far the Ottoman Empire stretched, Jews who lived within its borders remained under the ominous shadow of *dhimmi* status. They inherited the fundamental uncertainty of life under Muslim rule: the dual prospects of opportunity and restriction, protection and persecution.

---

[32] Maurice M. Roumani, *The Jews of Libya*, page 3.
[33] Abraham Ben-Jacob, 'Kurdistan,' *Encyclopaedia Judaica*, Volume 10, column 1298. Abraham Ben-Jacob published fifty-four Kurdish-Jewish poems (in Hebrew) in 1961, in his book *Kehillot Yehudei Kurdistan*.

On the one hand, Jews in the Ottoman Empire could aspire to high office and reputation. In 1585 a Marrano named Solomon Abenaish (ibn Ya'ish) became so successful in advancing Ottoman diplomatic interests that he was ennobled as the Duke of Mitilene. A decade after the death of Don Joseph Nasi, Duke of Naxos, Abenaish was given a renewal of the lease on Tiberias and the seven villages around it.[34] On the other hand, Jews in Ottoman lands lived with the constant prospect of discrimination. At any time, entire communities could suffer hardship at the whim of a Muslim ruler or a local official. In 1586 the senior Cadi (judge) in Jerusalem deprived Jews in the city of the right to worship in their synagogues. As the Jewish historian Solomon Grayzel wrote of Tripolitania, these and all other Jews in Ottoman lands depended on 'the whim or wisdom of the ruler.' They suffered as 'every internal disorder brought new persecution; every new tyrant exacted the last possible penny.'[35]

Sometimes the most tolerant of Muslim rulers turned against the Jews. Sultan Murad III, who succeeded Selim II in 1574, employed many Jews in positions of influence at his royal court. A Jew named Hodja Nessimi (Nissim) was chosen by the Sultan as director of the Ottoman mint – an appointment that reflected the trust bestowed upon Jews in financial matters during most centuries of Muslim rule.[36] Don Joseph Nasi, Duke of Naxos, was allowed to continue in his role of administering the wine tax. An Italian-born Jew, Solomon Nathan Ashkenazi, served as one of Murad III's physicians and conducted several important diplomatic negotiations for him.[37] Jewish comedians and actors were often hired to perform for

---

[34] Cecil Roth, *The House of Nasi: The Duke of Naxos*, page 133.
[35] Solomon Grayzel, *A History of the Jews from the Babylonian Exile to the Present*, page 730.
[36] Daniel M. Friedenberg, *Jewish Minters & Medalists*, page 6. With the conquest of Egypt by the Ottoman Sultan Selim I in 1517, a Jew of Spanish descent, Abraham de Castro, was appointed master of the Egyptian mint, where he coined the new Ottoman money. The last director of the Mamluk mint in Egypt had been a Jew, Isaac Hacohen Shalal, the head of the Jewish community in Cairo.
[37] A senior court official commented that 'Rabbi Salamone, because of his good conduct, takes part at present in most of the negotiations of this Porte.'

Murad III. The Sultan kept at court a redoubtable woman, Esther Kyra, described by Cecil Roth as 'the Jewish intimate of successive generations at the harem . . . still active despite her great age.'[38]

In 1579, Murad III eventually turned against the Jews, upset by what he considered the ostentatious clothing of Jewish women in Istanbul, one of whom was said to be wearing jewellery worth forty thousand golden ducats. As Cecil Roth has written, it was reported that 'the Sultan so resented the spectacle that, in a fit of childish rage, he issued orders for the extermination of all the Jews living under his rule.' Murad III's Jewish physician, Solomon Ashkenazi, then persuaded the Sultan's mother to intervene. He raised a large sum of money from his fellow Jews as a bribe, 'and the fickle monarch was induced to change his mind.' But Murad III did reassert the *dhimmi* rules that forbade Jews and Christians from wearing silk clothing. He also ordered non-Muslims to wear a cap and not a turban, which was to be reserved for true believers.[39]

The dangers faced by Jews in Ottoman lands were many. In the town of Amasiya, in the Black Sea region of northern Anatolia, a Blood Libel was spread by local Christians in the years between 1530 and 1545.[40] An Armenian woman reported seeing Jews murder a Christian boy in order to use his blood at their Passover meal. As a result, several Jews were arrested by the Muslim district

---

Edward Kossoy and Abraham Ohry, *The Feldshers*, page 134, note 3. The Ottoman imperial court in Istanbul was known as the Porte (also the High Porte and the Sublime Porte), after the gate to the Grand Vizier's quarters in the Topkapi Palace.

[38] Cecil Roth, *The House of Nasi: The Duke of Naxos*, page 189. Esther Kyra exerted considerable influence over the Sultan's wife, who, as Cecil Roth has observed, 'in turn dominated the Sultan.'

[39] Cecil Roth, *The House of Nasi: The Duke of Naxos*, pages 198-9.

[40] Abraham Haim, 'Amasiya,' *Encyclopaedia Judaica*, Volume 2, columns 794-5. The Amasiya Blood Libel was described by the scholar and historian Joseph ibn Verga, who settled in Edirne (Adrianople) after fleeing from Spain to the Ottoman Empire. In his published historical work, Joseph also wrote about the persecution of Jews in Christian countries – as his father Solomon ibn Verga had done while living in Christian Rome. Simon Marcus, 'Ibn Verga, Joseph (d.c. 1559),' *Encyclopaedia Judaica*, Volume 8, columns 1202-3.

governor – a notorious hater of the Jews – Mustafa, the son of
Sultan Suleiman the Magnificent. These Jews were imprisoned, tortured, found guilty and hanged. When the boy who had been
reported murdered was found alive and well, Mustafa reluctantly
agreed to punish the accusers. After hearing of the miscarriage of
justice in Amasiya, Moses Hamon, the Sultan's Jewish physician,
persuaded the Sultan to issue an edict forbidding local officials
from trying Blood Libel cases; henceforth, these cases were brought
before the Sultan himself in Istanbul.[41]

In Salonika, one of the great cities of the Ottoman Empire,
relations between Jews and Muslims were never easy. It was not
unusual for Muslims to produce false claims of debt against wealthy
Jews in an attempt to deprive them of their property. The historian
Maurice Goodblatt, after studying more than five hundred documents from Salonika in this period, concluded that government
officials 'frequently became accomplices in these evil schemes.' Jews
were even reluctant to live in Muslim neighbourhoods for fear of
being subject to night attacks – from Christians as well as Muslims.
In some cases, they depended on the warnings of danger they
received from friendlier Muslim neighbours. Rabbi Samuel de
Medina recorded one occasion when a Jewish merchant had been
welcomed into a Muslim home for the night, but was later urged by
his host not to continue his journey before daylight because his life
would be in danger.[42]

At the beginning of the Seventeenth Century an English visitor
to the Ottoman Empire, George Sandys, was a witness to the plight
of Jews under their *dhimmi* status in Jerusalem. 'Here also be some
Jewes,' he wrote in his account of his travels, 'yet inherit they no part
of the land, but in their owne country do live as aliens, a people

---

[41] In 1592 the Blood Libel was revived by Muslims in the Turkish town of Bursa,
where many Jewish refugees had settled after fleeing from Christian persecution in
Spain. A local Muslim, Mirza bin Hussein, accused eight Jews of having lured him
into their home and drawn blood from him. The Sultan, accepting the man's
story, ordered the eight Jews to be exiled to the Island of Rhodes.
[42] Morris S. Goodblatt, *Jewish Life in Turkey in the XVIth Century*, pages 124 and 215.

scattered throughout the whole world, and hated amongst whom they live; yet suffred, as a necessary mischiefe: subject to all wrongs and contumelies, which they support with an invincible patience.' Sandys added an observation from his personal experience: 'Many of them have I seene abused, some of them beaten; yet never saw I Jew with an angry countenance.'[43]

One outcome of the Jews' frustrated hopes was seen in the mid–Seventeenth Century, when a dramatic series of events unfolded in the Ottoman Empire. It began normally enough in 1662, when Sabbatai Zevi, a Jew from the city of Izmir (Smyrna), was living in Jerusalem. A heavy *jizya* tax imposition forced the Jewish community of Jerusalem – some one thousand people – to send Zevi overseas to seek alms on the community's behalf. On his return to Jerusalem three years later, Zevi – then twenty-nine years old – declared himself the Messiah.

Jews throughout Muslim and Christian Europe, Asia and North Africa were excited by the age-old messianic promise of redemption, looking eagerly forward to the year 1666, when it was widely believed that Zevi would be crowned 'King of the World.'[44] In the Persian city of Gorgan, on the southeastern corner of the Caspian Sea, Jews refused to pay the *jizya* tax, so certain were they that Zevi was the Messiah.[45] For hundreds of thousands of other Jews, Zevi became a beacon of hope in the darkness – a beacon that shone brightly for those suffering in the pogrom-plagued regions of Christian Eastern Europe.[46] Messianic claims were not new among the Jews; the most recent had emerged in 1530, in the Muslim-ruled city of Salonika.

---

[43] George Sandys, *A Relation of A Journey Begun in An: Dom: 1610*, quoted in Martin Gilbert, *The Routledge Historical Atlas of Jerusalem*, Fourth Edition, Map 15, page 25.
[44] Gershom G. Scholem, *Sabbetai Sevi*.
[45] Houman Sarshar, *Esther's Children: A Portrait of Iranian Jews*, page 67.
[46] One follower of Sabbatai Zevi in Muslim lands was Aleppo-born Raphael Joseph Chelebi (Halabi), the mint master in Cairo. A man of enormous wealth and deep religious convictions, Chelebi supported with his own money fifty students of Talmud and kabbalists. He wore the clothes of a penitent and often had himself flogged. Daniel M. Friedenberg, *Jewish Minters & Medalists*, page 6.

Zevi touched a widespread Jewish longing to change the status of Jews in both Christian and Muslim lands.

The Ottomans took immediate steps to crush what looked like was becoming a popular movement of discontent. They imprisoned Zevi in Edirne and forced him to convert to Islam, disillusioning his many followers. Zevi's movement rapidly declined, yet in Salonika some of his followers believed that he must have converted for a reason, and converted to Islam themselves. They continued to practise Judaism secretly, assuming that Zevi – who died in 1676 – would one day return to lead them.[47] These 'crypto-Jews' became known as Dönmeh. To this day, the Dönmeh living in Turkey are proud of their heritage.[48]

Zevi's movement made it clear that, although the Ottomans had offered Jews many opportunities since 1299, there was much left to be desired for the Jews who lived under Ottoman rule. Despite the haven it offered the Jews until the Nineteenth Century, the Ottoman Empire never provided a complete break with the *dhimmi* restrictions of the past, nor with the potential burden of the *jizya* tax. One Iraqi-born British Jew, Moshe Kahtan, recently commented on the life of Jews in Ottoman lands with some cynicism, but not without a kernel of truth: 'At the time of the Ottoman Empire the Jews' fate depended on the Governor's mood and whim and the amount of corruption that he exacted. So when there was a lull in the persecution – bless them – they called it "the golden age." It was not a golden age. It was an age when the Jews were persecuted less.'[49]

---

[47] Gershom G. Scholem, *Sabbetai Sevi*.
[48] One Dönmeh, Mehmed Djavid Bey, was among the leaders of the 1908 Young Turk constitutional revolution, 132 years after Zevi's death. Djavid Bey served as Minister of Finance in the reformed administration of Sultan Abdul Hamid II. Another Dönmeh, Dr. Nazim Bey, was a founding member of the Young Turk Committee of Union and Progress (CUP). He served as Minister of Education.
[49] Moshe Kahtan, *Daily Telegraph*, 15 April 2003.

7

THE EIGHTEENTH AND
NINETEENTH CENTURIES

'Scarcely a day passes that I do not hear of some act of tyranny
and oppression against a Jew'

Opportunities and setbacks went hand in hand for Jewish com-
munities living under Muslim rule in the Eighteenth Century.
In Istanbul, during the early years of the century, Jews were among the
typesetters at the first ever Muslim printing press, providing the skilled
labour needed to carry out the printing.[1] Yet in Jerusalem, another
Ottoman-ruled city, Jews suffered hardship in 1720 when Muslim
Arabs seized the local Ashkenazi synagogue, burned the Scrolls of the
Law and refused to return the synagogue to the Jewish community.[2]

In an account of his journeys through the Ottoman Empire, the
Swedish traveller Frederick Hasselquist described Jewish prosperity in
Jerusalem with a telling caveat. He noted that the rabbis of the city
gained considerable revenue from co-religionists 'throughout the
whole world,' as well as from Jewish pilgrims 'who come from far and
wide to pay their respects at the seat of their forefathers.' It was, however, the local Muslim authorities who 'draw the greatest part,' for
'Jews as well as Christians must constantly bring offerings to their
altars, if they will kiss their holy places in peace.'[3] In 1775 the Jews in
Jerusalem – and throughout the Ottoman Empire – submitted to an
increase in the *jizya* tax, so that the Ottomans could raise revenue for
their war with Russia.

Jews in other Ottoman lands experienced a similar combination of promise and hardship. In 1740, Rabbi Hayyim Abulafia, a

---

[1] Bernard Lewis, *The Middle East*, page 10.
[2] The synagogue was returned to the Jewish community ninety years later, in 1816.
[3] Frederick Hasselquist, *Voyages and Travels in the Levant in the Years 1749, 50, 51, 52.*

Jew from Izmir, travelled to Palestine and settled in the city of Tiberias. Jewish life had languished there since the land was leased to Don Joseph Nasi 180 years earlier, and for the previous seventy years all cultivation had ceased. The Muslim ruler of Galilee, Sheikh Dahir al-Amr, invited Rabbi Abulafia and a number of Jewish families to 'come up and take possession of the land,' and to revitalise the city and its surroundings.[4] This they did, planting vineyards and olive groves; in the words of Cecil Roth, they 'renewed in some measure the atmosphere of the autonomous Jewish settlement.'[5]

The Jewish community of Bukhara faced another kind of challenge. Being isolated in a desert oasis, far from any centre of vibrant Jewish life, the community was losing its Jewish identity amidst a vigorous and devout Muslim khanate. In 1793 the Jews of Safed sent an emissary, Joseph ha-Ma'aravi, to address the problem and to revive the Bukharan Jewish community. He travelled the 1,700 miles to Bukhara, crossing desert and mountains, and then sent for religious books from Istanbul, Leghorn (Livorno) and Vilna. The Khan of Bukhara subsequently agreed that there should be a community leader, the Nasi, who could serve as a communal judge and represent the community's needs to the Muslim authorities. This beneficial system continued until 1873, when Russian control was imposed on the Khanate.[6]

In Yemen, a brief resurgence of Jewish life occurred during one period of Zaydi Shiite rule, when Jews rebuilt their synagogues and were able to achieve important positions in Yemeni society. A prominent Jew, Rabbi Shalom ben Aharon ha-Kohen Iraqi, was made responsible for the mint and the royal finances. But because the Jews worked mostly as artisans, there was no class of wealthy property owners or successful middle-class traders to support a thriving

---

[4] The quotation echoes the biblical book of Hosea, one of the twelve Minor Hebrew Prophets.
[5] Cecil Roth, *The House of Nasi: The Duke of Naxos*, pages 134-5.
[6] Aviva Müller-Lancet, 'Bukhara,' *Encyclopaedia Judaica*, Volume 4, column 1473.

scholarly community. Yemen's Jewish communities were small and scattered, so that it was often impossible to obtain a quorum for prayer. Rabbi Shalom ben Aharon managed to help the Jewish community for a short time, by raising its prestige among the Muslims, but he quickly fell from favour as a result of the envy and hostility of local Muslim officials.[7]

These hardships and challenges were sometimes compounded by large events. In the Libyan hinterland, Jews became entangled in the revolt of local Berber tribes in the 1750s. Some of the small Jewish communities chose to participate in the revolt, but others were forced to provide the rebels with weapons and medicine. A number of Jews secretly paid the *jizya* tax to the Muslim authorities in Tripoli, hoping to avoid punishment when the revolt was crushed. In Tripoli itself, Jews suffered at other times under the occupation of two different invaders, the Tunisian ruler Ibrahim Sherif and the Algerian Ali Burghul. Under both rulers the situation became so dire that the Jewish community later celebrated its liberation with local Purims: the 'Purim Sherif' on the twenty-third of Tevet in the Hebrew calendar (to commemorate 19 January 1705) and the 'Purim Burghul' on the twenty-ninth of Tevet (to commemorate 20 January 1795).[8]

During the rest of the Eighteenth Century, Tripoli's Jewish community flourished under the rule of the Muslim Karamanli dynasty. Jews became successful as traders, effectively controlling the maritime trade in henna, wool and cereals with the Italian port of Leghorn (Livorno). They were also prominent in the trade across the Sahara, to the oases of the Fezzan, and south as far as the cities of northern Nigeria. They traded esparto grass, the alfalfa herb and ostrich

---

[7] Reuben Ahroni, *Yemenite Jewry: Origins, Culture, and Literature*, page 138.
[8] These Purims reflected the age-old Festival of Purim, which celebrated the saving of Persian Jews in ancient times from the mass murder decreed by the Grand Vizier Haman, as described in the *Book of Esther*: '. . . in the day that the enemies of the Jews hoped to have power over them, (though it was turned to the contrary, that the Jews had rule over them that hated them),' *Book of Esther*: 9:1.

feathers. Within Tripoli, Jews worked as silversmiths and goldsmiths, moneychangers and bankers, silk spinners, weavers and dyers. A few Jewish families in the city managed to become wealthy – those to whom the local Muslim authorities granted an official task, such as customs subcontractors or mint masters.[9]

The Eighteenth Century saw equally impressive commercial activity among the Jews of Morocco. In 1766, Sultan Sidi Mohammed III decided to turn the small Atlantic port of Mogador (now Essaouira) into a mercantile metropolis, and to make it the only Moroccan port other than Tangier open to European trade. In order to create a thriving port, he invited several Jewish families to settle there – some of Berber origin from the High Atlas Mountains, others from the cities of Sousse and Marrakech.[10] Five Jewish families came from Marrakech, among them the Pinto family, who brought to the city the cannons that still adorn the town walls.[11]

Several Jewish families in Morocco were able to achieve prominence in trade as well as in other fields. Members of the Benider family were active as ships' chandlers, providing shipping supplies to the British in Gibraltar. Jacob Benider, who was born under British rule in Gibraltar but lived in Tangier, served as the official interpreter at British consulates in several Moroccan cities, including Mogador, Salé, Safi and Agadir. In 1772 the Sultan of Morocco even sent Jacob Benider as Ambassador to London on a diplomatic mission.[12] Another Moroccan Jewish family, the Benoliel family, was active in diplomacy as well as commerce. Judah Benoliel, who died in 1839, was sent by the Sultan of Morocco on diplomatic missions

---

[9] Renzo De Felice, *Jews in an Arab Land: Libya, 1835-1970*, pages 7 and 8. De Felice lists the wealthy families as the Halfons, Hassans, Labis, Arbibs, Ambrons and Nahums, 'etc.'

[10] Daniel Schroeter, *The Sultan's Jews: Morocco and the Sephardi World*, page 13.

[11] Information provided by Barbara Barnett (herself a Pinto). When plague devastated Mogador in 1799, the Pintos went to England, where they went into the tobacco trade.

[12] Leon H. Spotts, 'Benider, Moroccan family,' *Encyclopaedia Judaica*, Volume 4, column 520.

to Sweden, Norway, Denmark and Belgium. He also negotiated peace between Sardinia and Morocco. It was at Jacob Benoliel's request that the Sultan authorised the reconstruction of the synagogue in Tangier.[13]

This general sense of calm changed for the worse as dramatic events heralded the approach of the Nineteenth Century. In 1791, Spain made war on Morocco and bombarded Tangier. After the fighting ended, the Sultan of Morocco, Moulay Yazid, made the Jews of Tangier sell all their household goods, in order to pay for the war and fund the added protection that Tangier would need against future attacks.[14] Only a year earlier, Moulay Yazid had turned against the Jews of Fez, who had hitherto prospered, especially as goldsmiths, lace-makers, embroiderers and tailors, and manufacturers of gold thread.[15] Moulay ordered the destruction of the synagogues, the plunder of the Jewish Quarter and the expulsion of Jews from the city. It was not until two years later, when Yazid was succeeded as Sultan by Moulay Suleiman, that the Jews were allowed to return to Fez, albeit to a much reduced area.[16]

Individual Jews also suffered; two examples from the end of the Eighteenth Century give a flavour of what a Jew could expect, however influential or successful he might be. In the first case, a Jewish businessman, Jacob Attali, reached high favour as the protégé of the Moroccan Sultan Mohammad. But the Sultan's successor, Moulay Yazid, decided to punish him for supporting the previous Sultan by having him beheaded. Not fatal but still disturbing for the Jewish community was the case of Isaac Pinto, a Jew who held the position of Chief of Customs in Tangier – the most lucrative office to which a *dhimmi* in Tangier could aspire. When Pinto died in 1792 the Sultan

---

[13] David Corcos, 'Benoliel, Moroccan family,' *Encyclopaedia Judaica*, Volume 4, column 544.

[14] A Jew, Yeshaya (Isaiah) Benamar, was brought by the Sultan from Fez to supervise the building of a new pier to replace the one that had been destroyed in the war.

[15] The Jews also held two monopolies, one over tobacco and the other over the minting of coins.

[16] David Corcos, 'Fez,' *Encyclopaedia Judaica*, Volume 6, column 1257.

immediately confiscated all of his possessions and forced his son to sell the family's home.[17]

In the first years of the Nineteenth Century, a Spanish Christian, General Domingo Badia y Lebich, travelled in the guise of a Muslim – under the name Ali Bey El Abassi – through North Africa and western Asia.[18] After leaving Morocco he travelled to Tripoli, where he observed a rejuvenated Jewish community. These Jews, he noted, were 'treated somewhat better than in Morocco. There are about two thousand who dress as Muslims do; only the cap and slippers must be black, and the turban usually deep blue.' He added that there were 'about thirty very rich families, the others being craftsmen or goldsmiths. Trade with Europe is almost entirely in their hands: they deal mainly with Marseille, Leghorn, Venice and Malta.'[19]

Such were the protective benefits of *dhimmi* status, but they were not always so evident. In 1806 a Belgian-born doctor, Louis Frank, became personal physician to the Bey of Tunis during the regency there. In an account of his experiences, Frank described the life of the Jews in Tunis and the effect of their *dhimmi* status. These Jews were the only subjects of the Bey who paid him a personal tax, and 'although this payment is claimed for their protection, nothing is more common than to see them being molested and even struck by the Moors.' Dr. Frank observed that 'they accept these mistreatments and blows with astonishing resignation,' and should a Jew 'dare to reply to his aggressors, he would most certainly run the risk of becoming involved in serious proceedings from which he could extricate himself only at the cost of a large sum of money.' Indeed, the insults hurled at Jews often had 'no other aim but this abusive and tyrannical extortion.'[20]

---

[17] Attali's brother only escaped execution by converting to Islam. M. Mitchell Serels, *A History of the Jews of Tangier*, page 4.

[18] *Bey* was originally a Turkish title for a chieftain, and then later for the ruler of a region or province. The first three Ottoman Sultans used the title *Bey*. From the Nineteenth Century onwards, *Bey* was used as a term of respect.

[19] Renzo De Felice, *Jews in an Arab Land: Libya, 1835-1970*, page 6.

[20] L. Frank, Tunis, *Description de cette Régence*, published in Paris, 1862, quoted in Bat Ye'or, *The Dhimmi*, pages 292-3.

No decade of the Nineteenth Century passed without such a threat or act of violence against Jews under Muslim rule. Sometimes violence took the form of the medieval Christian Blood Libel, but at other times it lacked even that pretence. In 1813 in Palestine, the leaders of the Jewish community in the Holy City of Hebron – the site of the Tomb of the Patriarchs, Abraham, Isaac and Jacob – were imprisoned and tortured until a ransom was paid to the Arab sheikhs who had abducted them.[21] The Jewish community of Hebron was too poor to pay the ransom; it took them more than a year to collect the money from Jewish communities in Germany, Holland and England.[22] In 1814, in the Russian-ruled Muslim city of Baku on the Caspian Sea, the Jews, who had been harassed by the local Muslims over many years, were subjected to a Blood Libel, being accused of using non-Jewish blood for the Passover meal. Only the intervention of the Russian Tsarist authorities saved them, offering them official protection and refuge in a nearby town.[23]

In Morocco in 1820, the Jewish Quarter of Fez was targeted by an invading Muslim tribe, the Udaya, who seized canvas, silk, silver and gold. The attack did not stop at plunder. Jewish women were taken to the Muslim quarter, where the young girls among them were raped. Many Jewish men were murdered while trying to protect their women from abduction. Leaders of the community and shopkeepers were tortured and forced to reveal where they had hidden their money. According to one source, when a man's wife was particularly beautiful, the invaders 'stole her from her husband to force him to pay a ransom.'[24] The persecution only stopped after the Udaya tribesmen challenged the Sultan, who bombarded them with his canon and drove them from Fez.[25]

---

[21] The four Jewish Holy Cities are Jerusalem, Tiberias, Safed and Hebron.

[22] Tudor Parfitt, *The Jews in Palestine, 1800-1882*, pages 39-48.

[23] Simha Katz, 'Baku,' *Encyclopaedia Judaica*, Volume 4, column 119.

[24] A. an-Nasiri, *Recherches approfondies sur l'histoire des dynasties de Maroc*, Paris, 1906, quoted in Bat Ye'or, *The Dhimmi*, pages 293-4.

[25] In commemoration of their deliverance, the Jews of Fez celebrated a special Purim – *Purim del Kor*, the Purim of the cannon balls – every year on the anniversary of the bombardment. David Corcos, 'Fez,' *Encyclopaedia Judaica*, Volume 6, column 1257.

A similar attack occurred in the Galilee city of Safed in 1838. The Jewish community there was devastated when Druze raiders from southern Lebanon, joined by Muslims from Safed itself, rampaged through the Jewish Quarter during the night, looting as they went. Women were raped and men tortured in an attempt to make them reveal the whereabouts of their 'hidden gold and money.' The next day Egyptian troops arrived, restored order, punished a number of local Muslims for the attacks and forced them to return much of the looted property.[26]

On some occasions, Muslim rulers themselves initiated violence against the Jews. In 1818, in the eastern Mediterranean port city of Acre, Pasha Abdalla – determinedly independent of his nominal masters in Istanbul – turned against one of his leading Jewish citizens, Haim Farhi. A well-off and deeply religious man, Farhi had opened his home to those in need, whether Jews, Christians, or Muslims. But when Abdalla accused him of building his private synagogue higher than the Acre mosque, Farhi was sentenced to death and executed. His body was denied a proper Jewish burial and thrown into the sea. When the tide washed the body up on the shore, it was thrown in again. Farhi's house was then ransacked and all his belongings taken away, leaving his family destitute. Abdalla also turned against the Jews of Safed and Tiberias, forcing them to hand over their valuable possessions. Only the intervention of the Austrian Consul in Aleppo, Baron Picciotto – a Jew – halted the Pasha's rampage.[27]

Five hundred miles east of Acre, the Jews of Baghdad suffered ill-treatment at the hands of another Muslim ruler, the local governor Daud Pasha. The governor's harassment, starting in 1817 and continuing for fourteen years, prompted hundreds of Baghdadi Jewish families to flee by ship from Basra to the Indian port of Surat, where they became active in the jute, cotton and tobacco trades. Jews fleeing from Baghdad also set up flourishing trading communities in Bombay and Calcutta, and later as far east as Rangoon, Hong Kong

---

[26] Tudor Parfitt, *The Jews in Palestine, 1800-1882*, pages 67-9.
[27] 'Haim "El Muallim" Farhi (1740-1818)': www.farhi.org/history.htm. *'El Muallim'* means 'The Teacher.'

and Shanghai. These communities were all led by Baghdadi Jewish families, including the Ezras, Eliases, Gubbays and Kadhouries.[28]

A number of events in the Nineteenth Century brought the plight of Jews in Muslim lands to the attention of Western Europe and the United States. One of these events was the forced conversion of Jews in the Persian city of Meshed in 1839. The Jews of Meshed had faced an imminent massacre by a Muslim mob, until Muslim notables saved most of them by declaring that the Jewish community would convert to Islam. Some of the converts fled to the Central Asian city of Merv, 150 miles to the north-east, where they were welcomed by the Sheikh of Merv and were allowed to return to Judaism.[29] Other refugees from Meshed went to Afghanistan to join the Jewish communities in Kabul, Herat and Maimana. There they began trading in animal skins, carpets and antiquities, and later produced liturgical and religious poetry of great beauty.[30]

In 1834 another event occurred that shocked the western Jewish world: the public execution of a seventeen-year-old Jewish woman, Sol Hachuel (also known as Zulaika Hajwal), in the Moroccan city of Tangier. The tragedy began when Sol befriended a Muslim woman who had ambitions to convert her to Islam – a particularly meritorious act under the code of Islamic law then prevalent in Morocco. When the woman's efforts failed, she denounced Sol to the Muslim authorities, claiming that the girl had indeed been converted, but had returned to Judaism.

Sol was brought before the Sultan's representative, the Basha (Governor) of Tangier, Arbi Esudio, and accused of having agreed to be converted to Islam. Sol declared: 'You have been deceived, Sir. . . . I never pronounced such words: she proposed it to me, but I did not consent.' She then told the Governor, in Ladino, in words that

---

[28] The Chief of Staff of the Indian Army's Eastern Command in the 1971 Bangladesh Liberation War, Lieutenant-General J.F.R. Jacob, was of Baghdadi-Jewish descent. He later became the Governor of two Indian States, Goa and Punjab.
[29] Bat Ye'or, *The Dhimmi*, page 88.
[30] W.J. Fischel, 'Afghanistan,' *Encyclopaedia Judaica*, Volume 2, column 327.

became her epitaph: *Hebrea naci y Hebrea quero morir* – 'A Jewess I was born, a Jewess I wish to die.' The Governor responded by offering Sol silk and gold if she agreed even then to convert to Islam. He then threatened her with punishment for apostasy: 'I will have you torn piece-meal by wild beasts. You shall not see the light of day, you shall perish of hunger, and experience the rigour of my vengeance and indignation, in having provoked the anger of the Prophet.'

Sol, unflinching, replied: 'I will give my limbs to be torn piece-meal by wild beasts; I will renounce forever the light of day, I will perish of hunger, and when all the evils of life are accumulated on me by your orders, I will smile at your indignation, and the anger of the Prophet: since neither he nor you have been able to overcome a weak female! It is clear that Heaven is not too auspicious to making proselytes to your faith.'

The Governor was indignant at Sol's reference to Mohammed – 'you have profaned the name I revere,' he told her – and sent her to prison, where she was held with an iron collar around her neck, and chains on her hands and feet. Her parents appealed to the Spanish Consul in Tangier, but his considerable efforts to have her set free were unsuccessful. Sol was then sent to Fez, for the Sultan to decide her fate. Her parents were made to pay a substantial sum for the cost of the journey, and threatened with five hundred lashes if they could not find the money. Fortunately for them, the Spanish Consul paid the charge.

In Fez, the Sultan appointed the Cadi – a senior Koranic judge – to determine Sol's punishment. The Cadi summoned the Jewish sages of Fez, who urged him to spare Sol's life. The Cadi replied that unless she agreed to convert to Islam she would be beheaded – and the Jewish community punished. Despite efforts by the sages to persuade her to convert in order to save her life and their community, Sol refused conversion and was found guilty. She was condemned to be executed in the main marketplace in Fez. The Cadi stated that the cost of the execution would have to be borne by her father.

A large crowd of local Muslims gathered to watch the execution, crying out as she was brought through the streets: 'Here comes she who blasphemed the Prophet – death! Death! to the impious wretch!'

At the scaffold, Sol was permitted to wash her hands and say the Shema prayer, 'Hear! O Israel, the Lord is God, the Lord is one . . .' Then one of the executioners cut her with his scimitar and, in the hope of persuading her to convert to Islam – apparently on the Sultan's orders – declared, 'There is yet time to become Mohametan, and save your life!' On seeing her blood she turned to him with the words, 'Do not make me linger – behead me at once – for dying as I do, innocent of any crime, the God of Abraham will avenge my death!' She was then beheaded.[31]

The Fez Jewish community had to pay to have Sol Hachuel's corpse, her head and the bloodstained earth given to them for Jewish burial in the Jewish cemetery. She was buried next to one of the great sages of Moroccan Jewry and declared a martyr.[32] Her story was told and retold by Jews all over the world as the tragedy of a Jew entrapped by Islamic enmity towards the infidel.

Jewish communities still suffered at the hands of Christian Europe, yet European travellers in Muslim lands were frequently shocked by what they witnessed of the treatment of Jews there. This was even apparent in Jerusalem, the holiest of Jewish cities. The French writer and diplomat Chateaubriand, who was in Jerusalem in 1806, wrote that local Jews were the 'special target of all contempt.' Despite their troubles, he added, 'they lower their heads without complaint; they suffer all insults without demanding justice; they let themselves be crushed by blows.'[33] In 1834, a British traveller, Robert Curzon, was also in Jerusalem. 'Many of the Jews are rich,' he recalled later, 'but they are

---

[31] Sixteen years later, Sol Hachuel's execution was the subject of a graphic painting by the French painter Alfred Dehodencq. The painting, which is in Paris, in the Musée d'art d'histoire du Judaïsme, is reproduced as the front cover of Andrew G. Bostom (editor), *The Legacy of Islamic Antisemitism*, which has a full account of the case – 'A Note on the Cover Art,' pages 13-16.

[32] Eugenio Maria Romero, *El martirio de joven Hachuel o la heroina Hebrea*: Gibraltar, Imprinta Militar, 1837. Published anonymously in London in 1839 as *Jewish Heroine of the Nineteenth Century: A Tale Founded on Fact*. Quoted by Andrew Bostom (editor), *The Legacy of Islamic Antisemitism*, pages 13-17.

[33] François-René Viscount de Chateaubriand, *Itinéraire de Paris à Jérusalem*, pages 426-7.

careful to conceal their wealth from the jealous eyes of their Mohammedan rulers, lest they should be subject to extortion.'[34]

Similar accounts of harassment and fear were recorded by visitors to other Muslim lands. In 1835 a British visitor to Algiers, Perceval Barton Lord, noted that any Muslim soldier, 'if so inclined, would stop and beat the first Jew he met in the street, without the latter daring to return or even ward off the blows.' Lord wrote that the victim's 'only resource was to run as fast as he could, until he had made his escape.' Complaint was, in his opinion, 'worse than useless,' for the Cadi of Algiers always summoned the soldier and asked him why he had beaten the Jew, to which the soldier would answer, 'Because he has spoken ill of our holy religion.' At that point, wrote Lord, the soldier would be dismissed 'and the Jew put to death.'[35]

Another traveller to North Africa in the early Nineteenth Century was a British orientalist, William Edward Lane. In his book *Manners and Customs of Modern Egypt*, published in 1836, he described the situation of the Jews in Cairo. They were 'detested by the Muslims far more than are the Christians,' he wrote. 'Not long ago, they used often to be jostled in the streets of Cairo, and sometimes beaten merely for passing on the right hand of a Muslim. At present they are less oppressed; but still they ever scarcely dare to utter a word of abuse when reviled or beaten unjustly by the meanest Arab or Turk; for many a Jew has been put to death upon a false and malicious accusation for uttering disrespectful words against the Kur'an or the Prophet.'[36]

European travellers expressed the same surprise and dismay at the plight of Jewish communities in Asia. A British traveller in Persia, Charles Wills, wrote that the Jews there were repeatedly humiliated by the Muslim population. 'At every public festival,' he wrote, and 'even at the royal salaam, before the King's face – the Jews are collected, and

---

[34] Robert Curzon, *Visits to Monasteries in the Levant*, page 208.
[35] Perceval Barton Lord, *Algiers, with notices of the neighbouring States of Barbary*, Volume Two, page 81. Lord added: 'It is true that the testimony of two Musulmans was required to the fact of the Jew having abused their religion, but on such occasions witnesses were never wanting.'
[36] William Edward Lane, *Manners and Customs of the Modern Egyptians*, page 554.

a number of them are flung into the hauz or tank, that King and mob may be amused by seeing them crawl out half-drowned and covered with mud. The same kindly ceremony is witnessed whenever a provincial governor holds high festival: there are fireworks and Jews.'[37]

Another Western traveller, the Romanian-born Jewish historian Israel Joseph Benjamin, visited the Persian Jews in 1850. He wrote that they were 'obliged to live in a separate part of town . . . for they are considered as unclean creatures.' He also noted that, 'under the pretext of their being unclean, they are treated with the greatest severity and should they enter a street, inhabited by Mussulmans, they are pelted by the boys and mobs with stones and dirt.' Jews were even 'prohibited to go out when it rains; for it is said the rain would wash dirt off them, which would sully the feet of the Mussulmans.' At other times, if a Jew was recognised as a Jew while walking in the streets, 'he is subjected to the greatest insults. The passers-by spit in his face, and sometimes beat him . . . unmercifully.'

Benjamin reported that if a Jew entered a shop, he was forbidden to inspect the goods that were on sale there. 'Should his hand incautiously touch the goods,' Benjamin wrote, 'he must take them at any price the seller chooses to ask for them.' Yet, on occasion, Persians entered Jewish homes uninvited to 'take possession of whatever pleases them. Should the owner make the least opposition in defence of his property, he incurs the danger of atoning for it with his life.' This demarcation in society – and the danger of any transgression – was equally apparent during the three days of the *Muharram*, an important period of mourning in Shia Islam. If a Jew dared to be in the streets during those days, Benjamin wrote, he was 'sure to be murdered.'[38]

The situation was also discouraging for Jews in the Bukharan Khanate, where in 1863 an intrepid explorer, Arminius Vámbéry – a

---

[37] Charles James Wills, *Persia as It Is: Being Sketches of Modern Persian Life and Character*, page 230.

[38] Israel Joseph Benjamin, *Eight Years in Asia and Africa, from 1846-1855*; also published in France as J.J. Benjamin, *Cinq années en Orient*; quoted in Bernard Lewis, *The Jews of Islam*, pages 181-183. It is the tenth day of *Muharram* (the first month of the Muslim year), and to some extent the days leading up to the tenth, that is the *Ashura*, the period of mourning for the Shia.

Hungarian Jew and a convert to Christianity – travelled while disguised as a Muslim ascetic. On his return to Hungary he wrote that the Jews of the Khanate were living 'under the greatest oppression and exposed to the greatest contempt.' He described how the head of the Jewish community in Bukhara, upon paying the collective *jizya* tax, was given 'two slight blows on the cheek, prescribed by the Koran as a sign of submission.' Some Bukharan Jews, hearing of the privileges accorded to Jews in Turkey, had made their way to Damascus and other places in Syria. But Vámbéry noted that 'this emigration can only occur secretly, otherwise they would have to atone for the very wish by confiscation or death.'[39]

Of all the places visited by outsiders during the Nineteenth Century, Palestine remained the focus of Western concern about the Jews. On 25 May 1839 the British Vice-Consul in Jerusalem, William Tanner Young, wrote a report comparing the condition of the Jews in Palestine to that of their counterparts in Egypt. Young wrote that the Governor of Egypt, Ibrahim Pasha, showed 'more consideration' for the Jews than the Christians did. Young also wrote that he had heard several Egyptian Jews acknowledge that 'they enjoy more peace and tranquility under this Government, than they have ever enjoyed here before.' But he then observed that, in contrast, 'the Jew in Jerusalem is not estimated in value much above a dog – and scarcely a day passes that I do not hear of some act of tyranny and oppression against a Jew.'

Young's task in Jerusalem was to follow the British Government's pledge 'to afford protection to the Jews generally.' In his report he informed the Foreign Secretary, Lord Palmerston, that he had succeeded in obtaining 'justice for Jews against Turks,' but added that it was 'quite a new thing in the eyes of these people to claim justice for a Jew.' Young went on to warn Palmerston: 'What the Jew has to endure, at all hands is not to be told.' But tell it he did: 'Like the miserable dog without an owner, he is kicked by one because he crosses his path, and cuffed by another because he cries out – to seek

[39] Arminius Vámbéry, *Travels in Central Asia*, pages 372-3. Vámbéry was born Armin Bamberger.

redress he is afraid, lest it bring worse upon him; he thinks it better to endure than to live in expectation of his complaint being revenged upon him. Brought up from infancy to look upon his civil disabilities everywhere as a mark of degradation, his heart becomes the cradle of fear and suspicion – he finds he is trusted by none – and therefore lives himself without confidence in any.'[40]

When the English traveller John Lowthian visited Jerusalem in 1843, Jews made up more than half of the city's population, yet still their situation appeared lamentable. 'What a painful change has passed over the circumstances and condition of the poor Jew,' Lowthian wrote, 'that in his own city, and close by where his temple stood, he has to suffer oppression and persecution.' Should a Jew have 'a little of this world's good in his possession, he is oppressed and robbed by the Turks in a most unmerciful manner; in short, for him there is neither law nor justice.'[41] Lowthian's words were reinforced two decades later, when an Italian geographer, Ermete Pierotti, spent a number of months in Jerusalem, where he observed that the local Muslims 'unfortunately hold the opinion that to injure a Jew is a work well pleasing in the sight of God.'[42]

Eventually the plight of Jews in Muslim lands became known far and wide. In 1854 the *New York Daily Tribune* published an article by Karl Marx that included a damning description of how Jews were treated in Jerusalem. The article was based entirely on what Marx had read in the British Museum in London, for he had never visited any part of the Ottoman Empire. Marx used the information he had read to draw wider conclusions about Islam's relationship to the outer world. 'The Koran and the Mussulman legislation emanating from it,' he wrote, 'reduce the geography and ethnography of the various people to the simple and convenient distinction of two nations and of two countries;

---

[40] Albert M. Hyamson (editor), *The British Consulate in Jerusalem*, pages 8-9.
[41] John Lowthian, *A Narrative of a Recent Visit to Jerusalem and Several Parts of Palestine in 1843-44*.
[42] Ermete Pierotti, *Customs and Traditions of Palestine, Illustrating the Manners of Ancient Hebrews*.

those of the Faithful and of the Infidels.' He explained that 'the Infidel is "*harby*," i.e. the enemy,' and that 'Islamism proscribes the nation of the Infidels, constituting a state of permanent hostility between the Mussulman and the unbeliever.'

In his article, Marx wrote, 'Nothing equals the misery and the sufferings of the Jews at Jerusalem.' They lived in 'the most filthy quarter of the town, called *hareth el-yahoud*, in the quarter of dirt, between the Zion and the Moriah, where their synagogues are situated – the constant object of Mussulman oppression and intolerance.' In addition, they were insulted and persecuted by the Christian inhabitants of the city. Marx added that the Muslims, 'forming about a fourth part of the whole, and consisting of Turks, Arabs and Moors, are, of course, the masters in every respect.'[43]

One of the first guidebooks to Jerusalem, published in 1871, gave a similar impression of Muslim attitudes towards the Jews. The book contained a particularly revealing entry about the al-Aqsa Mosque. Readers were told they could expect 'the Muslim guide' at the mosque to describe how, on the day of judgement, after the 'Anti-Christ' had been killed, 'the victors will then proceed to a general massacre of the Jews in and around the Holy City, and every tree and every stone shall cry out and say: "I have a Jew beneath me, slay him."'[44]

That such information caused concern was evident in a dramatic Western intervention. It took place after a notorious Blood Libel case in Damascus. An Italian friar had disappeared in that city together with his Muslim servant on 5 February 1840. Local Christians accused the Jews of murdering the two men in order to use their blood in the Passover meal. The charges were then brought by the French consul in Damascus, supported by the city's Egyptian Muslim governor, Sherif Pasha. Seven leaders of the Jewish community were arrested and tortured. Two died; one accepted Islam to save his life.

---

[43] Karl Marx, 'Declaration of War: on the History of the Eastern Question,' *New York Daily Tribune*, 15 April 1854 (written on 28 March 1854).
[44] Walter Besant and E.H. Palmer, *Jerusalem, the City of Herod and Saladin*. According to the book, the Muslim guide would also explain how 'the Messiah will break the crosses and kill the pigs' – the Christians – 'after which the Millennium will set in.'

Sixty-three Jewish children were imprisoned and many Jewish homes destroyed in the search for the bodies. It then emerged that the friar had been killed by a Muslim.[45]

To forestall any further Blood Libel accusations in Muslim lands, the British philanthropist Sir Moses Montefiore travelled with a Jewish delegation first to Cairo and then to Istanbul. There he persuaded the Sultan, Abdul Mejid, to declare the Blood Libel a fallacy and to forbid its propagation anywhere in the Ottoman Empire. The Sultan's decree was issued on 6 November 1840, addressed to the chief judge of Istanbul. Montefiore had prepared the draft and given it to Reshid Pasha, the Ottoman Minister for Foreign Affairs.[46]

The Sultan's decree was emphatic in its defence of the Jews and the Jewish religion. It began: 'An ancient prejudice has prevailed against the Jews. The ignorant believe that the Jews were accustomed to sacrifice a human being to make use of his blood at his feast of Passover. . . . The calumnies which have been uttered against the Jews and the vexations to which they have been subjected have at last reached our Imperial Throne.' The Sultan noted that Muslim theologians had examined Jewish religious books and found that the Jews 'are strongly prohibited, not only from using human blood, but even from consuming that of animals. It therefore follows that the charges made against them and their religion are nothing but pure calumny.'

The 'Jewish nation,' declared Abdul Mejid, 'shall possess the same advantages and shall enjoy the same privilege as are granted to the numerous other nations who submit to our authority. The Jewish nation shall be protected and defended.'[47]

A Muslim ruler had come to the rescue of the Jews.

---

[45] Rabbi Yehuda Alkalai, born in 1797 in the Ottoman city of Sarajevo, was so deeply perturbed by the Damascus Blood Libel that in 1843 he called for the adoption of Hebrew as the national language of the Jews, and for the purchase of land in Ottoman-ruled Palestine and the development of agriculture there, for both the absorption of new immigrants and the encouragement of Jewish national unity.

[46] Jonathan Frankel, *The Damascus Affair*, page 376.

[47] Quoted in full in Stanford J. Shaw, *The Jews of the Ottoman Empire and the Turkish Republic*, pages 200-1.

8

PROGRESS AND PERIL: TOWARDS THE TWENTIETH CENTURY

'A generous sovereign and protector of his Israelite subjects'
'Our most implacable enemy'

A remarkable improvement for Jews in the Ottoman Empire came in 1849, when Sultan Abdul Mejid granted official status to all Jewish and Christian communities under his rule. Extending the existing *millet* system of autonomous communities, he allowed Jews and Christians to establish organisations to regulate their communal life and represent their needs before local Muslim authorities. He followed this with a second, remarkable change: in 1856 he ordered an end to *dhimmi* status within the Ottoman Empire. Until the end of his reign, the Sultan proceeded to introduce new laws to weaken the *dhimmi* condition, including one decree issued in 1865 that allowed Jews in all of Libya's main towns to be represented in the local Ottoman counsels by their chief rabbi.[1]

Abdul Mejid's successor, Sultan Abdul Aziz, made further progress by finally breaking the grip of *dhimmi* subservience. On 12 December 1875, more than a thousand years after the Covenant of Omar, he issued a decree that circumvented the refusal of Islamic religious courts to accept evidence from Jews and Christians. All legal cases between Muslims and *dhimmis* were to be moved out of the religious Sharia courts – where such cases had to be heard, according to Islamic law – and into the civil courts.[2] The change reflected a basic tolerance in Ottoman society that was seen again in the following year, when a Jew from Mesopotamia, Menahem Saleh

---

[1] Renzo De Felice, *Jews in an Arab Land: Libya, 1835-1970*, page 9.
[2] Imperial *iradé* (decree), 12 December 1875: Bat Ye'or, *Islam and Dhimmitude*, page 75.

Daniel, was appointed Deputy for Baghdad to the first Ottoman Parliament in Istanbul.[3]

The benefits of Ottoman tolerance were already evident in Baghdad, where Jewish culture and scholarship were blossoming. The Beit Zilkha rabbinical college, which had been founded in 1840, produced graduates who served throughout Mesopotamia. In 1863 the first Hebrew-language printing press in Baghdad was established by a Jewish printer, Moses Baruch Mizrachi. The press printed a Hebrew newspaper, *Ha-Dover* ('The Speaker'), and three books. A second printing press was founded five years later, and went on to print fifty-five books in fourteen years.[4] A third press, founded in 1888 by the Baghdadi-Jewish scholar and writer Solomon Bekhor Huzin, printed books for prayer and communal use, as well as scholarly works from previous centuries that were formerly available only in manuscript form. In twenty-five years, seventy-five books were printed by Solomon Bekhor Huzin and his son Joseph Huzin.[5]

When Jews were granted autonomy under Muslim rule, Jewish communities were able to grow and thrive. This was apparent in Baghdad, where the Jewish population by 1884 was estimated at 30,000. It was also apparent in Egypt, where rulers since Mohammad Ali Pasha had invited foreigners – including Jews – to come and settle. After the Suez Canal was opened in 1869, Ismail Pasha, the Khedive of Egypt, made an added effort to encourage outsiders to settle in the country as a way of developing its economy. As he explained: 'My country is no longer in Africa; we are now part of Europe. It is therefore natural for us to abandon our former ways and to adopt a new system adapted to our social conditions.'[6] The age-old restrictions

---

[3] Menahem Saleh Daniel later founded a Jewish elementary school in Baghdad in 1910. Meir Basri, 'Prominent Iraqi Jews of recent times,' *The Scribe*, Issue 76, Spring 2003.

[4] This press was founded by Rahamim ben Reuben, who had gained printing expertise in Bombay, in British India, amidst a vibrant community of former Baghdadi Jews.

[5] Avraham Yaari, 'Baghdad, Hebrew Printing,' *Encyclopaedia Judaica*, Volume 4, column 93.

[6] Hugh Chisholm, 'Ismail Pasha,' *Encyclopaedia Britannica*, Eleventh Edition, page 875.

and humiliations of *dhimmi* status were set side, and those Jews who responded to the Khedive's call were granted special privileges in return for their skills and expertise.

Jewish enterprise flourished in the favourable conditions established by the Khedive. The Egyptian business world, the cotton trade, and manufacturing and retailing all gained in turn by the Jewish influx.[7] In April 1888, Khedive Tewfik awarded a contract to build, operate and manage a new Cairo-Helwan railway to a consortium of three Jewish bankers – Jacob Moise Cattaui, Felix Suares and Baron Jacques Levi Bohor de Menasche. Ten years later, members of the Cattaui dynasty helped to found and then direct the National Bank of Egypt. Among them was Baron Jacques, who also sat on the board of directors for the Egyptian Delta Light Railway and owned mercantile enterprises in Manchester, Liverpool, Paris and Istanbul. Another Cattaui family member was Felix Suares, who helped to finance agricultural development in the Nile Delta as a board member of the Agricultural Bank of Egypt, and who transformed a bankrupt company into the country's largest sugar production enterprise.[8]

The Jews made equally impressive contributions to Egypt's cultural life. A shining example was James (Yakub) Sanua, the son of an Italian Jew who settled in Egypt even before Khedive Ismail's call for immigrants. Born in Cairo, Sanua was a prominent writer, playwright, satirist and poet who laid the foundations of modern Egyptian theatre. His thirty-two plays were written not in classical but in colloquial Arabic, and had enormous popular appeal in Egypt. He became such an influential critic of the corruption and extravagance of the Khedive – demanding 'Egypt for the Egyptians' and calling for an end to the growing British influence in the country – that in 1878 he was exiled to Paris, never to return. His father, Raphael Sanua, by contrast, became a trusted adviser to the Khedive and his family.[9]

---

[7] Victor D. Sanua (editor), *Egyptian Jewry*, page 3.
[8] Samir W. Raafat, *Maadi, 1904-1962: Society & History in a Cairo Suburb*, page 17.
[9] Victor D. Sanua, '"Egypt for the Egyptians": The Story of Abu Naddara (James Sanua) 1839-1912, A Jewish Egyptian Patriot,' *Image Magazine*, September 1997.

Several thousand Jews made their way to Egypt in this period – including many who fled Tsarist Russia; all of them displayed a remarkable ability to adapt to new surroundings. A Romanian-born Jew, Max Herz, who reached Egypt in 1881, brought his architectural skills to the service of Islam. He became an architect at the Department of Waqf (the Religious Endowments Authority) and the director of the Islamic Art Preservation Committee. Herz undertook the restoration of many mosques in Egypt, including two in Cairo, and was responsible for the Egyptian Pavilion at the Chicago Universal Exhibition in 1892.[10] In the words of Ellis Douek, a descendant of a Jewish family that arrived in Egypt at that time, migrants like Herz 'had taken a leap of faith,' and 'not just in relocating themselves, but in understanding that the move, in order to succeed, had to involve taking up a new culture.'[11]

Another significant turning point for the Jews in Muslim lands came in 1860, when the first Jewish world organisation, the Alliance Israélite Universelle, was established in Paris. The founders of the Alliance (as it became known) were concerned at the remoteness of many Jewish communities outside Europe. They wanted an organisation that would respond to the needs of Jews wherever they were suffering, and would protect those who were discriminated against because of their religion. The Alliance also wanted to promote the kind of changes that were occurring in Europe at that time, where Jewish emancipation was leading to full participation of Jews in political, cultural, commercial and social life. In its manifesto, the Alliance announced that the organisation's aim was to 'serve as a most important stimulus to Jewish regeneration.'

In the coming decades, the Alliance fought for the rights of Jews everywhere – in Christian Europe, Tsarist Russia and the Balkans, and throughout the lands of Islam. The organisation's most powerful instrument was education; it built a network of schools that brought

---

[10] Samir Raafat, *Cairo, The Glory Years*, page 31.
[11] Ellis Douek, *A Middle Eastern Affair*, page 26.

European teachers and a European curriculum to Jews in Muslim lands whose education had previously been restricted to Jewish religious instruction. In every region of Muslim rule, these schools provided Jews with a sense of cohesion and opportunity, and helped to preserve Jewish identity by combating Christian missionary influence.[12] They also educated Jews who later became leaders of their communities at a time when such leadership would be most needed.[13]

In 1867 a French Jew, Charles Netter, suggested to the Alliance a means to help Jews from Persia and Eastern Europe build new lives as farmers in Ottoman Palestine. With the organisation's support, he went to Istanbul a year later and met the Grand Vizier of the Imperial State Council. Netter persuaded the Grand Vizier to procure a decree from the Sultan allowing the Alliance to lease land near Jaffa for a Jewish agricultural school. The Governor of Syria, Rashid Pasha, then authorised the purchase of a ninety-nine-year lease on 2,600 dunams (650 acres) of land.[14] Netter built a school on this land in 1870, which he named Mikve Israel ('The Hope of Israel'), serving as both principal and instructor there, and witnessing the beginnings of Jewish agricultural settlement in Ottoman Palestine.[15]

As the Alliance expanded its efforts, it received support from wealthy and prominent Jews around the world. The funding for its projects was massively boosted after 1874 by the charitable donations of the Austrian-born Jewish philanthropist Baron Maurice de

---

[12] The Alliance school system in the Ottoman Empire worked closely with Istanbul's Chief Rabbi, Moshe Lévi, to open two new elementary schools in Istanbul that were intended, in part, to offset the influence of Protestant missionaries.

[13] The first two schools in Morocco were opened in Tetuan in 1862 and in Tangier in 1869.

[14] Originally, a dunam (or *dönüm*), from the Turkish *dönmek* (to turn), was the amount of land one man could plough in one day. It was not precisely defined and varied considerably from place to place. It is still used, in various standardised versions, in many countries that were formerly part of the Ottoman Empire, including Israel, where 52 dunams is the equivalent of 11 acres.

[15] Israel Klausner, 'Charles Netter,' *Encyclopaedia Judaica*, Volume 12, columns 1001-2.

Hirsch. Like the founders of the Alliance, Hirsch wanted 'to improve the position of the Jews in the Ottoman Empire by instruction and education,' and allocated a total of eleven million gold francs to that end.[16] In the same year, the Alliance opened its first school in Baghdad. The school had been founded nine years earlier by David Sassoon, one of the wealthiest and most charitable of Iraqi Jews; it was his son, Sir Albert Sassoon, who gave the school as a gift to the Alliance.[17]

Towards the end of the Nineteenth Century, the Alliance Israélite Universelle had some cause for optimism in its work in the Ottoman Empire: Jews there were thriving under tolerant rule. They were to be found working as teachers at Istanbul University, as merchants and traders throughout the Empire, as Ottoman consular officials throughout Europe and as officers in the Ottoman Army – where kosher food was provided, and Sabbath observance allowed. The Jews of Ottoman Turkey found no barrier to advancement despite the Islamic faith of the Sultan and the majority of his subjects.

The Alliance's bulletin of 1893 expressed genuine enthusiasm in thanking Turkey. It read: 'There are but few countries, even among those which are considered the most enlightened and the most civilized, where Jews enjoy a more complete equality than in Turkey.' The Sultan had proved to be 'a generous sovereign and protector of his Israelite subjects.'[18] These words echoed the many telegrams of thanks that had reached Sultan Abdul Hamid II a year earlier, when the Jews had commemorated the four hundredth anniversary of the expulsion of Jews from Spain, and had also celebrated the welcoming of Jews into the Ottoman Empire. Istanbul's Chief Rabbi, Moshe Lévi, had visited the Sultan in person to present him with a statement

---

[16] Simon R. Schwarzfuchs, 'Alliance Israélite Universelle . . . ,' *Encyclopaedia Judaica*, Volume 2, columns 648-54.

[17] David Solomon Sassoon, *A History of the Jews in Baghdad*, page 171.

[18] Stanford J. Shaw, *The Jews of the Ottoman Empire and the Turkish Republic*, pages 208-10.

of gratitude, as well as the text of a special prayer that reflected a strong sense of communal well-being. The prayer was read in all the synagogues of the Empire.[19]

Yet for all the progress that the Alliance witnessed in Turkey, its leaders did not ignore the numerous threats – old and new – that still loomed over the Jews during the second half of the Nineteenth Century. In 1869 a new and menacing shadow was cast over Jewish life when the growing literature of European anti-Semitism reached the Ottoman Empire. It came with the publication in Beirut of a French forgery claiming to be the confessions of a Moldovian rabbi converted to Christianity, revealing the 'horrors' of the Jewish religion.[20] Such misrepresentation mirrored widespread hostility: Jews were regularly the victims of attacks throughout Muslim lands. Again and again during the second half of the century, violence disrupted the settled calm and creativity of Jewish life.

In Morocco, in 1862, an Arab mob broke into the Jewish Quarter of Elkasr Kebir, near Tangier, and desecrated the synagogues. Seventeen Torah scrolls had to be sent to Tangier for safekeeping, each one smuggled by two Jews. A year later, in the Moroccan town of Safi, a fourteen-year-old Jewish boy, Jacob ben Yuda Accan, was accused of murdering his master, a Muslim tax collector who had died after an illness of several days. Accan was innocent but confessed under the torture of more than 150 lashes. So also did another innocent Jew, Elliahou Lalouche, who was also given more than 150 lashes.

Under torture, both victims named two other Jews – equally innocent – who then confessed after similar torture. The families of these Jews protested outside the main mosque in Safi, while the Chief Rabbi appealed to the Cadi: 'Does the law of the *ulama* of Morocco

---

[19] Four years later, the new Sultan, Abdul Hamid II, gave Chief Rabbi Lévi his blessing and support as he worked to restore the Jewish community's earlier position as the most favoured minority in the Ottoman Empire. Lévi also strengthened the Jewish community's charities to help orphaned, elderly and poor Jews. (Stanford J. Shaw, *The Jews of the Ottoman Empire and the Turkish Republic*, page 207.)

[20] Quoted in Yehoshafat Harkabi, *Arab Attitudes to Israel*, pages 273-5.

decree death to all Jews?'[21] Despite this appeal, all the accused were executed without even the charade of a trial.

News of these events in Morocco caused concern in Europe, prompting Sir Moses Montefiore – who had protested in Istanbul after the Damascus Blood Libel – to take action on behalf of the Jews of Morocco. At the age of eighty, and with the support of the British Government, Montefiore visited Morocco in 1863. Travelling in style in a sedan chair, he met Sultan Mohammed IV and was given a legal assurance that the Jews would be better protected in the future, according to protective aspects of the *dhimmi* regulations. When two Moroccan Jews were arrested after accidentally splashing mud on a Muslim servant of the senior Spanish diplomat in Tangier, they were released through Montefiore's efforts.[22]

The Jews of Morocco could not see an end to such incidents of violence. Although some Jews thrived in this period – including the Bensusan family, successful traders who had links to Sephardi merchant houses in England – the familiar terrors of *dhimmi* existence were never far from the surface.[23] In the town of Entifa in 1879, a pious sixty-five-year-old Jew, Jacob Dahan, took in a poor Muslim woman during a severe famine. He fed and looked after her, and in return the woman worked in his house. But when the town's governor learned of the arrangement, he ordered Dahan to come before him and declared: 'Can a Jew have a Moorish woman to serve him? He deserves to be burnt!' Jacob Dahan was then taken outside, nailed to the ground and beaten so severely that he died.[24]

---

[21] *Ulama*, also spelled *ulema*, means a community of legal scholars of Islam; those who possess the quality of *ilm* (learning).

[22] David Littman, 'Mission to Morocco (1863-1864),' in Sonia and V.D. Lipman (editors), *The Century of Moses Montefiore*. During his visit, Montefiore gave £300 (more than £40,000 in the money values of 2010) towards the building of a Jewish girls' school in Tangier that would teach Spanish, Hebrew and sewing. M. Mitchell Serels, *A History of the Jews of Tangier*, pages 27-9.

[23] David Corcos, 'Bensusan . . . Moroccan family,' *Encyclopaedia Judaica*, Volume 4, columns 554-5.

[24] Letter from three Jews of Entifa, sent from Marrakech, to David Corcos in Mogador, 18 June 1880. Quoted in David Littman, 'Jews under Muslim Rule in the late Nineteenth Century,' *Wiener Library Bulletin*, Issue Number 28, 1975, page 72.

Jews were also victimised elsewhere in North Africa, where Muslim Arabs – like those who populated the majority of Ottoman lands outside Turkey – regarded the status of *dhimmi* as one that forbade true equality. In 1897 leading members of the Jewish community in Tripoli sent a letter to the President of the Alliance that gave a grim picture of Jewish life in rural Tripolitania. They wrote of how an Arab mob had destroyed the synagogue in the village of Zliten, and that forty of the robbers were imprisoned; 'a few days later they were set free without the slightest punishment; not only that, but they were not even made to return the objects stolen from the synagogue and discovered in their houses.' The letter also reported: 'Last Thursday a Jew on his way to his village was killed by Arabs and his companion was injured. . . . The authorities have not attempted to find the criminals.' The writers went on to explain: 'It is quite understandable that, to the Muslims, Jews are of no account, and our personal safety is in jeopardy and our belongings are not our own.'[25]

The Jews of another Libyan town had expressed the same fear and insecurity a year earlier. In a petition to the Chief Rabbi in Tripoli, Jews in the coastal town of Misurata described the local Arabs as 'our most implacable enemy' and revealed that they were contemplating fleeing in order to escape continual robberies and violent attacks. Then, in 1897, a series of attacks by local Arabs forced the Jews of Misurata to pay the Ottoman authorities to provide an army barracks to protect them. Once they paid, however, no barracks were built. The Jews protested the attacks before the local Muslim governor, who arrested a few local Arab chieftains, ordered them to pay compensation for the attacks and then released them. Many Jews, fearful of reprisals, abandoned the town altogether.[26]

Jewish life was no less precarious in Ottoman-ruled Kurdistan, where a severe drought in 1880 and a series of famines prompted

[25] Letter of 21 February 1897, quoted in David Littman, 'Jews under Muslim Rule in the late Nineteenth Century,' *Wiener Library Bulletin,* Issue number 28, pages 69-71.
[26] Renzo De Felice, *Jews in an Arab Land: Libya, 1835-1970,* pages 302-3, note 27.

Jews to flee southward to Baghdad. For Jews who remained in Kurdistan, conditions were harsh and unyielding. Robbery and murder were common occurrences. In order to safeguard their lives, Jews were compelled to pay a special tax to the tribal chief. As Abraham Ben-Jacob has written, 'because of their isolation from the outside world, no concern was shown for them; their persons and belongings were sold to feudal rulers.' Some chiefs sold Jews or gave them away as gifts; this servitude continued until the beginning of the Twentieth Century.[27]

Jews throughout the Muslim world continued to look towards their ancient homeland. Despite their own hardships and *jizya* tax commitments, they made great efforts to provide financial help to the Jews of Palestine and to religious institutions in the four Jewish Holy Cities – Jerusalem, Hebron, Safed and Tiberias. When Safed was destroyed by an earthquake in 1837, Jews from Damascus travelled sixty miles to help dig out the dead. Emissaries from the four holy cities also made their way to lands beyond Palestine, seeking alms from Jewish communities in the farthest reaches of the Muslim world.

Persecution and hardship led many Jews to take the further step of immigrating to Palestine in search of a better life. In Yemen, where Jews had been subjected to extremely harsh rule during much of the Nineteenth Century, Jewish immigration to Palestine began in 1882. A Yemeni artisans' quarter was established below the walls of Jerusalem, in the Arab village of Silwan. Beginning in the following year, however, the Ottoman ruler of Yemen refused to allow the emigration to continue, and for more than two decades Yemeni Jews could only make their way to Palestine clandestinely.[28]

---

[27] Abraham Ben-Jacob, 'Kurdistan,' *Encyclopaedia Judaica*, Volume 10, columns 1297-8.
[28] Sarah Szymkowicz, *The Virtual Jewish History Tour, Yemen*. The last thirty Jewish families of the Yemeni-Jewish village of Silwan were evacuated by the British Mandate authorities on 11 August 1938, two years after the outbreak of the Arab revolt in Palestine. Three of the four synagogues were later destroyed. In 2007, the fourth synagogue was inhabited by an Arab family (Nissan Ratzlav-Katz, *Arutz Sheva – Israel National News*, 16 May 2007).

The first emigration of Bukharan Jews to Jerusalem began even earlier, in 1868, and was unopposed by the Ottomans. In 1892 a Bukharan quarter was founded inside the city and became a centre of commerce and learning. The Bukharan Quarter was especially notable for its fine stone buildings and promenades. In the words of the historian Aviva Müller-Lancet, 'Bukharan folkways and costumes were long perpetuated by the community of Jerusalem, making it the most colourful and picturesque element in Jerusalem Jewry.'[29]

From Baghdad, Jews had been immigrating to Palestine since the first half of the Nineteenth Century. The earliest of these immigrants were from the Matalon family, arriving in 1818, and from the Ilbizravi family, arriving in 1830. Another family, the Yehudahs, headed by Shelomoh Yehudah, arrived in Palestine in 1854 and established two large religious academies in Jerusalem. At their own expense, members of the Yehudah family maintained all the academies' students and supplied them with their subsistence. The family also donated a substantial sum of money for the building of the first large Ashkenazi synagogue in Jerusalem, Tiferet Israel. Shelomoh Yehudah's son Saul later bought land in the village of Motza, near Jerusalem, where he established the first agricultural village outside the city walls.[30]

By 1890 the Jews had formed a majority in Jerusalem for more than thirty years. In Palestine as a whole – between the Mediterranean Sea and the Jordan River – there were as many as fifty thousand Jews living among an Arab population of more than half a million. The number of Jews was growing by two to three thousand each year, and although nearly all of the new settlers were refugees from Tsarist Russia, Jews from Muslim lands continued to arrive and settle as well.[31] Throughout Palestine, these Jews created a Jewish community – the Yishuv – that

---

[29] Aviva Müller-Lancet, 'Bukhara,' Encyclopaedia Judaica, Volume 4, column 1476.
[30] Abraham Ben-Jacob, 'Babylonian Jews in Israel,' The Scribe, Issue 5, Volume 1, May-June 1972.
[31] Immigrants in this period included Jews from Afghanistan, who set up a printing press in Jerusalem. The press published Judaeo-Persian books that included commentaries on the Bible, the Psalms and religious texts.

was active in farming and commerce. Jewish traders, teachers, artisans and labourers contributed to the steady growth of Jerusalem, turning it from a medieval backwater into a modern metropolis.

Some Arabs welcomed the growing prosperity that the Jewish newcomers brought. Others, however, were alarmed at the prospect of losing their majority status. Their concerns led to the first Palestinian Arab protest, on 24 June 1891. That protest took the form of a telegram sent from Jerusalem to the Grand Vizier in Istanbul; it made two requests: that no more Russian Jews should be allowed to enter Palestine, and that they should be forbidden to acquire land there.[32] Although some leading Arabs appear to have refused to sign the protest, others did.

It was not Russian Jews, but rather Jews from a Muslim land, Persia, who were to be the first victims of the Arabs' new anti-immigration mood. Over a period of two months, at the end of 1891 and the beginning of 1892, some 150 Jews arrived in Jerusalem after fleeing from Muslim persecution in their native Persia. The Muslim authorities in Palestine insisted on deporting them; the Jews were rounded up and held captive in a storehouse. Their plight was described with indignation in a letter written by a Presbyterian minister, A. Ben Oliel, to the British Consul in Jerusalem. 'Those inside were trying hard to force the doors open,' Ben Oliel wrote, 'while the police and a set of Moslem roughs were piling big stones against the doors, and the police striking any who succeeded in putting heads or hands out.'[33] The deportations followed soon afterward.

The Persian Jews had much to fear. It was in the same year that Jews in the Persian city of Hamadan were given a written set of rules to ensure that they understood and obeyed the restrictions imposed on them under their *dhimmi* status. There were twenty-two rules in all. While some were part of the long-standing *dhimmi* regulations, others were newly invented. The rules read as follows:

---

[32] Report from the British Consul in Jerusalem: National Archives, Kew, Foreign Office papers, FO 195/1727.

[33] Letter of 11 February 1892, printed in Albert M. Hyamson, *The British Consulate in Jerusalem in relation to the Jews of Palestine, 1838-1914*, Part Two, pages 478-80.

1. The Jews are forbidden to leave their houses when it rains or snows.[34]
2. Jewish women are obliged to expose their faces in public.[35]
3. They must cover themselves with a two-coloured *izar*.[36]
4. The men must not wear fine clothes, the only material permitted them being a blue cotton fabric.
5. They are forbidden to wear matching shoes.
6. Every Jew is obliged to wear a piece of red cloth on his chest.
7. A Jew must never overtake a Muslim on a public street.
8. He is forbidden to talk loudly to a Muslim.
9. A Jewish creditor of a Muslim must claim his debt in a quavering and respectful manner.
10. If a Muslim insults a Jew, the latter must drop his head and remain silent.
11. A Jew who buys meat must wrap and conceal it carefully from Muslims.
12. It is forbidden to build fine edifices.
13. It is forbidden for him to have a house higher than that of his Muslim neighbour.
14. Neither must he use plaster for whitewashing.
15. The entrance of his house must be low.
16. The Jew cannot put on his coat; he must be satisfied to carry it rolled under his arm.
17. It is forbidden for him to cut his beard, or even to trim it slightly with scissors.
18. It is forbidden for Jews to leave the town or enjoy the fresh air of the countryside.
19. It is forbidden for Jewish doctors to ride on horseback.[37]
20. A Jew suspected of drinking spirits must not appear in the street; if he does he should be put to death immediately.
21. Weddings must be celebrated in the greatest secrecy.
22. Jews must not consume good fruit.[38]

---

[34] To prevent the 'impurity' of the Jews being transmitted to the Shiite Muslims.
[35] Like prostitutes.
[36] An *izar* is a large piece of material with which Muslim women are obliged to cover themselves when leaving their houses.
[37] This right was generally forbidden to all non-Muslims, except doctors.
[38] 'Conditions imposed upon the Jews of Hamadan, 1892,' quoted in David Littman, 'Jews under Muslim Rule: the Case of Persia,' *Wiener Library Bulletin,*

The severity of these rules was such that an Alliance school teacher, Saul Somekh, after visiting Hamadan, wrote that the Jews of the city 'have a choice of automatic acceptance, conversion to Islam, or their annihilation.' Somekh observed that 'some who live from hand to mouth have consented to these humiliating and cruel conditions through fear, without offering resistance.' Somekh reported to his superiors in Paris that thirty of the most prominent Jews of Hamadan 'were surprised in the telegraph office, where they had gone to telegraph their grievances to Teheran. They were compelled to embrace the Muslim faith to escape from certain death. But the majority is in hiding and does not dare to venture into the streets.'[39]

The Alliance brought the situation to the attention of the European Powers, who pressured the Shah of Persia, Nasser al-Din, into challenging the mullahs of Hamadan. Within a few months, the edict was rescinded.

Not all the Oriental Jewish communities were as well-known or as prosperous as those of the Ottoman Empire and Egypt. In 1902 the Jews of Europe and the United States were made aware, with the publication of an article by Herman Rosenthal and J.G. Lipman in the *Jewish Encyclopedia,* of a group of Jews who had lived among Muslims for a thousand years and more, and who were poor in the extreme. These were the 'Mountain Jews' of Daghestan. Known as 'Judaeo Tats,' or 'Tats,' they sang an ancient song about themselves:

> And we, the Tats
> We, Samson warriors,
> Bar Kokhba's heirs . . .
> we went into battles
> and bitterly, heroically
> struggled for our freedom.

Issue number 32, 1979, pages 7-8.
[39] Letter of 27 October 1892, quoted in David Littman, 'Jews under Muslim Rule: the Case of Persia,' *Wiener Library Bulletin*, Issue number 32, 1979, page 7.

In the eyes of the Muslims among whom they lived, the Jews of Daghestan were *dhimmis*, yet they were respected as fierce warriors who never hesitated to defend, by sword or rifle, their families, their religion, the land they worked and their personal dignity. In dress and customs they were similar to the other tribes who maintained a fierce independence throughout the Caucasus.

The Jews of Daghestan believed that they were the descendants of the Ten Lost Tribes. Their language, Tat, Tatti or Judaeo Tat, was a combination of Persian and Hebrew. They may well have been the descendants of Persian-Jewish soldiers who – in the Fifth and Sixth Centuries – were stationed in the lowlands of the Caucasus by the Sasanian kings. Their task was to protect Persia from attacks by the marauding Huns and other nomadic invaders from the east. These Jews were later confronted by the invading Turkic hordes, and were forced to migrate further north to the mountains of Daghestan.[40]

According to the Russian Imperial census of 1897, there were 12,000 Jews in Daghestan. Rosenthal and Lipman gave a graphic account of what was known about them: 'They wear the Circassian dress, and always go heavily armed, even sleeping without having removed their weapons. Their houses, like those of the other inhabitants, are ill built and dirty, and on the walls one finds, together with brightly shining arms, smoked fish or mutton hung up to dry. The main occupation of the Daghestan Jews is agriculture; but little of the land is owned by them, it being usually rented of their Mohammedan neighbours, to whom they pay their rent in produce, usually tobacco. They raise in addition vegetables and grapes; and some of them are engaged in the tanning of hides; while a few are small traders.'

Rosenthal and Lipman also gave a vivid description of the Mountain Jews' relations with the Daghestani Muslims: 'The Mohammedans often attack and rob the homes of the Jews, destroy their burial-places, and molest their graves. The Jews, being compelled to rent the land of them, are completely at their mercy, and are obliged to pay very heavy taxes, which at times are almost unbearable.' This was the *jizya* tax. 'In

---

[40] See Map 17, page 371.

some places the Jews are reduced to great poverty; they live in dug-outs, are constantly abused and exploited, possess scarcely any property, and have not even the means to pay for the religious instruction of their children. The Mohammedan landowners require every able-bodied man and woman to work for them a certain number of days in each year, either in the fields, or tending cattle, threshing, repairing their houses, etc.' In one village the Jewish inhabitants had to give their Muslim landlords 'at least one hundred days each in the course of a year, and are obliged besides to furnish a certain number of eggs and chickens, as well as charcoal, sand, wood, salt, and shoes. They must also make many cash payments for various purposes.'[41]

Ten years after Rosenthal and Lipman gave the western Jewish world a glimpse of the exotic eastern Mountain Jews, Dr. Aaron Benjaminy, a Russian Jew who had grown up among these Jews, published a detailed study about them in several issues of the Hebrew Labour Party weekly newspaper, *Achduth*. His information was based on his personal experiences forty years earlier. He wrote of the six thousand Mountain Jews in the main city, Derbent, and enumerated town-by-town and village-by-village a total population of 26,000 Mountain Jews. Dr. Benjaminy also described one entirely Jewish village, Agloby. There were many entirely Jewish hamlets.[42]

A central feature of the life of the Mountain Jews was their family units, which had no fewer than thirty-two to thirty-four closely knit members, and often as many as seventy, living together in one large and well-fenced courtyard. In a village three to five such units might constitute the entire village. When in 1949 the Soviet Union denounced such 'obsolete and antiquated customs' as counter to 'socialist reality.' Itzhak Ben-Zvi, one of Israel's founders and its second President, responded indignantly in his book *The Exiled and the Redeemed* and defended this Jewish household system. He wrote of how it consisted 'in essence of primary organizational cells of

---

[41] Herman Rosenthal and J.G. Lipman, 'Daghestan,' *Jewish Encyclopedia*, Volume 4, page 411.
[42] *Achduth*, Issues No. 38-48, 1912: quoted in Itzhak Ben-Zvi, *The Exiled and the Redeemed*, page 52.

the Jewish communities . . . which carried on their precarious existence for so long in a hostile environment of Moslem fanaticism.'
Ben-Zvi stressed that 'the large families were a pillar of strength,
both materially and spiritually, for the Jews in general,' because
'they alone defended them against the onrush of Moslem as well as
Christian hordes.'[43]

One Western observer remained optimistic when pondering the attitude of Muslims towards the Jews, focusing on just how much could
be accomplished if that attitude were to change for the good. In
1898 the United States Consul in Jerusalem, Edwin Sherman Wallace,
wrote in his account of life in the city: 'Once the Turk gets over his
animosity towards his elder brother, the Jew, there will be nothing in
the way of the increase of the new city' – the Jerusalem suburbs that
were rapidly modernising the city. 'The Jew wants to come,' the
Consul noted. 'He is anxious to buy a plot of ground and build him
a home in or near the city of his fathers. He simply asks to be let
alone, freed from oppression and permitted to enjoy his religion.
The land of the city is ready for him.'[44]

The land of Palestine may have been ready, but whether Muslims
would accept a growing Jewish presence there was something on
which the coming century would cast grave doubt.

---

[43] Itzhak Ben-Zvi, *The Exiled and the Redeemed,* page 57.
[44] Edwin Sherman Wallace, *Jerusalem the Holy,* page 122.

9

THE FIRST YEARS OF THE TWENTIETH CENTURY AND THE EMERGENCE OF ZIONISM

'Considerable stiffness of mental fibre in a difficult environment'

For some Jews living in Muslim lands, the Twentieth Century opened auspiciously. In 1900 a young Istanbul rabbi, Haim Nahum, was appointed as a teacher of French at the Imperial Ottoman School of Engineering and Artillery. From that moment he was in contact with 'Young Turk' officers of the Committee of Union and Progress, who within a decade were to be the driving force for reform in the Ottoman Empire. The Young Turk Revolution of 1908 not only restored the constitution that had been subverted for thirty years, but also granted Jews within the Sultan's empire equal rights and parliamentary representation. Within a year of the Young Turks coming to power, Haim Nahum was appointed Chief Rabbi of the Ottoman Empire. He was able to ensure that the Jewish subjects of the Sultan were treated with respect.[1]

At the beginning of the Twentieth Century the Ottomans entered a period of fragmentation that required a greater reliance on their military to preserve the empire. In 1903 the Jews of the Libyan city of Tripoli were unable to pay the annual tax levied on them in lieu of military service, and were already in arrears for the previous year. At that point, military service was not compulsory for Muslims; the tax was a discriminatory measure. The Ottoman authorities arrested twenty Jews in an attempt to secure payment. In response, Jewish shopkeepers and craftsmen closed their premises. The Italian Consul – the most important foreign diplomat in the city – then warned the Ottoman

---

[1] Stanford J. Shaw, *The Jews of the Ottoman Empire and the Turkish Republic*, page 220.

authorities that Italy would hold them responsible if trade with Italy suffered as a result of the strike. Only then did the authorities agree to reduce the tax, and to match it more closely with the income of those who would have to pay it.[2]

After 1908 the Young Turks introduced conscription in their effort to sustain their rule. The situation worsened as the Ottoman Empire was challenged in both Europe and North Africa. Ottoman forces were defeated in Tripolitania in 1911 by the Italians and in the Balkans in 1912-13 by a combination of Greeks and Bulgarians. The cost of the Tripolitanian and Balkan wars led the Ottoman authorities to impose higher taxes and a three-year compulsory military service. In Palestine, this military service could be avoided for the payment of £28 (the equivalent of £2,500 in the money values of 2010). Many Jews in Palestine paid the tax, and thus, in the words of Norman Bentwich, 'enriched the Turkish exchequer; but still a considerable number were taken off into the army.'[3]

Jews volunteered to serve in the Ottoman Army as proof of their patriotism. The Istanbul-based Zionist newspaper *Hamevasser* repeatedly praised the participation of eighty Ottoman Jewish soldiers in the suppression of the Druze rebellion in southern Syria in 1910–11. This was a campaign in which more than fifty Jewish soldiers were wounded.[4] Another effect of conscription was to prompt a new wave of Jewish migration. Thousands of young Jewish men left the Ottoman Empire to avoid being taken into the army. Many chose to cross the Atlantic and settle in the United States. In 1909 a Jewish community was founded in Portland, Oregon, made up of Jews from Rodosto on the Sea of Marmara.[5]

---

[2] It emerged that of the 3,825 registered taxpayers, only 867 were able to pay even part of it. Renzo De Felice, *Jews in an Arab Land: Libya, 1835-1970*, page 302, note 25.
[3] Norman Bentwich, *Palestine of the Jews*, page 178.
[4] Aryeh Shmuelevitz, 'Zionism, Jews and the Ottoman Empire as reflected in the weekly *Hamevasser*,' in Tudor Parfitt with Yulia Egorova, *Jews, Muslims and Mass Media: Mediating the 'Other,'* page 30.
[5] Information given to the author by the Portland, Oregon, Sephardic Community, Ahavat Achim (Brotherly Love), 9 November 2001.

The forces of nationalism and modernity were transforming Jewish life in Persia just as they were in Ottoman Turkey. In 1906, under a new constitution and following an increase in the powers of the parliament (the Majlis), Persian Jews obtained equal rights with all other citizens, Muslim and non-Muslim alike. Advancements in constitutional rights provided, however, a sharp contrast to the animosity that Jews continued to face from extremist Muslims, even in non-Arab societies like Persia.

On 21 May 1910, four years after equality of religious worship was established in Persia, Jews in the city of Shiraz were confronted with an outburst of anti-Jewish sentiment that was harsh even by the standards of the time. An eyewitness, Nissani Macchallah, a young Jewish teacher at the Alliance school, saw a *sayyid* – a Muslim dignitary – beating two elderly Jewish men with chains.[6] When he intervened and remonstrated with the *sayyid*, the Muslim stabbed Macchallah to death.

As a result of protests from the European Powers, the *sayyid* was sentenced to three months in prison, and an order was promulgated that called for respect for Jewish lives. To avenge the *sayyid's* imprisonment, his followers falsely accused the Jews of killing a young Muslim girl near the Jewish cemetery. They also arranged for copies of the Koran to be thrown into the sewage of the Jewish Quarter in an attempt to provoke an anti-Jewish riot. On 31 October 1910 the director of the Alliance School in Shiraz, Tunisian-born Elie Nataf, sent a full account of what followed to his head office in Paris. A 'frenzied mob' headed for the Jewish Quarter, he wrote. It arrived at the same time as the soldiers who had been sent by the military governor to protect the Jews. But, 'as if they were obeying orders,' the soldiers were 'the first to break into the Jewish houses, thereby giving the signal to plunder.' Nataf continued: 'The carnage and destruction which then occurred for six to seven hours is beyond the capacity of any pen to describe.'

---

[6] *Sayyid* is also an honorific title given to male descendants of Mohammed through his grandsons, Hasan ibn Ali and Husayn ibn Ali.

As soon as the Jews of Shiraz saw the danger they were in, they buried everything of value in underground hiding places. They even dropped objects that could survive immersion in water into the pools in the courtyards. But as Nataf reported, all their efforts were in vain: 'The most concealed places were totally emptied. The assailants dived into the ponds to retrieve the objects there.' Not one of the 260 houses in the Jewish Quarter was spared. As for the looters: 'Soldiery, louts, *sayyids*, even women and children, driven and aroused less by religious fanaticism than by a frenetic need to plunder and appropriate the Jews' possessions, engaged in a wild rush for the spoils.' At one point during the looting, about a hundred men from a rural tribe who were in Shiraz to sell livestock 'joined the first assailants, thereby completing the work of destruction.'

The looting was not the end of that tragic day for the Jews of Shiraz: 'The thieves formed a chain in the street. They passed along the line carpets, bundles of goods, merchandise, gum, tragacanth,[7] opium, dried fruits, skins; demijohns full of wine, brandy; utensils, caskets containing valuable objects, anything, in a word, that was saleable. That which didn't have a commercial value or which, on account of its weight or size, could not be carried off was, in a fury of vandalism, destroyed or broken. The doors and windows of the houses were torn off their hinges and carried away, or smashed to pieces.' The rooms and cellars of the houses were 'literally ploughed up to see whether the substratum didn't conceal some wealth.'

The mob – 'these fanatics' – then turned against the Jews themselves. Most had managed to find refuge at the British Consulate or in the houses 'of Muslim friends' – those Muslims who, as in every episode of anti-Jewish violence, in all the countries where Jews were threatened, took their own risk to hide Jews and shelter them. But the Jews who had stayed in the Jewish Quarter to defend their houses were savagely attacked; twelve were killed and fifteen seriously injured. An 'unlucky' Jewish woman wearing gold rings in her ears was ordered

---

[7] Tragacanth (astragalus gummifer), also known as Goat's Thorn and Shiraz Gum, is used as a herbal remedy for cough and diarrhoea, and, in paste form, to treat burns. It is also used in leatherworking and as a stiffener in textiles.

by a soldier to surrender them. As Nataf described the incident, 'she made haste to comply and had taken off one of the rings when the impatient madman found it more expeditious to tear off the earlobe together with the ring.'

The riot was a devastating blow to the Jewish community. Five or six thousand Jews had lost everything except – in the words of Elie Nataf – 'the few tatters which they were wearing at the moment their quarter was invaded.' The local authorities seemed 'to have done only one thing – encourage the soldiers in conjunction with the populace to attack and plunder the Jewish quarter.'[8] This occurred in the same decade as the pogroms in the Christian empire of the Russian Tsars – pogroms that were similar in so many of their details, and that were sending millions of Jews to seek refuge in the United States, Canada and Western Europe.

Beyond Persia and Turkey, Jews living in Arab lands continued to suffer the kinds of harassment that had forced generations of their forebears to travel far and wide in search of refuge. In Kurdistan, where the Alliance was making progress in opening Jewish schools, there was still cause for discouragement.[9] A Jewish school was opened in Kirkuk in 1912, but during the same year, twelve Kurdish Jews were murdered. The news of the murders led many Jews to sell their fields and houses – for which they were forced to accept an inevitably low price – and to make their way westward to Palestine.

An important exception among Arab-ruled countries was Mesopotamia, where the Jewish community prospered due to the tolerance of Ottoman rule. In 1904 a leading rabbi and scholar in Baghdad, Ezra Reuben Dangoor, established one of the first Hebrew and Arabic printing presses in the city.[10] Another Baghdadi Jew, Sasson Heskel, was appointed Deputy for Baghdad in the Ottoman Parliament

---

[8] Report of 31 October 1910: quoted in full in Bat Ye'or, *Islam and Dhimmitude*, pages 403-5.

[9] The first Alliance school in Kurdistan was opened in Mosul in 1900. It was soon followed by a second school in the same city, opened in 1906.

[10] Rabbi Dangoor later became the Chief Rabbi of Baghdad after the First World War.

in 1908 – a post he held for ten years. He was sent to London in 1909 as part of a Turkish delegation, and later served in the Ottoman administration as Under-Secretary of State for Trade and Agriculture.[11] In the same period, the Jewish philanthropist Meir Eliahou built a large and modern hospital for the Jews of Baghdad, which the Ottoman Governor of the city, Nazim Pasha, formally opened in the presence of senior members of the government in 1910.[12]

An American traveller in Yemen witnessed the uncertainty that Jewish communities faced even under tolerant rule. In 1915, C. Wyman Bury acknowledged that Ottoman rule – which had resumed after the reconquest of Yemen in 1872 – 'has secured them tolerance.' But although Jews were recognised as 'an important economic factor' in Yemen's development, theirs was nonetheless 'rather a harried existence.' Because 'the Islamic code is rigidly enforced,' Bury feared that the Jews' position 'may yet be one of jeopardy.' He noted that the Jews were not allowed to have schools or synagogues, and so assembled at private houses for worship. In these circumstances, Bury had been impressed to see a Jewish cobbler teaching his children to read the Hebrew Scriptures in his shop, which he felt denoted a 'considerable stiffness of mental fibre in a difficult environment.'[13]

The situation for Jews was even more precarious in North Africa, where incidents of violence persisted into the Twentieth Century. The Sultan of Morocco had tried to solve this problem in 1892. He sent a strong letter to the Caid of Marrakech, quoting Mohammed's declaration, 'He who commits an injustice against a Jew shall be my enemy on the Day of Judgement,' and urging the Caid 'to commit this fault no longer.'[14] But from 1900 onward, Arab rebels began fighting the growing power of France, and they attacked not only French troops but Jews as well.[15] In 1903, forty Jews were killed in Taza. Four years

[11] Meir Basri, 'Prominent Iraqi Jews of recent times,' *The Scribe*, Issue 76, Spring 2003.
[12] Gourji C. Bekhor, *Fascinating Life and Sensational Death: The Conditions in Iraq Before and After the Six-Day War*, page 20.
[13] C. Wyman Bury, *Arabia Infelix, or the Turks in Yamen*, pages 30-1.
[14] Letter of 27 December 1892, quoted in David Littman, 'Jews under Muslim Rule in the late Nineteenth Century,' *Wiener Library Bulletin*, Issue number 32, 1979, page 75.
[15] For the Jewish communities in Morocco before 1948, see Map 9, page 364.

later, in 1907, at least fifty Jews were killed in Settat. That same year, in Casablanca – where 6,000 Jews formed a quarter of the population – thirty Jews were killed and two hundred Jewish women abducted, raped and then ransomed back to the Jewish community.[16]

The humiliations of *dhimmi* status were also continuing. In 1911 the head of the Jewish boys' school in Fez, Amram Elmaleh, wrote to the president of the Alliance in Paris about the degrading practice of the Chief Rabbi of Fez, Vidal Sarfaty, having to take off his shoes when entering the Sultan's palace. 'It is my opinion,' Elmaleh explained, 'that it would be impossible to obtain an order from the Sultan to allow Jews to enter the Palace with their shoes on. It is a concession which his pride would not permit, and quite contrary to the Muslim conception of the relative positions of the Jews and themselves.' Yet Elmaleh looked hopefully towards the future: 'With the passing of time and the penetration of modern ideas into the Muslim world . . . this mark of servitude imposed upon the Jews will eventually disappear.'[17]

Jewish life in Morocco suffered further setbacks with the establishment of French colonial rule in 1912. Only two weeks after the French flag was flown above Fez, the local Muslims sought to wreak vengeance against their new rulers, but, unable to challenge them militarily, they looked for a scapegoat and turned against the Jews. Rampaging through the Jewish Quarter, an Arab mob looted and burned for three days and nights. More than sixty Jews were killed – men, women and children.[18] Fifty Jews were wounded and ten thousand left homeless. On the first evening, two thousand Jews found shelter and safety in one of the Sultan's courtyards.[19] Had the French

---

[16] For this tragic period for Moroccan Jewry, recorded in Alliance Israélite Universelle documents, see David Littman, 'Jews under Muslim Rule – II: Morocco 1903-1912,' *Wiener Library Bulletin*, Issue number 29 (1976), pages 3-19.

[17] Letter of 30 January 1911, quoted in David Littman, 'Jews under Muslim Rule in the late Nineteenth Century,' *Wiener Library Bulletin*, Issue number 32, 1979, pages 75-6.

[18] David Corcos, 'Fez,' *Encyclopaedia Judaica*, Volume 6, columns 1255-8.

[19] David Littman, 'Mission to Morocco (1863-1864),' in Sonia and V.D. Lipman (editors), *The Century of Moses Montefiore*.

authorities not confiscated all weapons in the Jewish Quarter, under the pretext of halting the smuggling of arms, the Jews would have at least been able to defend themselves.

More Jews were killed in the pogrom in Fez than in the Kishinev pogrom in Tsarist Russia nine years earlier. Yet the Kishinev pogrom, in which forty-nine Jews were murdered, had led to widespread protest throughout the Christian world by Jews and non-Jews alike. The Fez pogrom was reported far less widely – and then ignored.

The first Zionist Congress was held in Basel in 1897 under the leadership of Theodor Herzl. Inspired by more than forty years of Jewish national aspirations in both emancipated and persecuted Jewish societies, the Congress inaugurated a movement for the establishment of a Jewish National Home, under Jewish self-rule. That movement became known as Zionism, a return to Zion, to Jerusalem; it inspired Jews all over the world by its promise of security, safety, relief, communal autonomy and nationhood.

The Jewish nation was to be established in the ancient Jewish homeland of Palestine, then under Ottoman rule, with Jerusalem as its focal point. This goal reflected an age-old hope, reinforced every year at the conclusion of the Passover meal, when Jews recalled the Exodus from Egypt in ancient times, and recited 'Next Year in Jerusalem.' Zionism aimed to turn that spiritual longing into a political reality, and with it to restore in Palestine a Jewish territorial identity, agricultural development and civic society.

The Zionist programme involved the use of diplomacy to persuade the Ottoman Turks to set aside land for the creation of the Jewish National Home. It also involved a search for European support – chiefly British, French, German and Italian – for a Jewish homeland in Palestine. Sustained immigration of Jews to Palestine had begun in the early 1880s. By 1897 at least one thousand Jews a year were making their way to Ottoman Palestine, mostly from Tsarist Russia and Romania. They went to till the soil and build Jewish national institutions, including armed self-defence units to ward off the spasmodic attacks by marauding Bedouin and Arab villagers.

Although Zionism at its foundation was predominantly an Ashkenazi movement – appealing principally to the persecuted Jews of Russia, and the more fortunate Jews of Europe and North America – it had from its outset a Sephardi and Oriental Jewish aspect. Two Algerian Jews were at the first Zionist Congress in Basel in 1897: M.E. Attali, who represented the Algerian city of Constantine, and Dr. Eugene Valensin, who represented the French city of Montpellier, where many North African Jews had settled. From Tunis a group calling itself 'Zionist Youth' sent greetings.

Two weeks after the end of the Basel Congress, a Jewish youth organisation in Constantine sent Herzl a letter, informing him that his determination 'to realize the Zionist ideal' had 'aroused an enormous response in Constantine.'[20] The number of declared Zionists in Algeria was small, fewer than four hundred by 1919, but the enthusiasm of the youth was real.

A second Zionist Congress was held in 1898, also in Basel. Messages of greeting were sent from 'Tunisian Zionists' and from 'the Zionist Group' in the Moroccan town of Mogador. Also in 1898, a Zionist association was established in the Egyptian port city of Alexandria. Two years later, two European Zionist emissaries wrote from Cairo to the Central Zionist Office in Vienna: 'A vague idea of our movement flutters among the native Jews, not only in Cairo, but in all of Egypt.'[21] By 1904, there were Zionist associations in Port Said, Suez, Tanta and Mansura. Several Egyptian Zionist newspapers were also being published in Egypt, some in French, others in Judaeo-Arabic and Arabic. Several hundred Jews throughout Egypt paid their *shekel* for membership in the World Zionist Organization.[22]

---

[20] Michel Abitbol, 'Zionist Activity in the Maghreb,' *The Jerusalem Quarterly*, Issue 21, Autumn 1981.

[21] Report of 13 June 1900, quoted in Jacob M. Landau, *Jews in Nineteenth-Century Egypt*, pages 275-7.

[22] The *shekel* was an ancient Israelite unit of weight and currency; it became the term for a small coin and is now the basic monetary unit of the State of Israel. The *shekel* was also the name of the certificate of membership in the World Zionist Organization, given to every Jew who paid the annual membership dues.

In Morocco, a predominantly Muslim country, Zionist associations were established in 1900 in Mogador and Tetuan. The association in Tetuan was helped by the efforts of a Russian-born physician, Dr. J. Berliawsky, under whose guidance a Hebrew-language library was also established. In Mogador, Zionist activity was stimulated by the spiritual head of the Jewish community, Rabbi Jacob Ifargan, and by a former resident, Moses Logasy, who had emigrated to England some years earlier. Returning to Mogador, Logasy sold shares in one of the founding institutions of the First Zionist Congress, the Jewish Colonial Trust, for the purchase of land in Palestine for Jewish farming villages. As a result of such fundraising efforts, the Mogador Zionists were entitled to send two representatives to the Fifth Zionist Congress, held in Basel in 1901.

Zionist associations soon proliferated in towns across Morocco. In 1903, in the coastal town of Safi, the leaders of a local Zionist association founded that year wrote to Herzl, addressing him as 'President of God!' They asked him, 'What exactly is Zionism? What is the task that we must perform in order to achieve the desired end?' They went on to ask for a copy, in Hebrew, of Herzl's book *The Jewish State* 'together with any other books WRITTEN IN HEBREW that shed light on Zionism. We are prepared to pay the price we are charged for them.'[23] As the historian Norman Stillman has commented regarding the Jews of Morocco and Tunisia: 'Word of the Zionist movement's birth in Europe fuelled the cherished hopes for national redemption that were an integral part of their religious conviction.'[24]

The Jews of Fez had an added reason to find inspiration in the Zionist movement. Theirs was a poor community, located in Morocco's main centre of Islamic zeal. Jews living in these conditions found much to hope for in the messianic aspect of Zionism – the proposed return of Jews to their ancient land, where they would have

---

[23] Letter of 17 March 1903: quoted in Norman A. Stillman, *Jews of Arab Lands in Modern Times*, pages 312-3.
[24] Norman A. Stillman, *Jews of Arab Lands in Modern Times*, page 72.

sovereignty. In 1908 a Hibbat Zion ('Lovers of Zion') society was founded in Fez; it later bought shares in the Jewish Colonial Trust and extended its activities to the nearby towns of Meknès and Sefrou.

Unfortunately, when the society asked if it could be protected by one of the European consuls in Fez, the request was turned down by Herzl's successor, David Wolffsohn – Herzl had died in 1904.[25] Ashkenazi Jews in Europe did not always understand the extent to which 'Oriental' Jews had urgent needs. For them, the Jews of the Muslim world remained an unknown element: remote, backward, provincial, even strange – not an integral part of the intellectual struggles and national aspirations of western Jews. In 1908, in Libya, the Jews of Benghazi appealed to the Jewish Territorial Association in London for help and protection after Arabs set fire to twenty Jewish shops. 'We can find no remedy to these sufferings,' the Benghazi Jews wrote, 'but to put ourselves in God's hands and yours, dear brothers.' Their letter led to no positive intervention.[26]

Even without the impetus of Zionism, Jews from North Africa had long been drawn to settle in Palestine. Individual families came not only to the four holy cities of Judaism – Jerusalem, Safed, Tiberias and Hebron – but also to Acre and Haifa, two busy ports and trading centres. In 1909, Jews from North Africa were among the founders of the first all-Jewish city, Tel Aviv. In Jerusalem there were an estimated 2,000 Jews from North Africa on the eve of the First World War, amidst a total Jewish population of 45,000. In Haifa, Jews from North Africa and their descendants made up a majority of the city's Jewish population.

In August 1911, the Tenth Zionist Congress welcomed to Basel a delegation of Jews from North Africa. At that time, Zionism had gained footholds in North Africa beyond its initial bases of support in Tunis and Morocco. In 1912 a Zionist society was founded in the Libyan city of Tripoli, drawing inspiration from a young photographer, Elia Nhaisi.

---

[25] Norman A. Stillman, *Jews of Arab Lands in Modern Times*, page 74-5.
[26] Renzo De Felice, *Jews in an Arab Land: Libya, 1835-1970*, page 25.

Although it did not last more than a year, the society was revived by
Nhaisi five years later, when it appealed for Italian Jews to send a chief
rabbi to Tripoli who was 'both a Zionist and scrupulously observant in
Jewish life.'[27]

Zionism was gradually developing support among Jewish communities in the Arab world. In Afghanistan, the leader of the local
Jewish community, Mula Agajan Cohen, spent six months in
Palestine in 1908. Upon his return – and until his murder in 1913 –
he encouraged his fellow Jews to immigrate there.[28] In Ottoman
Mesopotamia, too, Zionism entered its embryonic stages before
the First World War. A small Zionist society was organised in Basra
in 1913, and although it had only ten members, one of its founders
explained in a letter to the Zionist secretariat in Berlin that 'many
are anxious to enter into it but are afraid of the Turkish authorities.'[29]
A year later, three Jews in Baghdad sent money to the Zionist
Organization of Berlin asking for pamphlets and information.

News of Zionist activity also spread among the Jews of Yemen. In
1912, Samuel Varshavsky, a Russian-born Jew and an activist in the
Zionist Labour movement in Palestine, travelled to Yemen as an
emissary of the Palestine Office and of Palestine's chief Ashkenazi
rabbi.[30] He spent two years giving the Yemeni Jews his first-hand
account of Zionist work in the agricultural rehabilitation of
Palestine.[31] Several thousand Yemeni Jews, inspired by what they

---

[27] Renzo De Felice, *Jews in an Arab Land: Libya, 1835-1970*, pages 45 and 88.
[28] Mula Agajan Cohen was appointed a royal adviser by the King of Afghanistan,
Habibullah Khan, but in 1913 he was murdered by Muslims jealous of his power.
Reuben Kashani, 'The Jews of Afghanistan,' *Ariel: The Israel Review of Arts and
Letters*, No. 113, page 53.
[29] Letter of 13 September 1913, quoted in Norman A. Stillman, *Jews of Arab Lands
in Modern Times*, page 85.
[30] Varshavsky later took the surname Yavnieli.
[31] On reaching southern Yemen, Varshavsky was captured and robbed by
Bedouin tribesmen. He was then ransomed by the Jews of Habban. 'The Jews in
these parts are held in high esteem by everyone in Yemen and Aden,' Varshavsky
later wrote. 'They are said to be courageous, always with their weapons and wild
long hair, and the names of their towns are mentioned by the Jews of Yemen with
great admiration.' The Jews of Habban practised the martial arts known in
Hebrew as 'Abir.' Today, a descendant of Yemeni Jews, Yehoshua Sofer, teaches

learned, made their way to Palestine on the eve of the First World War and immediately after it.[32] At that time, some 270 Yemeni Jews were already working in the Jewish township of Rehovot. The *New York Times* reported in 1918 that the work of these Jews 'has proved a great success.' The same report also noted that many of the Jewish communities in Palestine included 'educated Jews and Jewesses' from Damascus and Beirut.[33]

There were some Jews who did not support the burgeoning Zionist movement, preferring instead local means of improving Jewish life. In Damascus, in 1910, the opening of a Hebrew National School and kindergarten was opposed by the director of the city's Alliance school. Like others in the Alliance, he viewed Zionist education as a threat to settled Jewish life and aspirations. Yet the new school enrolled five hundred pupils within a year, while the nearness of Syria to the Jewish community in Palestine spurred wider support for the idea of a Jewish National Home.

In all, ten to twenty thousand Jews from Muslim lands went to live in Palestine in the Nineteenth and early Twentieth Centuries. Norman Stillman has observed that, while these Jews were few in numbers compared with those who remained under Muslim rule, they 'represented sentiments and impulses that were more widespread among their communities of origin than their own actual numbers might seem to suggest.'[34]

From the outset, Muslims regarded Zionism with suspicion. On 29 April 1898 the Ottoman Ambassador in Washington, Ali Ferruh Bey, wrote to Istanbul in order to alert the Sultan that the aim of the

---

his family tradition of Abir, for which there are two schools, one in Jerusalem and the other in Tel Aviv. Sofer is best known in the world of martial arts as a master of Kuk Sool Won, a Korean martial art. Ken Blady, *The Jews of Habban, South Yemen (Jewish Communities in Exotic Places)*, page 32.

[32] These Yemeni Jews joined farming communities and founded their own farming villages. Itzhak Ben-Zvi, *The Exiled and the Redeemed*, page 31.

[33] 'Zionism Already Begun in Palestine,' *New York Times*, 9 June 1918.

[34] Norman A. Stillman, *Jews of Arab Lands in Modern Times*, pages 66-7 and page 66, note 4.

Zionists was 'to establish an independent government in Palestine.'[35]
In his letter, he urged Sultan Abdul Hamid to 'take certain measures
to rectify the error committed by his forefathers in allowing non-
Muslim communities to settle in Palestine.'[36] The Sultan took heed;
measures were instituted to restrict the sale of land in Palestine to
foreign Jews, and to oblige all Jewish visitors to leave cash deposits to
ensure that they would leave the country after their visit.

The steady influx of Jews to Palestine continued. As it did, fear
and anger mounted among the Arab majority. In 1902, Albert Antébi,
the Jewish Colonization Association representative in Jerusalem,
reported to the association that 'rancour' against the Jews was spread-
ing in the Ottoman administration, in the law courts and among
government officials. Antébi went on to state that 'the ill-will of the
local population coincides with the creation of Zionism.'[37] It was an
ill-will, however, that predated Zionism by many centuries. The
emergence of Zionism provided it with an excuse and a spur, a label
on which to attach age-old animosities.

From the Ottoman authorities in Istanbul came instructions in
1907 to impose strict limits on the sale of land to Jews in Palestine.
That year, Asaf Bey, the Kaymakam (local governor) of Jaffa, refused
to allow any further building in the Jewish farming communities on
the outskirts of the city. In addition, as one Zionist emissary wrote to
Zionist headquarters in Berlin, he imposed 'incredibly heavy' taxes
on the local Jews.[38] There were already six thousand Jews in Jaffa, living among a Muslim population of 38,000. On 16 March 1908, bitterness against these Jews led to a clash between Jews, Ottoman

---

[35] Ali Ferruh Bey had earlier served in Paris, London and St. Petersburg. His
father, with whom he had grown up, had been governor of the Sanjak of
Jerusalem. This was the Ottoman administrative district centred in Jerusalem that
included the coastal region from north of Jaffa to the Egyptian border at Rafah. Its
eastern edge was the western shore of the Dead Sea.
[36] Jacob Landau and Mim Kemal Oke, 'Ottoman Perspectives on American Interests
in the Holy Land': Moshe Davis (editor), *With Eyes Towards Zion*, page 265.
[37] Letter of 28 February 1902: quoted in Neville J. Mandel, *The Arabs and Zionism
before World War I*, page 42.
[38] Letter of 27 December 1907: quoted in Neville J. Mandel, *The Arabs and Zionism
before World War I*, page 26.

soldiers and local Arabs in which thirteen Jews were injured, some of them severely.[39]

In Istanbul, following the Young Turk Revolution of 1908, Turkish suspicions grew even further regarding the full extent of Zionist ambitions. One senior Muslim Ottoman politician, Gümülcine Ismail Bey, publicly expressed his fears that a Jewish State would be established not only in Palestine but also in Mesopotamia. Other Turkish politicians were suspicious that Zionism – the headquarters of which were then in Berlin – was really a plot to establish German power in the Ottoman Middle East.[40]

Within Palestine, Arab anti-Zionist sentiment was stimulated in 1911 by a new Arab newspaper, *Falastin* ('Palestine'), published in Jaffa. This publication committed itself to reporting what it saw as the continuing Zionist threat to Arab property and aspirations. In one of its first issues that May, the newspaper published an open letter denouncing Zionism as 'the source of the deceitfulness that we experience like a flood and which is more frightening than walking alone in dead of night. Not only this: it is also an omen of our future exile from our homeland and departure from our homes and property.'[41] Two years later, on 8 November 1913, the newspaper printed a poem by Sheikh Suleiman al-Taji, a founder of the Jaffa-based Ottoman Patriotic Party. The poem was entitled 'The Zionist Danger.' The first three of its six stanzas read:

> Jews, sons of clinking gold, stop your deceit;
> We shall not be cheated into bartering away our country!
> Shall we hand it over, meekly,
> while we still have some spirit left?
> Shall we cripple ourselves?

---

[39] In 1908, 2,097 Russian Jews reached Palestine. That same year, 103,387 reached the United States. In the ten years from 1905 to 1914, when 24,068 Russian Jews reached Palestine, 1,089,237 reached the United States. These Jews were seeking an escape from poverty and pogroms.

[40] Stanford J. Shaw, *The Jews of the Ottoman Empire and the Turkish Republic*, page 225.

[41] Quoted in Neville J. Mandel, *The Arabs and Zionism before World War I*, page 122.

The Jews, the weakest of all peoples and the least of them,
Are haggling us for our land;
how can we slumber on?
We know what they want
– and they have the money, all of it.

Master, rulers, what is wrong with you?
What ails you?
It is time to be awake, to be aware!
Away with this heedlessness
– there is no more time for patience![42]

The hostility of the Palestinian Arabs towards Zionism was seen most clearly – and effectively – in the anti-Zionist platform of the two Jerusalem Arabs elected to the Ottoman Parliament in April 1914. One of the two, Sayyid al-Husseini, warned: 'If we continue in our ways and they in theirs, then all our lands will pass into their possession.'[43] The other successful candidate, Raghib al-Nashashibi, promised voters: 'If I am elected as a representative I shall devote all my strength, day and night, to doing away with the damage and threat of Zionism and the need to prevent its implementation in Palestine.'[44]

Arab nationalism was on the rise. The purchase of land by Jewish immigrants in Palestine stirred anger among those who wanted to keep Palestine as part of a future Arab nation – as part of what was then called Greater Syria – independent from Ottoman Turkish rule. That anger was directed not only towards Jews, but also towards anyone who was willing to sell their land to Jews: both

---

[42] Quoted in Neville J. Mandel, *The Arabs and Zionism before World War I*, pages 175-6.
[43] Speech of 30 March 1914, quoted in Neville J. Mandel, *The Arabs and Zionism before World War I*, page 183.
[44] Quoted in Y. Porath, *The Emergence of the Palestinian-Arab National Movement, 1918-1929*, page 27.

Muslim and Christian Arabs, as well as absentee Arab landlords in Beirut. This conflict within Arab society as to whether to support or oppose Jewish national aspirations would continue in Palestine and far beyond throughout the next century.

10

JEWISH AND ARAB NATIONALISM: THE FIRST WORLD WAR AND AFTER

'Latent, deep-seated hatred'

In August 1914 war broke out among six Christian European empires – Britain, France, Russia and Italy on the one side, Germany and Austria-Hungary on the other. Two smaller Christian nations, Serbia and Belgium, were its first victims. Throughout August and September 1914, Germany pressed a Muslim country, the Ottoman Empire, to enter the war on its side.

Ottoman Turkey entered the conflict as an ally of Germany in October 1914. The Ottoman authorities at once took several thousand Jews and Christians from throughout Palestine to work as forced labourers for the Turkish war effort. These captives built roads, constructed railways and worked on military fortifications in Syria. Leading Jews were exiled from Palestine to Istanbul and Damascus, while more than ten thousand Jews fled by ship to Alexandria in the hope of finding security in British-ruled Egypt. They brought with them their Zionist ideals, and soon stimulated the development of a federation of Egyptian Zionist organisations.

Inside Palestine, the Jews were subjected to the autocratic rule, hostility and whim of Djemal Pasha, the Generalissimo of the Ottoman 'Army of Syria.' Djemal issued a proclamation against all Zionist enterprises, threatening severe punishment for anyone who showed public support for the Jewish national cause, or who flew the Jewish flag – the Star of David. Djemal then disarmed the Jewish self-defence force, hitherto sanctioned by the Ottomans, and with it the only protection the Jewish villages possessed against all-too-frequent attacks by Arab marauders. Finally, Djemal closed down the Anglo-Palestine Bank, the main source of funding for the Jews in Palestine.

The Jews suffered further hardship when the Turkish Army made its way southward through Palestine to the Sinai front. In the words of a British Zionist, Norman Bentwich, the army 'scoured the country-side for provisions and made pitiless requisitions. It cut down the trees and laid bare the forest of the colony of Chederah.'[1] The village of Chederah had been founded in 1890 by young Zionists from Vilna, Kovno and Riga, on land reclaimed from malarial swamps. More than half of its founders had died of malaria in the intervening twenty-five years. In 1916 the village's eucalyptus groves, needed to drain the swamps, were still young, and were essential for the survival of the village.[2]

The First World War also brought troubles for the Jews in the Ottoman province of Mesopotamia. As British troops landed in the south in November 1915, occupying Basra, the Ottoman Governor of Mesopotamia, Nur a-Din Pasha, arrested a number of Jewish and Christian leaders in Baghdad and expelled them to the northern city of Mosul. Those who remained in Baghdad did not fare well; when the value of Turkish securities fell in the money market, it was Jews who were accused, falsely, of profiteering and causing a financial crisis.

As British troops drew near to Baghdad in the first two weeks of March 1917, many more Jews were arrested by the Turks. They were accused of secretly supporting a British victory, tortured and killed. Meanwhile, eighteen thousand Jews were serving in the Ottoman Army, marching under the banner of the Crescent and reaching

---

[1] Norman Bentwich, *Palestine of the Jews*, pages 182-6. Bentwich later immigrated to Palestine, becoming Attorney General in the British Mandate administration.
[2] By 1961, Chederah (Hadera) was an Israeli town of twenty-six thousand people, more than six thousand of whom were Jews from Muslim lands who arrived after 1948.

officer rank even when they had never studied at a military academy. These soldiers fought – and died – on the battlefield for Turkey. A Jewish medical officer, Menahem Abravanel, fought at the Dardanelles, was decorated and survived the war.[3] But as many as a thousand Jewish Ottoman soldiers were killed in action.[4]

On 11 March 1917, British troops entered Baghdad. They were welcomed by the Jews as liberators, and for several years afterward their arrival was commemorated by the Jews of Baghdad as 'a day of miracle.'[5] After the British conquest of Amara, it was a Jewish merchant, Ezra Hardoon, who persuaded the Muslim tribes of Luristan, on the Mesopotamian-Persian border, to support the British. The Turks condemned Hardoon to death, but commuted this to a long prison sentence. After the war, the British gave him an honourary decoration in recognition of his help. He refused to accept any financial reward.[6]

On 2 November 1917, while the First World War was still being fought, and as British forces approached Jerusalem, the British Government issued its Balfour Declaration. This was a letter from the Foreign Secretary, A.J. Balfour, to the head of the British Zionist Federation, Lord Rothschild, promising British support for a Jewish National Home in Palestine in return for help in the Allied war effort. That promise would come into effect once the Ottoman Turks were defeated. The Zionists did not have long to wait.

For the Jews, the defeat of the Palestine part of the Ottoman Empire came in two stages. The first was the liberation of Tel Aviv and Jerusalem from Turkish rule in October-November 1917, by troops under the command of a British General, Sir Edmund Allenby. The second was the liberation a year later by Allenby's forces

---

[3] Another medical officer in the Ottoman Army, Eliahu Eliashar – in 1917 a recent graduate from the University of Beirut – served as a parliamentary representative of the Sephardi Jews in Israel's first Knesset (February 1949 to July 1951).
[4] Information provided by the Turkish historian Nayim Güleryüz, letter to the author, 18 January 2009.
[5] Peter Wien, *Iraqi Arab Nationalism*, page 49.
[6] Nir Shohet, *The Story of an Exile: A Short History of the Jews of Iraq*, pages 24-6.

of Tiberias, Safed and the many Jewish farming villages of the Jezreel Valley and Galilee.

The terms of Britain's Mandate for Palestine, drawn up by the British Colonial Secretary Winston Churchill, stated that the Jews were in Palestine 'of right and not on sufferance.'[7] Encouraged by this pledge, Jews accelerated their exodus from all over the Arab and Muslim world, as they did from Ashkenazi Europe and the Americas. Among the first to reach Palestine after the First World War were Jews from Muslim Kurdistan. In the seven years between 1920 and 1926, almost 2,000 Kurdish Jews emigrated to Palestine, an average of almost 300 a year. In 1935, 2,500 Kurdish Jews emigrated.[8]

Also reaching Palestine were several hundred impoverished Yemeni Jewish orphans who had been repeatedly subjected to forcible conversion. In 1923 forty-two Jewish orphans were forced to convert in the Yemeni port city of Hodeida. 'A few of them managed to escape into the wilderness,' stated a letter to Jerusalem from the Jewish community in Hodeida. But there 'they weep and scream because of their dreadful suffering.' Muslims in Yemen blackmailed Jewish neighbours who were known to be sheltering Jewish orphans by threatening to denounce them.[9]

For more than two years, the Arab armies had been led in their fight against Ottoman rule by Emir Feisal, the son of Emir Hussein, Grand Sharif of Mecca and leader of the Arabs of Hejaz. As the war was ending, Feisal saw Zionism as beneficial to the region. On 4 June 1918, near the Arab port of Akaba on the Red Sea, he signed an agreement with the Zionist leader Dr. Chaim Weizmann in which Feisal welcomed the Jews to their National Home in Palestine.[10]

---

[7] *Statement of British Policy on Palestine*, Command Paper 1700 of 1922, also known as the Churchill White Paper.

[8] Abraham Ben-Jacob, 'Kurdistan.' *Encyclopaedia Judaica*, Volume 10, column 1299. Ben-Jacob gives the figure for 1920 to 1926 as 1,900.

[9] Tudor Parfitt, *The Road to Redemption: The Jews of the Yemen, 1900-1950*, page 67.

[10] In 1921 the British excluded Transjordan from the Jewish National Home, giving it to Feisal's brother, Emir Abdullah.

Feisal was expecting to be given the throne of Syria and hoped to win Zionist support for Arab national ambitions. On 1 March 1919 he wrote to a leading American Zionist, Felix Frankfurter, stating: 'We Arabs, especially the educated among us, look with the deepest sympathy on the Zionist movement.' His letter continued: 'We will wish the Jews a most hearty welcome home.' Feisal then explained his understanding of Zionism: 'I hope the Arabs may soon be in a position to make the Jews some return for their kindness. We are working together for a reformed and revived Near East, and our two movements complete one another. The Jewish movement is national and not imperialist: our movement is national and not imperialist, and there is room in Syria for both. Indeed I think that neither can be a real success without the other.'

Feisal ended his letter by stating: 'I look forward, and the people with me look forward to a future in which we will help you and you will help us, so that the countries in which we are mutually interested may once again take their place in the comity of the civilized peoples of the world.'[11] In January 1921 he informed the British Government that, in return for the throne of Syria, with its capital in Damascus, he 'agreed to abandon all claims of his father to Palestine.'[12]

Among leaders in the Muslim world, Feisal was a striking exception. Palestinian nationalism was on the rise, and with it there came an upsurge in anti-Zionism that was spearheaded by Palestinian Arab leaders who saw Jewish land purchases in Palestine – which were encouraged at that time by the British Mandate authorities – as a direct threat to their hopes of statehood. The nationalism of the wartime Arab Revolt against Ottoman rule had stimulated the prospect of Arab sovereignty in an area spanning the whole Arabian Peninsula and Greater Syria – including Palestine.

Opposition to Zionism was seen in its most anti-Jewish form in the Palestinian Arab petitions presented to Winston Churchill when,

---

[11] Letter dated 1 March 1919, Central Zionist Archives: re-printed as a removable facsimile document in Martin Gilbert, *The Story of Israel*, page 13.
[12] Letter of 17 January 1921, T.E. Lawrence (Arab Affairs Adviser) to Winston S. Churchill (Colonial Secretary): Churchill papers.

as Colonial Secretary, he visited Palestine in 1921. These petitions demanded an immediate end to Jewish immigration. In one of them, the Haifa Congress of Palestinian Arabs characterised the Jewish people in the language of age-old stereotypes. 'The Jew,' the petitioners wrote, 'is clannish and unneighbourly, and cannot mix with those who live about him. He will enjoy the privileges and benefits of a country, but will give nothing in return. The Jew is a Jew the world over. He amasses the wealth of a country and then leads its people, whom he has already impoverished, where he chooses.'[13]

Jewish leaders within Palestine attempted to challenge this implacable hostility. They sought to build bridges between the Jewish and Muslim communities in the neighbouring countries of Lebanon, Syria, Egypt and Iraq – where Arab nationalism was gaining strength. But these efforts were countered by Muslim leaders who actively inflamed Muslims against Zionism. One such leader was Haj Amin el-Husseini, who became Mufti of Jerusalem in 1922. When anti-Zionist propaganda reached Iraq in 1925, he encouraged it. The spread of Arab national independence from Britain – Egypt in 1926, Iraq (formerly Mesopotamia) in 1932 – led to an intensification of anti-Zionism, and served to worsen the position of the Jews living in Arab lands.

Despite ominous developments in the wider world, the life of Jews in some Muslim countries was never better than in the 1920s. The Middle East seemed on the verge of a new openness. Russian-born Yechezkel Steimatzky was able to expand his chain of bookstores beyond Palestine, establishing stores in Beirut in 1927, then in Damascus, Baghdad, Cairo and Alexandria. Jews and Muslims alike browsed in these stores and bought the latest books and current newspapers.[14]

In Persia, Jews enjoyed greater freedom and tolerance after Reza Khan Pahlavi became Shah – with the support of Britain – in

---

[13] Palestinian Arab Congress, memorandum, 14 March 1921: Central Zionist Archives.
[14] Eri Steimatzky (Yechezkel Steimatzky's son), in conversation with the author, 2004.

1925. His social reforms opened new occupations to the Jews and allowed them to live outside the Jewish Quarters of towns.[15] Similarly, a Persian Jew, Ayyub Loqman Nehuray, represented the interests of Jews for more than thirty years as the Jewish delegate in the Persian Parliament. Nehuray secured leave for Jewish officers in the Persian Army on the Jewish High Holydays. Working with Armenian and Zoroastrian delegates, he also secured a law that enabled non-Muslim marriage and divorce to be regulated by their own religious authorities, liberating the Jews of Persia from their previous dependence on Islamic law.[16]

In neighbouring Iraq, after the establishment of the British Mandate there, Jewish community leaders played an important role in shaping the country's political destiny. One of the Jews who held high office in the first Iraqi Government was Sasson Heskel, the former Deputy for Baghdad in the Ottoman Parliament. Heskel was appointed Minister of Finance in 1920. On his appointment he invited a fellow Iraqi Jew, Abraham Elkabir, to become Assistant Accountant General. Elkabir accepted, explaining that while he had declined government service in Ottoman times, he was 'no longer serving a rotten and doomed administration. We will serve our own country with a glorious past and a promising future.'[17] The appointment of these Jews – the recognition of their Iraqi patriotism, and their optimism for the future of Iraq – was a sign of the level of trust that existed between Iraq's Muslim and Jewish communities.[18]

---

[15] On a visit to the Jewish community of Isfahan, Pahlavi also became the first Persian ruler since Cyrus the Great, 2,500 years earlier, to pay respect to the Jews by praying in a synagogue. Along with his liberalisation, Pahlavi turned against the Shiite clergy and banned Islamic dress. When women were seen veiled in the streets, their veils were compulsorily removed; women teachers were not allowed into the classroom even with headscarves.

[16] Houman Sarshar (editor), *Esther's Children: A Portrait of Iranian Jews*, page 264.

[17] Meir Basri, 'Prominent Iraqi Jews of recent times,' *The Scribe*, Issue 76, Spring 2003.

[18] In March 1921, Heskel was one of the two senior representatives of Iraq at the Cairo Conference, at which Winston Churchill, then Secretary of State for the Colonies, chose Emir Feisal to be ruler of Iraq, initially under a British Mandate.

The warm relationship between Jews and Muslims in Iraq was much in evidence after Emir Feisal was proclaimed the King on 11 July 1921. A month later, a banquet was held in his honour by the Jewish community in Baghdad. The London *Jewish Chronicle* reported that the banqueting hall 'was decorated with Arab and English flags, and on the walls were inscriptions in both languages – "Long live King Feisal" and "Long live the free Arab people."' The Baghdad Jewish boy scouts formed a guard of honour at the entrance of the hall, while pupils of all the Jewish schools in the city assembled along the streets around the building.

On the King's arrival at the banqueting hall, he was welcomed by the Haham (Chief Rabbi) of Iraq, Ezra Dangoor, who presented him with a copy of the Pentateuch in gold binding. In response, King Feisal announced: 'I thank my Jewish citizens, who are the mainspring of the life of the people of Iraq.'[19] Jewish poets then recited odes glorifying the King and his people.[20]

In the years ahead, King Feisal's support was of central importance to the tolerance shown to Jews by the Muslim population. Under his rule, Jews continued to play an influential role in the country's government. Sasson Heskel was elected a member of the Iraqi Parliament in 1925; he had already received high decorations from Feisal and the Shah of Iran, and had been knighted by King George V in 1923. One of Heskel's greatest contributions to Iraq was his role in the country's negotiations with the British Petroleum Company (BP), in which he successfully persuaded the company to pay Iraq for its petroleum in gold and not in banknotes.[21]

Another Jewish former Deputy in the Ottoman Parliament, Menahem Saleh Daniel, was appointed a Senator of the Kingdom of Iraq in 1925. He was succeeded as Senator by his son, Ezra Daniel, seven years later. Other Jews held positions of influence through the

---

[19] *Jewish Chronicle*, 23 September 1921.
[20] Nir Shohet, *The Story of an Exile: A Short History of the Jews of Iraq*, page 31.
[21] Tamar Morad, Dennis Shasha and Robert Shasha (editors), *Iraq's Last Jews*, page 4.

1930s and beyond.[22] From 1927 to 1948, Abraham Elkabir served as Accountant General of Iraq and Director General of Finance.[23] Likewise, Daud (David) Samra, who had been a judge in Iraq during the Ottoman period, served as Vice-President of the Iraqi High Court of Cassation from 1923 to 1946.[24] When the statutory time came for Samra's retirement, the Iraqi Parliament passed a special law – the first of its kind and the first for any Iraqi citizen – extending his term of office for a further five years.[25]

Zionist activity in Iraq in the 1920s was stimulated by a Jewish literary society that was formed in 1920. In 1921 a group from within the society set up a separate Mesopotamian Zionist Committee, which received permission to function from the Iraqi Government. In the years 1920 and 1921 a substantial sum – £16,434 sterling – was also donated for Jewish land purchase, agriculture and tree-planting in Palestine.[26] Much of this funding was provided by a single Iraqi Jew, Ezra Sasson Suheik.

Zionism aroused significant misgivings and tensions in Iraq. As Norman Stillman has commented: 'The Zionists enjoyed considerable sympathy from the poorer Jewish masses, who demonstrated their support in vocal public gatherings that offended Arab public opinion and frightened members of the Jewish upper class.'[27] One member of that upper class, Menahem Saleh Daniel, a Senator in the Iraqi Parliament, warned the Zionist Organization in London of the

---

[22] In 1932, Abraham Haim, the son of a rabbi and cantor, was elected as a deputy for Baghdad. He served eighteen years in the Iraqi Parliament, including as the rapporteur of the financial committee of the Chamber. He was also a member of Iraq's parliamentary delegation to the League of Nations when Iraq joined the League in 1932. He later headed the Iraqi Directorate of Pensions. Meir Basri, 'Prominent Iraqi Jews of recent times,' *The Scribe*, Issue 76, Spring 2003.

[23] In 1944, Elkabir represented Iraq at the Bretton Woods Conference in Washington that helped to establish a post-war global economic plan.

[24] Courts of Cassation could review and overturn the decisions of lower courts. Samra was also a lecturer at the Baghdad Law College for thirty-two years, beginning in 1919.

[25] Gourji C. Bekhor, *Fascinating Life and Sensational Death: The Conditions in Iraq Before and After the Six-Day War*, page 45.

[26] £16,434 is worth more than £330,000 in the money values of 2010.

[27] Norman A. Stillman, *Jews of Arab Lands in Modern Times*, page 86.

dangers of a Zionist policy. 'You are doubtless aware,' he wrote, 'that, in all Arab countries, the Zionist movement is regarded as a serious threat to Arab national life. If no active resistance has hitherto been opposed to it, it is nonetheless the feeling of every Arab that it is a violation of his legitimate rights, which it is his duty to denounce and fight to the best of his ability.' The Senator explained that Iraq 'has ever been, and now is still more, an active centre of Arab culture and activity, and the public mind here is thoroughly stirred up as regards Palestine by an active propaganda.'

Senator Daniel made it clear to the Zionist Organization in London that, 'in the mind of the Arab,' sympathy with the Zionist Movement 'is nothing short of a betrayal of the Arab cause.' He also pointed out the problems being created by the success of Iraqi Jews in commerce and government. In Baghdad, the success of Jews was 'nearly an outstanding feature of the town,' so much so that the Iraqi Jew was 'being regarded by the waking-up Moslem as a very lucky person, for whom the country should expect full return for its lavish favours.' The Iraqi Jew was, moreover, 'beginning to give the Moslem an unpleasant experience of successful competition in Government functions, which, having regard to the large number of unemployed former officials' – former Ottoman officials – 'may well risk to embitter feeling against him.'

Senator Daniel went on to describe the 'regrettable effects' of the arrival in Baghdad from Palestine of Dr. Ariel Bension, a representative of Zionist fundraising activities: 'There was for a time a wild outburst of popular feelings towards Zionism, which expressed itself by noisy manifestations of sympathy, crowded gatherings, and a general and vague impression among the lower class that Zionism was going to end the worries of life and that no restraint was any longer necessary in the way of expressing opinions or showing scorn to the Arabs.' This feeling, Senator Daniel wrote, was 'more Messianic than Zionistic.' To an observer, 'it was merely the reaction of a subdued race, which for a moment thought that by magic the tables were turned and that it were to become an overlord.'

Senator Daniel's forebodings of what harm Zionism might do were intense. 'In this state of raving,' he wrote, 'the Jews could not fail to occasion a friction with the Moslems, especially as the latter were then high up in nationalist effervescence.' A prominent member of the Iraqi Cabinet – a Muslim – had remarked 'reproachfully' to the Senator that, 'after so many centuries of good understanding, the Moslems were not at all suspecting that they had inspired the Jews with so little esteem for them.'[28]

Senator Daniel's ominous warnings presaged dangers that even he could not envisage. Two nationalisms, Arab and Jewish, were on a collision course. In 1922 the Iraqi Government refused to renew the permit of the Mesopotamian Zionist Committee, which had to operate unofficially for the next seven years. Meanwhile, Jews were joining their fellow Iraqis on the path to independence. On 7 March 1929 a Jewish journalist, Anwar Shaul, published an open letter in his weekly magazine *al-Hasid*, addressed to the British High Commissioner and Commander-in-Chief, Brigadier-General Sir Gilbert Clayton, demanding full independence for Iraq from Britain.[29]

Zionist activity continued to gain momentum in the Muslim world, but not without meeting significant obstacles. In the autumn of 1919, Joseph Joel Rivlin, a Palestinian Jew who had been exiled by the Ottomans to Damascus, reported that Zionist activity was flourishing in Syria. He wrote that more than two-thirds of Jewish schoolchildren in Damascus attended Zionist institutions, while more than five hundred Jewish teenagers attended classes organised by the Maccabi League, a branch of the worldwide Zionist sports movement.

The close proximity of Syria to Palestine meant that Jews there were well exposed to Zionist ideas. Hebrew newspapers from across the border were being widely read, and because Syria was a point of transit for Kurdish Jews on their way to Palestine, local Jews had frequent contact with Zionist immigrants. Damascus Jews often helped travelling migrants who were destitute, giving them shelter and paying for their train tickets from Damascus to the border of Palestine,

---

[28] Letter of 8 September 1922, quoted in Norman A. Stillman, *Jews of Arab Lands in Modern Times*, pages 331-3.

[29] Nir Shohet, *The Story of an Exile: A Short History of the Jews of Iraq*, page 32.

sixty miles away. From the border, these migrants then travelled to nearby Tiberias, where they worked in agriculture.

In his report, Rivlin mentioned that Zionism was even winning sympathy among local Arabs. One Arab newspaper in Damascus 'had begun to speak favourably about the Jews' until the authorities closed it down on the grounds that its editor had formerly been a Turkish spy. In particular, Rivlin stressed that there were two 'Arab notables' who were 'favourably inclined towards us.' These two men, Riyad Bey al-Sulh, the son of a prominent Syrian-Arab politician, and Hashim Bey, Chairman of the Drafting Committee for the Arab Constitution for Syria, had promised to disseminate the ideas of the Syrian Jews to 'their ardent nationalist friends.' Rivlin and the two men had 'a long conversation about our aspirations and rights and what would be our relations with the Arabs,' and as a result, Rivlin was hopeful of 'compromise between us and the Arabs.'[30]

These discussions were based on the expectation of Syrian independence – something the Arabs believed – wrongly – to be imminent. The French had no intention of giving up the control they had established over Syria following the defeat of the Ottoman Empire. Arab hopes for an independent Syria were dashed in July 1920, when France imposed its control over Syria. Zionist enterprises also suffered. In 1922 the French Mandate government ordered all Syrian Jewish schools to ensure that 'instruction in your school be in the Arabic language as opposed to any other, because it is the official language.'[31] Hebrew could be taught only as a foreign language; any school that continued to teach its curriculum in the Hebrew language – as many did – would be closed.

In Cairo, Zionism was also an increasing feature of Jewish life. In 1920, Albert Mosseri founded a pro-Zionist weekly, *Israël*, which for the next twenty years was the leading Jewish newspaper in Egypt, and

---

[30] Report of Joseph Joel Rivlin, August-September 1919, quoted in Norman A. Stillman, *Jews of Arab Lands in Modern Times*, pages 263-273.
[31] Instruction of 3 July 1922: quoted in Norman A. Stillman, *Jews of Arab Lands in Modern Times*, page 274.

was also read by Jews in other Muslim countries.[32] Yet the Egyptian Government, which finally won its struggle for independence from the British in 1926, looked with hostility at Jewish Zionist aspirations, just as it was hostile to the national identity of its own Christian Copts. Under the first Nationality Code, promulgated on 26 May 1926, Egyptian nationality was only to be for those who 'belonged racially to the majority of the population of a country whose language is Arabic or whose religion is Islam.'

Despite this denial of citizenship, the Jews of Egypt continued to participate in all aspects of Egyptian life. In 1923 the former Chief Rabbi of Turkey, Haim Nahoum Effendi, became Chief Rabbi of Egypt.[33] A distinguished scholar, lawyer, linguist and diplomat, he was one of the founders of the Egyptian Royal Academy of the Arabic Language, and was appointed a Senator in the Egyptian Legislative Assembly. At the request of King Farouk, Haim Nahoum translated into French all the Ottoman imperial decrees relating to Egypt, dating back to the Sixteenth Century. He also helped to revitalise the Society for the Historical Study of the Jews of Egypt.[34]

In 1924, the year after Haim Nahoum became Chief Rabbi, an Egyptian-born Jew, Joseph Aslan Cattaui, was made Finance Minister. He had already played a major part in developing the Egyptian sugar industry; his family had helped finance the railway system in Upper Egypt. Like Chief Rabbi Haim Nahoum, Cattaui later became a Senator.[35] Also in 1924, the stature of many attendees at the funeral of Jewish financier Moussa Cattaui Pasha revealed just how prominent Jews had become in Egyptian society. The leading Cairo newspaper wrote of the 'large number of dignitaries,' both foreign and Egyptian, who came to pay their respects; among them were the King's representative, Prime Minister Zaghloul Pasha,

---

[32] Norman A. Stillman, *Jews of Arab Lands in Modern Times*, page 70.

[33] The title *Effendi* was an Ottoman title of honour.

[34] Victor D. Sanua, 'Haim Nahoum Effendi (1872-1960),' *Image Magazine*, February 1998.

[35] Victor D. Sanua, 'The Contributions of Sephardic Jews to the Economic and Industrial Development of Egypt,' *Image Magazine*, March 1998.

two former Prime Ministers and the former Governor of Alexandria, who read a eulogy.[36] Then in 1928, Salvator Cicurel – later the President of Egypt's Sephardi community – captained Egypt's national fencing team at the Amsterdam Olympic Games. The team reached the finals, winning a silver medal.

But 1928 also saw an ominous development for Egyptian Jews: the formation in Ismailia of the Muslim Brotherhood, headed by Hassan al-Banna, which set its heart and its energies against Zionism. A populist movement with a strong Islamic fundamentalist message, the Muslim Brotherhood stirred up hatred not only against Zionism as a political and national movement, but against Jews as the bearers of an alien and destructive religion and ideology. Its very first topic for debate was 'The Subject of Palestine and the necessity of Jihad.'[37]

Not only Jewish nationalism, but Judaism, was under threat in the 1920s. In Yemen, a Nineteenth-Century decree for the forcible conversion of Jewish orphans was reintroduced in 1922. The conversion of a *dhimmi* orphan to Islam had always been considered a meritorious act. This followed the belief that every child, whoever his parents, was born into the *fitra*, or innate disposition, which was taken to mean that he was born a Muslim.[38] The ruler of Yemen, Imam Yahya, was in search of recruits for his orphanages that were in fact military training schools. For seven years the decree was rigorously implemented. When it was re-promulgated in December 1928, twenty-seven Jewish orphans were forced to convert to Islam within four months.

In a letter sent to the Board of Deputies of British Jews on 7 March 1930, the Jewish community in Yemen reported: 'The government has formally ordered that searches be carried out in all the towns and

---

[36] *Al-Ahram*, 19 May 1924.
[37] Ada Aharoni, Aimée Israel-Pelletier, Levana Zamir (editors), *History and Culture of the Jews from Egypt in Modern Times*, page 137.
[38] 'Allah's Apostle said, "No child is born except on Al-fitra (Islam) and then his parents make him Jewish, Christian or Magian (Zoroastrian), as an animal produces a perfect young animal: do you see any part of its body amputated?"' *Sahih al-Bukhari*, Volume 2, Book 23, Number 441; prophetic traditions collected by Muhammad ibn Ismail al-Bukhari (810–870).

villages for children, boys and girls, with no father, to arrest them and take them to a qualified police officer so that they should be instructed in the religion of Muhammad in conformity with the teaching of the Quran. Government agents have started to implement these orders. All children caught in the net are taken to the police officer who is charged with the task of indoctrinating them and offering them the moon if they convert to Islam.'

The letter described how, in spite of the authorities' attempts at bribery, 'these poor victims, deprived of all support and of any means of being purchased back, refuse to give up their faith.' But it went on to note that 'their persecutor gives them no respite, he frightens them with all kinds of threats, hits them on the back with a stick, slaps them and punches them until they cry, and finishes up by chasing them away and ordering that they be locked up.' The letter then stated: 'The unfortunate children find themselves locked up in dark cellars, bound in iron chains. The prison guards visit them frequently and threatened to kill them so that in the end the children gave up and betrayed their faith.'

On 3 January 1929 the capital of Yemen, Sanaa, became – in the words of the letter – 'the scene of a terrifying and impressive spectacle.' The events were recounted in full: 'Two young orphans, brother and sister, agreeable looking, were snatched away from their mother in full view of the Jewish population, despite the cries of the desperate family. The Jews got together and collected a sum of money in order to buy back the children. But this was in vain. The Quran prohibits Muslims from accepting money in order to prevent a conversion. The government has decided to convert all the orphans on pain of death. The brother and sister in question were so cruelly beaten that they had to convert. During the official ceremony hundreds of people accompanied the children. Around the children were fifty or so young children, gloomy and silent, as if it were a funeral procession.'[39]

---

[39] Tudor Parfitt, *The Road to Redemption: The Jews of the Yemen, 1900-1950*, pages 68-9.

The situation of the Jews everywhere under Muslim rule took a turn for the worse in 1929, when Palestinian Arabs, incited by Haj Amin al-Husseini, the Mufti of Jerusalem, claimed that the Jews in Palestine had designs on the Muslim Holy Places in Jerusalem, then under British protection. Specifically, they alleged that the Jews intended to restore the glory of the Temple of Solomon at the expense of the al-Aqsa Mosque and the Dome of the Rock.

That August, Haj Amin turned his followers savagely against the Jews.[40] The attacks began on August 23, when armed Arabs attacked individual, unarmed Jews walking in the Old City of Jerusalem. Two days later there was a sustained Arab attack on Jewish suburbs in Jerusalem; forty Jews were killed and four thousand fled their homes, many of which were then looted. In the village of Motza, just outside Jerusalem, six Jews were killed in their homes, and their bodies mutilated. In another attack the same day, more than sixty Jews were killed in the Jewish Quarter of Hebron, many of them women and children. Ten Jews were killed in Safed, while in the Jewish village of Hulda, most of the homes were destroyed.

Amidst the bloodshed and destruction, there were several acts of rescue by Muslims. During the riots in Hebron, even as the ferocious mob rampaged through the Jewish Quarter looking for Jews to attack, several Palestinian Arabs risked their own lives to save Jews. One of those who was saved later became the wife of an Israeli Minister of the Interior. She recalled how the Arab caretaker of her building had hidden her in a cupboard as marauders charged through the building looking for Jews, murdering the rest of her family.[41]

When the attacks ended six days later, 133 Jews had been killed. But the end of the attacks was not the end of the incitement. On

---

[40] The account and quotations that follow, relating to the events in Palestine in August-September 1929, are taken from the British Government's comprehensive enquiry, *Report of the Commission on the Palestine Disturbances of August, 1929* (known as the Shaw Report), Command Paper 3530 of 1930.
[41] Personal testimony of Mrs. Yosef Burg (born Rivka Slonim), an eighth-generation Hebron Jew, in conversation with the author, Jerusalem, 1972.

September 11, a Jerusalem Arab students' leaflet was widely circulated in the Muslim sections of the city. 'O Arab!' it warned, 'Remember that the Jew is your strongest enemy and the enemy of your ancestors since older times. Do not be misled by his tricks, for it is he who tortured Christ (peace upon him), and poisoned Mohammed (peace and worship be with him).' The leaflet went on to urge all Palestinian Arabs to boycott Jewish businesses in order to 'save yourself and your Fatherland from the grasp of the foreign intruder and greedy Jew.' Three weeks later, the British High Commissioner in Palestine, Sir John Chancellor, telegraphed to the Colonial Office in London that 'the latent deep-seated hatred of the Arabs for the Jews has now come to the surface in all parts of the country. Threats of renewed attacks upon the Jews are being made freely and are only being prevented by visible presence of considerable military force.'[42]

Within a year of the 1929 riots in Palestine, the British Government gave the Arab rioters a victory that they had hardly dared to hope for: it imposed the first severe restrictions on Jewish immigration to Palestine since the 1922 White Paper had stated, emphatically, that the Jews were in Palestine 'of right and not on sufferance.' The restrictions of this new White Paper set much stricter limits on Jewish land purchase and settlement building, pushing the prospect of a Jewish majority in Palestine far into the future.[43]

Encouraged by the White Paper, Arab violence in Palestine and the denunciation of Zionism that accompanied it had wide repercussions in the Arab world. In Baghdad, on 12 December 1929, anti-Zionism came to the fore when the chairman of the Zionist Organization and of the Jewish National Fund Committee in Iraq, Aharon Sasson, was summoned to appear before the Central Police. He was ordered to sign a declaration by which – in his words – he

---

[42] Telegram of 29 September 1929: National Archives (Kew), Cabinet Papers, CAB 27/206.
[43] Palestine White Paper of 21 October 1930: *Palestine Statement of Policy by His Majesty's Government in the United Kingdom*, Command Paper 3692 of 1930.

'obligated himself to stop collecting funds for the Jewish National Fund and to refrain from organizing a Zionist Society here.'[44]

A visit to Iraq in 1928 by a leading British Zionist, Lord Melchett, had already led to Arab anti-Zionist demonstrations in Baghdad. Following the 1929 riots in Palestine, there was further anti-Zionist agitation in Iraq. The Iraqi Government's response was to make Zionism illegal.

---

[44] Aharon Sasson, report of 18 December 1929, Baghdad: quoted in full in Norman A. Stillman, *Jews of Arab Lands in Modern Times*, pages 342-4.

THE NINETEEN THIRTIES

'Why do they call us dirty? I washed!'

For many Jews living under Muslim rule, the 1930s was a time of prosperity and opportunity. In the Muslim island kingdom of Bahrain, on the Persian Gulf, a Jew named Abraham Nonoo was elected to the Municipal Council in 1934. Nonoo, who had left Iraq as a young boy, built a gold and silver business by taking the gold and silver thread from dresses that had been thrown away, and melting them into ingots. He later imported gold from England and sold it to the local jewellery trade.[1] In the Yemeni capital, Sanaa, Rabbi Yihya ben Shalom Abyad, a biblical scholar, astronomer and physician, provided medical treatment to Jews and Muslims alike, treating free of charge those who could not pay. He also earned his livelihood as a silversmith and goldsmith.[2]

For the Jews of Egypt, the 1930s were a time of particular achievement. Some of the country's leading Jewish families financed the creation of both the Islamic Museum and the Museum of Modern Art. To house the latter, Elie Mosseri donated to the government one the finest Jewish mansions in Cairo. On 8 February 1931 the museum was opened by King Fuad.[3] Elie Mosseri, who was related to both the Cattaui and Suares families, was also the main shareholder of the Mena House Hotel at the Giza pyramids, and the King David Hotel in Jerusalem.[4]

---

[1] Nancy Elly Khedouri, *From Our Beginning to Present Day*, pages 78 and 80.
[2] Yehuda Ratzaby, 'Abyad, Yihya ben Shalom (1873-1935)': *Encyclopaedia Judaica*, Volume 2, column 198.
[3] Samir Raafat, *Cairo, The Glory Years*, page 109.
[4] The Mena House Hotel was taken over by the Egyptian Government in 1952. The first Egyptian-Israeli peace talks were held there in 1971.

An Egyptian-Jewish Athletics Team represented Egypt in the Maccabia Games held in Palestine in March 1935. On its return, it was met and congratulated by King Farouk's uncle, Prince Abdel Moneim.[5] That same year, Joseph Cattaui went to London as a member of the Egyptian delegation to negotiate the independence of Egypt.[6] He was one of many Jews in Egypt who held high places in society. When the banker Joseph Nissim Mosseri died in 1934, his funeral was attended by the Prime Minister, Abdel Fattah Yehia Pasha, and his entire Cabinet; five past and future Prime Ministers were also present. The house next to Mosseri's belonged to another Jew, the Egyptian court jeweller Meyer Eliakim, whose tenants at different times were the Jewish businessman David Ades and the Jewish bankers Abdullah and Maurice Zilkha.[7]

Another Egyptian Jew, Emanuel Mizrachi, was in charge of the royal estates of King Fuad. A keen gardener, Mizrachi introduced the South African Bird of Paradise flower to Egypt. Until a host insect could be found to pollinate the flower, Mizrachi had to do it by hand. In 1937 he played an important part in securing Egypt's financial independence, helping to negotiate the Montreux Convention, whereby Egypt was to be freed from the Capitulations and Mixed Courts imposed by twelve European nations fifty years earlier.[8]

One of the most remarkable Jews in Egypt in the 1930s was the filmmaker Togo Mizrahi, a founding father of the Alexandrian cinema. Several of his films were inspired by Arabic folktales and Arabic heritage, including *Children of Egypt* (1938). His masterpieces of comedy included several films starring a Jewish actor, Shalom; *Shalom the*

---

[5] For a photograph of the Prince congratulating Albert Salama, a member of the Team, see Ada Aharoni, Aimée Israel-Pelletier, Levana Zamir (editors), *History and Culture of the Jews from Egypt in Modern Times*, page 99.

[6] Victor D. Sanua, 'The Contribution of Sephardic Jews to the Economic and Industrial Development of Egypt,' *Image Magazine*, March 1998.

[7] Samir Raafat, *Cairo, The Glory Years*, pages 245-6.

[8] Samir Raafat, *Cairo, The Glory Years*, pages 172 and 178-9. The Capitulations and Mixed Courts that regulated them, were contracts signed between the Ottoman Empire and the European Powers, principally France and Britain, conferring rights and privileges in favour of their subjects resident in or trading with the Ottoman dominions.

Dragoman appeared in 1935 and *Shalom the Athlete* in 1937. One of Mizrahi's most popular films, *Sallamah* (1945), was set in the time of the Umayyad dynasty and starred Egypt's favourite singer, Oum Kalthoum. One of Mizrahi's greatest contributions was to turn the singer Laila Mourad into a legend in Egyptian culture, producing and directing five films in which she starred. Although Mourad converted to Islam before rising to fame, her parents were both Jewish; her father, Ibrahim Zaki Mordachi, was a famous religious cantor, singer and musician in 1920s Egypt.[9]

Throughout the 1930s, while so many Jews achieved success and prominence in Egyptian society, Jewish community life and culture also thrived. Nine Jewish schools in Alexandria and five in Cairo maintained a high standard of secular education, teaching French, English, Arabic, Hebrew and Italian. Ten per cent of the students, from poor families, attended free of charge. Two Jewish hospitals, one in each city, financed and maintained by the Jewish community, treated Jews, Muslims and Christians. An Egyptian Jew, Abram Bey Adda, founded an ophthalmic hospital that treated the eye diseases prevalent among poor Egyptians, and donated the hospital to the Alexandria municipality. There were more than sixty synagogues in Egypt, for a Jewish community of more than 60,000 Jews.[10]

More than half a century later, the writer Claudia Roden fondly recalled the 'vanished world' of Egypt in that period. In Zamalek, the Cairo district where she was born, the Jewish community had 'a happy and important place in the mosaic of minorities – which included Copts, Armenians, Syrian Christians, Maltese, Greeks and Italians, as well as British and French expatriates – living among the

---

[9] Communication from Mimi de Castro, 22 February 2009.

[10] In 1966, thirty years after Togo Mizrahi was at the height of his productivity, his Egyptian Films Company, together with all its films, promotional rights and distribution rights, was seized by the Egyptian authorities and sold. This was part of an uncompromising sequestration of Egyptian-Jewish assets. The deed of sequestration was dated 4 July 1966, thirty years after two of Mizrahi's most successful comic films were first released. There is a facsimile of the deed of sequestration in: 'Alex Cinema, Cinematographers': http://www.bibalex.org/AlexCinema/cinematographers/Togo_Mizrahi.html.

Muslim majority.' Claudia Roden remembered how on 'every Friday evening and on High Holidays, the Grand Temple was packed with people who came to hear Rabbi Nahum's famous speeches in French. By tradition the Prime Minister of Egypt always came for the Kol Nidrei prayer' – which took place at the start of the Day of Atonement, the most solemn twenty-four hours in the Jewish religious calendar.[11]

Despite the promise and security of Jewish life in countries like Egypt, uncertainty and foreboding began to loom large in January 1933 with the rise to power in Germany of Adolf Hitler and his Nazi Party. Hitler utilised radio broadcasts to beam his virulent hatred of Jews to Palestinian and Syrian Arabs, and to all the Muslim countries of the Middle East. A major attack in the propaganda focused on Britain's support for a Jewish nation in Palestine. By inflaming Arabs against Jews, the Nazi propaganda machine hoped to undermine French rule in Syria and British rule and influence in Palestine, Iraq and Egypt. Hitler's message was echoed by Italian Prime Minister Benito Mussolini, who sought to further his own an anti-British agenda in the Middle East. Italy, as the ruler of Libya, introduced discriminatory legislation directed at Libyan Jews in 1938, as it did against its own Italian Jews.

The persecution of Jews within Nazi Germany had ramifications for Jews throughout the Muslim world. In 1933 a group of Jews from Alexandria raised money to buy land in Palestine for a new village, Kfar Yedidia, for Jewish refugees from Germany.[12]

After the November 1938 Kristallnacht pogrom in Germany, in which a thousand synagogues were destroyed, more than ninety Jews killed, and countless Jewish homes and businesses looted,

---

[11] For fond memories of Egypt in this period, see Claudia Roden, *The Book of Jewish Food*, pages 3 and 8.

[12] In the same way, Egyptian Jews helped the many Jews who passed through Egypt from other lands. In 1934 and 1935, Pinhas Bouskeyla, son of the Chief Rabbi of Port Said, and the Jewish owner of the city's Hotel de France, gave food and shelter to Yemeni Jews on their way to Palestine. Ada Aharoni, Aimée Israel-Pelletier, Levana Zamir (editors), *History and Culture of the Jews from Egypt in Modern Times*, pages 113, 119, 123 and 124.

Egyptian Jews were able to help German and Austrian Jews who stopped at Port Said while en route from Italy to a distant haven, Shanghai. German-born Thea Woolf, who had gone to Egypt as a nurse in 1932, wrote: 'We formed three groups: one in Cairo, one in Alexandria, one in Port Said, so that every ship which laid anchor in Port Said was visited by a delegation from the Jewish hospitals, and we tried with the consent and even the help of the Port Authorities, to help those poor helpless fugitives as much as we could.' After some had recovered in hospital, 'we tried to find a way for them to stay in Egypt until the end of the war, and then helped them emigrate to their relatives in Palestine.'[13] The women of the small Jewish community at Port Said immediately set up a relief group, Union Féminine Israélite, rented an apartment in the harbour and stocked it with supplies for the refugees – including food, clothing, toys for the children, toiletries and medicine.[14]

Thea Woolf's experiences before and during the Second World War – which began in September 1939 with the German invasion of Poland – led her to reflect on 'the crucial and generous help the Egyptians extended to the Jewish refugees fleeing from Nazi persecution.' This 'marvelous and courageous collaboration,' she wrote, 'between Jews and Arabs to save Jews from the Holocaust is an historic fact concerning the Jewish-Moslem collaboration in Egypt which is still quite unknown.' Woolf expressed a hope that this collaboration 'may constitute a further link in strengthening the growing peace ties between Jews and Arabs in the Middle East.'[15]

In Iraq, the Jewish community – 120,000 Jews in all, two-thirds of whom lived in Baghdad – flourished in spite of the growing pro-German and

---

[13] Ada Aharoni, *Not in Vain: An Extraordinary Life* (the life of Thea Woolf), page 85.
[14] Letter of Jose Salmona: *IAJE Newsletter* (International Association of Jews from Egypt Newsletter), 2002, Volume 4. No. 1, Addendum. Pinhas Bouskeyla, son of the Chief Rabbi of Port Said, also joined forces with the owner of a Port Said department store to help the refugees. Ada Aharoni, Aimée Israel-Pelletier, Levana Zamir (editors), *History and Culture of the Jews from Egypt in Modern Times*, pages 113, 119, 123 and 124.
[15] Ada Aharoni, *Not in Vain: An Extraordinary Life* (the life of Thea Woolf), page 91.

pro-Nazi inclinations of King Ghazi I, who ruled from 1933 to 1939.[16] A number of Iraqi Jews occupied positions of power and influence, including Ezra Menahem Daniel, one of the five members of the Senate Praesidium. The Director of the Budget, Ezra Khedhouri, was also a Jew, as was the Director of Income Tax, Moshi Soffer. The Baghdad Chamber of Commerce was co-founded by a Jewish member of the Iraqi Foreign Ministry, Meir Basri, and of the Chamber's eighteen to nineteen board members, between nine and eleven were Jews.[17]

There were twenty-four synagogues in Baghdad in 1935; the Masuda Shemtob and Soffer synagogues were founded in that year, while the oldest, the 1,400-year-old Great Synagogue, dated back more than a hundred years before Islam. Among the Jewish schools in Baghdad were the Albert David Sassoon School for boys – one of nine Jewish boys' schools – and the Laura Kadourie School for Girls – one of two Jewish girls' schools. In Baghdad, Basra and Hillah, Jewish schools all received government subsidies. The Jewish community was protected by the guarantee in the Iraqi Constitution of 1925 that the Jewish Spiritual Council had the right to deal with all matters pertaining to Jewish marriage, dowry, divorce, separation, alimony and the attestation of wills.

By the mid-1930s, Jewish businesses in Iraq spanned a wide array of commercial activity. Among those advertising in the *Iraq Directory* for 1936 was Abdul Sattar S. Kaddouri, a commission agent who exported skins, wool, dates, grains and seeds, and who imported

---

[16] Far from Iraq, a community of Iraqi Jews was flourishing: the Jews who had reached Shanghai from Iraq in the late Nineteenth Century, forming a thousand-strong Sephardi community. The leading families – the Kadhouries, Sassoons, Dangoors and Hardoons – were major benefactors to the life of Shanghai, where five thousand Ashkenazi Jews, most of them refugees from the anti-Jewish policies of the Soviet Union in the 1920s, lived side by side with the Sephardi Jews. Renée Dangoor later recalled how her fellow Sephardi Jews 'all spoke Baghdadi Arabic and conducted their accounts and correspondence in Arabic.' They were, she added, 'without exception devout Jews who lived a strictly Orthodox life.' Renée Dangoor, in conversation with the author in 2000: quoted in Martin Gilbert, *From the Ends of the Earth*, page 124.

[17] Itamar Levin, *Locked Doors*, page 4.

hosiery, stationery and piece goods 'of every description.' More than
half of Kaddouri's fellow importers and exporters were Jews. The
directory also listed I. and C. Ades, agents for Ford, Ferranti, Michelin
and thirty-seven other foreign companies; Khedhouri A. Zilkha,
whose bank had been established in Beirut in 1899; Rubain M.
Mizrahi, an antique dealer; Ezra Murad Shamoon, a tobacco broker;
and two Jewish providers of carpenters' tools, Moshi Eliahou Hayek
and Eliyah Y. Fattal. Another Jewish entrepreneur, Haim H.
Nathaniel, provided an overland mail and passenger service by road
from Baghdad to Palestine, Syria and Iran, and a shipping service
from Basra to Haifa and Beirut.[18]

Jews who lived in Iraq during the 1930s often had fond memories of those years.[19] Aida Basri – great-granddaughter of the Chief
Rabbi of Iraq, Ezra Dangoor – wrote: 'My early memories of Baghdad,
of the street where we lived, were good. In our neighborhood we had
Muslim, Christian, Armenian and Jewish families. We lived in harmony and visited each other, especially on festivals. As young kids, we
played with the neighborhood kids; although we knew we were different, being Jewish.' Aida Basri had 'the most wonderful memories'
of attending a Jewish school. She acknowledged, however, that the
aim was to get 'a top education' and to sit British, French and
American examinations because 'we knew that sooner or later we
will have to leave.'[20]

Mordechai Ben-Porat, an Iraqi-born Jew, has recorded in his
memoirs the uncertainty that was present during his teenage years
in Adhamiya, north of Baghdad. In the local market, he recalled,
the stores were owned by Muslims and Jews, 'good neighbours working peacefully side by side.' Ben-Porat's father would go to his store
every day in Arab dress, 'a *zboon*, a long straight gown for men,

---

[18] *The Iraq Directory, 1936.*
[19] Rachel Shabi, *Not the Enemy: Israel's Jews from Arab Lands*, page 1. Shabi writes of
her father's home city 'and source of pride,' Basra: 'The city whose rivers he
paddled, on the banks of which he hung out with his friends – Muslim, Jewish,
who cared? – eating flamed spicy fish together.'
[20] Aida Zelouf (born Basri), letter to the author, 17 February 2008.

above that a dark *abaya* and a red *tarbush* on his head.'[21] Because of their distance from the Jewish community in Baghdad, Ben-Porat's family 'developed closer relations with our Moslem neighbours.' But underneath this idyll, there flowed dark currents. As Ben-Porat explained: 'A Moslem's right to harass a Jew was taken for granted; it would not have occurred to the victim to react or to report the matter to the police.'[22]

Another Iraqi-Jewish boy, Yitzhak Bezalel, witnessed harassment from Muslims first-hand. He remembered taking his grandmother to a Baghdad synagogue on the Day of Atonement, a day on which nothing made of leather could be worn. 'Arab hooligans,' he wrote, 'who knew that on this day Jews would walk barefoot, would spread broken glass on the streets, and many Jews would come to the synagogue with bloody feet.' The young boy also recalled: 'One day I ran home from school – an Arab had hit me because I was a Jew. "Grandmother, what does it mean to be a Jew?" I asked. "Never be ashamed of your Jewishness," she replied. Another time, Arab children shouted at us "Dirty Jews!" "Why do they call us dirty? I washed!" I asked. "They wouldn't care whether you are dirty or not," she replied. "It bothers them that you're a Jew. Be proud of this."'[23]

With the spread of Nazi radio propaganda from Germany, Jews were also the subject of Muslim antagonism in Lebanon. On 25 July 1933 a columnist for *al-Sahafi al-Ta'ih* ('The Wandering Journalist') compiled a digest of recent letters from Muslim readers. One

---

[21] *Abaya*: a Muslim woman's overgarment (also known as a *hijab*), usually black, that covers the whole body except the eyes, feet and hands. *Tarbush*: a man's tall, brimless, felt cap, usually red, with a silk tassel, worn either by itself or as the base of a turban.

[22] Ben-Porat also explained that because his family name, Murad, 'was obviously Jewish, we took another, Kazzaz' – the Arabic for 'silk dealer,' which had been his grandfather's profession. Mordechai Ben-Porat, *To Baghdad and Back*, pages 20-5.

[23] Bezalel also recalled: 'Another time the teacher asked us to make a contribution to the Iraqi Army. I asked grandmother for a shilling, but she refused. "You are a Jew, and not an Iraqi – first of all a Jew,"' Quoted in Ora Melamed (editor), *Annals of Iraqi Jewry: A Collection of Articles and Reviews*, pages 12-13.

reader had written: 'The Jews are a people of evildoers. They will eat up everything, and they will control the markets.' Another wrote: 'The Jews are an intriguing group that works in hiding to kill nationalism and the principle of freedom.' A third reader declared: 'If the Jews occupy our country, they will inflict distress and bring disasters over it.'[24]

Some Arabs, however, railed only against the activities and ideas of Zionism, feeling that it was wrong to oppose the Jews as a people. This sentiment was voiced in Syria on 2 November 1933 – the six-teenth anniversary of the Balfour Declaration – when a Syrian news-paper, al-Ayyam, expressed support for the measures being imple-mented by the French authorities to protect the Jewish Quarter of Damascus from Muslim attacks. The newspaper commented: 'There shall be no fear for the Jews of Damascus. In Damascus no one con-templates any aggression against an Israelite.' Any attack on the Jews of the city would be considered 'an attack against a part of the noble nation's ensemble.'[25]

Such high principles were not evident in Afghanistan following the assassination of the Afghan King, Nadir Shah, in November 1933. Although the King had been killed by a rival Afghan clan, the five thousand Jews of Afghanistan were made scapegoats, and a campaign began against them. They were forbidden to leave towns without per-mits and were made to pay a special poll tax – the jizya revived. In the town of Balkh, the gates to the Jewish Quarter were locked each night. This persecution arose in spite of the fact that Nadir Shah's predeces-sor, Amanullah Khan, who had ruled from 1919 to 1929, believed that the Afghan people were descended from the Tribe of Benjamin.

Similar hostility also appeared in Tangier in June 1933, but with-out any excuse or warning. A group of Muslims had attacked Jews whom they found walking in the streets. Jewish community leaders urged all Jews to be 'prudent' when walking in the city, and asked the

---

[24] Quoted in Götz Nordbruch, Nazism in Syria and Lebanon, page 24.
[25] Quoted in Götz Nordbruch, Nazism in Syria and Lebanon, page 148, note 54.

Moroccan authorities for greater protection. But ten months later, on 14 April 1934, Arabs responded to a march by Jewish boy scouts by mounting public demonstrations against the Jews. Fortunately for the Jewish community, April 14 fell on the Sabbath, when most Jews were at home.[26]

Arab nationalism was gradually succeeding in its aspirations: Egypt became fully independent from Britain in 1926 and Iraq followed in 1932. What would be the future of the Jews of Palestine, should they fail to become a majority in the land? This question was a source of deep concern for the Palestinian Jews.

On 23 August 1933 a Palestinian Arab newspaper carried an article commemorating the fourth anniversary of the 1929 riots in Palestine – riots in which 133 Jews had been killed, and several Arabs executed by the British for the murders. The author of the article, Emil al-Ghawri, was a Palestinian Arab civil servant. He wrote: 'Today is the anniversary of the August uprising, the flames of which were borne high on this day in 1929. That day was a day of brilliance and glory in the annals of Palestinian Arab history. This is a day of honour, splendour and sacrifice.' The Jews in Palestine had 'coveted our endowments and yearned to take over our holy places.' But no sooner had they 'begun marching along this shameful road than the Arabs stood up, checked the oppression, and sacrificed their pure and noble souls on the sacred altar of nationalism.'[27]

From a Muslim perspective, there was nothing so 'sacred' about Jewish nationalism – Zionism – which was seen by 1933 as an unacceptable challenge to Arab national aspirations, and to the deep-seated Islamic perception of the Jew as an infidel. British Mandate Palestine was still a predominantly Muslim land, both in terms of population and land ownership. In 1936 there were 940,000 Arabs

---

[26] M. Mitchell Serels, *A History of the Jews of Tangier*, pages 149-50.
[27] Quoted in Y. Porath, *The Emergence of the Palestinian-Arab National Movement, 1918-1929*, page 270.

and 370,000 Jews in the country. Of those Jews, 134,000 had arrived since Hitler had come to power three years earlier.[28]

In Palestine, Arab riots began once more on 15 April 1936, growing rapidly to a full-scale uprising against British rule. The rioters' main demand was a halt to Jewish immigration into Palestine. Yet Jews in all Arab lands were affected, as Muslim governments hastened to give strong vocal and emotional support to the uprising. By October 1936, eighty Jews had been killed by Arabs in the riots in Palestine – many while sitting in their homes or travelling by bus – and thousands of acres of Jewish-owned crops and orchards had been burned. In clashes with British troops, thirty-three British soldiers and more than 140 Arabs had been killed.

While the Arab uprising in Palestine was still in progress, the British Government set up a Royal Commission on Palestine – the Peel Commission – to enquire about the causes of the uprising and to make recommendations about what should be done. The commissioners recommended the partition of Palestine into two independent States, one Arab and one Jewish, with Jerusalem, Bethlehem and a corridor to the coast to be retained by Britain. In giving evidence to the Peel Commission on 25 November 1936, the Zionist leader Chaim Weizmann spoke about the plight of the Jews in Germany, Poland and elsewhere in Europe, describing them as 'six million people doomed to be pent up in places where they are not wanted.' He also made reference to 'the Jews in Persia and Morocco and such like places, who are very inarticulate, one hears very little of them.'[29]

On 7 January 1937 the head of the Jewish Agency for Palestine, Russian-born David Ben-Gurion, told the Peel Commission that he applauded the fact that the Arabs of Egypt and Iraq had achieved their independence. He went on to say that there was 'no conflict of interest between the Jewish people as a whole and the Arab people

---

[28] These figures are taken from the Palestine Royal Commission Report (the Peel Commission), Command Paper 5479 of 1937.

[29] Dr. Chaim Weizmann, evidence to the Royal Commission on Palestine, 25 November 1936: National Archives (Kew), Colonial Office papers, CO 733/342. Morocco had been under French rule since 1912.

as a whole. . . . We need each other. We can benefit each other.' It was the belief of the Zionists, Ben-Gurion added, 'that a great Jewish community, a free Jewish nation in Palestine, with a large scope for its activities, will be of great benefit to our Arab neighbours, and from the recognition of this fact will come a lasting peace and lasting cooperation between the two peoples.'[30]

Ben-Gurion's hopeful view was challenged six days later, when a leading Palestinian Arab, Awni Bey Abdel Hadi, gave his own evidence to the Royal Commission. 'Every Arab in Palestine,' he said, 'will do everything possible in his power to crush down that Zionism, because Zionism and Arabism can never be united together.'[31] It was not long before Abdel Hadi's words found resonance and support. On 26 July 1937 the British Ambassador to Egypt telegraphed to the Foreign Office in London about a recent conversation with the Egyptian Prime Minister, Nahas Pasha, who told him that 'Egypt could not regard with equanimity' the prospect of a Jewish State as her neighbour. 'Apart from question of defence etc,' Nahas told the Ambassador, 'who could say the voracious Jew would not claim Sinai next? Or provoke trouble with the Jewish community in Egypt itself?'[32]

In September 1937 the Mufti of Jerusalem, Haj Amin al-Husseini, organised a conference at Bludan, a summer resort in Syria, attended by 424 non-government delegates from Syria, Palestine, Lebanon, Transjordan, Iraq, Egypt and Saudi Arabia. It was chaired by a former Iraqi Prime Minister, Naji al-Suweidi.[33] The conference declared that Palestine was to be 'the holy region of our fatherland' and an integral part of the Arab nation. The Peel Commission's proposal to partition Palestine between Arabs and Jews was denounced as an attempt to prevent the union of Arabs in their struggle towards an Arab nation.

---

[30] David Ben-Gurion, evidence to the Royal Commission on Palestine, 7 January 1937: National Archives (Kew), Colonial Office papers, CO 733/342.
[31] Awni Bey Abdel Hadi, evidence to the Royal Commission on Palestine, 13 January 1937: National Archives (Kew), Colonial Office papers, CO 733/342.
[32] Sir Miles Lampson, telegram of 26 July 1937: National Archives (Kew), Foreign Office papers, FO 371/20810.
[33] Prime Minister of Iraq from November 1929 to March 1930.

In London, official government opposition to a Jewish State was also growing. On 4 July 1938 the Colonial Secretary, Malcolm MacDonald, told Dr. Weizmann that if Britain endorsed even a small Jewish State, 'We should lose much of the friendship of the authorities and peoples of a number of important surrounding countries like Egypt, Saudi Arabia, Iraq and Syria.'[34]

On 18 January 1939, in a secret memorandum for his Cabinet colleagues, Malcolm MacDonald rejected Churchill's 1922 formulation that, as MacDonald phrased it, 'all Jews as such have a right to enter Palestine.' MacDonald went on to explain: 'Arab detestation of the Jewish invasion into Palestine being what it is, it would be wholly wrong to suggest that this large Arab population should one day in their own native land and against their will come under the rule of the newly arrived Jews.'[35]

To appease pan-Arab sentiment, in March 1939 the British Government prepared a third Palestine White Paper – the MacDonald White Paper – introducing restrictions on Jewish immigration so that there could not be a Jewish majority in Palestine in the foreseeable future. The British Parliament voted by a large majority to accept these restrictions, despite a strong plea from Winston Churchill – who then held no political office – in favour of allowing Jewish immigration to continue.

Churchill told the House of Commons on 23 May 1939: 'So far from being persecuted, the Arabs have crowded into the country and multiplied till their population has increased more than even all world Jewry could lift up the Jewish population. Now we are being asked to decree that all this is to stop and all this is to come to an end. We are now asked to submit, and this is what rankles most with me, to an agitation which is fed with foreign money and ceaselessly inflamed by Nazi and by Fascist propaganda.'[36]

[34] Discussion on 4 July 1938: National Archives (Kew), Cabinet papers, CAB 24/278.
[35] Memorandum of 18 January 1939: National Archives (Kew), Foreign Office papers, FO 371/23221.
[36] *Hansard*, Parliamentary Debates, House of Commons, 23 May 1939.

Churchill was right on both counts. Between 1922 and 1939 more Arabs had entered Palestine than Jews. These were Muslim immigrants, including many illegals, from Morocco, Algeria, Tunisia, Libya, Egypt, Yemen, Iraq, Iran and Syria – as well as from Transjordan, Sudan and Saudi Arabia.[37] These immigrants were drawn to Palestine by its opportunities for work and its growing prosperity – opportunities and prosperity often created by the Jews there. In 1948 many of these Arab immigrants were to be included in the statistics of 'Palestinian' Arab refugees.

As far as Nazi and Fascist propaganda was concerned, since the beginning of 1939 the radio station at Bari, in southern Italy, had been regularly transmitting Italian and German radio propaganda to the Middle East. Intended to challenge British and French influence in the region, these broadcasts actively fostered hostility towards Jewish aspirations in Palestine. The Italians had even established close contacts with the Mufti of Jerusalem, Haj Amin al-Husseini.

The Arabs had hitherto been wary of Hitler, who, in his book *Mein Kampf*, first published in 1925, placed them on one of the lowest rungs of the 'racial ladder,' just above the Jews. But as Hitler began courting Arab support in opposition to the British and French, Nazi influence gradually took hold in the Middle East. At the end of 1937, Hitler prudently suggested omitting his racial ladder theory from the forthcoming Arabic translation of *Mein Kampf*.[38]

Nazi agitation was particularly prevalent in Iraq during the rule of King Ghazi. The Christian-owned newspaper *al-Alam al-Arabi*

---

[37] One striking official British statistic: immigration to Jerusalem from outside Palestine between 1922 and 1931 included 21,000 Arabs and 20,000 Jews. For the countries from which these immigrants came, see Martin Gilbert, *Historical Atlas of Jerusalem*, Map 43, page 77. For a detailed discussion and factual material on Arab immigration to Mandate Palestine, see Joan Peters, *From Time Immemorial: The Origins of the Arab-Jewish Conflict Over Palestine*, chapters 11-14.

[38] Letter from the German Propaganda Ministry, Berlin, to the German Foreign Ministry, 10 December 1937: Lukasz Hirszowicz, *The Third Reich and the Arab East*, pages 45-6.

('The Arab World') published daily extracts from the Arabic edition of *Mein Kampf*, with its virulent anti-Jewish venom, but without any reference to the anti-Arab 'racial ladder.' A pro-Nazi society, *al-Muthanna*, was established in Baghdad in 1935, with branches in Basra and Mosul.[39] It was headed by a well-known Muslim-Iraqi enemy of the Jews, Dr. Sa'ib Shawkat. The *al-Futuwwa* ('Chivalry') youth brigades disseminated anti-British and anti-Jewish leaflets.[40] The Iraqi Government, responding to public pressure, closed its borders to Jewish refugees from Germany.[41] Hitler's malign influence had penetrated to the heart of a proud Muslim land in which Jews had long held an honoured place.

On 16 October 1936, Haj Amin al-Husseini arrived in Iraq from Syria and took up residence in Baghdad. He had escaped from Palestine – where he was wanted by the British for having fomented the Arab riots that were causing many British deaths. Reaching Iraq with the Mufti were a group of his more fanatical followers. Under his encouragement, a 'Committee for the Salvation of Palestine' was established in Baghdad; it even extorted money from local Jews. The funds of the committee were used to send weapons and ammunition to the Palestinian Arab insurgents.

Anti-Jewish measures proliferated in Iraq. A quota was established restricting the enrollment of Jews in the national school system. The study of Hebrew and Jewish history was banned in Jewish schools. The three Jewish daily newspapers – *al-Misbah*, *Yeshurun* and *al-Hasid* – were closed down. On 16 September 1936, on the eve of the Jewish New Year, two Jews were shot dead in the street. On the Holy Day itself, another Jew was murdered in Baghdad and yet another in Basra. Two more Jews were murdered in Amara. Aharon Sasson, the Iraqi Zionist leader, was arrested and deported.

---

[39] The Al-Muthanna Club was named after Muthanna bin Haritha, leader of the Muslim conquest of Iraq in the Seventh Century.

[40] Liora Lukitz, *Iraq: Quest for National Identity*, page 94.

[41] It took enormous efforts on the part of the Jewish hospital in Baghdad to gain entry permits for a single Jewish physician and a Jewish midwife, both of whom sought refuge from Germany. Between 1933 and 1935, only six German Jewish doctors were granted admission to Iraq.

Nazi influence spread even to the Kurdish region in northern Iraq, where the persecution of Kurdish Jews – whose forebears had been in the country for two thousand years – reached an unprecedented level. In 1935 more than 2,500 Kurdish Jews left for a new life in Palestine.[42]

In 1937 the German Ambassador to Iraq, Fritz Grobba, invited the leader of the Hitler Youth, Baldur von Schirach, to visit Baghdad with eight members of his staff. Von Schirach had tea with King Ghazi, visited a number of schools and invited a group of Iraqi students who were undergoing military training to be his guests at the 1938 Nuremberg rally. They went, and returned to Iraq enthusiastic about the Nazi regime.[43]

In Palestine, attacks on Jews continued throughout 1938. On June 29 a bomb was thrown at a Jewish wedding party in Tiberias, wounding seven Jews, including three children. In an Arab attack on Kiryat Haroshet, a Jewish village at the foot of Mount Carmel, five Jews were killed, including two children aged eleven and two. On 1 November 1938 a British Mandate police report noted that although the Arabs of Palestine had not yet declared 'a complete "Jihad" (Holy War), yet Jihad had been preached in many village mosques in Palestine, Syria and Iraq.' If the British Government were to announce a policy 'which is adverse to Arab interest,' the report warned, 'a complete Jihad will be declared by the more prominent religious leaders of Islam.'[44]

Jewish life in Muslim lands in the 1930s had much to commend it, but with the rise of anti-Jewish sentiment brought on by Arab nationalism in Palestine, and by Nazism in Germany – with its propaganda beamed to the Muslim world – a new world was in the offing. The idyllic aspects of the past would vanish in the next decade.

---

[42] Nir Shohet, *The Story of an Exile: A Short History of the Jews of Iraq*, pages 41-4.
[43] Marina Benjamin, *The History of a Family, the Story of a Nation*, page 110. On 1 October 1946, at the Nuremberg Trials, Baldur von Schirach was found guilty of 'crimes against humanity' for his part in the deportation of the Jews of Vienna. He served twenty years as a prisoner at Spandau.
[44] Report of 1 November 1938: Criminal Investigation Department (CID), Mandate Palestine: National Archives (Kew), Colonial Office papers, CO 733/359.

12

THE SECOND WORLD WAR:
A TIME OF DANGER

*'Recognition of the right of the Arabs to solve the Jewish question in
accordance with Arab nationalist aspirations and in the same manner
as in the Axis countries'*

With the rise to power of Adolf Hitler in Germany in 1933, the
European powers faced the threat of German territorial
expansion. In March 1938, Germany annexed Austria, and in March
1939, German forces entered the Czechoslovak capital, Prague. In
April 1939, Germany's ally Italy, under Benito Mussolini, invaded
Albania. Then on 1 September 1939, German forces attacked Poland.
Honouring their recent treaty with Poland, Britain and France
responded by declaring war on Germany two days later. The Second
World War had begun.

Although the initial epicentre of the war was in northern Europe
and Scandinavia, the fighting soon encroached upon Muslim lands.
By 1940, Italian and German forces were battling the British and
Commonwealth forces in Italian-ruled Libya. Hitler and Mussolini
meanwhile continued to broadcast persistent radio propaganda to
Muslim lands, extolling the virtues of Nazism and Fascism, and blaming the Jews for the world's ills. Claiming to be patrons of Arab
national aspirations, Germany and Italy denounced France for its
Syrian Mandate and Britain for its Palestine Mandate.

Following the Franco-German armistice in June 1940, a collabo-
rationist regime was set up under Marshal Pétain, based in the
French provincial town of Vichy. With German acquiescence, Vichy
rule extended to French North Africa – Morocco, Algeria and
Tunisia – with its large Jewish communities. The Vichy authorities
imposed many anti-Jewish regulations. One of these was a quota
restricting the number of Jewish doctors who could practise medicine

in Vichy-controlled Algeria. A United States consular report described how the quota was 'violently criticized by the natives, for in the past, Jewish doctors were about the only ones who were willing to take care of the native sick, particularly in the towns.' This situation was 'especially acute' in the Muslim Quarter of Algiers.[1]

Jewish communities became a target of violence from the outset of Vichy rule. In Tunisia, local Arabs frequently attacked Jews. In August 1940, riots and looting were reported from four Tunisian towns: Keff, Ebba-Ksour, Moktar and Siliana.[2] To deflect Arab discontent away from France, the Vichy Foreign Minister, Paul Baudouin, ordered the French Resident-General in Tunisia, Admiral Estéva, to find 'quiet ways to indulge Arab sensitivities.' Arabs who had been convicted of pillage and theft during the anti-Jewish riots were released from prison. As a result, the riots resumed. Jews were attacked in Degache in November 1940 and in Gafsa a few months later.[3]

In May 1941 three days of anti-Jewish violence broke out in the Tunisian city of Gabès. It began when thirty Muslims attacked a synagogue in the Jewish Quarter, killing eight Jews and injuring twenty. Local Arab police made no effort to intervene while the violence continued. A Jewish survivor, Yosef Huri, recalled sixty-two years later the tragic fate of his neighbour, Afila Rakach, who was cooking dinner for her family in her small kitchen when a group of Arabs broke into her home: 'They grabbed a pot of boiling soup, poured it over her, tortured her in her house, stoned her, and then killed her.'[4]

Another Jew from Gabès, Tzvi Haddad, who lived near a coffee house at the end of a largely Arab street, remembered how his mother went to look for his sister when the riots began, but was assaulted as soon as she got out of her front door. He recalled: 'An Arab knocked her down and another grabbed her and tried to cut

---

[1] Report of the United States Consulate General in Algiers, 'Native Affairs in Algeria,' 22 June 1942: United States National Archive, Record Group 84/350/48/11/01, 1942: 840.1.
[2] See Map 11, page 366.
[3] Robert Satloff, *Among the Righteous*, page 84.
[4] Interview, 1 September 2003: Robert Satloff, *Among the Righteous*, page 85.

her throat.' Tzvi Haddad, hearing her screams, rushed out to find her covered in blood. Miraculously, she survived, but she carried a scar on her throat for the rest of her life.[5]

The Vichy police, fearing a total breakdown of their control, eventually brought the riots to an end. Admiral Estéva telegraphed his explanation of the riots to Vichy, explaining that German prestige, which had been on the rise 'for some time' – with German victories in the Balkans, North Africa and the Atlantic – 'leads Muslims to believe themselves to be more and more on top of the Jews, since the latter keep their confidence in Britain and America.' The presence of German soldiers in Gabès, Estéva noted, 'has without doubt, even without intervention on their part, let the Arabs believe they would be protected in the case of riots.'[6]

Although anti-Jewish sentiment rose significantly in French North Africa under Vichy rule, there were many Muslims there who stood by and assisted their Jewish neighbours. Their support was voiced even before the imposition of Vichy rule. One of the Muslim leaders in Algiers, Abdelhamid Ben Badis, had earlier founded an Algerian League of Muslims and Jews. After his death in the spring of 1940, his place as a conciliator between Muslims and Jews was filled by Sheikh Taieb el-Okbi. In November 1940 an Arab member of the Algiers municipal council protested publicly at the exclusion of a Jewish colleague from the annual Armistice Day commemoration. As it was a day of deep significance in the Pétainist calendar, his protest was ignored. He refused to participate.[7]

In early 1942, el-Okbi heard rumours that a French pro-Fascist group, the Légion Française de Combattants, was urging the Muslims in Algiers to launch a pogrom against the Jews. He immediately issued a formal prohibition on Muslims attacking Jews. The leader of the predominantly Jewish resistance in Algiers, José Aboulker, later

---

[5] Yad Vashem interview 3563297, quoted in Robert Satloff, *Among the Righteous*, page 85.
[6] Letter of 23 May 1941: Robert Satloff, *Among the Righteous*, pages 85-6.
[7] Robert Satloff, *Among the Righteous*, page 220, note 23.

recalled that when German agents had tried to push the Arabs 'into demonstrations and pogroms,' it had been in vain. When Jewish goods were confiscated and put up for public auction, Aboulker wrote, an instruction went around the mosques: 'Our brothers are suffering misfortune. Do not take their goods.' Not one Arab, Aboulker added, agreed to become an administrator of confiscated Jewish property.[8]

The Jews also benefited from similar support in Tunisia.[9] The Muslim ruler, Ahmed Pasha, the Bey of Tunis, showed his contempt for Vichy's anti-Jewish laws by granting exemptions to several leading Jews.[10] Ahmed Pasha's successor as Bey of Tunis was Muhammed al-Munsif, known to the French as Moncef Bey. Eight days after coming to the throne, he showed his support for his Jewish subjects by awarding the highest royal distinction to twenty prominent Jews. When the Germans occupied Tunisia at the end of 1942, Moncef Bey summoned his senior officials to his palace and told them: 'The Jews are having a hard time but they are under our patronage and we are responsible for their lives. If I find out that an Arab informer caused even one hair of a Jew to fall, this Arab will pay with his life.'[11]

At this time, a Muslim citizen, Khaled Abdelwahhab, who had studied in both France and the United States, saved several Jewish families in the Tunisian coastal town of Mehdia. They were being held by the Germans in an olive oil factory while the men of the families were taken away for forced labour. Abdelwahhab, the son of a former minister at the Tunisian court – who often entertained German officers at his home – had learned that the Jews were in danger. Through the night, he took all those at the oil factory, two

[8] Robert Satloff, *Among the Righteous*, pages 107-8.
[9] In May 2004, when the historian Robert Satloff visited Tunis, he was welcomed by Sidi Chedli Bey, the ninety-four-year-old son of the last hereditary ruler of Tunisia. Chedli Bey told him how, when his father was deposed in 1956, and his family's wealth and property were confiscated, Tunisian Jews – recalling his father's help for them in the Second World War – paid not only for his father's apartment but for Sidi Chedli Bey's own education. Robert Satloff, *Among the Righteous*, page 113.
[10] One of these Jews was the ophthalmologist Roger Nataf.
[11] Oral history interview, Yad Vashem, No. 3559094, quoted in Robert Satloff, *Among the Righteous*, page 113.

dozen in all, to his farm at Tlelsa, twenty miles inland from Mehdia. There they found safety, wearing the obligatory yellow star on their clothing, until the arrival of the British Army in early 1943.[12] Whenever a nearby German Red Cross unit visited Abdelwahhab, he told the Jews to remove their yellow stars in order to avoid any risks to them and to himself.[13]

A similar instance occurred in early 1943 in the Zaghouan Valley, deep in the Tunisian countryside. Jews brought there from Tunis were being forced to build a small military airstrip when fierce fighting erupted in the valley. In the turmoil, sixty Jews escaped. They made their way across nearby fields to the country estate of a former mayor of Tunis, Si Ali Sakkat, a member of the ancient Quraysh tribe of the Arabian Peninsula and a proud descendant of Mohammed. Si Ali opened his gates and took the refugees in, gave them food and a place to sleep, and kept them safe until the Allied armies reached his estate.[14]

In his researches into Muslim help for Jews in wartime North Africa, the historian Robert Satloff has found that Moncef Bey's Prime Minister, Mohamed Chenik, 'regularly warned Jewish leaders of German plans, helped Jews avoid arrest orders, intervened to prevent deportations, and even hid individual Jews so they could evade a German dragnet.' Acting in the name of Moncef Bey, Cabinet members found ways to give 'special dispensations' to some Jewish men to exempt them from forced labour, and intervened with the German authorities on behalf of Jewish hostages. Members of Moncef Bey's court also hid Jews who had escaped from German labour camps.[15]

Jews living in Europe suffered enormously during the Second World War. Several thousand of them, originally from Muslim lands – North Africa, Egypt, Syria and Iraq – were living in France when the war broke out. They had gone to France in the interwar years

---

[12] Robert Satloff, *Among the Righteous*, pages 121-37.
[13] Mordecai Paldiel, 'A righteous Arab,' *Jerusalem Post*, 3 April 2009.
[14] Robert Satloff, *Among the Righteous*, pages 114-9.
[15] Robert Satloff, *Among the Righteous*, page 112.

in search of work and opportunity. Starting in 1941, they were arrested by the Vichy police along with other foreign-born Jews then living in France – mostly from Poland – and sent to holding camps. From these camps they were deported to Auschwitz, where most of them were murdered. On the basis of the French deportation lists, it is possible to see the birthplaces of Jews from North Africa who were deported to Auschwitz with the active collaboration of the Vichy French Government and police.[16]

At least thirteen Jews who were born in Muslim lands were executed in France for their part in the French Resistance. Each was named in the official German lists of those executed. René Hayoun and Lucien Liscia were both born in Tunis, while six others were born in Algeria: Abraham Cohen, whose city of birth is not given; Isaac Zerbib from Ain Beda; Isaac Sellem from Bou Saada; and Chao Abecassis, Mardoche Amesellem and Isaac Ben Zimra from Oran. Elias Solomon was born in Beirut, Raphael Caraco in Bursa, Salomon Levy and Haim Liaser in Izmir, and Haim Hatem in Jerusalem – when Beirut, Bursa, Izmir and Jerusalem had been part of the Ottoman Empire.[17]

Of the Moroccan-born Jews living in 1940 in France, 153 were deported from Paris to Auschwitz and murdered there. The oldest was seventy-three-year-old Messaoud Aknine from Tangier. The youngest was Michel Dray, whose family had come from Casablanca. He was just twenty months old; born on 4 May 1942, he was deported to his death on 20 January 1944. His three siblings were deported with him: Jacqueline, aged three and a half; Simone, aged two and a half; and Leon; aged eight. Their parents, Marguerite and Marius Dray, had been deported to their deaths six months before their children. 'For six months,' writes Rabbi Serels about the four Dray children, 'they remained without parental love.'[18]

---

[16] Serge Klarsfeld, *Memorial to the Jews Deported from France, 1942-1944*; see also Map 8., page 363.
[17] Serge Klarsfeld, *Memorial to the Jews Deported from France, 1942-1944*, pages 642-654.
[18] Rabbi M. Mitchell Serels, 'Moroccan Jews on the Road to Auschwitz,' *Sephardim and the Holocaust*, pages 95-6.

As the war continued, Jewish communities in the Muslim world faced increasing difficulties. In 1942, fierce battles were fought in North Africa between British and Commonwealth forces on the one side, and German and Italian forces on the other. When the Italians drove the British from Libya for the second time at the beginning of 1942, Mussolini ordered the roundup of all Libyan Jews. More than two and a half thousand Jews were arrested and taken to two Axis-run camps, one at Giado, the other at Gharyan. Of the 562 Jews interned at Giado, more than a quarter died there, mostly of typhus. One survivor sharply contrasted the Libyan Muslim guards in the camp with the 'brutality' of the Italian guards. 'When they see a Jew,' Yehuda Chachmon recalled of the Arab guards, 'they don't talk to him, they don't torture him, they don't make trouble for him.'[19]

The Jews of Tunisia also suffered the oppression of European fascist rule. When Tunisia came under direct German rule for six months, starting in November 1942, Jews were rounded up and incarcerated in labour camps. They were also ordered to wear the Star of David. Plans for their deportation were interrupted only by the Allied victory in May 1943, which drove the Germans out of North Africa.[20]

Even Jewish communities untouched by the fighting became the targets of increased hostility during this period. On 8 January 1942 the British Ambassador in Cairo, Sir Miles Lampson, reported to the Foreign Office in London that 'anti-Semitism created by the Palestinian situation and intensified by Jewish monopolizing tendencies

---

[19] Oral history interview, Yad Vashem, No. 3562945, quoted in Robert Satloff, *Among the Righteous*, page 103.

[20] Rafael Uzan, then a teenager, was among those rounded up. Ten years later, the Israeli authorities gave him and his family, for their home in Israel, an abandoned Arab house in Safed. As he entered it for the first time, and saw the sandals of a young child on the floor, he turned to walk away from the house. But an 'inner voice' stopped him. 'Fool!' it said, 'You have a short memory. One pair of sandals and you give up? Have you forgotten how your Arab friends cheered and stamped. . . . How they cheered as the Germans dragged you half-naked through the market? The "klabs" and "son-of-dirty-Jew-bitches" they hissed after you were enough to build a bridge of curses from Nabeul to Jerusalem.' Irene Awret, *Days of Honey: The Tunisian Boyhood of Rafael Uzan*, page 229.

during the war, has certainly become a more or less permanent factor in Egypt.' In the Ambassador's view, the Zionist dimension was the culprit. 'As you are aware,' he commented, 'Jews have long enjoyed a privileged situation in Egypt, where many of them were on intimate relations with influential authorities including the Palace. But during the last few pre-war years the Palestine question began to create feeling against the Jews.' The Ambassador noted that Palestinian Arab refugees from the 1936 rebellion had stirred up feeling against the Jews. Pointing out that many Egyptian Jews were in British employ in the Allied headquarters, where army contracts and commercial orders were distributed, he reported that it was 'widely asserted that it was impossible for a Moslem to get an order without going through a Jew.'[21]

Anti-Jewish attitudes also drew significant strength from Nazi Germany. The Mufti of Jerusalem, who had been living as a fugitive in Iraq since 1936, wrote to Hitler from Baghdad on 20 January 1941, styling himself 'Grand Mufti of Palestine.' In his letter, Haj Amin al-Husseini offered his services to the Third Reich, sending Hitler a draft declaration three weeks later, setting out his conditions for Arab support. One condition was that Hitler agree to 'condemnation of the Jewish national home in Palestine as an illegal entity.' Another was 'recognition of the right of the Arabs to solve the Jewish question in accordance with Arab nationalist aspirations and in the same manner as in the Axis countries.' Yet another was 'prohibition of all Jewish emigration to Arab countries.'[22] Under Haj Amin's plan, the Arabs were to expel the Jews from Palestine and not allow them to join their fellow Jews in any Muslim country.

After the Mufti fled Baghdad in May 1941 – to avoid capture by the British – he went first to Iran, then to Italy and finally to Berlin, where he offered his help to Hitler in person. He then successfully pressed Hitler not to allow the transit of four thousand Jewish children

[21] Sir Miles Lampson, Cairo, 8 January 1942: Foreign Office papers, FO 371/31576.
[22] Memorandum brought to Berlin on 12 February 1941: Lukasz Hirszowicz, *The Third Reich and the Arab East*, pages 109-10.

from Bulgaria to Palestine, and was active in the formation of a Muslim SS Division in Bosnia, at the same time that individual Muslims in Bosnia and Albania were saving Jews from deportation. The most horrific of the Mufti's influences was the creation of an SS task force intended to kill the half million Jews in Palestine. At least 30,000 of those Jews were pre-war refugees from Germany and Austria.

In October 1942, 'Einsatzgruppe Egypt,' headed by SS Colonel Walter Rauf – who had used the mobile gas chamber to devastating effect in German-occupied Eastern Europe – was ready to accompany Rommel's troops from Athens to Palestine.[23] The plan was for the twenty-four-member killing squad to enlist the help of Palestinian Arab collaborators, just as they had enlisted the help of local Ukrainian, Belorussian, Lithuanian, Latvian and Estonian volunteers in Eastern Europe. Had German forces defeated the British in Egypt and crossed the Suez Canal, not only would the Jews of Palestine have been in grave danger, but also the Jews of Egypt, Lebanon, Syria and Iraq. Fortunately, with Rommel's defeat at El Alamein in November 1942 and the subsequent retreat of German and Italian forces from Egypt, the killing squad was disbanded.

Nazi influence became particularly strong in Iran – as Persia was known after 1935. Since the rise of Hitler to power in 1933, Reza Shah had reversed his earlier tolerance towards the Jews and turned his country more and more towards Germany. The Shah also stimulated anti-Jewish feeling among his Muslim subjects. Britain and the Soviet Union deposed him after jointly occupying Iran in August 1941 – hoping to forestall German control – but the Shah's replacement, his twenty-two-year-old son Mohammad Reza Pahlavi, found his father's pro-German influence difficult to eradicate.

In January 1942 the British Consul in Kermanshah, Vaughan Russell, informed the Foreign Office in London that the Muslims, largely 'pro-German in sentiment,' were reluctant to work for the occupation forces, but that the non-Muslims were glad to do so. 'It

---

[23] Klaus-Michael Mallman and Martin Cueppers, *Halbmond und Hakenkreuz: Das 'Dritte Reich,' die Araber und Palästina.*

has been reported to me several times,' he noted, 'that Moslems have warned pro-British Christians and Jews here of the fate which awaits them and their women folk "when the Germans come into Persia and drive the Anglo-Russian forces out of the country." Many reports have reached this consulate of Christians and Jews having been threatened by Moslems in this town with death "after the cursed British have been defeated."'[24]

The danger to non-Muslims was well understood in London; on 12 March 1942 the British Ambassador in Teheran, Sir Reader Bullard, was warned by the Foreign Office that the British authorities, military and civil, 'should wherever possible employ Moslem Persians, and should at least not concentrate exclusively on Christians and Jews, Armenians etc, since this tends to rouse Moslem feelings against them.'[25]

One of the most devastating setbacks for Jews in Muslim lands during the Second World War occurred in Iraq. The tragic chain of events began on 31 March 1941, with an anti-British revolt spurred on by the Germans and Italians. Headed by a former Iraqi Prime Minister, Rashid Ali al-Gaylani, the revolt ousted the pro-British Prime Minister, Nuri Said, and seized power in Baghdad. The Regent of Iraq, Abdul Illah, who had been ruling since the death of King Ghazi in 1939, was forced to flee to the British air base at Habbaniya – fifty-five miles west of Baghdad – and was then sent for safety to a British warship in the Persian Gulf.

Britain, being hard pressed by German and Italian forces in North Africa, called on British India to send troops to Basra. Meanwhile, Rashid Ali proceeded to restore the relations between Iraq and Nazi Germany that had been severed by Nuri Said in 1939. One of the leaders of his coup, Yunis al-Sabawi, the new Minister of the Economy and a prominent Iraqi nationalist lawyer, had translated *Mein Kampf* into Arabic. Among the active supporters of Rashid Ali was the Mufti of

---

[24] 'Memorandum,' 20 January 1942: Foreign Office papers, FO 371/75182.
[25] Note of 12 March 1942: Foreign Office papers, FO 371/75182.

Jerusalem, Haj Amin al-Husseini, who at that time was still living in Baghdad with a number of his Palestinian Arab supporters. From Berlin, the previously expelled German Ambassador to Iraq, Fritz Grobba, returned to Baghdad by air and offered Iraq a new era under the patronage of Germany. Rashid Ali promised the Germans vital fuel oil from the Mosul oilfields.

On 18 April 1941 the first British forces from India landed at Basra. By the end of the month, British warplanes from Habbaniyah were bombing Iraqi troop concentrations in Baghdad and Mosul. On May 2, Rashid Ali's troops began a siege of Habbaniya. Four days later, as British troops advanced to Baghdad from Basra, armed Iraqi rioters attacked one of the main Jewish hospitals in Baghdad, the Meir Elias Hospital. The building was looted, the pharmacist shot dead, the hospital accountant gravely wounded, and the doctors and administrative staff taken to prison. After the President of the Jewish community, Chief Rabbi Sasson Khedouri, intervened, the Inspector-General of Police ordered the Jews released and the rioters arrested.[26] But this did not prevent another attack. On the following day, May 7, a number of Arab youths burst into a circumcision ceremony, knives in hand, murdering a young boy and wounding his brother.[27]

In the last week of May, British forces were locked in battle with Rashid Ali outside Baghdad. On the night of May 29, outmatched and outwitted by a far smaller British force – 1,200 soldiers against at least 20,000 – Rashid Ali and the Mufti panicked, and together with the military and civilian leaders of the revolt, they fled under cover of darkness to Iran. Fritz Grobba and the German military mission left Baghdad the next morning.[28] But as soon as they had gone, the pro-Nazi Yunis al-Sabawi appointed himself Military Governor of Baghdad.

At ten in the morning of May 30, with British forces gathering

---

[26] Gourji C. Bekhor, *Fascinating Life and Sensational Death: The Conditions in Iraq Before and After the Six-Day War*, page 89.
[27] Violette Shamash, *Memories of Eden: A Journey Through Jewish Baghdad*, page 188.
[28] Robert Lyman, *Iraq 1941: The Battles for Basra, Habbaniya, Fallujah and Baghdad*, page 84.

outside Baghdad – but reluctant to reveal their weakness in numbers by entering the city – al-Sabawi summoned the Chief Rabbi, Sasson Khedouri, to his office, and ordered him to instruct the Jews to enter their homes and not come out again after noon that day. They had to have their bags packed, one suitcase for each family, and stand by to be taken to detention camps 'for their own safety.' Even as his order was being transmitted, Yunis al-Sabawi is said to have tried to arrange for members of the youth wing of the pro-Nazi *Katayib al-Shabab* militia to mark Jewish houses, shops and stores in red.[29] He also instructed the broadcasting station to issue a call to the Baghdad public to massacre the Jews. The broadcast was to go out at the noon deadline.

Knowing nothing of the imminent broadcast, but fearful of what the deadline meant, Sasson Khedouri asked the community leaders what he should do. They urged him to go to see the Mayor of Baghdad, Arshad al-Umari, a man they knew to be compassionate and fair. As he entered the Mayor's room, Khedouri swept off his rabbinical turban and flung it to the floor, thereby expressing his intense grief; baring one's head in the presence of a Muslim is the ultimate display of desperation. Al-Umari, a suspicious man with fear in his heart, picked up the turban and said to Khedouri, 'Tell me what the matter is.' Khedouri then told the Mayor about the deadline, pleading: 'Don't let them do this terrible thing!' The Mayor handed back the turban and told Khedouri: 'Please, put it back and go home. Tell your people not to worry. I shall take care of everything.'[30]

Al-Umari was as good as his word, taking immediate action by seizing control of the city. Yunis al-Sabawi fled to the Persian border and the inflammatory broadcast was never made. Violette Shamash has described the mood of the Jews on the following day: 'Much to our relief, the radio that Saturday evening reverted to playing Arab songs . . . and at 5.30 p.m. an announcer declared that an armistice had been signed. Half an hour later another bulletin broke the news

---

[29] Gourji C. Bekhor, *Fascinating Life and Sensational Death: The Conditions in Iraq Before and After the Six-Day War*, pages 90-1.
[30] Violette Shamash, *Memories of Eden: A Journey Through Jewish Baghdad*, pages 195-6.

that the Regent would arrive at the airport at ten o'clock the following morning.'[31] The armistice had been signed by the British forces and a Security Commission of leading Iraqis.[32]

Yet the dangers facing the Jewish community were only beginning; the British forces allowed the defeated Iraqi troops to return to their barracks without surrendering their weapons. Stung by their humiliating defeat, and already fuelled with anti-Jewish rage, al-Sabawi's followers decided to act. On June 1 a group of Jews were attacked and stabbed while travelling to the airport to welcome the Regent back to the city. A full-scale pogrom – the *farhud* – began at three o'clock that afternoon.[33]

Demobilised soldiers from Rashid Ali's forces and a few members of a pro-Nazi militia *Katayib al-Shabab* encountered a group of Jews on a bridge and attacked them with knives. One Jew was killed and sixteen wounded, in full view of Iraqi policemen who took no action. One witness recalled: 'In the streets, unsuspecting men had been seized and beaten to death; others had been slaughtered in their looted homes; some had been zealously protected by Arab neighbours.'[34]

The killings spread rapidly. Julian Sofaer, who was not quite seventeen, was told by a passing friend not to venture out because 'they have started to kill Jews.' Moments later, as the same friend reached the end of the street, Sofaer saw people gather around the boy. 'I learned later that he was killed. Another rumour had it that he was injured and taken to hospital where he was killed.' That night, Sofaer remembered, 'there were periods of ominous silence, I assume as victims were surrounded, followed by wild screams as an act of violence was perpetrated. This continued throughout the night.'[35]

---

[31] Violette Shamash, *Memories of Eden: A Journey Through Jewish Baghdad*, page 198.

[32] The Security Commission was headed by a committee that included Amin al-Asima, the chairman of the Iraqi Red Crescent Society.

[33] The word *farhud* means 'violent dispossession.' It is not an Arabic word, but is possibly of Persian origin, or deriving from the Hebrew word *pra'ot* (*hafra'ot*) (disturbances).

[34] Tova Murad Sadka, *No Way Back*, page 45.

[35] Julian Sofaer, letter to the author, 23 February 2009.

The violence found many willing hands: members of the Katayib al-Shabab militia, pro-Nazi students, Palestinian Arab followers of the Mufti, demobilised soldiers and policemen disloyal to the mayor. All participated and fought among themselves for their share of the loot. The victims, meanwhile, feared not only for their families but for their entire community. When a mob broke into the house of Heskel Haddad and he heard his father's cry of 'God save us!' he realised 'that "us" meant more than just a single Jew in jeopardy. This wasn't just another sickening but isolated outrage. The unseen sword hung over all of "us."'[36]

Mordechai Ben-Porat, who was eighteen at the time, has described how the Jewish neighbourhood in Adhamiya, north of Baghdad, was invaded by Muslims 'armed with vicious tools such as axes, knives and all manner of sticks and clubs.' As they approached his home, he could hear very clearly 'their strident voices and calls on Allah to sanction their murder of Jews – "Allahhou Akbar!" (God the Almighty), "Idhbah Al Yahud!" (Slaughter the Jews!) and "'Mal el Yahud – Halal!" (It is permitted to rob the Jews!).'

Ben-Porat and his family barricaded themselves into their home and climbed up to their roof to see what was happening. Ben-Porat later recalled: 'I watched as our "good" Moslem neighbours, living on the opposite side of the street, those to whom mother would offer occasional savoury dishes from her kitchen, participated in the general madness: they guided the raving attackers to our front door.' But at the very moment when the mob reached Ben-Porat's house, the wife of another Muslim neighbour, Colonel Taher Mohammed Aref, stopped them from proceeding. Holding one of her husband's guns and a hand grenade, she 'stood facing the menacing crowd. . . . Her determination and show of arms convinced them of her serious intent and they retreated.' Ben-Porat never forgot this woman's actions: 'It was an act of bravery and left an indelible impression on my mind.'

---

[36] Heskel M. Haddad, 'Shavuot in Baghdad in 1941 (The Farhod),' *Midstream*, May/June 2006.

Ben-Porat's mother, Regina, was attacked on the street by a young Arab 'brandishing a tar-smeared staff,' who hit her on the head several times until she fainted. But again help was at hand: a policeman revived her and then offered to take her home. 'It was yet another instance,' Ben-Porat recalled, 'of a kindly Moslem showing concern for someone not of his faith.'[37] Hundreds of Baghdadi Jews were protected in this way by their Muslim neighbours. Hundreds of others were given refuge in police stations loyal to the Security Commission.

Salim Sasson, a Jew who worked in an agricultural machinery firm in Baghdad, noticed the stark difference in the attitudes of his neighbours during the pre-war years: 'The Muslims sometimes showed us intimacy as if we were brothers and at other times could be hateful.' He had encountered that hatefulness on the day of the *farhud*, while attempting to visit a Jewish neighbour, Abdullah Elias: 'Three armed soldiers ran after me and one of them, wielding a knife, blocked my way. I fought with him and tried to get to Abdullah's door, but it was locked. The three men knocked me down, fired shots over my head, and the man with the knife plunged it into my chest and made a deep cut in my wrists. Then a Muslim woman walking by threw bricks at me in an attempt to finish me off. They left and as I lay helpless on the ground bleeding I looked over and saw that my mother was watching helplessly from our window.'

A taxi driver who was passing by, and who knew Salim Sasson, drove him to the hospital. But as he lay outside the hospital on a stretcher, his troubles resumed: 'Two Muslim workers picked me up and as they carried me inside they decided to have a game of it by throwing me up in the air and catching me and then they laughed while I writhed in pain.' His life was then placed in serious danger when two Iraqi soldiers approached: 'One of them put his bayonet at my throat and spat at me: "You dirty Jew." He then asked his partner, "Shall I finish him off?" His friend replied, "To hell with him. He's

---

[37] Mordechai Ben-Porat, *To Baghdad and Back*, pages 28-9.

already finished."' Salim Sasson was taken into the hospital and survived. While he was there he saw many wounded Jews succumb to their injuries.[38]

On June 2, in an attempt to defuse the volatile situation in Baghdad, the newly returned Regent appointed as Prime Minister Jamil al-Madfai, a man known to be well-disposed towards the Jews. At noon that day, the Regent also ordered the Kurdish division, which had remained loyal, to enter Baghdad and open fire on the rioters. His order was obeyed. The Kurdish soldiers acted with unrestrained zeal, shooting the rioters without mercy and dispersing the mobs. Yunis al-Sabawi and two of his closest collaborators were arrested at the Iranian border, and hanged in Baghdad on the morning of July 20, at the entrance to the Jewish Quarter.

This brought an end to the violence, but the *farhud* marked the beginning of the end of the vibrant life of Iraqi Jewry: 178 Jews had been murdered in Baghdad and nine outside the city. Several Muslims who had tried to come to the defence of their Jewish neighbours were also murdered. Several hundred Jewish women and young girls were raped. More than 240 Jews were orphaned and at least two thousand Jews were badly wounded. In addition, 911 Jewish homes and 586 Jewish-owned shops and stores were looted, as were four ancient synagogues.[39]

Abraham Elkabir, who served in the Iraqi administration for a quarter of a century, later reflected – while living in Israel – on what went wrong between the Muslims and Jews. He traced Muslim hostility to three factors: the Palestine issue, the Mufti of Jerusalem's campaign in Iraq identifying Jews and Zionists, and the 'anti-Semitic tendencies' of the British officials and other Westerners in Iraq. He recalled a speech by Dorothy Thompson, Secretary of the American Friends of the Middle East, to an audience of the women's branch of the Iraqi Red Crescent Society: 'She warned the Arabs to beware of

[38] Tamar Morad, Dennis Shasha and Robert Shasha (editors), *Iraq's Last Jews*, pages 34-40.
[39] Gourji C. Bekhor, *Fascinating Life and Sensational Death: The Conditions in Iraq Before and After the Six-Day War*, pages 92-3.

the Jews.' The Hitler regime in Germany had also given 'an addi-
tional and greater stimulus to the embryonic anti-Jewish movement.'
The striking German military successes in the early stage of the war,
the formidable German propaganda machine led by the Mufti and
assisted by the Iraqi pro-Nazi broadcaster Younis Bahri, and the savage attacks of the *farhud* all 'had a tremendous effect on the population already infected by the anti-Semitic virus.'

Elkabir also commented on a social divide between many Jews
and Muslims in Baghdad. The 'beautiful villas' of the Jews 'were photographed and published in the proximity of some miserable looking Arab huts. Well-dressed beautiful Jewish ladies were a striking
contrast to the then-veiled Muslim women and the bare-footed Arab
female milk sellers. . . . For every two Muslims walking along Rasheed
Street, the great artery of Baghdad, you would certainly find a well-
dressed Jewish passer-by.' Envy and frustration, Elkabir noted, 'prevented people's looks from taking account the Jewish dwellers of the
slums and the wealth of Arab politicians and nouveaux riches.' The
large number of Jews in higher education had likewise become a
cause of envy.[40]

Other observers confirmed the persistence of that bitter divide.
In November 1942 one of the leading Arab experts in the Jewish
Agency, Eliahu Epstein (who later took the surname Elath), went to
see the British Ambassador to Iraq, Sir Kinahan Cornwallis, who was
then in Jerusalem. Epstein asked Cornwallis to use his influence to
persuade the Iraqi authorities to allow seven hundred Polish Jewish
orphans, then waiting in Teheran, to cross through Iraq to Palestine.
The orphans had the necessary British entry permits to Palestine,
but the Ambassador declined. He told Epstein that 'to those Iraqis
who objected to Jewish immigration into Palestine, age made no difference, since "a little Jew is bound to become an adult."'[41]

---

[40] Abraham Elkabir, manuscript notes, quoted in Peter Wien, *Iraqi Arab
Nationalism*, pages 49-50.
[41] Report of 11 November 1942: Central Zionist Archives, Z4/14797.

Such ill-feeling was evident to Iraqi Jews. Among those who left Iraq immediately after the *farhud* were Julian Sofaer, his mother and his sister. They spent three days in the passport office, filling out forms and getting them stamped. When their passports were refused, Sofaer returned with his grandfather, Abraham Haim, a former representative for Iraq at the League of Nations. He later recalled his grandfather's outrage: 'He proceeded to give them a dressing down and asked: "do you think that you can hold your heads up among nations when you rob, rape women and kill innocent people as you have?" On being told that this was perpetrated by the mob, he replied that it was perpetrated by the police, the army, the students and the mob. . . . He was requested to calm down, offered coffee and cigarettes, and the final form was stamped. We got our passports.' For Julian Sofaer, the *farhud* then became 'a tragedy which turned out to be a blessing in disguise – it got us out of that dreadful country and away from its destructive, treacherous and savage people.'[42]

Slowly and cautiously, the Jews who did not leave Iraq in the wake of the *farhud* began to rebuild their lives, repair their damaged properties and create an even wider network of medical facilities, schools and cultural activities. But their community was divided. The intellectuals, professionals and leading merchants were confident that, as loyal Iraqi citizens, they could return to their privileged status of the pre-war years, and participate fully in Iraqi life. A second group, the Jewish Communists, looked to revolutionary socialism as the way forward; the Soviet Union under Stalin was then part of the Grand Alliance fighting Nazi Germany. A third group, the Zionists, were convinced that the only way forward was emigration to Palestine,

---

[42] Sofaer continued: 'Am I being unfair? Possibly, but please remember: when the Egyptians threw out their King, they put him on his yacht and told him to go away. In 1958 the Iraqis murdered the entire royal family, including those who attended them, and dragged the mutilated body of the Regent in the streets of their capital.' Julian Sofaer, letter to the author, 23 February 2009.

where half a million Jews – although still without statehood – already had their national institutions, and were actively participating in the Allied war effort.

Many Jews wished to leave Iraq but had yet to find the means to do so. Salim Sasson eventually emigrated a year after the terrible events of the *farhud*. He obtained a permit to enter the United States and travelled with his mother by flying boat to Palestine, then by air via Egypt, Sudan, Liberia and Brazil to New York. Three months after reaching the United States, Sasson was drafted into the United States Army. He won the Bronze Star serving in Europe, fighting against the Germans.[43]

In March 1942, Shaul Avigur, the head of the Jewish Agency's clandestine immigration project – 'Aliyah Bet' (Immigration B) – travelled from Tel Aviv to Baghdad in a British Army transport unit. There he witnessed at first-hand the plight that the Iraqi Jews faced, fearing as they did a repetition of the June pogrom nine months earlier. Avigur returned to Tel Aviv convinced that there would be a mass emigration from Iraq. He reported to the head of the Jewish Agency, David Ben-Gurion, that there was 'an urgent need to help the Jews in Baghdad.'[44]

Shaul Avigur's conviction was reinforced in unequivocal terms by another Jewish emissary from Palestine, Enzo Sereni. After spending ten months undercover in Iraq, Sereni came to understand the monumental impact of the *farhud*; he described it in a letter to Avigur in Tel Aviv. 'In the course of these two days in June 1941,' he wrote, 'the dream of Arab assimilation was shattered, and the belief of the Jews that they could live normal lives in the Iraqi Diaspora came to an end. The desire to flee grew. Had all the roads not been closed, had some door been open – all of Iraq Jewry would have fled, even those who for many years had believed in and avowed their Iraqi loyalty.'

---

[43] Tamar Morad, Dennis Shasha and Robert Shasha (editors), *Iraq's Last Jews*, page 41.
[44] Quoted in Tad Szulc, *The Secret Alliance*, page 206.

Sereni concluded: 'For many, particularly the youth or those who had been affiliated in the past with the Hebrew or Zionist movement, Palestine now seemed the sole and complete answer.'[45]

---

[45] Letter of 3 February 1943, Central Zionist Archive, quoted in Moshe Gat, *The Jewish Exodus from Iraq, 1948-1951*, pages 21-2. On his return to Palestine from Iraq, Enzo Sereni, who until 1939 had taken a major part in the clandestine emigration of Jews from Nazi Germany, volunteered for special service with British Intelligence. Parachuted into northern Italy on 15 May 1944, he was captured almost immediately. On 18 November 1944 he was executed in Dachau concentration camp.

13

TOWARDS LIBERATION, AND AN UNCERTAIN FUTURE

'Under pressure of a new nationalism'

In November 1942, as German troops were driven out of Egypt, an Anglo-American force landed in North Africa as part of an Allied invasion plan. Making a major contribution to the success of that plan was a five-hundred-strong Algerian Jewish Resistance group. The group was headed by José Aboulker, who had organised an uprising that paralyzed Vichy French communications and captured strategic points in Algiers on the eve of the Allied landings.

In the immediate aftermath of the North African landings, local Muslims took advantage of the chaos that followed by turning on the Jews, who for two and a half years had already suffered under the severity of Vichy discrimination. A Moroccan Jew, Maurice Marrachi, set out a long list of Muslim 'abuses of power' in letters to American and British authorities. His list included the burglary of Jewish homes, extortion of money and, in a coy allusion to rape, 'passing the night in the company of the mistress of the house.'[1]

A British journalist, Philip Jordan, described similar crimes after he entered the Tunisian town of Gafsa with the Allied troops a few hours after the town had been abandoned by the Germans. 'All the Jews in the town,' he wrote in his diary, 'have been pillaged by the Arabs acting under German encouragement. Even the doors and windows have been stolen. It is horrible.'[2] According to the German

---

[1] Letters of 20 December 1942 (to the American authorities) and 19 February 1943 (to the British authorities): National Archives (Kew), Foreign Office papers, FO 443/43.

[2] Philip Jordan, *Jordan's Tunis Diary*, page 208.

military archives, it was Italian soldiers who had encouraged the Arabs to loot the Jewish homes and shops. The German military police, having confiscated the loot, gave it to a local Arab charity.[3]

Angered at the Jewish relief and delight at the Allied liberation, Arab troops who had been part of the Vichy forces locked the gates of the Jewish Quarter in Rabat, making thousands of Jews prisoners.[4] At the same time, following the Allied liberation of French North Africa, the Free French Forces (*Forces Françaises Libres,* the FFL) kept the Vichy laws against the Jews on the statute book. On learning of this during a visit to Algiers early in 1943, Winston Churchill insisted that the laws be repealed. It was not a moment too soon. Particular hostility had been shown towards those Jews who had enabled the Allies to come ashore. Bernard Karsenty, one of the members of the Jewish Resistance group that had received the American commander of the land forces, General Mark Clark, on a secret visit before the November 1942 landings, was forced to flee the country. The brothers Lucian and José Chich, who had also helped the Allies, were threatened. Seven Jews were imprisoned.[5]

Other persecutions by local Muslim rulers continued. On 27 April 1943 the United States Vice Consul in Casablanca reported that 'it seems indubitable that there is a systematic persecution of the Jews by the Pasha of Beni-Mellal.' Jews had been expelled from their homes and shops for up to a week, and 'arbitrary economic measures' had been directed against them, including a ban on any Jewish trade in vegetables or poultry. There had also been random arrests and beatings. Britiz ben Shalom Elfassy was beaten and imprisoned for asking an Arab to pay for the rental of a bicycle. David Cohen, who was half-blind, was sentenced to six weeks in prison for not saluting a Muslim official.[6]

---

[3] Military Archives (Freiburg), RH-26-90, Afrika Division, File N. 61: quoted in Robert Satloff, *Among the Righteous*, page 218, note 52.
[4] Michel Abitbol, *The Jews of North Africa During the Second World War*, pages 145-6.
[5] Letter of Colette Aboulker (José Aboulker's sister), submitted to the British Foreign Office, 16 January 1943: Foreign Office papers, FO 371/36244.
[6] Philip H. Bagby, American Vice Consul, Report of 27 April 1943, 'Persecution of Jews at Beni Mellal': United States National Archives, Record Group 84/Entry 2998/Box 1.

Six months later, Jews were attacked in Fez. The British consul in Rabat reported to London soon afterward that 'a fairly serious riot' had occurred in Fez, 'originating I am told in an attempt by young Moors to molest a young Jew's girlfriend . . .'[7]

While the persecution of Jews continued, so did Jewish efforts to immigrate to Palestine. In 1943, Jews reached Palestine after fleeing from Yemen. The following year, Jews escaped illegally from Afghanistan and travelled both to Iran and to India before they too reached Palestine. Egypt refused to issue transit visas to allow Jews to travel overland through Cairo. From Libya, Jews were able to make their way legally to Palestine in 1944, when the British Mandate authority issued them twenty Palestine certificates. The first group of Libyan Jewish immigrants went to a kibbutz.

Encouraged by the successful emigration of their fellow Jews, Libyan Jewish youngsters enrolled in Zionist agricultural training to prepare for life in Palestine. Two Zionist youth clubs, Ben Yehuda and Maccabi, which had been closed by the Italians, were reopened. Two farms were established in Libya where young Libyan Jews underwent training for eventual farming life in Palestine. One of the farms was at Colonia Vardia, six miles outside Tripoli, the other in Zawia, twenty-five miles from Tripoli. Jewish history, the history of Zionism and modern Hebrew were taught in the Jewish schools in Tripoli and Benghazi.[8]

A few months after the first twenty Palestine certificates were issued in Tripoli, Libyan Jews were allocated another twenty; twelve went to Zionist agricultural pioneers. Britain proceeded to allow a steady wave of Libyan Jews to leave for Palestine.[9]

In many Muslim lands, the conditions that had prompted Jewish migration to Palestine remained unchanged as the Second World War came to an end. A report from the British Embassy in Kabul,

[7] Letter of 26 October 1943: Foreign Office papers, FO 443/43.
[8] Maurice M. Roumani, *The Jews of Libya*, pages 43-4.
[9] Renzo De Felice, *Jews in an Arab Land: Libya, 1835-1970*, page 364, notes 11 and 12.

sent to London on 29 December 1944, described the 3,350 Jews of Afghanistan as 'on the whole poor and of indifferent quality.' Jealousy at Jewish trading success, especially in karakul wool, had led to their expulsion from Andkhoi and Mazar-i-Sharif in 1934. A successful Jewish trading firm in Herat, with representatives in Kandahar, was being forced to sell half its shares each year to the Afghan National Bank. Some two hundred Jews had applied to emigrate, but, the British Embassy reported, 'it is doubtful if they will be able to find any countries willing to welcome them as immigrants.'[10]

The situation of Jews in all Muslim lands quickly worsened. A new and disastrous turning point came on 22 March 1945, with the formation of the Arab League in Cairo. The League's first resolutions included a restriction on Egyptian Muslim contact with those who were called 'supporters of Zionism,' that is, all Egyptian Jews. In the months that followed, anti-Zionist incitement and anti-Jewish violence spread throughout the Arab world. On 2 October 1945 the main Arab newspaper in the Libyan city of Tripoli published a startling account of a meeting in Damascus between Muslim religious leaders. These leaders had spoken of rumours about a United Nations plan to partition Palestine between Arabs and Jews, and according to the newspaper had declared that 'news of this sort aroused their scorn and led them to support any action aimed at eliminating the Jews from Arab countries.'[11]

The Muslim world, inspired by Arab nationalism but inflamed by Jewish nationalism, still considered Palestine as an Arab country and part of the Muslim patrimony, in which Jews could live only as a subject people. Further anti-Jewish riots broke out in Egypt on 2 November 1945 and continued on the following day. The British Embassy in Cairo sent two accounts to London of the information it had received from the Egyptian Director-General of Public Security. A 'crowd of roughs' had looted the shops of two Jewish-owned firms and a synagogue had been set on fire. The demonstrations in both

---

[10] 'Note on the Jews in Afghanistan,' letter from G.F. Squire to Anthony Eden, 29 December 1944: Foreign Office papers, FO 371/45207.

[11] Renzo De Felice, *Jews in an Arab Land: Libya, 1835-1970*, page 365, note 16.

Alexandria and Cairo had 'all been anti-Jewish and definitely not anti-British.' Five people had been killed and two hundred injured.[12]

The President of the Jewish community in Egypt, Salvator Cicurel, one of Egypt's pre-war sporting legends and the head of the Egyptian Chamber of Commerce, did his utmost to preserve the normalcy of Jewish life.[13] It was a hard task. The Mufti of Jerusalem, Haj Amin al-Husseini, arrived in Egypt after fleeing in 1945 from France, where he was wanted as a war criminal, and wasted no time in stirring up anti-Zionist sentiment. Legislation against Jews proliferated. An Egyptian Companies Law, promulgated on 29 July 1947, insisted that seventy-five per cent of all employees in enterprises must be Egyptian. As eighty per cent of Egyptian Jews had held foreign passports for many generations, this new law was a blow and a setback.

Egypt was not the only country to be affected by the wave of anti-Zionist and anti-Jewish feeling. Starting on November 4 and continuing for four days, there were anti-Jewish riots in Tripoli and in six other Libyan towns. The violence was intensified by two particularly inflammatory false rumours: that the Grand Cadi and the Mufti of Tripoli had both been murdered, and that the Jews had set fire to the Sharia court. The *New York Times* was emphatic, however, that the 'thirst for blood was greater than the thirst for loot or revenge.'[14]

The only deliberate acts of arson were committed against the Jews. During the riots, ten synagogues were looted and burned. In areas with mixed Arab and Jewish populations, the doors and shops of non-Jews had been marked in advance with special signs. On the first evening, the *New York Times* reported four days later, attacks that were 'premeditated and coldly murderous' were carried out by

---

[12] Telegrams of 2 and 3 November 1945: Foreign Office papers, FO 371/45394.
[13] Salvator Cicurel's niece was married to Pierre Mendès-France, a future Prime Minister of France.
[14] Clifton Daniel, 'Tripoli Riots are Laid to Poverty; Looting Stirred Many Arab Attacks, At Height of Attacks on Jews, Some Slayings were Result of Lust for Blood, British Seek Sources of False Rumors,' *New York Times*, 14 November 1945.

'individual Arabs' and small gangs who broke into Jewish homes and shops.[15] It was also reported that one Jew confronted the mob at his door with a meat cleaver, but the weapon was taken from his hand and used to cut open his chest.[16]

On the evening of November 5, as the attacks continued, the British authorities, who had been in control of Libya since the defeat of the German-Italian forces there in 1943, imposed a curfew. Despite this, on the morning of November 6, large-scale Arab attacks and looting were carried out against Jewish homes and businesses in the city. The nature of the killings was described by a Jewish eye-witness: 'In order to carry out the slaughter, the attackers used various weapons: knives, daggers, sticks, clubs, iron bars, revolvers, and even hand-grenades. Generally, the victim was first struck on the head with a solid, blunt instrument and, after being knocked down, was finished off with a knife, dagger, or, in some cases, by having his throat cut.'[17]

That night, the killing of Jews spread east of Tripoli to the towns of Zawia and Zanzur. In Zanzur, 40 of the 120 Jews of the town were murdered. In Zanzur and Amrus, according to one eyewitness, 'after having killed or injured their victims, the attackers poured benzine or petroleum over them and set them on fire, and ultimately those killed were so charred as to be unrecognizable. Grenades were used especially at Amrus against the synagogues as well as the houses. On some of the bodies signs of unimaginable cruelty could be discerned.'[18]

The Jewish leaders in Tripoli appealed to the British to send troops who would halt the attacks. After a forty-eight-hour delay, the British military commander took decisive steps: a State of Emergency was proclaimed; crowds carrying sticks or other offensive weapons were forbidden to gather; and British soldiers began patrolling the streets, searching passersby and entering Arab houses. On November 7 the

---

[15] Clifton Daniel, '74 Tripolitanian Jews Slain in Arab Riots,' *New York Times*, 8 November 1945.

[16] Clifton Daniel, 'Tripoli Riots are Laid to Poverty; Looting Stirred Many Arab Attacks, At Height of Attacks on Jews, Some Slayings Were Result of Lust for Blood, British Seek Sources of False Rumors,' *New York Times*, 14 November 1945.

[17] 'Anti-Jewish Riots in Tripolitania,' Central Zionist Archives, S/25/6457.

[18] 'Anti-Jewish Riots in Tripolitania,' Central Zionist Archives, S/25/6457.

British began arresting Arabs accused of attacking Jews and plunder-
ing Jewish homes. At Beni Ulid, the British evacuated the Jews from
their Quarter as the attackers gathered for a final assault. In several
other towns, the British surrounded the Jewish Quarters with a protective guard. Jewish self-defence was also effective in keeping the Arab
attackers out of the Jewish Quarter of Tripoli – the Hara – where several thousand Jews from other parts of the city had taken refuge.

A total of 129 Libyan Jews were killed during the four days of
attacks. One Arab lost his life during an attack on the Jewish Quarter.
Twenty Jewish women were widowed and ninety-three children
orphaned. In Tripoli alone, 150 Jews were seriously injured. In
Misurata (Kussabat), many women and girls were raped, and then,
in order to save their lives, were forced to denounce Judaism and
embrace Islam. In the destruction of shops, an estimated 4,200
Jewish traders and artisans were made destitute. More than four
thousand Jews fled their homes and took refuge in camps set up by
the British Military Administration, where more than ten thousand
were being fed each day during the first week after the attacks.

During the Libyan pogrom, there were many instances of Muslims
showing kindness and courage. On November 11 the Libyan Jewish
newspaper *Settimana Israelitica* reported that 'many Arabs' had risked
their lives by saving Jews from the attackers by offering refuge in
their homes.[19]

In the weeks following the attacks, efforts were made by the
Muslim leadership to distance itself from the rioters and to build
bridges with the Jewish community. On November 12 the Mufti of
Tripolitania, Mohammed Abdul Assaad el-Alem, issued a *fatwa* order-
ing believers to return what had been stolen from the Jews.[20] On
November 27, encouraged by the British, a meeting was held in the
British Military Administration hall in Tripoli between leading mem-
bers of the Arab and Jewish communities. An Arab-Jewish Committee

---

[19] Maurice M. Roumani, *The Jews of Libya*, page 49.
[20] Renzo De Felice, *Jews in an Arab Land: Libya, 1835-1970*, page 369, note 26.

for Co-operation and Reconstruction was established, under two senior community leaders, the Muslim Cadi, Sheikh Mahmud Burchis, and the Jewish leader Halfalla Nahum. 'All wise and sensible people on both sides,' said the Cadi, 'condemn such acts in the most absolute terms and desire only tranquility and peace.' In reply, Halfalla Nahum stressed the need for 'rebuilding mutual trust between the Arab and Jewish communities.'[21]

These were fine words, but the British Military Administration remained sceptical, writing in its annual report for 1945: 'Leading Arab personalities severely censured this shameful aggression. But no general, deep-felt sense of guilt seems to animate the Arab community at large: nor has it been too active in offering help to the victims.' This British report also referred to a new element in the relations between the Jews and Arabs of Libya: the 'self-assertiveness' of Libyan Jewish Zionists. 'The growth of Zionism,' the report concluded, 'must be considered one of the motives behind the anti-Jewish riots.'[22]

Zionism had indeed made progress among the Jews of Libya, helped by the wartime presence of soldiers from the Palestine-recruited Jewish Brigade. The imminent prospect of a National Home had given the Jews a sense of pride and a hope for a secure future. Jews would no longer have to put up with being second-class citizens, but that was how the Muslims among whom they lived considered them: the eternal, born *dhimmis*, subject to one form or other of the Covenant of Omar.

The British report was also correct in noting that Zionism had been a cause of the riots. Two of the premises damaged in the Tripoli riots were the head office of the Maccabi Club and the clubhouse at the Maccabi sports field, whose football, basketball, tennis and swimming facilities were a centre of the sporting activity of Zionist youth. Also damaged was the Zionist youth training farm outside Tripoli.[23]

---

[21] Renzo De Felice, *Jews in an Arab Land: Libya, 1835-1970*, pages 192-206.
[22] British Military Administration, Tripolitania, *Annual Report, 1945*, pages 11 and 13.
[23] It later emerged that on the morning of November 4, the British security officer for Tripolitania had been warned that an anti-Jewish demonstration supporting the rights of Palestinian Arabs was being planned. 'The Arab Anti-Jewish Riots in Tripolitania, 4-7 November, 1945,' Central Zionist Archives, S/25/10.165.

On November 4 news had been published in the local Tripoli news-paper, *Tarabulus el Gharb*, of anti-Jewish and anti-Zionist demonstra-tions in Syria, Lebanon and Egypt; this served to fan the flames of the existing anti-Jewish feeling.

In the immediate aftermath of the Second Word War, the Jews in Palestine were determined to bring an end to British rule. At the same time, the independent Muslim States of Egypt and Iraq put pressure on their own Jewish populations to denounce Zionism, and to renounce all solidarity with Jews in British Mandate Palestine.

The Jews in Palestine were facing local Arab attacks on an increas-ingly bloody scale. But despite the growing violence, Jews from Muslim lands, in common with Jewish survivors from the Holocaust in Europe, made enormous efforts to reach Palestine. There were risks and obsta-cles in every attempt. On 8 October 1945 the Palestinian Jewish news-paper *Davar* published a report on fifty Iraqi Jews who had just crossed the border from Lebanon without permits. At seven in the morning, 'two British officers from the Transjordan Frontier Force saw a group of about fifty Jews near Kfar Giladi. When they were about to investi-gate the matter, they were pushed aside by members of the Kibbutz who had absorbed the group into their settlement.' Undeterred, the British surrounded the kibbutz. At three in the afternoon there was shooting, and eight kibbutzniks were wounded. The British withdrew and the Iraqi Jews were safe.[24]

In Aden, as a result of radio broadcasts and the prevalence of loudspeakers in cafés, the illiterate among the Arab population had, in the words of an official British Government report, 'begun to take an interest in outside affairs . . . and in particular events connected with Palestine.' News was reported 'of Arab lorries being driven at Jews walking in the desert.' In one such incident, a Jew was killed.[25]

In March 1946 the head of the Jewish Agency, Dr. Chaim Weizmann, was questioned by the Anglo-American Committee of

<hr />

[24] Mordechai Ben-Porat, *To Baghdad and Back*, page 39.
[25] *Report on the Commission of Enquiry into the Disturbances in Aden in December, 1947*, paragraphs 30 and 32.

Enquiry 'regarding the problems of European Jewry and Palestine.' In the course of his presentation, Weizmann spoke of the Jews under Muslim rule, telling the committee: 'There are pogroms in Baghdad, Tripoli and even Cairo.' He acknowledged that previously 'the Muslim world has treated the Jews with great tolerance,' but he added that the Jews 'must not close our eyes to the fact that this greater humanitarian tradition is under pressure of a new nationalism.'[26]

---

[26] Evidence taken by the 'Anglo-American Committee of Enquiry regarding the problems of European Jewry and Palestine,' Weizmann Archive.

14

THE UNITED NATIONS PALESTINE PARTITION RESOLUTION

'There is nothing in our religion that says we should protect the Jews'

On 24 November 1947 the Political Committee of the United Nations General Assembly debated Resolution 181: the proposed partition of Palestine into two independent States, one Jewish and one Arab. The Jewish State would be in the areas predominantly lived in by Jews. The Arab State would be in areas predominantly lived in by Arabs.

During the debate, the chairman of the Egyptian delegation, Dr. Muhammad Hussein Heykal Pasha, warned the committee that 'the lives of one million Jews in Moslem countries would be jeopardized by Partition.' The partition of Palestine, he believed, 'might create anti-Semitism in those countries even more difficult to root out than the anti-Semitism which the Allies tried to eradicate in Germany.' If the United Nations voted to partition Palestine, Heykal Pasha cautioned, 'it might be responsible for very grave disorders and for the massacre of the large number of Jews.'

Heykal Pasha continued by arguing that a million Jews were living 'in peace' in Egypt and other Muslim states, enjoying 'all rights of citizenship.' He insisted that these Jews had 'no desire to emigrate to Palestine.' But he added: 'If a Jewish State were established, nobody could prevent disorders. Riots would break out in Palestine, would spread through all the Arab States, and might lead to a war between two races.'

The representative of the Palestinian Arab Higher Committee, Jamal al-Husseini, was equally threatening. 'It must be remembered, by the way,' he told the committee, 'that there are as many Jews in the Arab world as there are in Palestine whose positions, under such conditions' – following Partition – 'will become very precarious, even though the Arab States may do their best to save their skins.' Governments 'in general,' he added, 'have always been unable to prevent mob excitement and violence.'[1]

Five days after these dire warnings, on 29 November 1947, the United Nations General Assembly adopted Resolution 181: the establishment of two States in a partitioned Palestine, one Jewish and the other Arab. As with the British plan in 1937, Jerusalem, Bethlehem and a corridor to the sea were to be excluded from both States, and would be 'established as a *corpus separatum* under a special international regime and shall be administered by the United Nations.'[2]

From the moment of the promulgation of the United Nations Partition Resolution, pressure against the Jews living in Muslim lands intensified. It was fuelled by refusal of the Arab States to grant international legality to a Jewish State, and also by the rising anti-Jewish violence inside Palestine. This violence was stimulated by outside Arab propaganda and military intervention, even while the British Mandate was still in place. Although the United Nations resolution offered an Arab State as well as a Jewish one, the Arabs of Palestine rejected their own statehood; encouraged by the existing Arab States, they demanded sovereignty in all of Palestine, not in a partitioned country.

In Aden, then under British rule, a Muslim mob attacked the Jewish Quarter in the Crater district on the evening of 2 December 1947. Both in the Crater district and in the town of Sheikh Othman, six miles inland from Aden, Arab rioters – many marching under banners proclaiming 'Long Live Palestine' – set fire to Jewish shops and homes, and attacked Jews wherever they could find them. One

---

[1] Quoted in: Frank S. Adams, 'Arabs and Zionists Warn of Fighting: In Final Appeals to UN, Each Pledges War to Finish if Turned Down on Palestine,' *New York Times*, 25 November 1947.
[2] United Nations Resolution 181: United Nations Documentation Centre, reference A/RES/181 (II)/(A + B).

victim was Salam ben Yichye Terem, whose family owned a sewing business. He had just left his home in Sheikh Othman and was returning to get something when he was set upon by ten Arabs, who beat him up and then threw him off the top of a building. He fell to his death. 'He was known as a very good singer,' his great-niece later recalled, 'and had many friends.'[3]

The violence in Aden continued for three more days, as the British struggled to restore order by resorting to rifle and machine-gun fire, tear gas and armoured cars. In the afternoon of December 3, an attempt was made by a British Royal Air Force officer, Wing Commander Donald Pocock, to rescue Jews who were in danger from fire in a burning house. The British official enquiry related that, together with 'a leading Jew named Armando,' Pocock formed a protective cordon with British troops and Arab troops of the Aden Protectorate Levies. The Aden Protectorate troops turned against those they were meant to be defending. 'About twelve people came out of the house. As they came into the cordon there was a burst of fire, and a girl and a man within two feet of her were shot dead.'[4] This was one of several occasions when the Aden Protectorate Levies, who 'did not like to shoot their own people,' shot and killed Jews instead.[5]

By the time the British had quelled the Aden riots, eighty-two Jews had been killed. Of 170 Jewish-owned shops, 106 had been destroyed. Hundreds of Jewish houses, as well as the synagogue and the Jewish schools, were burned to the ground. Thirty-eight Arab rioters and an Arab member of the Levies were also killed in the Levies' clashes with the rioters.[6] Selim Benin, President of the Jewish community and

---

[3] Tammy Kovler, letter to the author, 20 July 2009.
[4] *Report on the Commission of Enquiry into the Disturbances in Aden in December, 1947,* paragraph 104.
[5] Selim Benin, Chairman of the Jewish Emergency Committee, told the British enquiry of another such incident. As he and his family tried to escape from their own house, which was on fire, to the house next door, his father-in-law 'was shot dead by Levies.' *Report on the Commission of Enquiry into the Disturbances in Aden in December, 1947,* paragraph 94.
[6] *Report on the Commission of Enquiry into the Disturbances in Aden in December, 1947,* paragraphs 229 and 232.

Chairman of the Jewish Emergency Committee, later told the British commission of enquiry: 'We never expected such things to happen – we were all the time living friendly with the Arabs.'[7]

Some 650 Aden Jews sought damages for the loss of their property. From London, the Central British Fund for Relief and Rehabilitation sent a British Jew, Arthur Diamond, to help them in their claims. Diamond wrote a full report of his seven-week experience. The families of the Jewish Adenites, he noted, 'have been resident for at least a thousand years.' Referring to the majority of the Aden Jews, he explained that 'whatever they possessed was in the form of stock in their shops, household goods, and buildings if they owned them, and it was possible, therefore, for a man wealthy by local standards to find himself possessed of nothing but a nightshirt if his house and shop were burned down.'[8]

When the future President of Israel, Itzhak Ben-Zvi, visited the Jewish Quarter of Aden three years later, he noted in his diary: 'Numerous half demolished buildings, including the school building, which was destroyed in the riots of 1947, immediately strike the visitor's eye: the marks of devastation and destruction are too striking to be ignored.' Among the buildings that had been 'gravely damaged' was the synagogue that stood at the entrance to the Jewish Quarter. Selim Benin showed Ben-Zvi 'the traces of the bullets that hit his residence, when his own father was killed.'[9]

Also in December 1947, anti-Jewish violence erupted in the Syrian city of Aleppo, where there had been a Jewish presence for eight hundred years, since the Twelfth Century.[10] All eighteen synagogues in the city were destroyed, as well as five Jewish schools and the Jewish

---

[7] *Report on the Commission of Enquiry into the Disturbances in Aden in December, 1947,* paragraph 51.

[8] Arthur Sigismund Diamond, 27 April 1948: quoted in full in Norman A. Stillman, *Jews of Arab Lands in Modern Times,* pages 500-3.

[9] Itzhak Ben-Zvi was then head of the Jerusalem-based Institute for the Study of Oriental Communities in the Middle East. 'Aden Diary,' in Itzhak Ben-Zvi, *The Exiled and the Redeemed,* page 277. In fact, it was Benin's father-in-law who was killed.

[10] Elie Kedourie, *Democracy and Arab Political Culture,* page 37.

orphanage and youth club.[11] The Syrian authorities – in their second year of independence from France – legitimised the violence with edicts that denied Jewish citizens the civil protection granted to other Syrians. As many as six thousand of Aleppo's seven thousand Jews fled the city. Some crossed the border southward into Lebanon, where they settled; others made their way to Palestine, or to Europe and the United States.[12]

On 2 December 1947, in Cairo, the Muslim Brotherhood newspaper *al-Ikhwan al-Muslimun* ('The Muslim Brotherhood') published a demand by the Arab League that the Jewish residents of all 'Arab territory' contribute money to the Arab armies. The catalyst for this demand was a report that a senior official of the Jewish Agency, in a speech in Tel Aviv, had stated that the Jews of Egypt had contributed ten million Egyptian pounds to the new Jewish State. In response to this speech, the leader of the Muslim Brotherhood, Hassan al-Banna, urged the Jewish citizens of Egypt to prove their loyalty to Egypt by opposing Zionism. The Arab League commented in its newspaper: 'We did not expect that they would do exactly the opposite thing and give their money, Egypt's money, to the Zionists.'[13]

Three days later, on December 5, an angry mob converged on the Jewish Quarter in Cairo, determined to wreak havoc. The Egyptian Government, itself afraid of being challenged by the Muslim Brotherhood, declared a state of emergency and banned all public demonstrations.[14] But much damage had already been done. Edna Anzarut, a young girl at the time, later recalled how the riots 'were terrifying, and would start in a flash.' She remembered 'hearing the scream of the mob when I was at school, and realizing that it was not safe to go home, as no one knew where the riots would spill over.' She also

[11] Siegfried Landshut, *Jewish Communities in the Muslim Countries of the Middle East*, pages 59-60.

[12] Hayyim J. Cohen, 'Aleppo': *Encyclopaedia Judaica*, Volume 2, columns 562-5.

[13] Report of 20 December 1947 from Jefferson Patterson, American Embassy, Cairo, to the Secretary of State, Washington: quoted in Norman A. Stillman, *Jews of Arab Lands in Modern Times*, page 505.

[14] Norman A. Stillman, *Jews of Arab Lands in Modern Times*, page 147.

recalled that when her mother's office boy, a Muslim, collected her from school, he would 'carry me on his shoulders and face the angry crowds – yelling at them that I was his daughter.'[15]

The street demonstrations eventually subsided, but newspaper incitement continued. So too did radio propaganda, broadcast to Egypt from a Palestinian Arab radio station near Jerusalem. On December 7 the station issued a warning to all Jews living in Arab countries: 'In spite of statements and declarations in which they denounce Zionism, the Arab League countries may yet ask them to define their attitude once and for all towards Zionism.' A week later, on December 14, the Muslim Brotherhood's newspaper declared: 'We have great traditions, but there is nothing in our religion that says we should protect the Jews and forfeit our liberty and dignity.'[16] The Brotherhood also called for the reintroduction of the *dhimmi* laws, which had been repealed by Egypt's Mohammad Ali dynasty a century earlier, allowing both Egyptian society and Egyptian Jewry to flourish.[17]

Even the tiny island kingdom of Bahrain, then under British protection, was the scene of violent attacks on the Jews. The representative of the British Government in Bahrain – the British Resident, Charles Belgrave – recalled in his memoirs that the Jews there 'were quiet, law-abiding, timorous people and in the past there had been no friction between them and the Moslems.' He described Jewish life in Bahrain as modest and peaceful: 'For many years there was a Jewish member on the Manama Municipal Council. They owned a few shops in which they sold piece goods, several of them were moneychangers and a few of the young men were employed as clerks in an office. Many of the Jewish women acted as

---

[15] Edna Turner (née Anzarut), letter to the author, 18 April 2009.
[16] Report of 20 December 1947 from Jefferson Patterson, American Embassy, Cairo, to the Secretary of State, Washington: quoted in Norman A. Stillman, *Jews of Arab Lands in Modern Times*, pages 507-8.
[17] Ada Aharoni, Aimée Israel-Pelletier, Levana Zamir (editors), *History and Culture of the Jews from Egypt in Modern Times*, page 139.

hawkers, taking goods for sale to the Arab ladies.' Although 'two or three of the Jews were prosperous merchants they were not a rich community and some of them, especially the Persian Jews, lived a hand-to-mouth existence.'[18]

That settled existence was cruelly interrupted when a riot broke out in the capital Manama. Beginning on December 5, Jewish shops and homes were looted, the synagogue destroyed and many Jews attacked and beaten up. During the riot, Belgrave, his British police driver and a British police officer fought off a mob that attacked a Jewish family who lived above their shop in the bazaar. Visiting Jewish homes after the police had quelled the riot, Belgrave was shocked to see that the houses 'had been stripped of their contents, and what could not be removed had been smashed.'[19] When the synagogue was desecrated, the Torah Scrolls were stolen.[20] 'Miraculously,' writes the historian Norman A. Stillman, 'only one elderly woman was killed.'[21]

In the months leading up to Jewish statehood, nowhere in the Muslim world was safe for Jews. On 9 January 1948 the British Ambassador in Damascus, Philip Broadmead, reported to London that since the United Nations' Partition Resolution there had been 'a clearly marked tendency on the part of the Syrian press to incite the public against Jews living in Syria.' A recent outbreak of cholera had been ascribed 'to intentional pollution of water supplies by Jews.'[22] In addition, Jewish merchants and commercial concerns had been 'accused of failing to contribute to the fund for the liberation of Palestine'

---

[18] The Jews of Bahrain were originally from Iraq, Persia and India.

[19] Charles Belgrave, *Personal Column: A History of Bahrain*, pages 148-51.

[20] In 1985, a local Bahraini approached David Nonoo, a leading member of the small remaining Jewish community, and confessed that a member of his family had stolen the Torah Scrolls in 1948, but was returning them because his family 'were all experiencing much misfortune by holding on to something not rightfully theirs': Nancy Elly Khedouri, *From Our Beginning to Present Day*, page 15.

[21] Norman A. Stillman, *Jews of Arab Lands in Modern Times*, page 147.

[22] The poisoning of wells was a frequent charge against Jews in medieval Christian Europe. A notorious accusation of well-poisoning occurred in Zurich in 1348, exactly six hundred years before the Syrian charge.

– from the Jews – while publicity had been given to 'the dismissal of certain Jewish Government employees.'[23]

Throughout North Africa, Jews felt the same pressure of Arab nationalism and hatred towards Zionism. On 22 January 1948 the President of the Federation of Jewish Societies of Algeria, Elie Gozlan, expressed his worries in a letter to the World Jewish Congress's Committee for Refugee Aid in New York. He wrote of how the French authorities and 'above all the Muslims' suspected Jews of 'complicity with the fighting going on lately in Palestine.' The Muslims, he wrote, 'do not hesitate to accuse North African Jewry of sending money, arms, and men to the Zionists.' He then added: 'What prudence the Jews must show in dealing with the Palestinian affair!'[24]

Gozlan also described the general mood among both Muslims and Jews: 'A serious movement is stirring the Muslim masses in North Africa (we have 12 million Arabs as opposed to barely half a million Jews). . . . A deep malaise reigns in North Africa, separatist ideas are making headway, and if one speaks of an exodus, it is necessary to specify that there is anxiety in many hearts.' Zionist emissaries on clandestine missions had been 'traversing North Africa from the heart of Tunisia to Morocco, preaching the exodus to Jews of modest or unfortunate circumstances, saying: "Go to Algiers where boats are ready to take you to Palestine, and you will have nothing to worry about." These unfortunates do not hesitate to respond to this command.' As a result, Elie Gozlan wrote, Algiers had seen 'an influx of thousands of poor people – women, old people, children, people without the means of existence having sold everything, sick people many of whom have contagious diseases (tuberculosis, trachoma, ringworm etc) . . .'

Such reports had already aroused concern among the American-Jewish leadership for the fate of Jews in Muslim lands. On 18 January

---

[23] Letter of 9 January 1948, reproduced in facsimile in Itamar Levin, *Locked Doors*, page 234.

[24] Letter of 22 January 1948: quoted in full in Norman A. Stillman, *Jews of Arab Lands in Modern Times*, pages 509-10.

1948 the President of the World Jewish Congress, Dr. Stephen Wise, wrote an article entitled 'Crime of Arabs is Genocide.' In the article he urged the United States Secretary of State, George C. Marshall – who had been Chief of Staff of the American forces during the Second World War – to find some way in which the United States could intervene to protect those in danger. 'Between 800,000 and a million Jews,' Wise wrote, 'in the Middle East and Africa, exclusive of Palestine, are in "greatest danger of destruction" by Moslems being incited to holy war over the partition of Palestine.' Wise stressed the words 'greatest danger of destruction.'[25]

As the declaration of Jewish statehood drew nearer, another American reached a similar conclusion. A twenty-two-year-old traveller, Robert F. Kennedy – whose father had been the United States Ambassador in London when war broke out in 1939 – wrote an article in the *Boston Globe* after returning from a visit to Palestine. Kennedy noted of the Arabs of Palestine: 'They are willing to let Jews remain as peaceful citizens subject to the rule of the Arab majority just as the Arabs are doing in such great number in Egypt and the Levant States, but they are determined that a separate Jewish State will be attacked and attacked until it is finally cut out like an unhealthy abscess.'[26]

---

[25] World Jewish Congress, New York, 18 January 1948: World Jewish Congress archive.

[26] Robert F. Kennedy, *Boston Globe*, 3 June 1948. Twenty years later, in 1968, Robert Kennedy, then a presidential candidate, was assassinated. His brother, President John F. Kennedy, had been assassinated in 1963.

1. A Jewish woman brings her merchandise to sell at the Sultan's
Harem, Istanbul, 1714. [*Israel Museum*]

2. A Jewish doctor in a Muslim land: a Seventeenth-Century print. [*Beth Hatefutsoth, Tel Aviv*]

3. A Jewish merchant in a Muslim land: a Seventeenth-Century print. [*Beth Hatefutsoth, Tel Aviv*]

4. A pre-1914 cast iron manhole cover of the Alliance Israélite Universelle school system: Jerusalem, photographed in 1984 still covering the manhole. The Hebrew letters stand for 'All Israel are brothers.' [*Martin Gilbert*]

5. The Yambol Synagogue, Istanbul. [*Israel Museum*]

6. A Jewish official in the Ottoman Empire, before 1914. [*Israel Museum*]

7. A Jewish wedding in Izmir, Ottoman Turkey, 1910. [*Israel Museum*]

8. Jewish delegates from the Tenth Zionist Congress, held in Basel, Switzerland, in 1911. [*Beth Hatefutsoth, Tel Aviv*]

9. Jewish women in the Moroccan city of Tetuan, 1925. [*Beth Hatefutsoth, Tel Aviv*]

10. Jewish girls in Tunis, 1931. [*Beth Hatefutsoth, Tel Aviv*]

11. Jewish boy scouts in Alexandria, Egypt, 1932. [*Ada Aharoni; Elie Patan private collection*].

12. Egyptian Prince Abdel Moneim congratulates the Maccabiah team, Cairo, 15 March 1935. [*Ada Aharoni*]

13. A wedding ceremony at the Neve Shalom Synagogue, Cairo, circa 1935. [*Ada Aharoni*]

14. The synagogue and Jewish Quarter in Zawia, Libya, after the pogrom of 1945. [*Maurice Roumani*]

15. A Jewish home in Zawia, looted during the 1945 pogrom. [*Maurice Roumani*]

16. Libyan Jewish schoolgirls. [*Maurice Roumani*]

17. Libyan Jewish schoolboys. [*Maurice Roumani*]

18. A Jewish woman searched at the dockside, before leaving Tripoli. [*Maurice Roumani*]

19. Libyan Jews leaving Tripoli by ship. [*Maurice Roumani*]

20. Hashid Camp, Aden: Yisrael Yeshayahu – a Yemeni-born emissary from Israel – with a Yemeni girl soon to leave for Israel on Operation Magic Carpet, 1949. [*Jewish Agency Archive*].

21. Operation Magic Carpet: Yemeni Jews on the plane from Aden to Israel. None of them had ever flown before. [*Beth Hatefutsoth, Tel Aviv*]

22. Tented camps in Israel for new immigrants from Muslim lands.
[*Gourji C. Bekhor*]

23. A Jew from Yemen at work on the Tel Aviv–Jerusalem highway,
1948. [*Jewish Agency Archive*]

24. Iraqi Jews on the plane to Israel, after losing their Iraqi nationality, 1951. [*Gourji C. Bekhor*]

25. Iraqi Jews landing at Lod Airport (now Ben Gurion Airport), Israel, 1951. [*Gourji C. Bekhor*]

26. Jewish refugees from Egypt, saying their morning prayers on board a ship arriving at Haifa Port. [*Burt Glinn: Magnum Photos*]

27. Two elderly Jews on Djerba Island, Tunisia, 1958. [*George Rodger: Magnum Photos*]

28. Jews from Morocco celebrate the festival of Mamouna in Jerusalem, 1984. [*Martin Gilbert*]

29. Memorial to the eighty-two Jews killed in Aden in December 1947: Holon, Israel, 2009. [*David Kovler*]

15

THE CREATION OF THE STATE OF ISRAEL, 14 MAY 1948

'The Zionist fortress will fall after the first attack'

On 14 May 1948, Israel declared its independence. Two days later, a *New York Times* headline warned: 'JEWS IN GRAVE DANGER IN ALL MOSLEM LANDS: Nine Hundred Thousand in Africa and Asia Face Wrath of Their Foes.'[1]

These ominous words reflected a sense of foreboding that had spread among Jews in Arab countries from the moment Israel declared independence. Hatred of Zionism had been integral to the Arab States' world view for three decades, and on May 14 that hatred became a hatred of Israel. Three Baghdadi Jews later recalled the 'bad omens' that appeared in their city overnight: 'army troops on the main routes, demonstrations, threats in newspapers and radio, plottings against Jews in the streets and market places.' They remembered how 'Jews walked liked shadows, terrified about their own destiny and that of their brothers in the Land of Israel.'[2]

The *New York Times* article, published on 16 May 1948, also reported ominous events in Lebanon, where 'Jews have been forced to contribute financially to fight against the United Nations partition resolution in Palestine. Acts of violence against Jews are openly admitted by the Press, which accuses the Jews of "poisoning wells" etc.'[3] Even more worrying was the rapidly approaching conflict between

---

[1] Mallory Browne, 'Jews in Grave Danger in All Moslem lands,' *New York Times*, 16 May 1948.
[2] Shlomo Sheena, Yaacov Elazar and Emmanuel Nahtomi, *A Short History of the Zionist Underground Movement in Iraq*, page 33.
[3] *New York Times*, 16 May 1948.

Arab and Israeli forces. On May 16 – two days after David Ben-Gurion declared independence in Tel Aviv – the five armies of Egypt, Syria, Lebanon, Iraq and Transjordan began their advance against the new Jewish State.

In Egypt, King Farouk had met a delegation of Egyptian Jewish leaders on the eve of the Arab-Israeli war and assured them of his commitment to protect the Jews.[4] Never a strong character, however, the King was unable to stem the rising tide of anti-Israel feeling in his country. The Egyptian Prime Minister, al-Nukrashi Pasha, decided to proclaim a state of emergency and arrest all Communists, declaring that all Jews were potential Zionists and that all Zionists were in fact Communists.

The Prime Minister's orders dealt a massive blow to the Jewish community. Hundreds of Jews were arrested in the hours after Israel's declaration of independence, and hundreds more were arrested as Egyptian troops advanced through the Gaza Strip – which they occupied – and deep into Israeli territory.[5] Before the end of the year more than six hundred Jews had been arrested and had their property sequestered by the government.[6] Those arrested in Cairo were interned in a former United States air base near the city. Those arrested in Alexandria were taken to Camp Aboukir, near the Mediterranean shore.[7] Another group of Jews was sent to the Sinai

---

[4] Norman A. Stillman, *Jews of Arab Lands in Modern Times*, page 151.

[5] One of those arrested on the evening of 14 May 1948 was Habib Vidal, the owner of a printing shop and the custodian of the synagogue at Helwan. Without being charged or brought to court, Vidal was sentenced to fifteen months in the Huckstep Prison, in the Egyptian desert. Shortly before he was released his daughter was allowed to hold her marriage ceremony in the prison. Habib Vidal's son later recalled: 'Father came to the ceremony handcuffed,' and after the family intervened, 'the Colonel in charge of the prison gave him a concession: one hour without handcuffs.' Samuel J. Cohen (Habib Vidal's nephew), manuscript, 'My Exodus from Egypt,' Tel Aviv, 10 May 2009.

[6] Barry Rubin, *The Arab States and the Palestine Conflict*, page 202. Some have put the arrest count as high as a thousand.

[7] Benjamin Bright, 'The Exodus revisited,' *Jerusalem Post*, 24 April 2006. Egyptian-born Abraham Matalon was arrested on the Friday night after Israel's declaration of independence. He was taken to Aboukir and kept in internment for a year and

coastal village of el-Tor, where they were interned in a former British quarantine station. Conditions there were harsh in the extreme.

The Egyptian Government also asked the Chief Rabbi of Egypt, Haim Nahum Effendi – then seventy-six years old and almost blind – to order that prayers be recited in every synagogue in Egypt for the victory of the Egyptian Army over the Israeli forces. He refused to do so.[8] Then on May 25, the Government issued a proclamation stipulating that no Jew could leave Egypt without a special visa from the Ministry of the Interior. This even applied to the many thousands of Jews who held foreign passports. As it turned out, the special visas were 'very scarce.'[9]

Relations between Jews, Christians and Muslims in Egypt had hitherto been accepting, even cordial. Elie Amiel, a basketball player for Alexandria's Jewish Maccabi team, had become a member of the Egyptian national basketball team after the Second World War. He played for Egypt both at home and overseas; his Muslim teammates gave him the nickname 'The Invincible.' It was only when the anti-Zionist campaign gained momentum that demands by the authorities forced him to leave the team.[10]

Another Egyptian Jew, Levana Zamir, enjoyed good experiences in the small town of Helwan, today a part of greater Cairo, in the years before the turmoil. She later recalled: 'When I left Egypt I was twelve years old and my best friend was a Muslim girl. . . . It was perfectly natural. As my mother said, there was a full harmony between Jews, Christians, and Muslims, and together we built Helwan.' A traumatic turning point came on 18 May 1948. 'At midnight, Egyptian police came into our house and they opened everything, they took

---

a half, until after Egypt's defeat. He later recalled: 'There was never a formal accusation, but we knew we were imprisoned for being Zionists.'

[8] Victor D. Sanua, 'Haim Nahoum Effendi (1872-1960),' *Image Magazine*, February 1998.

[9] Ada Aharoni, Aimée Israel-Pelletier, Levana Zamir (editors), *History and Culture of the Jews from Egypt in Modern Times*, page 143.

[10] 'Elie Amiel, 1925-2001,' obituary: *IAJE Newsletter* (International Association of Jews from Egypt Newsletter), 2002, Volume 4. No. 1, pages 5-6. Elie Amiel emigrated to Israel, where he continued his basketball career.

everything. In the morning, I went to school and my teacher told me they had taken my uncle to prison. "They say we are Zionists," my mother explained.' Levana Zamir's uncle was freed nearly two years later, when he was brought in handcuffs to a ship leaving for France. The family left Egypt for good in 1950: 'All our money was finished and we left for France with nothing.'[11]

Suzy Vidal recalled the events in Cairo following Israel's declaration of independence. 'Pandemonium broke loose' during an attack on the Jewish Quarter, she wrote. Her uncle Jacques, 'seeing the crowd close in on him, called out in Arabic the name of a patriotic paper to a newspaper vendor. Because of his dark complexion they believed he was one of theirs. They turned on their heels to hound another victim.' Two other relatives were not so fortunate: 'My youngest aunt, Lydia, who was pregnant, and her husband Joe, convinced they would reach home two streets away unharmed, took the small alley that led to the Synagogue. But the crowd was already there at the side door screaming and hunting the enemy. My aunt and uncle were both beaten up and left on the pavement. We still don't know by what miracle they escaped death and how the baby was safe.'[12]

Edna Anzarut, looking back fifty years later, wrote that 'the atmosphere was of anguish and fear. Every week, more and more of my parents' acquaintances and friends were arrested, forcibly taken from their homes for interrogation and internment.' As the 'witch hunt' against Zionists and Jewish Communists intensified, her parents decided to get rid of all their Hebrew books. 'The thought of destroying books, any books, was something intolerable, but it had to be done. The books could not be burnt – the smoke would have alerted the people who were watching our home. There was no safe

---

[11] Levana Zamir's family, the Mosseris, had emigrated from Italy three hundred years earlier, and still held Italian passports after being refused Egyptian ones. Benjamin Bright, 'The Exodus revisited,' *Jerusalem Post*, 24 April 2006.

[12] Sultana Latifa (Suzy Vidal), *The Jasmine Necklace*, page 67. Also a communication from Suzy Vidal, 2 January 2009. Lydia was nineteen at the time of the attack. She and her husband managed to leave Egypt before the baby was born, by ship from Alexandria to Haifa. The baby was a girl, Aliza, born in Israel, who lives in Israel today with her own children and grandchildren.

hiding place. Every single evening, after the Muslim hired help had left, my Dad, my Mum and I would tear Hebrew books, most of which were valuable and very old prayer books. We were weeping as we did this. They had to be torn into tiny pieces and we then flushed them down the toilet, night after night after night.'[13]

Amidst all the political turmoil, incitement and violence, relations between Muslims and Jews were still possible. In the Aboukir internment camp, Egyptian-born Abraham Matalon met the leader of the Muslim Brotherhood in Alexandria, who had also been imprisoned. 'At first,' Matalon remembered later, 'I didn't know he was a member. We embraced, and we started meeting every day. He said he wanted to learn Hebrew, and I wanted to learn Koran, so this is how we spent our time. I wanted to have a dialogue with the Muslims, and they loved me for it! I did the call to prayer in the camp and the soldiers admired it, they even answered me. And they knew I was a Zionist, but they did not manifest any attitudes against me. They said we are friends in life. When you come to talk to your enemy, you see that he is a different person, you can see his human side.'[14]

Like the Egyptian authorities, the Iraqi Government was implacable in its opposition both to Israel and to any Jews who might try – as did tens of thousands – to fulfil the ancient Jewish longing for a return to the Jewish homeland. Babylon (Iraq) had been the first Jewish place of exile 2,534 years earlier. But more than three hundred Jews were arrested in the first days of the Arab-Israeli war. They were brought to trial before military courts martial and fined or imprisoned. The charge against them was that they had given support to Israel.

One of those arrested, Shafiq Ades, was the richest Jew in Iraq. In the past, he had lunched with Government ministers and dined with the Regent. Ades was accused simultaneously of being a Zionist and a Communist. For the main charge against him, that he had sold arms to Israel, the military court presented no evidence. Ades

---

[13] Edna Turner (née Anzarut), letter to the author, 18 April 2009.
[14] Quoted in: Benjamin Bright, 'The Exodus revisited,' *Jerusalem Post*, 24 April 2006.

was refused the right to a proper defence, fined five million Iraqi
pounds and sentenced to death. He was hanged in public on 23
September 1948, in front of his mansion in Basra.[15] Mona Yahya,
whose family lived in Iraq at the time, later wrote about the incident:
'Crowds gathered to watch the spectacle and their cheers incited
the hangman to a repeat performance. The next day, close-up shots
of the hanged man covered the front pages of the Iraqi newspapers.
His neck was broken, his corpse dangled over his puddle of excre-
ment. He was labelled the Serpent, the Traitor, the Spy, the Zionist,
the Jew, while his estate worth millions was appropriated by the
Ministry of Defence.'[16]

That July, Zionist affiliation was made a criminal offence in Iraq.
Jews were removed from many areas of Iraqi public life, which they
had served so patriotically and so well for three decades. Jewish bankers were forbidden to continue offering their services. Wealthy Iraqi
Jews were forced by the government to pay money towards the Iraqi
war effort against Israel.[17] On 19 October 1948 the Cairo daily newspaper *al-Ahram* reported that the Iraqi Government had ordered the
wholesale dismissal of all Jewish officials and employees in government offices. Within a year, ninety-five per cent of all Jews in official
positions in Iraq had been dismissed: 1,500 in all, some of whom had
been in government service for as long as thirty years, from the first
days of Iraqi self-government.

Arrests and trials continued throughout 1948 and into the following year. One Jew arrested in 1948 was fifteen-year-old Uri
David, who was falsely accused of anti-government activity. He was
held for eight years in a prison deep in the Iraqi desert, where he
was often beaten 'black and blue.'[18] In March 1949 another Iraqi
Jew was sentenced to five years hard labour because a scrap of
paper with a Hebrew inscription from the Old Testament had been

---

[15] Hayyim J. Cohen, *The Jews of the Middle East, 1860-1972*, pages 33-4.
[16] Mona Yahya, *When the Grey Beetles Took over Baghdad*, page 115.
[17] Nissim Kazzaz, *The End of a Diaspora: The Jews in Iraq during the Twentieth Century*,
pages 287-293.
[18] Uri David, communication to the author, 22 February 2009.

found in his home. That same month, ten Jews were sentenced to three years hard labour because of an allegation that they had danced the Hora, an Israeli dance. Then in April, a sixty-year-old Jew was sentenced to seven years' hard labour because he had received a letter from his son in Israel. He died as a result of his brutal treatment in prison.[19]

Despite the actions taken against Jews supportive of Israel in countries like Egypt and Iraq, the prevailing opinion in the Arab world was that the State of Israel was doomed. King Abdullah of Trans-Jordan expressed it succinctly: 'The Zionist fortress will fall after the first attack.' Azzam Pasha, Secretary of the Arab League, declared publicly: 'This will be a war of extermination and a momentous massacre which will be spoken of like the Mongolian massacres and the Crusades.'[20] Yet at the end of the first week of June 1948, it was clear that the Arab nations attacking Israel had been over-confident. Although Iraqi forces were within sight of the Mediterranean Sea north of Tel Aviv, and Egyptian troops had reached the southern-most suburb of Jerusalem, the Arab armies were not yet succeeding in their aim of driving the Jews into the sea.

The realisation that the State of Israel might survive led to an intensification of anti-Israel and anti-Jewish feeling throughout the Arab world. There was a genuine disbelief and indignation at the Jews' ability to defend themselves. In the Moroccan town of Oujda, on the border with Algeria, five Jews were stabbed to death and thirty more injured during a mob rampage in the Jewish Quarter on June 7. Many small shops were destroyed and homes looted. That evening, in the nearby town of Djerada, thirty-nine Jews were killed and thirty seriously injured, out of a total Jewish population of one hundred.[21]

---

[19] 'Memorandum on the Treatment of the Jewish Population in Iraq,' submitted to the United Nations Secretary General, Trygvie Lie, 22 October 1949: copy in the British Foreign Office papers FO 371/75183.
[20] Both quotations from: Barry Rubin, *The Arab States and the Palestine Conflict*, pages 200-1.
[21] André Chouraqui, *Between East and West*, pages 181-2.

In Libya, where eighteen Jews had been murdered during Israel's first days, anti-Jewish feelings boiled over in a dramatic fashion. On June 12, a day after the first truce was declared in the Arab-Israeli fighting, several thousand Arabs from Tripoli's poorest area rushed towards the Jewish Quarter armed with iron crowbars, knives and sticks embedded with razor blades. They called out: 'If we cannot go to Palestine to fight Jews, let's fight them here.'[22] But at the gate of the Jewish Quarter, the Jews were waiting with stones and explosives. The mob eventually retreated, though not after many had been injured and some killed by the determined defenders.

The rioters then moved to parts of Tripoli where Jews and Muslims lived side by side; they raided and plundered Jewish shops and homes at will, burning whatever loot they could not carry off with them. Among the Jewish businesses destroyed were sawmills, craft workshops and a large garage. Many other buildings were attacked across the city, including a synagogue that had already been looted and burned during the riots of 1945. It took three days for the British to restore order. By that time fourteen Jews had been killed: seven old men, six women and one child. One Jewish woman had been raped and twenty-two Jews had been seriously injured. The Arab dead were between three (the British figure) and thirty (the Jewish figure). More than 1,600 Jews were made homeless. Three hundred Jewish families were destitute after losing everything they owned.

Attacks on the Jews also continued in Egypt, where on the night of June 19–20, bombs were thrown into Cairo's old Jewish Quarter. Twenty-two Jews were killed in the blasts and forty-one wounded. In the Levi family, only one eight-year-old boy, Yossef Levi, survived.[23] Two days later the Egyptian daily newspaper *al-Ahram* published a full report, with photographs, accusing the Muslim Brotherhood of responsibility.[24] The authorities managed to restore order and a

---

[22] Quoted in Maurice M. Roumani, *The Jews of Libya*, page 58.
[23] Yossef Levi emigrated to Israel. In 1996 he was living in the Israeli coastal town of Herzliya.
[24] Ada Aharoni, Aimée Israel-Pelletier, Levana Zamir (editors), *History and Culture of the Jews from Egypt in Modern Times*, page 143.

month later a British diplomat reported that the Jews, 'both rich and poor, carry on their normal activities in satisfactory conditions, although they are apt to be nervous of their position.'[25]

In spite of the return to order, an Egyptian Arab wrote a revealing letter to the *Bourse égyptienne* newspaper on July 22: 'It would seem that most people in Egypt are unaware of the fact that among Egyptian Moslems there are some who have white skin,' he wrote. 'Every time I board a tram I see people pointing at me and saying "Jew, Jew." I have been beaten more than once because of this. For that reason I humbly beg that my picture (enclosed) be published with an explanation that I am not Jewish and that my name is Adham Mustafa Galeb.'[26]

Fourteen-year-old Rosa Molcho witnessed the persistent anti-Jewish violence first-hand. On 22 September 1948, while lying in bed in Cairo, Rosa heard shouting in the street outside. Going to the window, she heard her mother, Aimée Mizrahi – a volunteer guard in the Jewish Quarter – calling out to the neighbours that there was a bomb, and that they should leave their homes and run. A former Egyptian Jewish soldier in the British Army, Jacques Lévy, who had defused two earlier bombs, was called to defuse this one. It exploded as he was working on it and he was killed instantly. Running into the street, Rosa found her mother mortally wounded. Aimée Mizrahi died in her daughter's arms.[27]

The first truce in the Arab-Israeli war – which came into force on 11 June 1948 – broke down twenty-seven days later, on 8 July 1948. Fighting quickly intensified on the Egyptian front in the Negev, and on July 15, Israeli aircraft bombed military targets in both Cairo and Alexandria. The following day, as reported by the British Embassy in Cairo to the Foreign Office in London, 'violent anti-Jewish speeches'

---

[25] 'The Position of Jews in Egypt,' G.L. McDermott, 2 July 1948, to the Foreign Office, London. National Archives, Kew, Foreign Office papers, FO 371/69259.

[26] Letter of 22 July 1948: quoted in Yaakov Meron, 'The Expulsion of the Jews from the Arab Countries . . . ,' Malka Hillel Shulewitz (editor), *The Forgotten Millions: The Modern Jewish Exodus from Arab Lands*, page 92.

[27] Rosa Molcho, recollections, in conversation with the author, Tel Aviv, 17 May 2009.

were delivered in the mosques of Cairo by members of the Muslim Brotherhood. After Friday prayers the speakers voiced their hatred and were 'evidently doing their best to incite the population against the Jews as a whole.' During and after the Israel air bombardment, 'attacks were made in various parts of Cairo on individual Jews' and on a number of Christian foreigners; three Egyptian Jews 'and two others, probably Egyptian Jews,' were killed.[28]

On 18 July 1948 a second truce was declared between the Israeli and Arab forces. A day later a bomb went off in the centre of Cairo that damaged two department stores. The government fanned the flames of popular anger by blaming the explosion on 'an aerial torpedo from a Jewish aircraft,' although no aircraft had been sighted over the city. A Muslim member of one of the two department store boards, Hasan Rifat Pasha – a former Egyptian Government minister – stated emphatically that the explosion 'could not possibly have been caused by a bomb from the air.'

The bomb blast signalled the beginning of what the British Ambassador Sir Ronald Campbell called an 'orgy of looting.' In the days that followed, attacks on Jews escalated as 'groups of students and the riffraff of Cairo indulged in Jew-baiting and assaults on a considerable number of foreigners, including British, causing deaths and injuries.' Even a number of 'fair-skinned' Egyptians, the Ambassador reported, were unable to escape 'molestation in the streets by students and others who have mistaken them for Jews.' Members of the Muslim Brotherhood worsened matters by distributing pamphlets in Cairo, 'exhorting the public to boycott Jews and generally make life unbearable for them.'[29] Anti-Jewish and anti-foreign protests soon proliferated in mosques and newspapers, heightened because it was Ramadan, the Muslim holy month of fasting and prayer.

The violence in Cairo grew more intense in August and September, with bomb attacks on Jewish-owned cinemas and retail stores. Leading

---

[28] Telegram from Sir Ronald Campbell to the Foreign Office, London, 19 July 1948. National Archives, Kew, Foreign Office papers, FO 371/69182.

[29] Telegram from Sir Ronald Campbell to the Foreign Office, London, 23 July 1948. National Archives, Kew, Foreign Office papers, FO 371/69259.

members of the Jewish community, in an attempt to prove their loyalty to Egypt, condemned Zionism and donated almost a quarter of a million United States dollars to the Palestine Fund welfare appeal for Egyptian troops fighting against Israel.[30] Such efforts were in vain. On September 22 a number of bombs were thrown into the old Jewish Quarter. According to a report in the *New York Times*, nineteen Jews were killed and sixty-two wounded, and many Jewish shops looted.[31] The attacks did not stop there; between 1949 and 1952, anti-Jewish riots became a regular feature of life in Cairo. Suzy Vidal later recalled how, 'standing on the roof of the Extaday Hotel,' her family 'watched the traditional riots of Cairo as one would a movie.'[32]

Anti-Jewish violence in Libya also persisted throughout the summer of 1948. When a bomb was thrown in the Jewish Quarter in Zliten, two Jewish children were blinded. Reprisals led to an increase in tension and the arrest of thirty Jews for possessing arms.[33] Tensions had already been exacerbated by first dozens, and later many hundreds of Arabs from French North Africa, who passed through Libya on their way to join the Arab armies attacking Israel. The Jewish community of Tripoli had called on the British military authorities to protect them, leading the British to establish a bus service from Tripoli to the Egyptian border that sped up the transit of Muslim volunteers. But this was not a complete solution; some Jews making their way to Tripoli across the hinterland were murdered. From the same hinterland, Jews were soon fleeing en masse in the opposite direction: from Gharyan the whole community left, abandoning their homes and their land for good.

One Muslim ruler, Sultan Muhammad V of Morocco, sought to calm the anti-Israel mood of his population and protect his Jewish

---

[30] A quarter of a million dollars was more than $5 million in the money values of 2010.

[31] Julian Louis Meltzer, '. . . 14 DIE IN CAIRO EXPLOSION 10 Jews Included in Toll . . .' *New York Times*, 23 September 1945.

[32] Suzy Vidal-Pirotte, *Extaday: a Childhood in Cairo, 1939-1949*, quoted on the back cover.

[33] One of the arrested men, Lillo Mahluf, committed suicide while in custody.

subjects. Speaking at the start of the first Arab-Israeli war, which began in May 1948 with five Arab armies attacking Israel simultaneously, the Sultan called publicly on 'all of you, Moroccans, without exception' for calm and for the preservation of public order. At the same time, he distanced himself from Zionism and warned his Jewish subjects to do likewise. The 'only goal' of the Arab armies, he said, was 'to defend the first *qibla* of Islam' – Jerusalem, Mohammed's initial direction for Muslim prayer – 'and to re-establish peace and justice in the Holy Land, while preserving for the Jews the status that has always been accorded them since the Muslim conquest.'

The Sultan was calling for a return to the Covenant of 'Omar, rather than a massacre or expulsion. Once the Arab armies were victorious against Israel, the Jews of Palestine would be allowed to live as *dhimmis*, free to practice Judiasm, protected, but subservient. Nor would the Jews of Morocco be in any danger of attack. That, the Sultan explained, 'is why we enjoin our Muslim subjects not to let themselves be incited by the undertaking of Jews against their brother Arabs in Palestine to commit any act whatsoever that might disturb public order and safety.'

Muhammad V wanted his Muslim subjects to know that 'the Moroccan Israelites who have lived for centuries in this country which has protected them, where they have found the best welcome, and where they have shown their complete devotion to the Moroccan throne, are different from the rootless Jews who have turned from the four corners of the earth towards Palestine, which they want to seize unjustly and arbitrarily.' The Jews of Morocco, he went on to warn, should refrain from any act that is 'liable to support the Zionist aggression or show their solidarity with it; because in doing so they would be violating their particular rights as well as their Moroccan nationality.'[34]

In Bahrain, Sheikh Sulman – the Sultan – also displayed comparative tolerance towards the Jews. With the establishment of the

---

[34] Proclamation of 23 May 1948, Rabat. Quoted in full in Norman A. Stillman, *Jews of Arab Lands in Modern Times*, pages 511-4.

State of Israel, he announced that any Jews who wished to do so could leave Bahrain, but could take neither money nor belongings, and could not return to Bahrain. They would have to abandon their homes and businesses. Following this announcement, many members of Bahrain's Jewish community went by boat to Bombay and then on to Britain. Only a dozen Jewish families remained in Bahrain. One of the few Bahraini Jews who went to Israel, returned to Bahrain and was arrested, imprisoned for a year, but then allowed to remain in Bahrain.[35]

Another Muslim ruler, the Shah of Iran, Mohammad Reza Shah, also refused to adopt a violent anti-Zionist stance. Starting in 1944 several Zionist youth organisations had been legally established in Iran. At the same time, Jewish refugees from Nazi persecution and Soviet exile had been making their way freely through Iran in their journey towards Palestine.

In the period leading up to the establishment of Israel, when Jews throughout the Arab world were entering their worst years, the Jewish community in Iran found opportunities and fulfilment under the Shah's tolerant rule. Jewish newspapers and schools were unrestricted in what they could write and teach. The American Jewish Joint Distribution Committee ('The Joint') was allowed to help Jewish social welfare cases, and to give medical assistance to Jewish schoolchildren, many of whom went to Alliance schools. In 1947 the Jewish Ladies Organization of Iran was founded to extend financial help to those in need, including a growing number of Jewish refugees from Iraq.[36] One of the founders, Shamsi Hekmat, an Iranian-Jewish woman, was for many years the treasurer of the Iranian Women's Organization and a pioneer of women's rights in Iran.

The Iranian-Jewish historian, physician and early Zionist, Habib Levy, called this period the 'golden age' of Jewish life in Iran. In the words of another Iranian Jew, Houman Sarshar, who

---

[35] Charles Belgrave, *Personal Column: A History of Bahrain*, pages 148-51.
[36] Support for the organisation's work came from The Joint in the United States: Houman Sarshar, *Esther's Children: A Portrait of Iranian Jews*, page 424, and Baruch Gilead, 'Iran,' *Encyclopaedia Judaica*, volume 8, column 1440.

left the country with his parents in 1978 – on the eve of the Iranian Islamic revolution – Jews living under the rule of Mohammad Reza Shah 'became some of the leading contributors to the country's full blown industrialization and Westernization campaign. Banking, insurance, textiles, plastics, paper, pharmaceuticals, aluminium production, liquor distillery and distribution, shipping, imports, industrial machinery, and textiles were all segments of Iran's then new and booming national industry that were either established by Jews or financed and directed under their leadership.'[37]

Even for those Jews who were not affected by violence during the Arab-Israeli war, life under Muslim rule was no less uncertain and precarious. In Iran, where the Jewish community flourished, pros-perity and opportunity did not bring an end to discrimination. An Iranian Jew recalled many years later that when he was a young schoolboy, 'not a day passed when I was not beaten up. I would go to school with a chain around my belt and some sand in my pocket to throw in their eyes.'[38]

Even deeper problems were evident in Libya, where poverty stalked the 36,000-strong Jewish community. By the middle of 1948, sixty per cent of all Libyan Jews were living on welfare provided by Jewish communities in Europe and the United States. Likewise, almost all the Libyan Jews who had left their coastal and inland towns to seek refuge in Tripoli were living off whatever the local Jewish community could provide. They joined a third of Tripoli's twenty thousand other Jewish inhabitants who were in the same position already.

In a letter that July to the United Nations Security Council, a group of Libyan Jews wrote of their situation as 'unbearable materi-ally, economically, as well as morally. We live under the spectre of the pogroms, our minds are full of fear at the danger that disorders may break out at any moment. . . . We have knocked on all doors to escape from this hell on earth, but we have found that the local authorities

---

[37] Houman Sarshar, *Esther's Children: A Portrait of Iranian* Jews, page xix.
[38] Communication to the author, 29 June 2009.

prevent all Jews from leaving the territory. . . . We appeal to you, the Supreme World Organization, to help us, make our lives secure, and free us from this hell on earth where twice in a year and a half we have been assaulted by conscienceless bloodthirsty masses and have lost our lives and goods.'[39]

Two Yemeni Jews, Hannah and Saadya Akiva, gave a similarly bleak account of Yemen in the aftermath of the Second World War. Speaking to the historian Bat Ye'or, they recalled how it was forbidden for a Jew to work in agriculture, to write in Arabic, to possess firearms, or to ride on a horse or a camel. Jews could only ride on donkeys, and even then they were obliged to ride sidesaddle in order to jump to the ground whenever they passed a Muslim – as in the early days of the Covenant of Omar more than 1,200 years earlier.

In the streets in Yemen, Jewish pedestrians had to pass Muslims on the left. Although Jewish cobblers made shoes for Muslims, they were not allowed to wear them. Hannah and Saadya Akiva explained: 'The Arabs forbade us to wear shoes, so that we hid them when, as children, we went searching for wood for cooking. When we were far enough away, we put on our shoes; on returning we took them off and hid them in the branches. The Arabs frequently searched us, and if they found them, they punished us and forbade us to collect wood. We had to lower our heads, accepting insults and humiliations. The Arabs called us "stinking dogs."'

Some of the harshest aspects of Islamic *dhimmi* practice were re-imposed on the Jews of Yemen. Most notably, Jewish children who became orphans before they were fifteen were forcibly converted to Islam. Hannah and Saadya Akiva recalled the considerable efforts made by the Jews to help children avoid this fate: 'The families tried to save them by hiding them in bundles of hay. Afterwards, the children were sent to villages where they hid with another family and were given other names. Sometimes the children were put into coffins and the Arabs were told they had died with their parents. Then they were helped to escape.'

---

[39] Quoted in Renzo De Felice, *Jews in an Arab Land: Libya, 1835-1970*, pages 226-7.

Hannah recalled the fate of one of her uncles, who worked for Muslims. He was married with four children. 'One day the Arabs wanted to convert him and locked him in a room.' There they tied him up and forced him to swallow meat that Jews were not allowed to eat – probably camel meat. 'They beat him terribly, then they went to sleep. My uncle was able to free himself from his bonds and escape. He returned home and cried continuously. He was questioned, but didn't reply, and tears flowed all the time. He refused to eat or drink. He died two days later. When he had been prepared for burial, one saw that his body was covered with wounds. We learned the whole story later because the Arabs told it to us secretly.'[40]

The Jewish community in Yemen was even subjected to a variant of the Christian poisoning of the wells accusation of past ages. The accusation spread through the capital city of Sanaa in the aftermath of a palace coup on 17 February 1948, during which the ruler of Yemen, Imam Yahya – Yahya Muhammad Hamid ed-Din – had been assassinated. The Jews were accused of murdering two young Muslim girls and throwing their bodies down a well. The leaders of the Jewish community were seized in their houses, beaten, taken to prison and chained together by their ankles. A mob burst into the Jewish Quarter, looting and robbing. Only the timely intervention of one of Imam Yahya's sons, Prince Sayf ul-Islam al-Hassan, prevented loss of life: the prince sent soldiers into the Jewish Quarter to protect the Jews and force the rioters to leave.[41]

In a letter from nearby Aden, the British Governor, Sir Reginald Champion, telegraphed to the Colonial Secretary in London that 'the two Arab girls may have been murdered by Arabs to justify attack on the Jewish Quarter for loot. Considering the apparent provocation and widely advertised anti-Jewish tension elsewhere, I think the Sanaa Jews are lucky not to have suffered a pogrom.'[42] Anti-Jewish tension was also appearing in other towns across Yemen, as the

---

[40] Interview of 8 October 1982: Bat Ye'or, *The Dhimmi*, pages 380-382.
[41] Tudor Parfitt, *The Road to Redemption: The Jews of the Yemen, 1900-1950*, pages 188-90.
[42] Telegram of 30 April 1949: Colonial Office papers, CO 4918/78009/1, document 58.

Arab-Israeli war fanned the flames of Muslim anger. A letter from a Jew in Sanaa, sent on 10 January 1949, reported that in the town of Dhamar, Jews were beaten and robbed 'because of one thing – that the Israelis are waging war on the Arabs in Palestine and are trying to conquer the whole of Palestine.' The letter from Sanaa contained the plea: 'Who can pull us out of this iron furnace?'[43]

The answer to that question was another of the Imam Yahya's sons, Imam Ahmad bin Yahya, who, in 1949 and 1950, allowed 44,000 Jews to leave Yemen for Israel. The Israeli-organised emigration – code-named Operation Magic Carpet – was conducted entirely by air. None of those who left Yemen for Israel had ever flown before. The airlift was supervised by Israeli-sent emissaries, including the Yemeni-born future Speaker of the Knesset – the Israeli Parliament – Yisrael Yeshayahu.

The rescue of the Jews of Yemen proceeded in two phases: taking the Jews from Yemen to Aden – then under British control – and flying them from Yemen to Israel. At first the Jews coming from Yemen made their long and dangerous way to Aden overland, but then the Imam allowed them to fly from Sanaa to Aden. The first group of Yemeni Jews to be flown through Aden arrived in Aden on 6 March 1949. On the following day the *Manchester Guardian* included a report of the plight of those who had come overland, quoting 'Jewish sources' who said that 'emaciated Jews arriving here all tell the same story of a ninety-mile trek to avoid capture and imprisonment in Yemen.' The overland arrivals 'say that rabbi and prominent members of the Jewish community in Yemen are imprisoned in chains.'[44]

In November 1948, Israeli forces began to push back the Arab invaders, including the largest and most successful of the five armies, that of Egypt. Israel's War of Independence ended in the first months of 1949. On February 24, Israel signed an armistice agreement with Egypt, on March 23 with Lebanon, on April 3 with Jordan and on

---

[43] Letter of 10 January 1949: quoted in Tudor Parfitt, *The Road to Redemption: The Jews of the Yemen, 1900-1950*, pages 188-9.
[44] *Manchester Guardian* (Manchester, England), 7 March 1949.

July 20 with Syria. Iraq, alone among those who had attacked Israel, declined to sign an armistice; in March 1949, Iraq withdrew its forces from Israeli soil.

On 2 February 1949, three days after Britain belatedly agreed to recognise Israel as an independent State, the British military administration in Libya allowed Libyan Jews to travel to Israel. This brought an end to a travel restriction that had been in force since the start of the Israel War of Independence. In Tripoli, the British authorities issued 8,000 exit permits within a few days. Between April 1949 and December 1951, more than 31,000 of Libya's 36,000 Jews left Tripoli on Israeli ships. Most of those who remained had property and other financial interests that they did not want to sell at absurdly low prices.

When the United Nations voted on 21 November 1949 to give Libya independence within fourteen months, even the Jews who did not want to lose their property felt the need to leave, fearing what an independent Muslim Libya might do to them. From the Libyan province of Cyrenaica, where more than five thousand Jews lived, fewer than three hundred remained by mid-1950. In all, 31,343 Libyan Jews emigrated to Israel, some through Italy, but most by ship from Tripoli to Haifa: forty-two ships in all made that journey within a year.[45]

Haim Abravanel, who was about to be put in charge of organising the emigration from Libya to Israel, wrote about the activities and mood of February 2, the first day of legal emigration: 'It was snowing for the first time in Tripoli and under the white flakes blown by the wind thousands of poor Jewish wretches ran towards the street where the police offices were, the Municipality and the Community offices, to get their passports at last.' At the same time, 'they were selling, liquidating everything: furniture, business assets, work tools etc. Without even knowing how they would reach Israel, unless it was through Italy, they wanted to leave immediately.' Abravanel continued: 'An indescribable excitement reigned everywhere and especially in the Jewish quarter.' The municipal authorities 'were deluged in the incessant

---

[45] Renzo De Felice, *Jews in an Arab Land: Libya, 1835-1970*, pages 223-8 and 232.

and determined throng animated by a single desire: to leave Libya.'[46] In a few days, more than eight thousand passports were issued.

This scene in Tripoli was being repeated across the Arab world. Jews whose ancestors had lived in uneasy harmony with Muslims for so many centuries, amid alternating prosperity and peril – succeeding and even flourishing when they were allowed to, and always making the best of their lot – judged that the moment had come when, as Arab hostility mounted, they must leave their homes and roots and prospects, and make a new life beyond Muslim control. They did not wish to be *dhimmis* any more. Finally they had a choice.

Between 1949 and 1952, more than 25,000 Jews left Egypt. Of these at least 15,000 went to Israel. The Egyptian authorities would not allow them to travel the 130-mile journey overland from the Suez Canal to the Egyptian-occupied Gaza Strip, and to use the Gaza crossing into southern Israel. Instead, with the tacit acceptance of the Egyptian Government, Israeli emissaries accompanied the Jewish refugees by sea via Genoa or Marseille, on a journey of more than two thousand miles. The money for the sea journey was provided by the American-Jewish Joint Distribution Committee in the United States and by the Jewish Agency in Jerusalem. Some wealthy Egyptian Jews also helped finance the move.

From the area that had been British Mandate Palestine, 726,000 Arabs were made refugees in 1948, having lost their homes, their lands and their livelihoods. The number of Jews who were forced to leave Arab lands after the establishment of the State of Israel was 850,000. While the Arab refugees were protected as refugees – and remain protected until today, along with their several million descendants – the Jews from Arab lands made new starts in life, bereft of the financial benefits and international sympathy of refugee status, either for them or for their descendants.

---

[46] Haim Abravanel, recollections, April 1950, Central Zionist Archive, S/20/555, quoted in Renzo De Felice, *Jews in an Arab Land: Libya, 1835-1970*, pages 229.

Despite facing severe economic difficulties and a war that caused much destruction and impoverishment, the young State of Israel took in 580,000 Jewish refugees from Muslim lands from the first days of its independence, as well as more than 100,000 survivors of the Holocaust in Europe. All of these refugees came with nothing, and were taken in, sheltered, fed, housed and found places in the workforce, despite the heavy financial costs to the Israeli Government.

The Jews living in Muslim lands in 1948 might have hesitated to make their way to a land at war, or to trust the emissaries who came from the new Jewish State to promote such a long and often hazardous journey. But they did not hesitate, even in the lands and towns and homes in which their families had lived for so many generations. They knew what their situation would be if they remained where they were. They knew that under Muslim rule their existence would be harsh and full of danger.

16

IRAQ, 1948–1952

'The treatment of the Jews of Iraq is not creditable to the Iraqi Government'

In Baghdad, most of the Jewish communal leadership, headed by Chief Rabbi Sasson Khedouri, an opponent of Zionism, hoped that with the end of the Israeli War of Independence the Jewish community could look forward to an easing of existing tensions and a relaxation in anti-Jewish rhetoric and attacks. But more and more Iraqi Jews, including many non-Zionists, doubted that such an attitude was realistic. On 14 November 1948, while Iraqi troops were still on the battlefield, an Iraqi law had added 'Zionism' to communism, anarchism and immorality in a list of offences whose propagation was punishable by seven years in prison or a heavy fine.[1]

Iraqi Zionists were not deterred. On 8 March 1949, as the Iraqi forces were returning from their Palestine war front, a British diplomat reported from Baghdad to London that 'many younger men, of the "white collar" class, roughly those aged thirty and younger, would be interested in emigrating to Israel, in the belief that they would have better opportunities there than in Iraq.'[2]

Individual Iraqi Jews and small groups began to cross the frontier into Iran, in defiance of the martial law that was then in force. Between March and December 1949, some 1,500 made the crossing; two thirds went on to Israel. All had been in danger of being captured and taken to prison in Baghdad.

---

[1] Law No. 11 of 1948 (amending Law No. 51 of 1938): *Gazette*, 14 November 1948, Government of Iraq, Baghdad, page 591.
[2] Report of 8 March 1949, National Archives, Kew, Foreign Office papers, FO 371/75128.

On 24 August 1949 a telegram reached the Zionist emissaries in Teheran, describing the events of the previous few days in Iraq. 'The persecution of Jews intensifies,' the telegram reported. 'Leading figures in the community have been arrested in Hillah. The head of the community in Khanaqin, the ritual slaughterer, and other notables have been placed under arrest on charges of abetting the flight of Jews. The state of the prisoners is appalling. They are being punished by hard labour.'[3] The ritual slaughterer died a few days later, as a result of torture.

On 3 October 1949, the Day of Atonement, the Iraqi police surrounded the synagogue in the town of Amara, on the Tigris River, and arrested ten worshippers, including the head of the local Jewish community. In the words of a former British official in the Iraqi Government, Stephen Longrigg, this incident was symptomatic of 'an increase in hostile pressure' on the Jews. For the Arabs, Longrigg noted, 'the sight of the terrified community aroused in some the worst instincts of spite and bullying.'[4]

The arrests and torturing continued. On October 12 the clandestine Zionist emissaries in Baghdad sent a coded message by radio telegram to their head office in Tel Aviv, stating that they no longer had any way 'of dealing with the situation.' The message noted that all the signs indicated that the new Iraqi persecutions 'may be a mass phenomenon, and the arrests and torture will affect hundreds if not thousands of Jews.' Nine days later, on October 21, a further coded message from the Zionist emissaries reported: 'Dozens of searches have been conducted in the homes of leaders and commanders' – the leaders of the clandestine movement. Three girls and one boy had died as a result of torture. 'Teachers have been arrested in schools. The Secret Police are resorting to brutal torture.'

The telegram then detailed the nature of the torture being inflicted on those who had been arrested: '1. They fetter the prisoners' hands with chains, string them up, and whip them. 2. They dip

---

[3] Telegram of 24 August 1949: quoted in Shlomo Hillel, *Operation Babylon*, page 214.
[4] Stephen Longrigg, *Iraq, 1900-1950*, page 353.

their hands and feet in boiling water. 3. They burn them with hot irons all over their bodies.' Those tortured 'have reached a state of hysteria, and some are hardly recognizable.'[5]

On October 23 large numbers of Jews gathered in the streets of Baghdad to protest about the continued arrests of Jews, and about the widespread hostility and harassment of Jews by the Muslim population. Two days later, most Jews in Baghdad stayed in their houses to observe a special day of fasting and prayer, and to continue their protest about the situation.[6] Shlomo Hillel, who was monitoring the day of fasting from Tel Aviv, later recalled that it 'surprised everyone – and none more than the Jews themselves – because the strike that accompanied it shut down the Jewish community to a man. Not a child appeared at school; shops and businesses remained shuttered; and even the Jews employed in government service stayed out of work. The police – who regarded the strike as a provocation if not outright insurrection – responded by escalating their violence.'[7]

An Iraqi Jew who had left Baghdad ten months earlier, and who pretended to have just arrived in Israel – since no one could be smuggled out at that moment – gave a well-attended press conference in Tel Aviv. In it he gave details based on the most recent messages received from Iraq. As a result of this press conference, news about the plight of Iraqi Jewry appeared in many newspapers in Western Europe and the United States. 'ANTI-JEWISH DRIVE IN IRAQ DESCRIBED,' was a headline in the *New York Times* on October 26, followed by a sub-headline: 'Escaped Merchant Says 350 Were Seized in 9 Days and 70 Per Cent Were "Tortured".' The article began: 'A 35-year-old Jewish merchant who said he had fled Baghdad told a Government-sponsored press conference tonight about what he described as a wave of anti-Jewish terror in Iraq.'[8]

---

[5] Telegrams of 12 and 21 October 1941: quoted in Shlomo Hillel, *Operation Babylon*, pages 216-7.
[6] Norman A. Stillman, *Jews of Arab Lands in Modern Times*, pages 158-9.
[7] Shlomo Hillel, *Operation Babylon*, page 223.
[8] Gene Currivan, *New York Times*, sent from Tel Aviv, 25 October 1949, printed 26 October 1949.

As the publicity spread, the Israeli Ambassador to the United States, Elyahu Elath (formerly Epstein), helped organise protest demonstrations at the Iraqi Embassy in Washington and the Iraqi Mission in New York. But when, on November 4, Elath asked George McGhee, the United States Assistant Secretary of State for Near Eastern, South Asian and African Affairs, if the United States would raise the question of the plight of Iraqi Jewry at the United Nations, McGhee replied that he 'strongly' recommended not raising the issue, because 'a debate in the General Assembly would stir up feelings and do Iraq's Jews more harm than good.'[9]

The situation of the Jews in Iraq was not raised at the General Assembly. But the head of the Iraqi delegation at the United Nations, Tawfiq al-Suweidi, was made to understand the strength of Israeli feeling. In December, the British Ambassador to Iraq, Sir Henry Mack, sent a full report of the situation of the Jews to the British Prime Minister, Clement Attlee. 'The condition of the Jews in Iraq,' wrote the Ambassador, 'has deteriorated since May 1948.' Almost eight hundred Jewish civil servants had been dismissed, including 261 from their posts at the Iraqi State Railways, 159 from the Ministry of Social Affairs and 117 from the Ministry of Education. Martial law had been 'grossly abused to the detriment of Jewish individuals, and the Jewish community does not now enjoy such equality of economic opportunity as it did in the past.'

The Ambassador added: 'The treatment of the Jews of Iraq is not creditable to the Iraqi Government, and they cannot be defended against charges of discrimination, but they have maintained order in circumstances of some difficulty and so prevented any repetition of the killing and looting of Jews which took place after the defeat of the Iraqi Army in 1941.' The Ambassador went on to warn: 'It is, I fear, inevitable that the Jewish community in Iraq will live in some insecurity, and it seems probable that this ancient community will decline in number and influence.'[10]

---

[9] Quoted in Shlomo Hillel, *Operation Babylon*, page 220.
[10] Sir Henry Mack, telegram of 12 December 1949: Foreign Office papers, FO 371/75182.

There was a moment of hope for the Jewish community in Iraq when Ezekiel Shemtob was appointed its acting head. He replaced the elderly Chief Rabbi Sasson Khedouri, who had been reluctant to take a lead in community protest, and had tried to dampen Jewish student ardour. Iraqi politics were also changing to the advantage of the Jews. On 9 December 1949, Nuri Said was replaced as Prime Minister by Ali al-Ayubi Jawdat, who, on December 18, nine days after taking office, lifted the martial law that had made emigration all but impossible for seven months, since 15 May 1948.

Although Jews still needed permission to leave Iraq, the ending of martial law made it possible for them to leave the cities legally, and then to attempt to cross the border into Iran. Israeli emissaries in Iraq worked strenuously to facilitate that escape. In January 1950 they arranged for 1,058 Iraqi Jews to cross the border into Iran. Other Jews made their own way, often helped by Arab smugglers, after having bribed Iraqi policemen and officials.[11]

On January 27, Ezekiel Shemtob went to see Prime Minister Ali Jawdat and received assurances from him that the Jews would again be issued passports to allow them to leave the country legally. Ali Jawdat also promised that the prison sentences passed on Jews in October, November and December would be reviewed, and that penalties for trying to leave the country illegally would be relaxed.

In the first week of February, Jawdat resigned and was succeeded as Prime Minister by Tawfiq al-Suweidi. The Jews of Iraq had reason to expect a further easing of their situation. Tawfiq was a friend of the new head of the Jewish community, Ezekiel Shemtob, who lived next door to him in the Karimat villa district of Baghdad. Although a Muslim and an Arab, al-Suweidi had studied at the Alliance Israélite Universelle school in Baghdad, a Jewish school whose reputation for first-class education had led several leading Muslim families to choose it for the education of their sons. On February 15, ten days after becoming Prime Minister, Tawfiq told Shemtob that he would allow Jews to leave and would issue them with special documents – *laissez-passers* – with

---

[11] Shlomo Hillel, *Operation Babylon*, pages 197-205.

which to leave. This was an important step forward. When Shemtob then asked that Jews who wished to leave be given full Iraqi passports, as Jawdat had offered, Tawfiq agreed.

That February another 1,020 Iraqi Jews left the country, most of them for Israel. On 7 February 1950 a headline in the *New York Times* read: 'JEWS LEAVING IRAQ IN A STEADY FLOW: Heavier Traffic across Border into Iran Is Attributed to Lifting of Martial Law. Most are Zionists. Attitudes Fluctuate.' The article, sent from the Iranian border city of Khorramshahr two weeks earlier, began: 'This crossing point for Iraqi Jews leaving the country is getting a steadily heavier traffic as Jews in Baghdad, principal centre of Jewish population in Iraq, in Basra and the adjoining southern areas close out their affairs and prepare to leave the country.'[12]

On March 2, while the Jews were celebrating Purim – the liberation from the threat of extermination in ancient Persia – they had cause for yet another celebration. On that day, the Iraqi Minister of the Interior, Saleh Jabr, introduced to Parliament the Revocation of Citizenship Bill, which would allow Jews to leave Iraq 'for good.' The one condition was that they give up their Iraqi citizenship in perpetuity, something that was acceptable to the vast majority of those who wished to leave. The Bill was passed that same day. One of the Israeli emissaries then in Baghdad, Iraqi-born Mordechai Ben-Porat, later recalled that an Iraqi Jewish police officer, Salman Dabby, was asked by the Iraqi commander of the police department in charge of citizenship revocation 'to investigate, before the Bill is ratified, the general opinion of the Jewish community.' Dabby's report was emphatic: if the Government oppression of the Jews in Iraq continued, 'the pace of registration would quicken.'[13] The Bill came into force two days later.

By the end of May 1950, at least ten thousand Iraqi Jews had crossed the border into Iran. These Jews – no longer citizens of Iraq – were taken to a refugee camp near Teheran administered by

---

[12] Albion Ross, *New York Times*, sent from Khorramshahr 24 January 1950, printed 7 February 1950.
[13] Mordechai Ben-Porat, *To Baghdad and Back*, page 185.

the American-Jewish Joint Distribution Committee and financed in part by a Jewish businessman of Iraqi origin, Saleh Shlomo Chitayat. From Teheran the refugees were flown to Israel. Among those who left Iraq through Iran at this time was five-year-old Avi Shlaim. As Professor of International Relations at the University of Oxford, he later recalled 'an atmosphere of panic,' in which 'Jews felt threatened, there were attacks.' In his view, his family left Iraq because of 'hostility at a popular level to the new State of Israel' – not due to any official Iraqi discrimination or expulsion.[14]

On 8 April 1950, the last day of Passover, the Zionist organisation in Iraq called on all Iraqi Jews who wished to do so to register for emigration. Within three weeks, 47,000 Iraqi Jews had presented themselves at registration centres in the main synagogues. There, they had to sign a formal and in many ways formidable declaration, which read: 'I declare willingly and voluntarily that I have decided to leave Iraq permanently and that I am aware this statement of mine will have the effect of depriving me of Iraqi nationality and of causing my deportation from Iraq and of preventing me forever afterward from returning.'[15]

The Iraqi Government decided to allow Jews of military age to leave. This important decision was a result of an arrangement with the only Jewish member of the Iraqi Senate, Menahem Saleh Daniel, made in return for the transfer of his substantial estates – valued at five million pounds sterling – to the Iraqi Government.[16] The airlift was far less efficient, however, than the one from Yemen had been. Those who had registered and signed the declaration and not been found a place on a plane were in the dangerous situation of being stateless, and without work. Some had even sold their homes.

Jewish emigration from Iraq was regularised in spring 1950, when the Iraqi Government allowed Near East Air Transport Company – the United States air charter company that had just completed the flights

---

[14] Avi Shlaim, quoted in the *Jerusalem Report*, 25 July 2008.
[15] Joseph B. Schechtman, *On Wings of Eagles*, page 112.
[16] Note of 4 February 1951: British Foreign Office papers, FO 371/91689.
£5 million in 1951 was the equivalent of at least £100 million in 2010.

from Yemen – to airlift Jews from Iraq to Israel. That spring, however, a problem arose that cast a shadow over the exodus of Jews from Iraq. The problem had nothing to do with the Iraqi Government, which had accepted that it had underestimated the number of Jews who wanted to leave the country; having predicted a maximum figure of ten thousand, it was prepared to allow ten times that number of Jews to leave if they wished to do so. The new and grave problem was Israel's inability to absorb so many newcomers at a time when at least a hundred thousand survivors of the Holocaust in Europe were also desperate to reach the new State. This predicament led to a slowdown in the rate at which Jews were admitted to Israel from whatever source, and created a bottleneck of Jews inside Iraq who, having obtained permission to leave, were suddenly left stateless.

An intimation that this problem would arise had been given to Shlomo Hillel, one of the Israeli organisers of the Iraqi Jewish emigration, and himself a clandestine emissary in Iraq. Hillel went to see the Treasurer of the Jewish Agency, Levi Eshkol (later Israel's second Prime Minister) in Jerusalem. The Jewish Agency was responsible for the absorption of all new immigrants to Israel. With a forthrightness that astonished Hillel, Eshkol said to him: 'Tell your good Jews that we'll be delighted to have them all, but they mustn't rush. Right now we lack the ability to absorb them. We don't even have tents. If they come, they'll have to live in the street.' When Hillel protested, Eshkol told him: 'You don't know what you're bringing these people into. You must make it absolutely clear to them that conditions are very difficult, downright primitive. Otherwise they'll be bitter – and rightly so. I don't want them protesting outside my window . . .'

On March 27, a few days after being rebuffed by Eshkol, Shlomo Hillel went to see the Israeli Prime Minister, David Ben-Gurion, who was totally supportive of the mass emigration from Iraq. 'Tell them to come quickly,' Ben-Gurion said to Hillel, and went on to ask: 'What if the Iraqis change their minds and rescind the law? Go and bring them quickly.' Hillel returned to Iraq, and did what he could to expedite the emigration. But the Jewish Agency held the purse strings; it still insisted on halving the rate of intending immigrants leaving Iraq.

Angry that Israel was slowing down the rate of emigration, Mordechai Ben-Porat, then the senior Zionist emissary in Iraq, telegraphed to his superiors in Tel Aviv to explain the plight of the Jews who had already applied to leave. They were in 'the worst way,' he explained. Citizenship had been revoked from 26,000 Jews. 'Have you taken into consideration,' he asked those who were slowing down the emigration, 'that there will be a revolt against us.' A revolt 'by the families who have left their jobs, sold their homes, and are waiting impatiently for the day when they can leave?' Angrily, Ben-Porat went on to ask: 'Why have you allowed us to deceive the Jews by promising them unlimited immigration?'[17]

Jews in Iraqi provincial towns who had applied to leave were thrown out of their homes by local officials, and even by neighbours. Reaching Baghdad as refugees, they were housed and fed in synagogues that were converted into emigration centres. The Israeli Foreign Minister, Moshe Sharett, warned his Cabinet colleagues on August 28 that the existing, reduced quota of between 2,500 and 3,000 Iraqi Jews a month was highly insufficient considering the 'emergency situation that has come into being in Iraq' and the 'capriciousness of the regime.' Sharett was concerned about the ability of the Iraqi authorities to 'resort to brutal means that cause the loss of human lives.'

The Israeli quota for Iraqi Jews remained in force. One Zionist emissary in Baghdad, Ronnie Barnett, reported to Tel Aviv on September 22 about a new influx of Jews who had applied to leave and had all the necessary documentation: 'A few thousand have arrived from (been driven out of, is more accurate) the provincial cities without a penny to their names. They loiter about everywhere in a frightful state.' First they used up the funds they had been given to pay for the flight out of Iraq – to Cyprus and then on to Israel – 'then they become a burden on the community.' Barnett added: 'I assume you know that there have been about fifty cases of infant deaths.'[18]

---

[17] Telegram of 17 July 1950: quoted in Shlomo Hillel, *Operation Babylon*, page 265.
[18] Shlomo Hillel, *Operation Babylon*, page 265.

That September, the government of Tawfiq al-Suweidi fell, and Nuri Said became Prime Minister of Iraq for the eleventh time. To the surprise of the Jews who had already applied to emigrate – of whom, on November 23, eighty thousand were reported to be waiting to leave, Nuri, hitherto not regarded as a friend of the Jews in any respect, made considerable efforts to accelerate the flow of emigration. His first idea was that the Iraqi Government would finance the direct flight of Jews from Baghdad to Israel using British Overseas Airways Corporation (BOAC) planes, which were capable of carrying 50,000 emigrants a month. But for this, BOAC needed the approval of the Israeli Government, which was unwilling to increase its 2,500 to 3,000 a month quota.

On a State Visit to Jordan at the beginning of 1951, Nuri Said produced a second plan. He asked the Jordanian Government if the Iraqi Jews could travel by road from Iraq across Jordan to Israel, using Iraqi Army lorries that would be protected by Iraqi soldiers. King Abdullah of Jordan and the Jordanian Prime Minister, Samir Rifai, told Nuri Said 'in definite terms' that they would not agree to his proposal. Nuri Said then insisted that Rifai went with him to the residence of the British Ambassador to Jordan, Sir Alec Kirkbride, to obtain confirmation that Britain supported the plan.

In his report of the meeting, Kirkbride explained that he had made it clear that he had no instructions from the Foreign Office in London to support the plan. There then followed what Kirkbride called 'an absurd wrangle' between Nuri Said and Rifai, 'which ended in their both losing their tempers.' Rifai was insistent that 'the passage of Jews through Jordan would almost certainly have touched off serious trouble amongst the very disgruntled Arab refugees who were crowded into the country.'[19] He then warned Nuri: 'Either the Iraqi Jews would have been massacred or the Iraqi guards would have had to shoot the Arabs to protect the lives of their charges.'

---

[19] Following the Arab-Israeli War of 1948–9, there were 350,000 Palestinian Arab refugees in refugee camps in Jordan, 280,000 on the West Bank (which Jordan had annexed in 1948) and 70,000 in former Transjordan (pre-1948 Jordan east of the river).

When Rifai said that he did 'not want to be party to such a crime,' Nuri replied – according to Kirkbride's report – 'with such a violent outburst' that he feared the two Prime Ministers would come to blows in his study.[20]

Thwarted in both of his plans to get rid of the Jews who were trying to leave Iraq, Nuri Said contemplated a third option: putting them in detention camps in the Iraqi desert until plans could be made for them to leave. Fortunately for the Jews, and prudently for Nuri Said's reputation, the Regent of Iraq, Abdul Ilah, refused to allow this. Even more fortunately for the Jews, at that very moment the Israeli Government raised the immigration quota to 13,500 a month. It was not a moment too soon. By 13 January 1951, a total of 85,893 Iraqi Jews – some two thirds of the country's total Jewish population – had registered for emigration to Israel. Of these, 35,766 had been deprived of their Iraqi nationality, but only 23,345 had been flown to Israel. At the earlier rate of immigration permitted by Israel, it would have taken four months to clear the backlog and another two years for all of the remainder to be able to make the journey.

Then disaster struck. On 14 January 1951, just as Israel increased the quota, a grenade was thrown into the midst of a group of Jews standing in the courtyard of the Masuda Shemtob Synagogue, one of the main emigration registration centres in Baghdad. The group was about to leave for the airport. Five Jews were killed and fourteen injured. The Iraqi Government accused the Zionists of throwing the fatal grenade, producing a variety of reasons to explain why the Jews had done it: to discredit Iraq, to pressure Israel into speeding up the airlift, or to panic the Jews who had not yet registered to leave so that they would hasten to do so. The Zionist emissaries in Baghdad, and the mass of Iraqi Jews, were convinced that the grenade had been thrown by Arab extremists. Those extremists, they believed, were eager to accelerate the emigration and happy to kill

---

[20] Telegram of 16 January 1951: Sir Alec Kirkbride to the Foreign Office, London: National Archives (Kew), Foreign Office papers, FO 371/91689. Kirkbride's published account of this meeting is in his book *From the Wings: Amman Memoirs*, page 115.

Jews in the process, or simply to frighten rich Jews – who had not wanted to abandon their assets – into leaving and thereby enriching the Iraqis.[21]

The Iraqi Government set a deadline of 9 March 1951 for the completion of Jewish registration for departure, and another deadline of May 31 for the emigration itself to be completed. After the failure of his air, land and detention camp schemes, Nuri Said threatened to drive the stateless Jews of Iraq across the border into Kuwait, unless they left by the March deadline. 'The Iraqis are in earnest about this,' the British Ambassador reported from Baghdad on 24 January 1951. 'Their real fear is a general war which would find them with a large number of stateless and disloyal persons, many of them without means of support, within their border. They are also genuinely afraid of a popular outburst against the Jews similar to that of May 1941.'[22]

In the seven weeks between the grenade attack of 14 January 1951 and the deadline of March 9, almost 30,000 more Jews signed up for emigration, surrendering their Iraqi citizenship. Initially, at the insistence of the Iraqi authorities, the planes carrying emigrants could not fly to Israel direct – which would create a precedent of direct flights from an Arab State to Israel – but had to fly via Cyprus. On March 10, the day after the registration deadline, another blow was struck at the ancient, determined and tormented Jewish community. At a secret session of the Iraqi Parliament, Nuri Said secured the passing of a law – Law No. 5 of 1951 – whereby the assets of all Jews who were leaving and had renounced Iraqi citizenship – 103,866 by that time – were frozen and put under Iraqi Government control.[23] Overnight, 80,000 Jews were made destitute.

When Law No. 5 was voted on, the six Jewish members of the

---

[21] For an account of the grenade episode and the documentation concerning it, see Norman A. Stillman, *Jews of Arab Lands in Modern Times*, page 162 and note 49.
[22] Telegram of 24 January 1951: Foreign Ofice papers, FO 371/91689.
[23] Law No. 5 of 1951, 'A Law for the Supervision and Administration of the Property of Jews who have Forfeited Iraqi Nationality,' *Gazette*, Government of Iraq, Baghdad, page 17.

Iraqi Parliament had not been allowed into the Parliament building. They protested publicly, and one of them resigned. But as Marina Benjamin, a historian of the Jews of Iraq, has written: 'Their power had already faded: even now their parliamentary colleagues were muttering behind their backs, what need the small number of loyalist Jews remaining in Iraq would have for six deputies once their co-religionists had departed.'[24]

As much as $150 million was confiscated from the Jews in this way, but possibly much more. Although some individuals succeeded in smuggling out 'considerable sums . . . often via the Beirut black market,' writes Norman Stillman, 'many were reduced to paupers.'[25] Those leaving could take with them only what they could carry in their suitcases and bundles, along with 50 dinars ($140) in cash for each adult, and a maximum of 30 dinars ($84) for each minor.[26] Searches at Baghdad airport were rigorous.

From March 12 onward, the Iraqi authorities finally allowed the planes to fly directly from Baghdad to Lod Airport in Israel.[27] The pressure to leave continued. By June 1, eighty-four thousand Iraqi Jews had emigrated and twenty thousand were still waiting to leave. But there was yet another cruel setback for Iraqi-Jewish emigration. At the end of 1951, following the show trials of a number of Zionists who had been accused of carrying out the January explosion, two Jews – Yosef Basri and Shalom Saleh Shalom – were hanged in public, in the heart of Baghdad, to enthusiastic public joy. One of the executed men had claimed in court that the confession used against him had been extracted under the most terrible torture.

The Zionist emissaries then back in Israel had hoped to be celebrating the success of Operation Ezra and Nehemia – the final flights of which left Baghdad in February 1952. They were instead devastated by the executions. Not one of the twenty-five emissaries, Shlomo Hillel

---

[24] Marina Benjamin, *Last Days in Babylon*, pages 214-5.
[25] Norman A. Stillman, *Jews of Arab Lands in Modern Times*, page 163. In the money values of 2010, US $150 million was approximately $1,230 million.
[26] In the money values of 2010, $140 was $1,150 and $84 was $690.
[27] Now Ben-Gurion Airport.

recalled, 'could find it in his heart to celebrate the successful conclusion of the undertaking that had rescued over a hundred thousand of our people from a country where the death of a Jew was
cause for exaltation.' The Psalmist had written of his ancestors'
ancient dispersion from Jerusalem to Babylon: 'By the waters of
Babylon, there we sat down, yea we wept, when we remembered
Zion.'[28] Shlomo Hillel reflected, 'And so were we fated to weep in
our hour of redemption as well.'[29]

By the end of 1951, a total of 113,545 Jews had left Iraq legally.
Another 20,000 had left illegally. Only about 6,000 Jews were still
living in the country, able, as Professor Stillman writes, 'to return to
relatively normal, comfortable lives for at least another decade.'[30]

---

[28] Psalm 137.
[29] Shlomo Hillel, *Operation Babylon*, page 285.
[30] Norman A. Stillman, *Jews of Arab Lands in Modern Times*, page 164.

17

EGYPT, 1951–1961

'We the "Yahud" were considered the "enemy"'

The first tremors of an earthquake that was to shake the remaining 70,000 Jews of Egypt to their core came in October 1951. The Wafd Party government, having already whipped up anti-British feeling, demanded the withdrawal of British troops from the Suez Canal Zone and unilaterally revoked the Anglo-Egyptian Treaty of 1936. In the months that followed anti-Jewish violence intensified.

Edna Anzarut was targeted while driving with her mother to a favourite painting spot outside Cairo: 'The first stone that was hurled at us hit the windshield,' she later recalled. 'An angry crowd suddenly appeared from everywhere, and started pelting our car with stones. Their faces deformed by fury and hatred, they shrieked "Yahoodi, Sahyooni, Bannatte el Kalb" – "Jew, Zionist, daughters of dogs." My mother was able to reverse without hitting anyone and escaped what had become an angry mob.'[1]

On 26 January 1952, 'Black Saturday,' thousands of Egyptians rampaged through a large part of the European sections of Cairo. The mob was incensed over the continuing presence of British troops in the Suez Canal Zone. As was often the case during nationalist demonstrations, it was the Jews, however, who ended up being victims of the unrest. Many Jewish businesses were attacked; in a single day of rioting an estimated £10 million of Jewish property was destroyed.[2]

---

[1] Edna Turner (née Anzarut), letter to the author, 18 April 2009.
[2] Approximately £500 million in the money values of 2010.

Suzy Vidal remembered that day in vivid detail: 'All of a sudden an enormous BOOM of people barging into our building froze us into terror. They were screaming and yelling in search of Jews who lived there.' The family fled to the roof, where 'fires and smoke were on the right and on the left.' It seemed to the Vidals that their 'last hour had come,' but unexpectedly 'a great silence fell on the frenzy in our building.' The mob had gone elsewhere. Abdou, the Muslim hall porter, 'had stopped the enraged crowd by solemnly stating that no Jews lived there. They believed him, leaving the building to hunt for another Jewish hideout.'[3]

Anti-Jewish attacks of this kind were almost always instigated by the extremist Muslim Brotherhood. Fortunately for the Jews, the Egyptian Government feared the Brotherhood's Islamic fundamentalist appeal and moved against the organisation with severity; the leader of the Muslim Brotherhood, Hasan al-Banna, was assassinated in February 1952. Egyptian Jews were no longer a target for official persecution by the Government. Although Egyptian law held that 'activities' carried out for the benefit of a country with which Egypt had broken relations was an offence that could lead to loss of citizenship, Zionism as such was not made an offence in the Egyptian criminal code.

The Government of Egypt underwent a significant change on 23 July 1952, when the Free Officers Movement, led by Colonel Gamal Abdul Nasser, forced King Farouk into exile and took control of the country in a bloodless coup. Lucy Calamaro, who was eight years old in 1952, later recalled: 'I remember the revolution because the Muslims burned all of the Jewish shops and stole what was inside. I remember it so well because for a whole week we did not leave the apartment.'[4] But to the relief of the seventy thousand Jews still living in Egypt, the new Government proved to be more tolerant than its predecessor. It was not long before Egyptian Jews felt confident they could look forward to easier times, and perhaps even a return to the life and leisure of the 1920s and 1930s.

---

[3] Sultana Latifa (Suzy Vidal), *The Jasmine Necklace,* page 90.
[4] Quoted in: Benjamin Bright, 'The Exodus revisited,' *Jerusalem Post,* 24 April 2006.

The leader of the new Egyptian Government, General Neguib, visited Jewish schools and synagogues. Two Jewish industrialists, Aslan Cattaui Bey and Victor Zagdoun, served on the board of the prestigious Mohammed Ali Club, of which another leading Egyptian Jew, Sir Simon Rolo, was a respected member. Several Jewish newspapers were still being published. Football matches organised by the Maccabi Club were played without harassment. Property that had been seized by the Egyptian Government during the Israeli War of Independence was returned to those of its owners who still lived in Egypt. Jews who had been held in detention, other than those accused of being Communists, were released.

Nevertheless, there were many small indications that all was not well for the Jews. In May 1953 the weekly Jewish newspaper *le Menorah* ('The Candelabra') was closed down by the authorities. The newspaper's assets were confiscated, and its editor, Jacques Maleh, was held in prison for forty days without access to any legal representation. He was then given the choice of a life sentence in prison or permanent exile from the country. He chose the latter.[5]

In June 1954, General Neguib was replaced by his fellow army officer Colonel Nasser, the leader of the Free Officers who had overthrown King Farouk. Like Neguib, Nasser had no animosity towards the Jews. His slogan was: 'The religion for God, and the homeland for all.' He had even become an enemy to the still-thriving Muslim Brotherhood, which had tried to assassinate him. But in July 1954, a month after Nasser came to power, Egypt's relations with Israel – and the fate of all Egyptian Jews – were suddenly placed in grave danger. The cause for alarm was the 'Lavon Affair,' a clumsy attempt by the Israeli secret service – the Mossad – and at least one Israeli Government Minister, Pinhas Lavon, to implicate the Muslim Brotherhood in acts of terror. The plan was to have Israeli agents explode bombs against Egyptian, American and British targets while at the same time making the attacks look like a Muslim Brotherhood operation.

---

[5] 'Jacques Maleh (1906-1989),' obituary, *IAJE Newsletter* (International Association of Jews from Egypt Newsletter), 2002, Volume 4. No. 2, pages 6-7.

The first bomb exploded in a post office in Alexandria on July 2. Several more exploded on July 14: at a British-owned theatre and at the United States Information Agency libraries in Alexandria and Cairo. Little damage was done and no one was killed or injured. But nine Israeli agents, all former Egyptian Jews, were arrested. One died under torture and another committed suicide. After a trial, which lasted from 11 December 1954 to 27 January 1955, two of the Israeli agents, Moshe Marzouk and Shmuel Azar, were sentenced to death and hanged.[6]

A Jewish Member of Parliament in Britain, Maurice Orbach, had flown to Egypt to speak with Nasser before the trial. Nasser assured Orbach that he 'had every desire to conclude a peaceful settlement with Israel, if it were not for his radical opponents, who were determined to overthrow the regime and accuse him of treason.'[7]

Meanwhile, the Egyptian Government had begun a secret roundup of Egyptian Jews, starting on 22 July 1954, in the aftermath of the Lavon Affair. Myriam Schechter, who was almost nineteen years old at the time, later remembered what became known as the 'Cairo Mishap.' The incident occurred at the Central Tram Station, where Jewish youth congregated each Saturday 'to decide on the activities for the evening.' Myriam Schechter recalled: 'I was on my way there to meet my date, when a friend, coming in the opposite direction, grabbed my arm. . . . He led me to someone's house where by ones and twos, some of our friends tiptoed in grimly. There had been a dragnet at the station, and all the Jewish young men arrested and taken to prison. My date spent the night in a cell with a murderer, playing chess with him through the night, afraid to fall asleep. The Jews were in shock. The aftermath of the so-called "Cairo Mishap" paralyzed us.'[8]

---

[6] Israel admitted responsibility for the bomb attacks in 2005, when the Israeli President, Moshe Katzav, honoured the nine Egyptian Jewish agents who had been involved.

[7] Michael M. Laskier, *The Jews of Egypt, 1920-1970*, pages 125-30. In March 1979, twenty-five years after the Lavon Affair, another Egyptian President, Anwar Sadat, took the risk of making peace with Israel. He was assassinated in October 1981 by officers opposed to the peace treaty with Israel.

[8] Myriam Schechter Wolf, letter to the author, 11 January 2009.

—

Jewish life in Egypt was soon dealt another blow with the onset of the Suez War in 1956. The Suez Canal and the land on both sides of it – the Suez Canal Zone – had been under British control since the end of the Second World War. But for the Egyptian Government under Nasser, complete control of the Canal was an overriding desire. On 26 July 1956, Cairo Radio announced that Egypt was nationalising the Canal, hitherto owned and administered by an international consortium under the authority of Britain and France.

In the days following the Canal's nationalisation, Suzy Vidal witnessed a sinister anti-Jewish mood that appeared in Cairo alongside anti-British unrest. In the streets she 'kept hearing the word *Yehud* – Jews – and the hate-filled looks were clear.' At the same time 'an insidious then gradually violent anti-Jewish campaign was launched in the newspapers and the radio.' By the time the university term started at the beginning of October, she had noticed 'a strange ostracism settled vis-à-vis the Jewish and foreign students,' and was forced to wonder: 'Where had the companionship gone, the enjoyment of one another's difference?'[9]

On October 29, Israeli forces advanced towards the Suez Canal in retaliation for continued terror attacks on Israel from the Egyptian-controlled Gaza Strip. Their advance was part of a secret agreement already made between Britain, France and Israel. In accordance with that agreement, Britain and France called on the Israeli forces to halt, and landed at Port Said to 'protect' the Suez Canal waterway, nationalised by Egypt three months earlier. The Suez War had begun.

On the first day of the Suez War – known in Israel as the Sinai Campaign – a young Egyptian Jew, André Aciman, heard Cairo Radio announce a 'decisive victory over the enemy.' England, France and Israel had been 'thoroughly defeated.' The 'crushing march' of Egyptian forces to Haifa and Tel Aviv 'was already under way,' and the combined Arab armies would celebrate victory by the end of the

---

[9] Sultana Latifa (Suzy Vidal), *The Jasmine Necklace*, page 99.

year on the shores of the Sea of Galilee.[10] The reality on the ground was very different. 'As night settled on that first doomed day,' Vivianne Silver has written, 'we could see flares in the darkened skies. . . . Bombs were falling on Cairo.'

At the sound of each bomb landing in Cairo, Vivianne Silver heard her father, Joseph Schinasi, exclaim: '"*Ils sont là. Nous sommes sauvés*" ("They've arrived. We are saved.").'[11] Each time his hopes were swiftly dashed. Yet it was two months later that her father came home 'absolutely jubilant, and joyfully said to us, "*Les visas du Canada sont arrivés. Nous sommes sauvés!*" ("The visas from Canada have arrived. We are saved!").' Vivianne Silver adds: 'This time, we were indeed saved!'[12]

In Israel, while the Suez War was still being planned, Shaul Avigur had devised a Mossad plan named Operation Tushia ('Cunning'). Its aim was to rescue as many of the 70,000 Jews in Egypt as possible from the cities on and near the Suez Canal Zone, and also from Cairo and Alexandria – once British forces reached those two cities. In the event, as a result of United States pressure, British and French forces were halted just south of Port Said and failed to capture any other city. But three Mossad operatives, headed by Lova Eliav – who had earlier been an organiser of the clandestine emigration of Holocaust survivors from Europe – were able to enter Port Said. There, under the protective eye of the British military authorities, they assembled about a hundred Jews, then travelled with them in two fishing boats across the Eastern Mediterranean to Haifa.[13]

For the vast majority of Egyptian Jews, however, such an escape was impossible. Trapped in the midst of a war, they endured a situation that was tense in the extreme. Professor Moshé Matalon, then a schoolboy, recalled almost half a century later 'the dramatic experience of being in Cairo during the Sinai Campaign, when we the "Yahud" were considered the "enemy" and we had carefully to obey

---

[10] André Aciman, *Out of Egypt: A Memoir*, page 167.
[11] Vivianne M. Schinasi-Silver, *42 Keys to the Second Exodus*, page 73.
[12] Vivianne M. Schinasi-Silver, *42 Keys to the Second Exodus*, page 75.
[13] Tad Szulc, *The Secret Alliance*, pages 244-5.

the blackout in order not to give the authorities an excuse to blame us of treason.'[14]

Within hours of the start of the Suez War, many hundreds of Egyptian Jews had been arrested. Samy Harari, leader of the Maccabi fan club in Cairo, was among them. He was beaten up and badly injured while in captivity, and never fully recovered. Others escaped such violence but were not spared the anti-Jewish mood. Harari's cousin Samuel Cohen later recalled how one of his Muslim neighbours was 'joyful' at the widely believed claim that Egyptian forces were already in Tel Aviv and 'were slaughtering the Jews and the Zionists.'[15]

Ronald Cohen, an eleven-year-old schoolboy, was awakened one night at about midnight. He later recounted: 'The secret police were there. They placed my mother under house arrest. Next morning we found an "X" carved in a stone outside our house: we had been identified as Jews.' He also remembered other distressing experiences: 'I was traumatized at school when a Jewish boy had a stone thrown at him and was bleeding from the head and my parents pulled me out of school. I never went back.' Ronald Cohen continued: 'I also remember how upset I was when I saw a Government-sponsored poster showing a Star of David with a snake coiled around it.'[16]

On 22 November 1956 a new Egyptian Nationality Code barred all so-called 'Zionists' from Egyptian nationality. On the following day an inflammatory proclamation was read out in all mosques, declaring: 'All Jews are Zionists and enemies of the State.'[17] Four days later, on November 27, the *Jerusalem Post* reported that Jews arriving by plane in Paris 'confirmed that expulsion orders were being issued to Jews in Egypt by the thousands.'[18]

The Israeli Foreign Minister, Golda Meir, wrote the first of two letters to the United Nations Secretary General on November 27 – the

---

[14] Letter from Professor Matalon: *IAJE Newsletter* (International Association of Jews from Egypt Newsletter), 2002, Volume 4. No. 2, page 1.

[15] Samuel Cohen, in conversation with the author.

[16] Sir Ronald Cohen, in conversation with the author, 18 September 2009.

[17] Law No. 391 of 1956: see *Revue égyptienne de Droit International,* Volume 12 (1956), page 80.

[18] *Jerusalem Post,* 27 November 1956.

second followed three days later – protesting 'the action taken by the Egyptian Government against the Jewish Community in Egypt.'[19] On December 21 the United States' representative to the United Nations, Henry Cabot Lodge Jr., declared that he and his Government shared 'the concerns about reports of the plight of Jews in Egypt' and put on record the United States' policy of 'abhorring such practices as have been alleged.'[20]

Within a few weeks, pressure from the United States forced the Anglo-French forces to withdraw from Egypt altogether. The last of the British troops left on 19 June 1957. Within a year Israel had evacuated the Sinai Desert and pulled back to its 1949 borders.

The Suez War had dire consequences for Egypt's 70,000 Jews. Three thousand Jews were arrested and detained without trial. More than 24,000 were served with deportation orders and forced to leave Egypt within a few days. Those who were deported were not allowed to sell their property or take their capital with them.

Robert Khalifa, who was ten years old in 1956, has described how the school behind his house was turned into a detention centre for British and French nationals who were also being expelled and 'Israeli sympathizers.' He writes: 'These so-called sympathizers were just the prominent members of the Jewish community.' When the expulsions began, Jews who had properties and businesses tried to have family members and acquaintances look after their bank accounts and assets. 'However,' Robert Khalifa adds, 'the people who were asked and even begged did not always accept for fear of giving reason to be ordered to leave Egypt. In fact, many people who took the risk and accepted to supervise businesses or properties supposedly only temporarily were also later kicked out.'[21]

One of those arrested, imprisoned, and then deported was Pinhas Bouskeyla, who twenty-two years earlier had given refuge in

---

[19] Israel Foreign Ministry Archive, Jerusalem.
[20] National Archives, Washington.
[21] Robert Khalifa, letter to the author, 25 November 2007.

his Port Said hotel to Jewish refugees from Yemen.[22] Another Jew expelled after the Suez War was Moise Lévi, who a mere six months earlier had been auctioning King Farouk's treasures on behalf of the Egyptian Department of Confiscated Properties.[23] He was deported not because he was a Jew but because he held a British passport. His fine villa in the Maadi suburb of Cairo was bought at a 'bargain basement price' by a Muslim who leased it to Said al-Taji al-Farouki, a Palestinian Arab whose lands near Ramla (in former British Mandate Palestine) had been confiscated by the Israeli Government. Lévi went to Britain.[24]

The Jews lost not only their homes and their property, but also their community and culture. Nouri Farhi, who was fourteen in 1956, saw a cousin and his wife – 'good Egyptian citizens, who had done nothing wrong to Egypt' – imprisoned and then expelled. Farhi's uncle had already been expelled in 1948 'with his family, few clothes and without money,' after being imprisoned for sixteen months and having his printing house confiscated. Looking back more than fifty years later, Nouri Farhi reflected: 'So we left Egypt. . . . We also left our past, our history, our grandparents' graves, our synagogues.'[25]

For many Egyptian Jews, the arrests and expulsions interrupted previously harmonious relations with neighbouring Muslims, and at the same time inspired a new and deep bitterness. Isaac Shama, whose relations with the Egyptians had always been good, was arrested and accused of being both a British and an Israeli spy. His son David later recalled a brief visit Isaac made to his family from prison, when one of the Egyptian policemen escorting him 'was crying (his eyes were red and wet).' David recounted how the policeman 'told me in

---

[22] Ada Aharoni, Aimée Israel-Pelletier, Levana Zamir (editors), *History and Culture of the Jews from Egypt in Modern Times*, page 159, note 29.
[23] In the two government sales of King Farouk's property, jewels and valuable possessions, Moise Lévi (Maurice Levy) – for the previous twenty years one of Egypt's leading auctioneers – obtained the concession to conduct the auctions. One auction was held at the Koubeh Palace in 1954 and the other at the Abdine Palace in January 1956. Samir Raafat, *Cairo, The Glory Years*, pages 230-1.
[24] Samir W. Raafat, *Maadi, 1904-1962: Society & History in a Cairo Suburb*, page 231.
[25] Nouri Farhi, letter to the author, 12 December 2008.

Arabic in a very gentle voice that my father will be alright and that Allah will watch over him.' He remembered 'being very confused at this because I truly hated these people who were hurting my father, and yet this policeman was being kind to me.'

Isaac Shama was tortured, tried, sentenced to death and then expelled. As he sailed from Egypt with his family, with nothing but the clothes they were wearing, his son recalled: 'My parents were so happy they were laughing and crying and could not seem to control their emotions. . . . I was happy, but angry. In fact I became very belligerent at Arabs in general and I was looking for confrontations anywhere I could find them. . . . All I wanted was vengeance for what was done to us.'[26]

As the expulsions continued, Suzy Vidal watched as her community of friends and family began to shrink and disappear. One of her father's cousins was deported after being accused of spying. All Egyptian Jews who were French and British subjects were given a maximum of ten days to leave, and were each allowed to take with them only two suitcases and ten pounds. Suzy Vidal later wrote: 'My childhood friend Jacqueline and her family were in that "enemy group."' The result was a pitiful sight: 'One after another of the friends and families that had survived 1948 and 1952 left, preferring two suitcases and £10 to the constant threats and uncertainty for the future.'

Suzy Vidal and her family left Egypt for Italy; her father left shortly after her. On her way across the tarmac to the plane she waved her scarf to show him that everything had gone well. 'Leaving our sunshine, our habits and our customs behind, that scarf was the flag of defeat, of the unforeseeable and of deep heartache. It was the parting of the roads that were never to meet again.'[27]

The exodus of Jews from Egypt was given further impetus later in 1957. Starting on November 1, and continuing for almost three weeks, 486 Egyptian Jews were arrested under 'Military Proclamation

---

[26] David R. Shama, letter to the author, 18 March 2008.
[27] Sultana Latifa (Suzy Vidal), *The Jasmine Necklace*, pages 100-4.

No. 4.' Their property and assets were sequestered and handed over to Egyptian administrators.[28] A number of Copts and Muslims were also seized under this proclamation, but their property was never taken from them.[29]

The Jews who left Egypt between 1956 and 1958 found sanctuary and rebuilt their lives in many lands. Among the largest groups, thirty-five thousand went to Israel, fifteen thousand to Brazil, ten thousand to France, nine thousand to the United States, another nine thousand to Argentina, and four thousand to Britain. Egypt's loss was these countries' gain. Egyptian Jews had been an integral part of the very lifeblood of Egypt for many generations, dating back to before the earliest years of Islam.

In the years that followed, legislation continued to impoverish the Jews who remained in Egypt, forcing many of them to leave. On 20 July 1961, almost eight hundred Jewish-owned companies, banks and industries were taken over by the Egyptian State.[30] That same day, Ministerial Decree No. 1276 nationalised the predominantly Jewish-owned Egyptian Delta Land and Investment Company that had developed the Maadi villa suburb in southern Cairo.

In 1961, a Jewish couple, Marguerite de Botton and her husband Charles Victor Castro, owners of one of Cairo's finest mansions, the Villa Castro, decided to leave Egypt. The Villa Castro was requisitioned. It later became the official residence of President Sadat; among his visitors there were Henry Kissinger and Presidents Nixon and Carter. Other former Jewish-owned mansions became the Russian, Afghan, Saudi Arabian and Canadian Embassies. The historian of Cairo, Samir Raafat, has reflected: 'Giza's riverfront Jews may have left the country, but standing as testament to their presence are their grand homes, now used as embassies, courtly homes of the rich and famous, or the official residence of the nation's President.'[31]

---

[28] *Egyptian Official Gazette*, No. 88, 1 November 1957.
[29] Jimena (Jews Indigenous to the Middle East and North Africa), International Rights and Redress Campaign, 'Country Narratives,' page 2: www.justiceforjews.com.
[30] Samir Raafat, *Cairo, The Glory Years*, page 251-2.
[31] Samir Raafat, *Cairo, The Glory Years*, page 247-8.

The few hundred Jews who did not immediately leave Egypt faced persistent discrimination. At Victory College – as Victoria College was renamed after the Suez War – André Aciman was 'the last Jew' in the school. In Arabic class he was given a poem vilifying Jews to learn by heart. He later recalled how, when he complained to his teacher that a fellow student had called him *kalb al-'Arab* – dog of the Arabs – 'she did not give me time to finish my complaint. "But you are the dog of the Arabs," she replied in Arabic, smiling, as if it were the most obvious thing in the world.'[32]

Robert Khalifa had a similar experience while studying at the Lycée Français. As a member of the compulsory cadet force, he did so well in military training that he was to be promoted sergeant. But on graduation day in 1963 he was not called to the dais. He later recounted: 'After the ceremony was over, the Principal called me and spoke down to me like I was a servant and I had some contagious disease. Apparently the officer who had recommended that I be promoted did not look at my file closely enough and had not noticed that I am Jewish.'[33]

Robert Khalifa and his family immigrated to Canada before the year's end. André Aciman and his family left in 1964. On his last night in Alexandria, André Aciman sat on the sea wall for the last time. He later described the emotions of that moment: 'I stared at the flicker of little fishing boats far out in the offing, always there at night, and watched a group of children scampering about on the beach below, waving little Ramadan lanterns . . . followed by another group of child revellers who were flocking along the jetty past the sand dunes, some even waving up to me from below. I waved back with a familiar gesture of street fellowship and wiped the light spray that had moistened my face. And suddenly I knew, as I touched the damp, grainy surface of the sea wall, that I would always remember that night. . . .

'I wanted to come back tomorrow night, and the night after, and the one after that as well, sensing that what made leaving so painful

---

[32] André Aciman, *Out of Egypt: A Memoir*, pages 228 and 237.
[33] Robert Khalifa, letter to the author, 25 November 2007.

was the knowledge that there would never be another night like this, that I would never . . . feel the baffling, sudden beauty of that moment when, if only for an instant, I caught myself longing for a city I never knew I loved.'[34]

Lucette Lagnado, who left Egypt with her family in 1963, felt the same way. The dedication in her family memoir is taken from the Bible: 'And the Children of Israel wept and said: "Who will feed us meat? We remember the fish that we ate in Egypt free of charge, and the cucumbers, melons, leeks, onions, and garlic. But now, our life is parched, and there is nothing we have nothing to anticipate but manna."'[35]

In her memoir, Lucette Lagnado wrote of her family's last night in Egypt: 'My father took me for a walk. Hand in hand, we made our way across the boardwalk passing one beach after another. Every once in a while, he would stop and turn and face the sea. He didn't say a word. There were countless cafés, and even in March, we could see nighttime revelers relishing the breeze of an Alexandria evening, smoking and drinking beer or arak, the liqueur whose smell I loved, but which was so strong I couldn't touch a drop.'

The next morning the Lagnados made their way to the dock, where their ship was expected to sail around noon. 'There were many other families like us, sitting in small chairs, surrounded by mountains of suitcases. They spoke a dozen different languages, Arabic and French, of course, the two most common languages, but also English, Greek, Italian, and Spanish. But that was Egypt, of course. Or it had been. Suddenly, "foreigners" weren't welcome in the very place where most of them had felt so profoundly at home. After months of frenzied activity, there was nothing left to do. Nothing except to sit back on our deck chairs, and gauge how it had all come to this – decades in the life of a family, reduced to two dank cabins situated too close to the roaring engines of a small unsteady boat, along with the twenty-six suitcases that contained all their worldly belongings.'

The Lagnados arrived in France 'with exactly $212 – the sum total

---

[34] André Aciman, *Out of Egypt: A Memoir,* page 240.
[35] Numbers 11:4-6.

that we'd been allowed to take with us out of Cairo.' It was soon spent. 'For Dad, who had spent a lifetime investing in the stock market and building a nest egg, what was most painful was finding himself destitute, dependent on charity for himself and his family to survive. My father was used to giving alms, not taking them. He had dreaded that moment but had been helpless to avoid it. . . . Most of the Jewish refugees of the Levant found themselves in exactly the same straits: they saw their social status and wealth vanish overnight. They went from being solid members of the bourgeoisie to beggars.'[36]

The Egyptian exodus of 1956 continued into the early to mid-1960s, and brought the remarkable story of a sometimes uneasy, sometimes fulfilling, but always creative two-thousand-year-long Jewish presence in Egypt almost to an end. By 1966 there were fewer than a thousand Jews remaining in the country.

On 10 September 1994 a seven-word notice in Cairo's *al-Ahram* newspaper told of the death in Switzerland of 'René Joseph Cattaui Bey, former Egyptian Senator.' René Cattaui was ninety-seven years old. He had become an Egyptian senator in 1938, when his father Joseph Cattaui Pasha had resigned due to ill health. In the words of Samir Raafat, the historian of Cairo, *al-Ahram* gave René Cattaui 'none of the usual accolades once attributed to his famed forebears.' Raafat has commented: 'The spirit of this important dynasty is no more. It is as though it passed into the back pages of history, a ghost for what had once stood for riches, glamour and power.'[37]

---

[36] Lucette Lagnado, *The Man in the White Sharkskin Suit*, pages 159-60, 164 and 173.
[37] Samir Raafat, 'Dynasty: The House of Yacoub Cattaui,' *Egyptian Mail*, 2 April 1994.

18

THE EXODUS CONTINUES, 1950–1967

'A growing desire to leave the country for Israel'

The existence of Israel was a powerful incentive for Jews to leave Muslim lands, inspiring in them the hope that they could live their lives free of anti-Jewish sentiment. In Syria, four thousand of ten thousand Jews left their homes and moved to the new Jewish State between 1948 and 1953. The extraordinary pull that Israel exerted was underscored by the fact that these emigrants from Syria travelled secretly, in order to evade a national ban on immigration to Israel.

Many Jews who wished to leave Syria went across the border to Lebanon – the only Arab country whose Jewish population increased after the Israeli War of Independence, from 5,200 to 9,000. Lebanon's mixed Muslim-Christian population was the most tolerant to Jews of any population in the Arab world. At a reception held by the Lebanese Jewish community in Beirut at Passover in 1951, all the nation's leading politicians were present, including the Prime Minister, Sami as-Solh, a Muslim.[1] But for Jews who defied Syrian law and attempted to make their way to Israel, escape was nearly always fraught with peril. In one tragic incident, in November 1950, thirty Syrian Jews found a group of smugglers willing to take them in a small boat from the Mediterranean shore to the coast of Israel. They were all murdered at sea.

In 1954 the Syrian Government lifted its ban on emigration to Israel for any Jew prepared to abandon his property without selling it.

---

[1] Kirsten E. Schulze, 'The Jews of Lebanon' in Tudor Parfitt (editor), *Israel and Ishmael: Studies in Muslim-Jewish Relations*, pages 91-3.

Yet because Syria wanted to avoid strengthening the population of Israel with an influx of Syrian Jews, such periods of sanctioned emigration were brief. For the many Jews who, as a result, could not find a way out of Syria, life was harsh. Don Peretz visited Syria in 1957 as an emissary of the American Jewish Committee – founded in 1906 to uphold the civic rights of Jews in any part of the world. He reported that the 5,300 Jews of Syria, who lived in the cities of Damascus, Aleppo and Kamishli, were mostly poor and dependent on charity sent by Jews from outside the country. They were also living, he wrote, 'if not in terror, certainly in constant fear, bedevilled by Syrian security forces.'[2]

There was a second brief lifting of the emigration ban in 1958, but again the Syrian authorities insisted that all their property had to be abandoned by every family when they left. By the beginning of 1959 the Jews of Syria were effectively captives: some three thousand in Damascus, fifteen hundred in Aleppo and five hundred in Kamishli, on the north-eastern border with Turkey. A long period of isolation from the rest of the Jewish world had begun. Israel, despite its common border with Syria, was completely out of bounds and out of reach.

The situation of Jews in Iraq steadily worsened following a coup on 14 July 1958. Among those killed in the upheaval were the Prime Minister, Nuri Said, and the Regent, Abdul Illah. Among those on the new rulers' wanted list was Tawfiq al-Suweidi, the former Iraqi Prime Minister who had allowed mass Jewish emigration. One of his friends was a Jew, Jamil Shemtob, whose father Ezekiel had been the head of the Baghdad Jewish community at the time of the emigration. Jamil Shemtob decided to risk his life in order to save his Arab friend. He took al-Suweidi to his own home, keeping him there in safety until the danger had passed.

Jamil Shemtob and his family stayed in Iraq, hopeful, like the five thousand other Iraqi Jews who remained, that they could maintain

---

[2] Quoted in Norman A. Stillman, *Jews of Arab Lands in Modern Times*, page 164.

and preserve the traditions of Iraqi Jewry in the new republic.[3] But in February 1963 the Baath Party came to power, and nine months of political turmoil led to a severe deterioration in the situation of the Jews. Travelling abroad, even for medical treatment, became nearly impossible. Almost no Jews were allowed to study at the universities. Much Jewish property, both individual and communal, was confiscated. Baghdad's ancient Jewish cemetery, which had existed for a thousand years, was destroyed. And then, in a decree reminiscent of the harshest days of *dhimmi* status, Jews were made to carry special yellow identity cards, so that, as Shlomo Hillel has commented, 'no one would mistake them for true sons and daughters of Iraq.'[4]

The Baath Party fell from power in November 1963, encouraging the remaining Jews of Iraq to look forward once more to better times. The period of respite was, however, all too short; in July 1968 the Baath Party returned to power, and was not to be dislodged for forty-five years. Iraqi-born Mira Rocca later recalled the tribulations of her aunt, Naima Soussa, even before the Baath Party returned. 'By 1966,' she wrote, 'it was impossible to get an exit visa, and my aunt, a wealthy widow, was desperate to leave. A grandmother in her sixties, she had some unfinished business in Khanaqin, one of the exit points for illegal departures. The sale of some property had been agreed with her late husband, but not concluded, and when the buyer offered to help smuggle her into Iran it seemed a heaven-sent opportunity. Naima travelled to Khanakin, signed, and waived all payment.'

Naima Sousa had put all her savings, jewellery, banknotes 'and a stash of gold coins' in a money belt, knowing the risk she was taking. Once the property sale was complete, the buyer stalled for time and then denounced her. 'The police found the money belt and sent Naima to Baghdad where she was thrown in jail. She appealed to the police chief, a friend of her son Maurice, who went to see his colleague, the Minister of the Interior. The Minister was outraged

---

[3] Mordechai Ben-Porat, 'Jamil Shemtov' (obituary), *Nehardea: Journal of the Babylonian Heritage Centre*, No. 16, Spring 2008. Jamil Shemtob later changed his name to the more Israeli-sounding Shemtov.
[4] Shlomo Hillel, *Operation Babylon*, page 291.

that he should be pleading the case of a Jewess. She was ordered to pay a 5,000 dinar fine (£63,000 in 2010) and they confiscated her money belt.'

There was no trial. Naima Soussa's detention was 'indefinite.' But as her niece later commented, 'she was spared the torture others suffered to elicit confessions of spying for Israel.' Remembering those Jews, Mira Rocca wrote: 'Some died in custody. It was a scary time: Jews were being publicly hanged on trumped up charges.' Naima Soussa languished in prison for two years while her family members in the United States lobbied lawyers and Senators. In London, Mira's mother managed to interest Amnesty International in the case, and, 'eventually, the combined pressure on the Iraqi regime bore results.' Naima Soussa's release came on the condition she 'voluntarily' donate to the Iraqi Government all that remained of her late husband's estate: farms, properties, businesses and bank accounts. 'Denied permission to go home and pack or to visit her husband's grave one last time, she was taken to Baghdad airport in a cattle truck.'[5]

Change was also on the horizon in Iran, where ninety-five thousand Jews were living in 1948, the descendants of one of the most ancient communities in the Jewish world. Arabs living in Iran made efforts to incite the local Iranians against Jews, and extreme Muslim organisations circulated anti-Jewish leaflets. Yet the Iranian Government refused to join in or even imitate the rhetoric that was rampant in the Arab world. In March 1950, Iran granted de facto recognition to Israel and sent a special representative there with negotiating authority.

Without internal impediment or harassment, 25,000 Iranian Jews emigrated to Israel in 1950 and 1951. Many of these immigrants were members of Zionist youth movements who wanted the opportunity to use their youth and energy to build up the Jewish State. The Iranian Government showed further tolerance towards the Jews in March 1950, when it took immediate steps to halt an attack on Jews that had broken out in the predominantly Arab province of Iranian

---

[5] Mira Rocca, communication with the author, 23 July 2009.

Kurdistan, along the Iraqi border. Twelve Kurdish Jews were murdered. As soon as the violence was stopped, the Iranian Government offered protection to any Jews in the affected area who wanted to move to the capital, Teheran, or even to Israel; more than one thousand Kurdish Jews went to Israel.

In 1951 the Iranian Government briefly shifted direction. A new Iranian Prime Minister, Mohammed Mossadeq, permitted an increase in anti-Jewish propaganda by the Muslim clergy, on whose support he depended politically. But when Mossadeq was overthrown in 1953 and the Shah regained power, anti-Jewish propaganda came to a halt. The number of Jews leaving for Israel fell steadily, from 4,856 in 1952 to 1,109 in 1953, and then to only 128 in 1955. The Shah became the first Muslim leader to recognise the State of Israel.

Close cooperation between Iran and Israel was evident throughout the 1950s and 1960s. Israeli contracting firms were active in Iran, particularly in reconstruction work after the Kazvin earthquake of 1962. The Israeli national airline, El Al, maintained a regular flight schedule between Teheran and Tel Aviv. Trade between Israel and Iran was carried out both by air and by sea, with sea trade proceeding through the Persian Gulf, the Arabian Sea and the Red Sea to the Israeli port of Eilat at the head of the Gulf of Akaba. Israeli agricultural experts worked in Iran, and Iranian Muslim agricultural students studied in Israel.

The Shah was finding it more and more difficult to control Iran's Shiite Muslim fundamentalists. In 1963 there were clashes between government forces and supporters of the Shiite clergy. During these clashes, anti-Jewish leaflets were circulated and Jews were assaulted. The number of Jews leaving for Israel rose to more than two thousand a year, and then fell again when the Shah's authority was restored – to 966 in 1966 and 462 in 1967.

The influence of the Muslim clergy with regard to the Jews became pervasive. Hayyim J. Cohen, Senior Lecturer on Contemporary Jewry at the Hebrew University of Jerusalem, has recorded one example that indicates the prejudice Jews faced in everyday life: a Muslim vegetable store owner would not allow a Jew to touch his vegetables, but would pick them out for him, 'for fear that the Jew might render all his fruit and vegetables unclean.'[6] This prejudice also had an institutional element. Although Jews had the right, collectively, to vote for one Jewish delegate in the Iranian House of Representatives (the Majlis), they could not, despite their large numbers, have more representation or participate in the election of other delegates. Nor could a Jew become a member of the Iranian Government or a judge.

In Afghanistan, Zionist activity had been illegal since 1948, and no emissaries from Israel had been permitted to enter the country. Starting in 1951, however, the Afghan Government changed its policy and allowed the Jews to leave for Israel. Four thousand had left by 1967; only three hundred remained. Throughout the mass emigration, the pressure to leave was continuous. Those Jews who stayed in Afghanistan were exempted from the country's Military Service Law, but were forced to pay a tax, reminiscent of the *jizya*, for not serving. Government service and government schools were both closed to Jews.[7]

The plight of the Jews of Yemen had also been alleviated by mass emigration. Between June 1949 and September 1950, a period of sixteen months, 44,000 Yemenite Jews had flown from Yemen to Israel.[8] This astonishing airlift operation comprised 430 flights. First called Operation on Wings of Eagles, and then renamed Operation Magic Carpet, it was carried out by the American charter airline the Near East Air Transport Company. At the height of the exodus in the autumn of 1949, eleven aircraft were flying around the clock.[9]

In December 1950, Itzhak Ben-Zvi, one of Israel's founders, and soon to be its second President, flew overnight from Israel to Aden

---

[6] Hayyim J. Cohen, 'Iran,' *Jewish Encyclopedia*, Volume 8, columns 1439-1443.
[7] Hayyim J. Cohen, 'Afghanistan,' *Encyclopaedia Judaica*, Volume 2, column 328.
[8] The British Acting Governor of Aden estimated that 42,069 Jews went by air from Hashid Camp to Israel between June 1949 and 27 May 1951: 'Jews Air Lift from Hashid Camp,' Colonial Office papers, CO 725/101/2.
[9] Joseph B. Schechtman, *On Wings of Eagles*, pages 52-7 and 70-2.

on one of the planes of Operation Magic Carpet. The journey took eight hours. On his arrival, he was driven to Hashid Camp – known in Hebrew as Mahane Geula ('Camp Redemption') – the assembly centre for Yemeni Jews who had been brought to Aden from all over Yemen to await the journey to Israel. There were then 2,100 refugees in the camp. Within seven days that number rose to 3,000. During the previous twelve months, thirty thousand Yemeni Jews had passed through on their way to Israel, funded by the American-Jewish Joint Distribution Committee and the Jewish Agency for Israel. Before Hashid Camp was established, eight thousand Yemeni Jews had already made their way to Israel through Aden.

Conditions in Hashid Camp were far from ideal. When the influx of refugees was at its height, in September and October 1949, between seventy and eighty per cent of the refugees there had been suffering from eye diseases. During those two months alone, three hundred people died in the camp – half the total number of deaths there for the year.

More than two hundred residents in Hashid Camp had come from Najran, a Saudi Arabian town beyond the Yemen border. Upon their reaching Yemen, the King of Saudi Arabia had asked the new Imam of Yemen, Zaydi Ahmad, to send them back to Saudi Arabia, since they were his subjects. The Imam had agreed to detain them, but refused to send them back.

While in Aden, Ben-Zvi heard 'with grave concern of the poisonous propaganda against Jews and Israel' that was being conducted by Arab refugees from Palestine who were reaching Yemen. Some of these Arab refugees, crossing into Yemen from Saudi Arabia, were appointed to positions in the Yemen police. It was they, Ben-Zvi learned, who had informed the Saudi King about the Jews from Najran. Ben-Zvi lamented 'the incessant flood of anti-Jewish propaganda that goes unchallenged.'[10]

The imperative for Jews to emigrate was particularly strong in Libya.

---

[10] 'Aden Diary,' in Itzhak Ben-Zvi, *The Exiled and the Redeemed*, pages 272 and 279.

On 5 October 1950 a Libyan Jewish newspaper in Tripoli reported that 'one finds even among the wealthier groups a growing desire to leave the country for Israel, and transfer to Israel their industrial plant and businesses. Now even among the young of the richest Jewish families there is a greater interest in the Zionist movement for youth immigration.'[11]

On 24 December 1951, Libya declared independence from the post-war British administration. Israel had already cast its vote in support of Libyan independence in the United Nations, helping to make Libya the first Muslim nation established after the founding of the Jewish nation of Israel. Yet the remaining four thousand Jews of Libya – the remnant of a forty-thousand-strong community – were not welcome as part of the new sovereign State.

On 20 October 1952 the Libyan weekly *Al-Libi* ('The Libyan') wrote bitterly about the Jews who remained in the country: 'They dominate the largest commercial and industrial activities and exploit all means with their skilful and enterprising methods.' They 'called themselves' Libyan citizens 'in order to exploit this status and attain their goals.' The paper went on to ask, 'Could these Jews be sincere?' It answered its own question with the words: 'We have never heard of a single Jew actively participating in the cause of our Country and we have never seen a Jew sacrificing his person or goods for the Country!' What then did the Jews represent? The Jewish community in Libya 'represents a form highly dangerous for the common cause of the Arabs and constitutes an insidious disease in the body of the nascent Country.'

The *Al-Libi* article continued by insisting that the Jews of Libya were 'a link in world Zionist policy.' Like Jews in the rest of the world, they 'believe only in the principle of amassing wealth and are faithful to no other country besides Israel.' Every penny that the Jews of Libya earned 'is a heavy brick of Arab blood building up Israel, and if they were allowed to arrange things as they would like they would move to Israel every facility for reconstruction in Libya and would

---

[11] Quoted in Renzo De Felice, *Jews in an Arab Land: Libya, 1835-1970,* page 231.

demolish it and leave it in ruins in order to build up Israel.'Whenever there was an occasion for them to talk about the 'initiative' in Israel, 'they show pride in its revival and progress, without any concern for our feelings.'[12]

Within two years, the Libyan Government had abolished the rabbinical court and dismissed the last four Jews serving in the police force. The catalyst for these moves came in the early months of 1953, when the Government sought admission to the Arab League. Since its foundation eight years earlier, the Arab League, with its own administrative structure and leadership, provided all Arab-Muslim regimes with a sustained anti-Israel policy and rhetoric.

The first restrictions imposed in Libya after its admission to the Arab League were all Israel-related: the suspension of the postal service to Israel, the closing down of the Jewish Agency as Israel's immigration office, and the expulsion of the Jewish Agency's representative in Libya, Meir Shilon. Obstacles were created for the renewal of expired passports. On 30 March 1957 the Libyan Government began to enforce a law forbidding any individual or corporation in Libya 'to make personally or indirectly an agreement of any nature whatsoever with institutions or persons residing in Israel.' The penalty was eight years in prison or a heavy fine. A Government office was set up to confiscate from any Jew, Muslim or foreigner, goods bearing the slightest resemblance to a Star of David.

Regina Waldman, a young Jewish girl living in Libya, who was nine old in 1957, recalled an incident in her own school. A teacher asked the children in an arithmetic lesson: 'If you have ten Jews and you kill five, how many do you have left?' That, she reflected many years later, 'was my first taste of hate.'[13]

On 9 May 1957 the Libyan Government issued a decree ordering all Libyan Jews with relatives in Israel to register with the Libyan Boycott Office, the main pressure group opposing Arab trade with Israel. Since more than ninety per cent of Libyan Jews had left the

---

[12] Renzo De Felice, *Jews in an Arab Land: Libya, 1835-1970*, page 387, note 4.
[13] Regina Waldman, 'A Jewish Woman from Muslim Society Reflects on Life in Islamic Lands,' *JIMENA* (Jews Indigenous to the Middle East and North Africa).

country between 1949 and 1952, this decree applied to almost every Jewish family in Libya.[14]

Pressure against the Libyan Jews mounted. On 31 December 1958 the Jewish community – hitherto an autonomous body charged with maintaining contact with the authorities – was abolished. A Muslim commissioner was appointed to supervise the Jewish community's activities. There followed a takeover by the Libyan Government of the main Jewish school, and then, in April 1960, the enforced closure of the Alliance Israélite Universelle school, which for more than sixty years had been a focal point of Jewish and western education. A protest by the United Nations Educational, Scientific and Cultural Organization (UNESCO) at the closure of the Alliance school was ignored by the Libyan authorities. The Maccabi sports club, the only surviving pro-Zionist organisation, was closed down.

Libyan newspapers kept up a barrage of venom, which they directed against the Jews as a people. 'A settling of accounts between the Jews and Islam is indispensable,' declared *El-Raid* ('The Guide') on 15 August 1960. 'The Jews are the authors of the misfortunes of all colonialist countries,' was the message from *Tarabulus al-Gharb* ('Western Tripolitania'). 'Peace is impossible,' asserted *Al-Libi*, 'so long as Jews are permitted to exercise their implacable hatred of the Arab world and the lands of Islam.'[15]

One further effort was made by the Libyan authorities to isolate the Jews, and to weaken their links both with Israel and with the 31,343 Libyan Jews who had emigrated there. On 21 March 1961 a law was passed that sequestered for the Government 'all goods and property in Libya belonging to organizations or persons resident in Israel or connected to them by professional affiliation.' Fortunately for the Jews, the setbacks created by this law were countered by a general economic upsurge as a result of the oil boom. The six thousand Jews remaining in Libya, like all Libyan citizens, benefited from the country's newfound prosperity.[16]

---

[14] Maurice M. Roumani, *The Jews of Libya*, page 189.
[15] Quoted in Maurice M. Roumani, *The Jews of Libya*, pages 192-3.
[16] Renzo De Felice, *Jews in an Arab Land: Libya, 1835-1970*, pages 265-9.

—

From the establishment of the State of Israel in May 1948, pressure had been mounting on the Jews of Morocco, who were made to feel unwelcome in the land where their forefathers had lived since before Roman times. The anti-Jewish pogroms in Oujda and Djerada on 7 June 1948, in which forty-three Jews were killed and sixty seriously injured, accelerated the exodus of Jews from the country.[17]

Jews also suffered setbacks in nearby Tangier, an international port city that had been under joint French, British and Spanish administration since 1923; 15,000 Jews lived there among 45,000 Muslims. The Muslims were demanding union with Morocco; on 15 March 1952 mass street demonstrations turned violent. In an attack mainly directed at European interests, many Jewish-owned shops were among those looted and burned.[18] It took another four years before union with Morocco took place. Meanwhile, between May 1948 and September 1956, more than 90,000 Moroccan Jews decided to leave.

Several Jewish organisations were active in Morocco both before and after 1948: the Jerusalem-based Jewish Agency, the American-based World Jewish Congress, the Hebrew Immigrant Aid Society (HIAS), and Zionist youth groups, among them Habonim, Bnei Akiva and Hashomer Hazair. In October 1954, Arthur Greenleigh, the executive director of HIAS, returned from a visit to Casablanca. He reported to his board of directors: 'The situation for all non-Moslems in Morocco is extremely tense. The Moslems are determined to drive out the French and achieve independence. . . . In the meanwhile the economic and political situations have rapidly deteriorated. Jews who have lived for centuries in the interior have found it necessary to move into the bigger cities to save their lives. Jewish businessmen have been threatened with death unless they make substantial financial contributions to the terrorists . . .' Greenleigh warned: 'Morocco is now an armed camp – no non-Moslem

---

[17] André Chouraqui, *Between East and West: A History of the Jews in North Africa*, pages 181-2.

[18] M. Mitchell Serels, *A History of the Jews of Tangier*, pages 168.

is safe on the streets at night and every day . . . someone is killed by terrorists.'[19]

As a first step in the departure of Moroccan Jews for Israel, HIAS set aside a substantial contingency fund for an emigration programme. In 1954 only 8,171 Jews had been allowed to leave for Israel. In 1955 that number rose to 24,994. The Jewish Agency was allowed to open an emigration holding camp in Casablanca. Even larger numbers of emigrants were expected. But on 3 March 1956, Morocco became independent from France, and Sultan Sidi Mohammed ben Yusef became its ruler.[20] One of the first actions of the new Moroccan Government was to order the Jewish Agency to halt its emigration activities and close down the emigration camp. The last group of Jews, 12,000 in all, was allowed to leave officially by September 1956.

The appointment of a Moroccan Jew, Léon Benzaquen, as Minister of Posts and Telegraph raised Jewish hopes of becoming an integral part of the new kingdom. But in July 1956 an internal HIAS report warned that there appeared to be 'clear evidence' that either the nationalist Istiklal Party or the Government, or both, had 'initiated a policy of disrupting Jewish community life in the country.'[21]

In early 1955 the Israeli Mossad chief, Isser Harel, appointed Shlomo Havilio as his senior representative in Morocco.[22] It was Havilio who launched the highly secret Operation Misgeret ('Framework'). Its agents – mostly Israeli Army officers who spoke French or Arabic – were inserted into Morocco to train some two hundred local Jewish youth in methods of self-defence. The Mossad also organised a mass movement of Jews out of Morocco. Would-be emigrants were taken on long journeys hundreds of miles overland across the Moroccan desert and smuggled across the borders of the small Spanish enclaves on the Atlantic coast. The Spanish dictator, General Franco – who was widely believed to be descended from Jews forcibly converted to Christianity

---

[19] Tad Szulc, *The Secret Alliance*, page 218.
[20] Later titled King Mohammed V.
[21] Tad Szulc, *The Secret Alliance*, page 224.
[22] The Mossad, short for ha-Mossad le-Modiin u'le-Tafkidim Me'Yuhudim (Institute for Intelligence and Special Tasks).

in the Fifteenth Century – allowed the emigrants unimpeded transit. Ships crowded with Moroccan Jews travelled again and again, under cover of darkness, from Atlantic and Mediterranean ports in North Africa to France.

Many of the Moroccan Jewish emigrants were from the remote and poverty-stricken mountain villages in the interior: 'primitive' Jews, as HIAS emissary Raphael Spanien described them, whom no other country but Israel would accept. Of the 270,000 Jews in Morocco, Spanien estimated, only between 25,000 and 50,000 were 'Westernized.' Among the 50,000 who had emigrated to Israel in the previous decade 'there is not even one doctor.'[23]

Between 1956 and 1961 more than 35,000 Moroccan Jews left clandestinely for Israel under the auspices of the Mossad. In 1960, the same year that he masterminded the capture of Adolf Eichmann in Argentina, Isser Harel, travelled to Morocco as a tourist. His visit there convinced him that many Jews wished to leave, and he appointed Alex Gatmon to be in charge of the Mossad operations in Morocco, under Ephraim Ronel in Paris.

The undercover departure of Jews to Israel was soon underway. On 11 January 1961, however, the *Egoz*, a small ship carrying emigrants from the Moroccan coast to Gibraltar, sank in heavy seas. Forty-three emigrants, half of them children, and their Israeli escort and Spanish crewman were drowned. Until then the *Egoz* had made thirteen safe crossings. Hearing of the tragedy, David Ben-Gurion instructed the Jewish Agency and the Mossad to find another way to get the remaining Jews who wished to emigrate to Israel out of Morocco.

It was not long before an imaginative solution presented itself. The plan – whose codename was Mural – had its origins with a senior Jewish Agency official, Naftali Bargiora, before it was passed on to a British Jew, David Littman, a man of determination and energy. Two weeks after the sinking of the *Egoz*, Littman knocked on the door of the Oeuvre de Secours aux Enfants (OSE) office in Geneva, and was

---

[23] Raphael Spanien, Report, February 1955: HIAS (Hebrew Immigrant Aid Society) archive.

received by Professor Jacques Bloch, the Director. 'What can I do?' Littman asked. Bargiora had found the man for the job.

Six weeks later, Littman flew to Casablanca with his Egyptian-born Jewish wife, Gisèle Orebi – then stateless – and their five-month-old daughter. Littman began an operation that would facilitate the departure, between June 26 and July 24, of 530 Moroccan Jewish children. During three months of preparation, Littman was helped by both Mossad contacts and the local Misgeret to encourage parents to register their children for a summer holiday with a Swiss children's organisation – something entirely legal, such as going to Marseille for a few days to watch a football match. The children received collective passports – dozens of children on a single passport. On reaching Switzerland they were to be taken to holiday camps and later sent on to Israel. In the end, three of the five convoys went directly to Israel.[24] David Littman had been a conduit to a new life, and is remembered and honoured to this day.

The Moroccan Government took a hard line towards the departure of Moroccan Jews for Israel. Moulay Ahmed Alaoui, the Minister of Information, described Jewish emigration as a 'betrayal and desertion' of Morocco. In addition, he declared: 'It was unjust that Moroccans should take the place of Palestinian Arabs in Israel, and that is why we stop the Jews leaving.'[25] Echoes of Nazism could also be heard. In March 1961, when a cinema in Casablanca screened a dramatised version of *Mein Kampf*, the audience applauded when an actor in the film exclaimed: 'We must exterminate the Jews.'[26]

The public mood in Morocco remained ugly. In March 1961, after a group of Moroccan Jews carrying forged passports were stopped by the police as they approached the border with the Spanish enclave of Melilla, the Istiklal Party's newspaper, *al-Alam*, stated that 'any Jew

---

[24] Communication from David Littman, 24 October 2003, and the film *Operation Mural: Casablanca 1961*, which had the first of many showings in Tel Aviv on 29 May 2008.

[25] Quoted by Tad Szulc, *The Secret Alliance*, page 248.

[26] Quoted by Tad Szulc, *The Secret Alliance*, pages 248-9.

attempting to emigrate to Israel deserves the death penalty.'[27] This harsh suggestion was ignored, but the fact that it had been made raised yet more fears among the Jews who wanted to leave Morocco.

Under instructions from Ben-Gurion, Israeli diplomats and Mossad operatives began secret negotiations with King Mohammed V's son and successor, King Hassan II, who came to the throne on 3 March 1961. One of the diplomats, Walter Eytan, and a deputy head of the Mossad, Shmuel Toledano, later gave accounts of these efforts. The Mossad chief in Morocco, Alex Gatmon, and later Raphael Spanien of HIAS, played central roles in discussions, some of which occurred with Eytan in Paris, and were concluded in Geneva. The Moroccan authorities wanted $100 for each emigrant. The Israeli Finance Minister, Levi Eshkol, opposed the payment, arguing that the Israeli economy could not face the burden. Ben-Gurion overruled him.[28]

The negotiations were concluded on 25 November 1961. With King Hassan's agreement, the emigrants could travel on collective passports – similar to those devised by David Littman for Operation Mural – making the potentially large number of individual passports unnecessary. The first of the new collective passports was signed two days later by General Oufkir, head of Moroccan National Security. It was agreed that although the emigrants would end up in Israel, their official final destination would be declared as France and Canada.

Just three days after the agreement was signed, a French steamship, the *Lyautey*, sailed from Casablanca for Nice. On board were 105 Moroccan Jews. This was the beginning.

Operation Yakhin,[29] another legal conduit for Jewish emigration, brought a further 100,000 Moroccan Jews to Israel between 1962 and 1964, at a cost of up to $10 million paid to the Moroccan authorities.[30] Briefly, on December 14, when the astonishingly high

---

[27] Quoted by Tad Szulc, *The Secret Alliance*, page 260.
[28] Tad Szulc, *The Secret Alliance*, pages 261–71.
[29] Yakhin was the name of one of the two main pillars that supported King Solomon's Temple in Jerusalem.
[30] In the money values of 2010, $10 million was $300 million.

numbers of would-be emigrants became known, King Hassan halted the emigration, only to permit its resumption nine weeks later. In June 1962, as public unease grew at such a large exodus, the King restricted the number of emigrants to 120 people a day. The rescue plan continued until all those Moroccan Jews who wished to leave had done so.[31]

One positive outcome of the Moroccan exodus saga was the close relationship that developed between King Hassan and Israel, via the Mossad, which led to the secret visits of Yitzhak Rabin and Moshe Dayan to Morocco – Rabin in October 1976, Dayan in September 1977. These visits were the catalyst for the negotiations that culminated in the visit to Jerusalem of President Anwar Sadat of Egypt in November 1977, and the Israeli-Egyptian peace treaty of 1979.

Morocco and Libya were not the only countries in North Africa to witness a mass exodus of Jews. On 20 March 1956, Tunisia achieved its independence. The country's new ruler, Habib Bourghiba, had no animosity towards Jews, of whom there were then 100,000 living among his Muslim fellow-countrymen. He even included a Jew in his first Cabinet. Yet Islamic extremism was on the rise, fuelled by the country's successful struggle for independence against France, and both nationalism and extremism quickly converged to exert pressure on the Jews.

The new Tunisian Government introduced a nationalist policy of 'Arabization' that ensured priority in jobs and services to Muslims. In 1958 the Jewish Community Council, the protective arm of the Jewish community, was abolished. During the economic crisis that soon beset the country, many Jews – as was often the case in times of

---

[31] David Littman explained his experience in Operation Mural and the role of the Mossad in these events in an interview with Xavier Cornut for a Moroccan newspaper, whose editor put the questions and provided the title: 'L'agent secret humanitaire,' *Le Soir Echos*, Casablanca, 23, 24, 25 and 26 March 2009 (republished in *Israel Magazine*, No. 10, Ashdod, June 2009, pages 250-254). See also Xavier Cornut, 'The Moroccan Connection,' *Jerusalem Post*, 23 June 2009, pages 13, 19; Cornut quotes at length from Samuel Segev, *The Moroccan Connection* (in Hebrew), Tel Aviv, 2008. Segev is also the author of *Operation Yakhin* (Ministry of Defence, Tel Aviv, 1984).

economic instability – were made scapegoats and arrested.[32] Within a few years of Tunisian independence, 70,000 Jews had left the country. More than half of them went to Israel; 30,000 went to France.

Israel and France also gained large numbers of new citizens as a result of the exodus of Jews from Algeria. In 1963, a year after Algeria became independent from France, the Algerian Nationality Code reserved the right of Algerian citizenship for those people living in Algeria whose fathers and paternal grandfathers had 'Muslim personal status.' This law ended at a stroke the security of the sixty Jewish communities still living in Algeria, each with its own rabbis, synagogues and schools. Unimpeded by the Algerian Government, which was glad to see them go, Algeria's Jews departed; 25,681 went to Israel and more than 125,000 to France.[33] An ancient Jewish community was at an end.

---

[32] Terence Prittie and Bernard Dineen, *The Double Exodus*, page 22.
[33] *JIMENA* (Jews Indigenous to the Middle East and North Africa), International Rights and Redress Campaign, 'Country Narratives,' page 5: www.justiceforjews.com

19

THE SIX-DAY WAR OF 1967
AND ITS AFTERMATH

*'The Jewish communities living in Islamic countries do not appreciate the
Muslims' good treatment and protection over the centuries'*

Israel's vulnerability within its 1949 ceasefire lines encouraged
Egypt and Syria to plan a military campaign aimed at bringing
about the Jewish State's final defeat and destruction. The Soviet
Union had begun providing both of the would-be aggressors with
substantial quantities of arms and ammunition. Israel's intelligence
services, desperate to counter any attacks, were constantly seeking
information about what preparations were being made against them.

On 18 May 1965, in Damascus, an Egyptian-born Jew, Elie Cohn,
was hanged for spying for Israel. He had indeed been a spy. Before
his trial he had been terribly tortured; at the trial itself he had been
denied a proper defence. After the execution, which took place
before a vast crowd in Martyrs' Square, in the centre of Damascus,
his body was left hanging for six hours, wrapped in a white robe, for
all to see. 'The day will come,' he wrote in his last letter to his wife,
about their children, 'when they will be proud of me.'[1]

Elie Cohn had been born in Alexandria in 1924. His parents had
earlier immigrated to Egypt from the Syrian city of Aleppo. Cohn,
who was fluent in Arabic, had learned both Hebrew and French at
school. In 1954, two years after the Muslim Brotherhood began its
virulent anti-British and anti-Jewish campaign, many of Cohn's
friends were implicated in an Israeli spy ring. Most were imprisoned,
some were executed. Elie Cohn was arrested and imprisoned, but
subsequently acquitted. On his release he left Egypt to join his

---

[1] Quoted in E. Ben Hanan, *Elie Cohn, Our Man in Damascus*, page 180.

family, who had immigrated to Israel in 1948. In Israel he married Nadia, a Jewish immigrant from Iraq. Then he became an Israeli spy, and was sent to Syria.

In Damascus, Elie Cohn befriended several leading Syrian politicians. Protected by their friendship, he had been able to send back to Israel topographical sketches of the Syrian defences on the Golan Heights, the text of Syrian military operational orders, and details on the nature and effectiveness of the country's armaments. This information proved invaluable when Syrian forces opened their attack on northern Israel on 6 June 1967, two years after Cohn had been hanged for spying.

The Six-Day War of 1967 was the second Arab attempt since 1948 to destroy Israel. In 1948 five Arab armies had taken part in an invasion they imagined would lead to an easy victory. In 1967 two countries, Egypt and Syria, devised the plan of attack, and at the last moment persuaded King Hussein of Jordan to participate. As the attackers waited for what they hoped would be an auspicious moment, the war threats, especially those made by Egypt, incited a swift and violent upsurge in anti-Jewish hostility and violence throughout the Arab world.

During the days leading up to the war, Jews living under Muslim rule were surrounded by war fever and anti-Israel denunciations. In the Libyan city of Tripoli, where five thousand Jews were still living, religious radio broadcasts and the Friday sermons in mosques on 2 June 1967 were dominated by proclamations of *jihad* – 'holy war' – against Israel. On June 3 it was announced that a week of support for the Palestinian Arab cause would begin on June 5. To the alarm of the Jewish community, the three other main minority groups in Tripoli, the Italians, Maltese and Greeks, announced their support for Palestine Week.

News reached Tripoli just after ten in the morning of June 5 that Israel had carried out a preemptive air strike on Egyptian aerodromes. Demonstrations, riots and violence began at once. Radio Cairo was quick to broadcast to Libya, calling on the population of

Tripoli to murder the Jews. Throughout Tripoli, Jews were hunted down in the streets and attacked in their shops and homes. The rioting continued for three days, during which time many shops were looted and set on fire.

An Italian journalist, Giorgio Fattori, reached Tripoli after the rioting was over and reconstructed the events from eyewitness testimonies. He reported that during the rioting on June 5 some Arab youths had run through the streets 'marking the doors of Jewish houses with white chalk.' Three Jews were stabbed to death 'under the terrified eyes of foreigners.' Although some Jews were smuggled out of the riot area by Libyan Muslim families, 'every so often someone was caught and quickly had his throat slit.' More than a hundred Jewish shops were destroyed. A Jewish girl tried to get to the market with her face covered like an Arab woman, but 'she was recognized and killed on the spot.'

Jews with foreign passports were compelled to seek protection at their embassies. More than a thousand were taken for safety to a Libyan Army base, the Gurgi Camp, on the outskirts of Tripoli. Three or four thousand were in hiding. Giorgio Fattori reported that on June 6 an old Maltese man 'was mistaken for a Jew and stabbed eight times.'[2] In all, seventeen Jews were killed. Thirteen were from two families: those of Shalom Luzon and Emilia Baranes Habib. These victims were taken out of Tripoli by a Libyan official who told them, reassuringly, that he was escorting them to a camp where Jews were being assembled for their own safety. Once they were outside the city he killed them.[3]

Among those who did their utmost to save the Jews in Tripoli was the Italian Ambassador to Libya, Cesare Pasquinelli. 'Israel has done marvelously,' he wrote home when the war was over, 'but here it is the Jews (a few thousand of them) who have to pay for it by being hunted down by the mob if they leave their homes. . . . It is incredible

---

[2] Report of Giorgio Fattori, *La Stampa*, 18 June 1967: quoted in Renzo De Felice, *Jews in an Arab Land: Libya, 1835-1970*, pages 275-7.
[3] Renzo De Felice, *Jews in an Arab Land: Libya, 1835-1970*, page 277.

that we must still see this after the Nazi infamy.'[4] Another generous foreigner helped Regina Waldman, who was nineteen years old in 1967. While the riots were at their height, she was allowed to hide in the home of a British engineer. She later recalled: 'From my hiding place, I watched the fires consume my father's warehouse. Killing people, rampaging and burning Jewish properties went on for days. I lived in hiding for a month before returning home.'[5]

When the riots came to an end, more than four thousand Libyan Jews were expelled, and their property, including their bank accounts, expropriated by the government. Because they held Italian citizenship, a legacy of Italian rule, they were allowed to go to Italy, 4,100 in all. The Libyan Government was happy to see them go. Many were taken directly from the Gurgi Camp to the port or the airport, escorted by police to protect them from mob attack.[6]

Regina Waldman later described that journey from the Gurgi Camp in graphic detail: 'We were only allowed to take a few suitcases and very little money. The day we left, armed soldiers put us on a truck to escort us "safely" to the airport. Instead, they dumped us on the side of the road. We boarded an airport bus, which then stopped in the middle of the desert. The driver said that there was engine trouble and the conductor allegedly went to get help and left us alone, once again. I looked to my father for support, but he was frozen in horror. I darted off the bus and ran to find help. As I ran my whole body shook with fear, but anger drove me forward.'

When Regina Waldman reached the petrol station, the bus conductor was holding the phone. 'After struggling with him,' she recalled, 'I snatched the phone out of his hand and called the British engineer who had hidden me. I turned to leave but now the door was blocked by three men, including the conductor. I was petrified. My throat tightened. My heart was pounding. I forced my way through the door and ran back to the bus. Gasoline was everywhere,

---

[4] Renzo De Felice, *Jews in an Arab Land: Libya, 1835-1970*, pages 277-8.
[5] Regina Waldman, 'A Jewish Woman from Muslim Society Reflects on Life in Islamic Lands,' *JIMENA* (Jews Indigenous to the Middle East and North Africa).
[6] Renzo De Felice, *Jews in an Arab Land: Libya, 1835-1970*, page 279.

the driver held a box of matches in his hand. The plan was to burn the bus with my family in it. Just then, the British engineer drove up. My family jumped into his car and we sped off to the airport. Upon arrival, the porters refused to load our luggage and spit on us. Our flight took us to Rome, where my family still lives.'[7]

For the two hundred Jews who remained in Libya after this new exodus, life became even bleaker than before. New anti-Jewish measures were introduced by Colonel Muammar Gaddafi, who became the ruler of Libya following an army coup in September 1969. All Jewish men were arrested and taken to police stations. A law was promulgated confiscating Jewish property, while all remaining Jewish-owned bank accounts were blocked. Libyan newspapers continued their invective by denouncing those 'who have been fighting against us and have been our enemies from time immemorial.' There was even a call for the destruction of all Jewish cemeteries, some of which had graves dating back many hundreds of years. It was the 'unavoidable duty of the city councils,' declared one newspaper, 'to remove their cemeteries immediately, and throw the bodies of the dead, which even in their eternal rest soil our country, into the depths of the sea. Where those dirty corpses are lying they should put buildings, parks and roads. Only then can the hatred of the Libyan Arab people towards the Jews be satiated.'[8]

Colonel Gaddafi eventually allowed the Jews to leave, and 'made sure,' in the words of Maurice Roumani, the historian of Libyan Jewry, 'that their religious patrimony of twenty-one Jewish cemeteries and sixty-four synagogues, a testimony to their past, was erased for ever from Libyan soil.'[9] All Jews who had passports promptly left Libya, never to return. Those who remained were, for the most part, elderly people without any relatives abroad. By 1972 there were fewer than forty Jews in Libya; by 1977 only sixteen; by 1982 only ten. In 2010 there were none.

----

[7] Eric Fingerhut, 'Forgotten refugees, Effort under way to focus on Jews of Arab lands,' *Washington Jewish Week*, 26 July 2007.
[8] Maurice Roumani, *The Jews of Libya*, page 207.
[9] Maurice Roumani, *The Jews of Libya*, page 217.

—

As Iraqi forces drove westward through Jordan on 6 June 1967 to join in the hoped-for victory over Israel, there was celebration and jubilation in the cities of Iraq. The population listened with rapt attention to martial music and bulletins that reported a series of decisive Egyptian victories in the south. On June 7, however, after an Israeli air strike on the Iraqi desert air base H-3, the popular mood turned from joy to anger. The cheers for victory quickly transformed into curses against 'Zionist agents' and a supposed Jewish 'fifth column' inside Iraq itself.

Jews throughout Iraq were arrested, tortured, and forced to pay money to their tormentors. The Jewish sports ground endowed by the former Jewish Senator, Ezra Menahem Daniel, was confiscated by the Ministry of Defence on the absurd charge that it was being used as a meeting place for Jews conspiring against Iraq. It was turned into a sports ground for the Iraqi Army. A new law – Law No. 64 of 1967 – gave the State the right to seize and administer Jewish property. Preachers in the mosques described the Jews as harmful germs that must be destroyed. Iraqi television showed comic programmes about traitors to Iraq who were given traditional Jewish names: Heskel, Shaul, Moshe, Ezra, Zion and Shalom. Jews were continually stopped in the streets by the police and searched.

On July 10 a former Iraqi Prime Minister, Tahir Yahya, returned to power in Baghdad. From that moment, the situation became even worse. Jewish students at Al-Hikma University were attacked and beaten up by Muslim students. A university education was refused to all Jewish schoolchildren who had completed their secondary schooling. Jewish traders were denied any further import licenses without paying a punitive tax. When Muslim dealers and traders refused to pay money that they owed to Jews, the Jews did not dare to complain, fearing for their lives.

Throughout the year of his second term of office, which lasted until July 1968, Tahir Yahya made life for the Jews even more intolerable than before. On 3 March 1968 he instituted a law and regulations that effectively forced the Jews into penury. Jews could not sell their cars or furniture. All licenses given to Jewish pharmacists were cancelled, and their pharmacies ordered to close down within fifteen days. All commercial offices in Baghdad had to dismiss their Jewish employees. Muslim-owned offices and shops were warned not to cooperate in any business ventures with Jews. The Daniel Market and other valuable Daniel properties – endowed to the Jewish community under a trusteeship by Ezra Menahem Daniel before his death – were sequestered by the government, despite the Court of Cassation's judgement that the property belonged to the Jewish community.[10]

Poverty, isolation and fear had become the plight of the remaining Jews of Iraq.

Within two days of the start of the Six-Day War, as Israeli troops began their advance through the Sinai Desert towards the Suez Canal, two hundred of the one thousand Jews still in Egypt were arrested and held in prison. At one police headquarters, Jews were kept without water for forty-eight hours. In Abu Za'abal prison outside Cairo, Egyptian police officers kicked and whipped Jewish prisoners, forcing them to call out anti-Israeli slogans.[11]

Moura (Marco, now Marc) Amin Khedr was among the Jews arrested in Cairo. He recalled thirty-five years later how, at two in the morning of June 6, he was suddenly awoken by his mother. '"Wake up, wake up Marco." I put on my clothes, half asleep and I didn't know what I was doing. The house was dark; no lights and at the front door were two men. They said we were to come for questions which wouldn't take long, only for a few minutes. They took me and my father. We were taken outside to a waiting car which drove us to the Abdin prison in downtown Cairo. I was only nineteen years old! The prison cell was dark. At the door, a guard was standing. The door had a strong metal bar at the top, as a safety measure against escape. Inside the cell, we saw a few more Jews, about eight or more.'

---

[10] Gourji C. Bekhor, *Fascinating Life and Sensational Death: The Conditions in Iraq Before and After the Six-Day War*, pages 148-157.
[11] Terence Prittie and Bernard Dineen, *The Double Exodus*, page 24.

Early in the day on June 7, Marc Khedr and the other Jewish prisoners were taken by truck to the Abu Za'abal camp. 'We were taken to a big gate, through it we saw a large table, three soldiers sitting. We formed a line and one by one, approached the table. One of the soldiers said: "*Ya yahoudi ya ibn il Kalb, esmak eh*," "You Jew, son of a dog, what's your name?" We then emptied our pockets and were given sackcloth to wear, a blanket and an aluminum plate. No knives or forks. We had to eat with our hands. The building was two stories high: the Jewish prisoners were on the second floor and the Muslim Brotherhood and anti-Nasser Egyptians and Palestinians from Gaza (who were supposedly collaborators with Israel), were on the first floor.'

Marc Khedr was taken to the second floor. 'I was shocked. There were people, young and old, running round and round a small yard, like dogs, and behind them, a soldier beating them with a big belt. They were screaming. It was my turn to run. It felt like a bad dream! You heard the voices scream, "Down with Israel. Long live Gamal Abdul Nasser. Palestine is Arab. Down with the Jews and with the Zionists," repeated over and over. We were then taken to our cell, which was made for twenty persons, although sixty were crammed in it. . . . We were all Jews. The first thing we did was to introduce ourselves. I didn't know anyone. Night time came. We had nothing to eat. We heard the bombs. It was very dark. We wanted to sleep but couldn't, mainly because we were stuffed together like sardines, very close to each other. Each person had enough space for about two and half tiles. The other person's feet were in your face. If you wanted to pass by to go to the bathroom, you had to step over several bodies and by the time you returned your place was already taken by someone else!'

On the morning of June 9, the fourth day of the war, another some two hundred Jewish prisoners arrived by train from Alexandria. 'They looked as if they had been beaten badly. We were divided in two groups and taken outside to the yard where stones and rocks were scattered. No talking was permitted. They asked us to separate the big rocks from the small ones. There was no particular reason for this. All they wanted was to keep us busy and humiliate us by forcing us to do meaningless work. The routine was the same nearly every day.'

After eight months the Jewish prisoners were transferred to a camp at a-Tur, on the Gulf of Suez coast of Sinai. Visitors were allowed once a month; Marc Khedr had his first home-cooked meal when his mother was allowed to visit. 'Gradually we were allowed to receive food every two weeks. . . . During the next two years, our condition improved. We were allowed to leave our cells to go into the yard all day. We played soccer, exercised, ran and even constructed a tennis court! In the evening, we would play poker by using hand made cards from the packets of Belmont cigarettes. . . . In the playground, Muslim and Jewish prisoners mingled together. Strange, but we got along fine with little or no conflict. We had one thing in common: we hated Nasser since he had imprisoned and brutalized us all, Muslim and Jew.'

The Jewish prisoners played soccer against the Muslim prisoners. 'As the months and years passed, I was very worried that we were never going to be released and was even thinking of escaping. One day, we were taken by truck to court. The Judge told us the reason we were in prison was because we were Zionist spies for Israel.' By the third year in prison, 'we began hearing rumors of our release. One day, an announcement was made and we were divided into groups and mine was the last one to exit the gate. The Captain was concerned that, upon our release, we would come back and bomb the prison! He tried to be nice to us! We were taken directly to the airport where we boarded a plane to Paris, because the French government agreed to give us temporary asylum.'

After spending eight months in Paris, Marc Khedr moved to San Francisco in 1971. 'It is good to be in America,' he wrote thirty-one years later. 'I entered the concentration camp when I was nineteen years old – promised only to be for a few minutes – and came out when I was twenty-two. Precious three years and three months were wasted. I am writing this so that the whole world knows what the Egyptian authorities did to us simply because we were Jews, even Egyptian indigenous Jews who were in Egypt over three thousand years before the Arabs invaded and conquered the whole Middle East in the Seventh Century.'[12]

Ovadia Yerushalmy was not much older than Marc Khedr when the Six-Day War broke out. Twenty-two years old, he was a student of economics and political science at the University of Cairo. He later recalled being at home with his mother when two police officers came to his house and asked him to go with them to the police station 'for five minutes' to verify something in his identity card. 'The five minutes lasted two years.' After two days and nights in a police cell with thirty other Jews, without food, he and the others were handcuffed in pairs and taken to Abu Za'abal prison. Conditions there were harsh in the extreme, with no soap, no toothpaste and no change of underwear allowed for three months. There were regular beatings by the guards.

After eight months in Abu Za'abal prison, Yerushalmy was transferred to the prison camp at a-Tur, in Sinai, where some eighty Jews were incarcerated. In his crowded cell one day, a prison officer came in and ordered another Jewish prisoner to undress and then sodomise his brother in front of their father. 'The officer left the cell after warning us not to say what happened.' The eighty Jews endured such humiliations for two years, until they were told that they would leave the country, and were taken to Cairo airport. There, Yerushalmi found his parents, who gave him a small suitcase and ten United States dollars. He was then put on a plane to Paris. His parents left a few months later. Like so many Egyptian Jews imprisoned at this time, Yerushalmy was tormented – and remains so to this day – by how he and his fellow Jews were so ill-treated.[13]

---

[12] Marc Khedr (Moura Amin Khedr), 'This is my life: my internment at Abu Zaabal and Tora concentrations camps,' written August 2002, revised October 2004; sent to the author, 7 February 2009. Suzy Vidal, who left Egypt after the Suez War a decade earlier, commented when she read Marc Khedr's testimony: 'These Jews who were unwise enough not to leave (and I now bless my mother Esther for her panic inciting us to leave) went through hell and most of them refused to tell their story. Therefore I am grateful to Mark Khedr who did so. It was a trauma to relate this story. But he is right, the world must know what was done to these men.' Suzy Vidal, letter to the author, 7 February 2009.

[13] Ovadia Yerushalmy, manuscript, 'The Longest Five Minutes in My Life,' Tel Aviv, 10 May 2009. He now lives in Israel.

By 1970 all Egyptian Jews who were not in prison had been allowed to leave. Only a few hundred Jews remained in all of Egypt. One of the most productive, cultured and creative Jewish communities in the world was almost at an end. President Nasser then ordered Egyptian Jewry's contribution to the life and prosperity of modern Egypt to be erased from all Egyptian history books.[14]

The troubles facing Jews in Muslim lands only deepened when Israel emerged victorious from the Six-Day War. In Lebanon, the 7,000-strong Jewish community found itself in a particularly difficult situation: many Arabs from Palestine, kept as refugees for twenty years, had turned from exhilaration at the prospect of Israel's defeat to anger at her rapid victory. Lebanese Jews felt more insecure than they had for many years. A total of 5,200 Jews – two-thirds of the community – decided to emigrate. Most went to France, where many of them had relatives. Others rebuilt their lives in Italy, Britain, Canada, Israel and South America.

In the immediate aftermath of the Six-Day War the situation of Jews in Muslim lands was widely reported. An article in the weekly *Jewish Chronicle* on 16 June 1967 gave a sombre roundup of the news as received in London: 'Numbers of Jews have been brutally killed and there has been considerable damage to property.' The article reported that in Tripoli 'sixteen Jews were thrown to their deaths from roofs and balconies,' and the Jewish driver of an American School bus 'was burned to death in his cab by an Arab mob.' In Aden, 'Arabs beat to death Mr. Mayer Awadh Shao, an elderly Jew,' and set the Aden synagogue on fire.[15]

On 22 September 1967 the World Islamic Congress met in the Jordanian capital, Amman. Only thirteen weeks earlier, Jordan had been forced to withdraw from its eighteen-year occupation of the West Bank and East Jerusalem. In a statement about Jews living in Arab

---

[14] Ada Aharoni, Aimée Israel-Pelletier, Levana Zamir (editors), *History and Culture of the Jews from Egypt in Modern Times*, page 157.
[15] Jewish Chronicle Foreign Staff, 'Many Jews murdered in Arab countries,' *Jewish Chronicle*, 16 June 1967.

countries – there were no Jews in Jordan – the Congress chose words that were full of threat. 'The Congress is certain,' the statement read, 'that the Jewish communities living in Islamic countries do not appreciate the Muslims' good treatment and protection over the centuries. The Congress declares that the Jews residing in Arab countries who contact the Zionist circles or the State of Israel do not deserve the protection and care which Islam provides for the free non-Muslim subjects living in Islamic countries.' These Jews were warned that 'Muslim Islamic Governments should treat them as aggressive combatants. Similarly, the Islamic peoples, individually and collectively, should boycott them and treat them as deadly enemies.'[16]

In Morocco, following the riots after the Six-Day War, King Hassan II hastened to protect his Jewish minority, and punished the angry mobs who turned to violence after Israel's victory.[17] But elsewhere in the Muslim and Arab world, wherever Jews still lived, Jewish communities were accused of dual loyalties: a true loyalty to Israel and a false loyalty to their country of residence. In every case, the alleged false loyalty was to a country in which Jews remained second-class citizens, the remnants of once vast *dhimmi* populations.

On 17 July 1968, scarcely a year after Israel's victory on the battlefield, the Baath Party returned to power in Iraq. On that day the ruling Revolutionary Council appointed a senior army officer, General Ahmad Hasan al-Bakr, as the country's new President. Al-Bakr had taken part in Rashid Ali's revolt against Britain twenty-seven years earlier.

---

[16] Quoted in Maurice Roumani, *The Case of the Jews from Arab Countries: A Neglected Issue*, page 53.

[17] The King had shown his readiness to protect the Jews earlier in the year. In Tangier, an Arab had attacked the city's Chief Rabbi, Yamin Cohen, near his home, severely wounding him in the neck. The attacker claimed to be sent by Allah to revenge the Israeli capture of East Jerusalem in June 1967. Without hesitation, King Hassan II ordered his own personal physician to travel to Tangier and save the Rabbi. Muslims, as a mark of respect, would then stop the Rabbi on the street when he returned from the synagogue on Friday night and ask for his blessing. M. Mitchell Serels, *A History of the Jews of Tangier*, page 171.

The repressive measures instituted against Iraq's remaining 5,000 Jews by the former Prime Minister, Tahir Yahya, were intensified. In October the Revolutionary Council announced that it had arrested a spy network that had been operating in Iraq on behalf of 'Zionism and Imperialism.' Most of those arrested were Jews. Yet the Iraqi Jews who had not left during the mass exodus twenty years earlier had neither close contact with Israel nor a positive interest in Zionism; they were Iraqis first and foremost, and had stayed in Iraq for that reason. Even when there were no obstacles to their leaving, the possibility of a new life in Israel, the United States, Canada or Western Europe had not tempted them to leave.

Seven of the Iraqi Jews arrested in October 1968 died while in custody after being severely tortured. They were Nissim Yair Hakham Nissim, an accountant; Fuad Yaakov Shasha, a merchant; Daud Sassoon Zubaida, a road-making contractor; Choua Soffer, a registrar of trademarks; Akram Ezra Bahir, a clerk; Azzouri Yaakov Jouri, a wealthy merchant; and Shamoun Mislawi, a poor newspaper seller.[18]

The other Jews who had been arrested in October 1968 were brought to trial in January 1969 before a special military court. The proceedings were held in secret. The court never allowed the accused to appoint lawyers, nor did it allow lawyers to take on their defence. One of the prisoners, Jack Atrakchi, was forced to lie on the ground in the prison yard as a truck was driven over him. It crushed and killed him before the eyes of the other prisoners. After that, the authorities could obtain any 'confession' they desired.

Nothing was known of the course of the interrogations or the trial until just after midnight on January 26, when Baghdad Radio broadcast selections from the trial proceedings. Shlomo Hillel, a former clandestine Zionist emissary in Iraq, was then Deputy Director-General at the Israeli Foreign Ministry, in charge of the ministry's Middle Eastern desk. On being given details of the broadcast, he realised that it portended a sinister outcome. He at once assembled

---

[18] Gourji C. Bekhor, *Fascinating Life and Sensational Death: The Conditions in Iraq Before and After the Six-Day War*, pages 162-7.

such staff members as he could, hoping to make use of the time difference between the Middle East and the United States – where it was still early evening – 'to try to mobilize some kind of force to stop the words that, once pronounced, would never be retracted.'

It was too late. 'As if jeering at our impotence,' Hillel later recalled, 'at seven o'clock the next morning the voice of the chief justice of the special military court boomed out on our radio sets, announcing that fourteen traitors, caught red-handed, had been condemned to death and already executed.'[19]

The executions had taken place in the prison at midnight. In the moments beforehand, other Jewish inmates had heard the prisoners crying loudly together: 'We are innocent,' 'We are innocent,' 'We are innocent,' and then making their last prayer to God, the prayer that reaffirms a Jew's faith in God: 'Hear! O Israel, the Lord is God, the Lord is One.' The other inmates then heard the loud sounds of the electric gallows, each noise signifying that one of the Jews had been executed. The whole procedure was carried out hurriedly and without ceremony – even, according to one report, without proper measures being taken to ensure that each prisoner was dead. In the early hours the corpses were transported to Tahrir Square.

On the morning of 27 January 1969 the Jews in Baghdad switched on their radios and television sets and, to their horror, heard jubilant announcements calling on all citizens of Baghdad to go to Tahrir Square to see the suspended corpses. The scene was later broadcast on Iraqi television, showing the hanging men with their faces uncovered. There were nine Jews, each wearing a placard around the neck bearing his name, profession, city and the word 'Jew.' The day was declared a national holiday. Crowds of Baghdadis surrounded the gallows, dancing, chanting and even picnicking. The Baghdad correspondent of *Le Monde* estimated that a million people went to see the bodies, gathering in the square and all the streets leading towards it.[20]

---

[19] Shlomo Hillel, *Operation Babylon*, page 293.
[20] *Le Monde*, 28 January 1969.

In Israel, Shlomo Hillel called a press conference – broadcast by the BBC – to protest the executions. Hillel later reflected: 'I doubt whether in all the two thousand five hundred years of Jewish history in Iraq, there had been anything to match the sheer malevolence of executing nine Jews on the same day.' Even the Egyptian Government condemned the hangings as 'doing harm to the Arab cause.'[21]

When the day of festivity in Baghdad came to an end, the corpses of the nine executed Jews were handed to the Iraqi Chief Rabbinate for secret burial. The nine Jews were Ezra Naji Zilkha, a sixty-year-old porcelain merchant from Basra; Charles Raphael Horesh, a forty-five-year-old commission agent who worked in Baghdad; Fouad Gabbay, a thirty-five-year-old forwarding agent who worked in Basra; Yeheskel Gourji Namerdi, a thirty-two-year-old clerk employed by the British Overseas Airways Corporation in Basra; and five students from Basra, aged between seventeen and nineteen: Sabah Haim Dayan, Daoud Ghali, Naim Khedouri Helali, Heskel Saleh Heskel and Daoud Heskel Barukh Dellal. As Iraqi law prohibited the execution of people under the age of twenty, the military court had – it seems – forced those under twenty to declare a higher age in their 'confessions' in order to carry out their executions.

At the same time as the executions in Baghdad, two Jews had also been hanged in Basra: Yeheskel Eliahou Dellal, a forty-eight-year-old merchant, and Yeheskel Raphael Yacoub, a forty-two-year-old banker. Their corpses were likewise suspended, with faces uncovered, in a Basra square, to the delight of a large crowd that danced and sang as had the crowds in Baghdad. After the executions, at least ten Jews were held incommunicado in Iraqi prisons for several months.[22]

Odette Ishayek, then twenty years old (later Odette Masliyah), recalled four decades later another 'terrible incident' that occurred at this time. Iraqi police had entered a Jewish home and killed four children and their parents. 'Only one daughter was spared as she

---

[21] Shlomo Hillel, *Operation Babylon*, page 294.
[22] Gourji C. Bekhor, 'The Baghdad Hangings,' *The Scribe*, Issue 9, Volume 2, January-February 1973.

was out of the house. People said that this was done in retaliation for something that had happened in Israel. The Iraqi government put two Iraqi Jews on British television to talk about their free life in Iraq and that no one was harming them.'

A new and massive exodus was underway. The six thousand Jews who had still been living in Iraq after 1951 were on the move. Odette Ishayek's uncle, Naim Shemie, an accountant in Baghdad, arranged for Odette's family to be smuggled out of the country with help from his Kurdish contacts in the north who came to Baghdad to buy and trade. Odette later recalled: 'Father was very scared. We paid about $1,000 for each member of the family: Dad, Mom, my sister and myself.'[23] It was November 1969. 'I did not tell any family or friends. I could not say anything in school. I took one small suitcase. We could not give away any of our things as we feared someone will discover that we are trying to escape. . . .

'It was the month of Ramadan, so we could not eat. My mother reminded us not to talk unless necessary so as not to attract attention. We tried to look calm and not scared. In a few hours, we arrived to the meeting place with our contact person.' A Jeep arrived. 'Dad sat beside the driver and the three of us sat in the back. We were instructed that whenever the Jeep drove past a busy street or a checkpoint, we need to duck, so as not to attract any attention. At some point when we were approaching a checkpoint, the driver suggested to my Dad that he say that he is going to a family wedding and give a Muslim family name. I could already see that my father was sweating, as he is not used to lying. The fear that overtook him was immense. Luckily, we were not stopped or questioned.'

The Ishayek family eventually approached the border of Iran. 'We started walking on a muddy path. The rain started to fall and it became very slippery with every step that we took. My sister and I lost our shoes in the mud, but continued to walk on our bare feet. I think we walked at least a couple of hours till the dawn started to appear. I imagine that we were close to the Iranian border; our guide said that we have

---

[23] The equivalent of $20,000 each in 2010.

to wait until the Iranian guards came to get us. After a while he started hinting to my father that the initial sum that he charged us was not sufficient. He asked for more money. That really made me mad. I tried to talk, but my mother quickly whispered to me that we have no choice, and having three women there, my father had better pay what he was asked.'

The Iranian border guards arrived, and the Ishayeks were safe. The family then spent a month in a Jewish Agency hostel in Teheran, after which they were flown to Tel Aviv. 'In the aftermath of us leaving Iraq,' Odette Masliyah later recalled, 'we heard that our house had been confiscated on the day after we left. Two of our second cousins were taken to prison and were never seen again.'[24]

In the West, persistent efforts were being made to secure the release of those Jews still imprisoned in Iraq. Bertha Fattal, an Iraqi-born Jew living in London, enlisted the help of Arthur Goldberg, a Jew and a former United States Supreme Court Judge. Goldberg took action at once. From London, he telephoned the Aga Khan IV, head of the Ismaili Muslims, who was then on holiday in Iceland. The Aga Khan telephoned his nephew, Sadr el-Din, a senior Red Cross official, who flew from Iran to Baghdad to intercede with the Iraqi Government. When the Iraqi officials told him that there were no Jews in prison, Sadr el-Din insisted on going to a prison in person. 'To the prisoners' surprise,' Bertha Fattal later noted, 'they were ordered out. They were so scared thinking they might be put to death and did not have the remotest idea that they were going to be released.'[25]

The exodus from Iraq continued. On 12 December 1971 the *New York Times* published a report sent from Baghdad nine days earlier, under the headline: 'IRAQI JEWS LEAVE IN A STEADY FLOW; 5 or 6 Families Going Weekly Despite Eased Conditions.' The article began: '"It's so terribly lonely here now," an aging Iraqi Jew said, tears coming to his eyes. He has sent his family abroad and hopes to follow soon.'[26]

---

[24] Odette Masliyah, letter to the author, 18 February 2009.
[25] Bertha Fattal, 'Bertha's Memoirs,' manuscript, pages 93-4.
[26] *New York Times*, 12 December 1971.

Jamil Shemtob, who had saved the former Iraqi Prime Minister, Tawfiq al-Suweidi, had been among the Jews who remained in Iraq after the 1958 coup, hoping that Jewish life would continue and flourish. But in 1970, as the Iraqi Government's treatment of the Jewish community became harsher, he decided to flee to Iran with his family. He was caught and his entire family was arrested. He tried to leave Iraq again after being released from prison, but the police arrested him once more. He was accused of spying for Israel, interrogated and tortured. The family's property was expropriated. On being released from prison for the second time, Shemtob tried to leave Iraq yet again. This time he was successful, travelling north to Iraqi Kurdistan and then crossing the mountain border into Iran. Flying from Teheran on 9 September 1971, he and his family landed safely in Israel.[27]

On 18 February 1973 a *New York Times* headline read: 'HALF BAGHDAD'S JEWS SAID TO APPLY TO LEAVE; PROPERTY SEIZED.' The article began: 'Half the members of the tiny Jewish community in Baghdad have applied for passports to leave Iraq in recent weeks in the face of a crackdown by Iraqi authorities, according to a first-hand account.'[28] That same day, in Montreal, an Iraqi-born Jew, Naim Kattan, spoke in the Spanish and Portuguese Synagogue at a memorial and protest rally for nine more Jews who had been murdered in Baghdad. 'Once again,' he said, 'we assemble in this Sanctuary in sorrow, and in anger. Once again, from a country which to many of us here this evening was "our home and native land,"[29] from that country we hear, through thick prison walls and through tight censorship, the tragic and heart-rending cries of brothers and sisters in anguish and distress. Once again, the United Nations Charter on Human Rights is trampled arrogantly under foot, and once again the champions of Arab causes conveniently turn their heads the other way.'

---

[27] Mordechai Ben-Porat, 'Jamil Shemtov' (obituary), *Nehardea: Journal of the Babylonian Heritage Centre*, No. 16, Spring 2008. On reaching Israel, Jamil Shemtob had changed his name to the more Israeli Shemtov.
[28] 'According to a first-hand account': *New York Times*, 18 February 1973.
[29] Words from the Canadian national anthem, *Oh, Canada*.

The names of the nine murdered Jews were Yaacoob Abdul Azziz, Dr. Ezra Khazzam, Azoori Shamash, Shaul Rejwan, Yaacoob Rejwan, Victor Abu Dahoud, Sakim Sadka, Naji Chitayat and Shaul Shamash. In all, from 1968 to 1972, more than fifty Iraqi Jews had been judicially murdered.[30]

Naim Kattan continued: 'The formula at Qesr el-Nihaya prison is consistent: daily sessions, each lasting several hours at a time, of beatings and torture, physical humiliation and degradation, on and on, until the victim is finally broken in both body and spirit, and he pleads for death to end it all. What a sad ending to a great historic past! A once-flourishing Jewish community whose feet were deeply embedded in the soil of Iraq, a community which for hundreds of years was a beacon of Jewish enlightenment and learning, flashing its bright rays to many parts of the Diaspora, while at the same time contributing to the economic life of the country which was its home. A community of 150,000 just over twenty years ago and today numbering only 400 souls.'[31]

Naim Kattan had left Baghdad in 1947 on a scholarship to the Sorbonne. He wrote in 2004: 'When I visit the Babylonian or Assyrian galleries in the Louvre, the British Museum, the Pergamon Museum in Berlin or the Royal Ontario Museum in Toronto, I relive my childhood excursions to Babylon and Niniveh. So many civilizations blossomed in that country! The traces they left are richer and more meaningful than all the oil wells. And I think to myself: what a waste! A country that cannot hold on to all its citizens!'[32]

Marina Benjamin, a British Jew of Iraqi origin, expressed similar sentiments when she visited the land of her grandparents, Regina Sehayek and Elazar Levy, in 2004. Reflecting on the life of Iraqi Jews between the two World Wars, Marina Benjamin wrote: 'They were well-connected, urbane, bent on self-advancement. It was a soaring

---

[30] Their names are given in Gourji C. Bekhor, *Fascinating Life and Sensational Death: The Conditions in Iraq Before and After the Six-Day War*, pages 161-7.
[31] *The Scribe*, Issue 10, Volume 2, March-August 1973.
[32] Naim Kattan, *Farewell Babylon*, page 8.

peak to attain after centuries of being merely tolerated – but also, a dizzying height from which to fall.'[33]

The new exodus from Iraq was spurred on by persistent anti-Jewish feeling that often spilled over into violence. In Baghdad, in the first week of April 1973 a mob broke into the house of Abraham Nissim al-Saigh, an elderly, wealthy bachelor. He was murdered in his home. Also in April, a mob broke into the house of Reuben Qashqoush, a dealer in spare parts for cars. He and his family had passports, airline tickets and travellers' cheques for a flight out of Iraq two days later. Most of their luggage was already packed. Reuben Qashqoush, his wife Clementine, and three of their four children – their two sons Fuad and Samir, and their daughter Joyce – were slaughtered in their home. The killers then left with a considerable amount of the family's belongings and valuables.

The lone survivor from the Qashqoush household, twenty-two year old Dora, was refused permission to leave Iraq. As her case became widely known, protests ensued around the world, culminating in a mass demonstration in Tel Aviv. World student organisations urged that Dora be allowed to leave; she had after all been about to leave when her family was murdered. Even the Indian Prime Minister, Indira Gandhi, added her voice to the protests. Finally, Dora was allowed to leave.[34] One more Iraqi Jew joined the vast Iraqi Jewish Diaspora.

The President of Iraq's Jewish community, Meir Basri, also left the country at this time. He had been imprisoned after the 1973 October War, when – following a surprise attack on Israel by Egypt and Syria – Iraq sent an artillery unit to fight against Israel on the Golan Heights. Twenty-five years earlier, Basri had been selected as Iraq's Finance Minister. The outbreak of the first Arab-Israeli War in

---

[33] Marina Benjamin, *Last Days in Babylon*, page xix.
[34] Gourji C. Bekhor, *Fascinating Life and Sensational Death: The Conditions in Iraq Before and After the Six-Day War*, pages 176-7.

1948 ended that appointment. In October 1974 he and his family received permission to leave Iraq. His daughter Aida Zelouf later recalled: 'My father was a writer; he had to leave most of his library there. We had to leave everything behind.'[35]

By the early 1970s, the once flourishing Iraqi Jewish community – which dated back 2,600 years – had dwindled to fewer than three hundred members. Jews were no longer welcome in the land of their first exile, Babylonia. Shlomo Hillel contemplated his own family's place in this dramatic change after he met his cousin Fahima, who was finally emigrating from Iraq, through Israel to Canada. Hillel recalled how their talk turned to the far-off days of life in Iraq: 'I waxed nostalgic about the family, the food, the romps by the river, but most of all our innocence. How far we had come since the days when we believed that closing the shutters and barring the doors was enough to keep evil at bay.'[36]

Shlomo Hillel asked his cousin if she and others had believed that Israel had forgotten those many thousands of Jews who had decided not to leave Iraq in 1950. Fahima responded that she had heard his voice over the BBC on the day of the hangings in January 1969. 'I knew that you hadn't and wouldn't ever abandon us.' For the 'longest time,' she added, 'I nursed a grudge. I felt that all the horrible things that were happening to us were because of Israel, because of your dream and your wars. You celebrated the victories, and we paid the price of those wars. Now I can see that we were saved because of the existence and efforts of Israel.'[37]

Many other Jews who left Iraq in this period later reflected on the difficult lives they had left behind. Edwin Shuker, who emigrated at the age of sixteen in 1971, recalled that 'a good week was when no one was arrested.'[38] Linda Masri Hakim, who left Iraq in 1972, had recurring nightmares that she was still stuck there. 'When I wake up,' she commented, 'I touch my pillow and say, "Thank God I am not in Iraq."'

---

[35] Aida Zelouf, letter to the author, 17 February 2008.
[36] Fahima was the sister of Jamil Shemtob and daughter of Ezekiel Shemtob.
[37] Shlomo Hillel, *Operation Babylon*, page 296.
[38] Edwin Shuker, in conversation with the author, 23 February 2009.

Linda wanted to 'close the book' on the history of the Jews in Iraq and 'forget about perpetuating the memory.' She explained: 'This is my attitude because we can't go back – in the same way that European Jews could not go back to Europe after the Holocaust.'[39]

In Syria, following the 1967 defeat of the Syrian forces and the loss of the Golan Heights to Israel, new regulations were imposed on the country's 3,500 Jews. These new laws harked back to a much earlier time when the Covenant of Omar could be burdensome in the extreme. There were twelve laws in all. The first: 'The Jewish right to emigrate is completely forbidden. This applies even to Jews in Syria who hold foreign passports.' The second: 'Jews are forbidden to move more than three kilometres from their place of residence. Those wishing to travel further must apply for a special permit.' The third: 'Identity cards issued to Jews are stamped in red with the word Mussawi (Jew).'

The fourth and fifth laws, respectively: 'Jews are normally subject to a 10 p.m. curfew' and 'Jews are allowed six years elementary schooling only.' The remaining laws, in sequence: 'Jewish houses in the town of Kamishli are to be marked in red'; 'Jews are barred from jobs in the public service, public institutions and banks'; 'Government officials and military personnel are forbidden to buy in Jewish shops'; 'Foreigners may not visit the Jewish quarters unescorted by a government official'; 'Jews are forbidden to own radios or telephones, or to maintain postal contact with the outside world'; and 'No telephones may be installed in Jewish homes.' The twelfth and final regulation: 'The property and possessions of deceased Jews are confiscated by the government. Their heirs must then pay for its use. If they cannot, it will be handed over to the Palestinian Arabs.'[40]

In addition to these twelve draconian regulations, which were strictly enforced, only two Jewish schools were allowed in Damascus.

---

[39] Tamar Morad, Dennis Shasha and Robert Shasha (editors), *Iraq's Last Jews, Stories of Daily Life, Upheaval and Escape from Modern Babylon*, page 167.

[40] There were then more than 100,000 Palestinian Arabs living in United Nations (UNRWA) refugee camps in Syria, most from the war of 1948, some from the war of 1967.

Their directors and most of their teachers were Muslims. Exams were usually ordered to be held on the Jewish Sabbath, so that observant Jews could not take part in them.

The plight of the Jews of Syria soon became well publicised. In 1970, during a meeting in Paris of the International Conference for the Deliverance of Jews in the Middle East, there was a dramatic moment when a Jewish escapee from Syria – masking her face to protect her identity and the family she had left behind in Syria – spoke of the harsh conditions under which the Syrian Jews were living.[41] In the following year, the World Jewish Congress, based in Paris, stated that 'apart from the Jewish problem in Soviet Russia, the Syrian plight has become our problem No. 2.' The Congress sent out a memorandum with details of the 'tragic situation of the Jews in Syria and request for immediate action by all our affiliates.'[42]

Those who attempted to help Syrian Jews escape their isolation incurred deadly risks. In September 1971 the head of the small Jewish community in Lebanon, Albert Elia, was kidnapped in Beirut. Elia had been active in helping Jews escape from Syria through Lebanon. It was widely believed that he had been seized by the Syrian secret police – the Mukhabarat – and taken to prison in Syria. His two children, who were then living in Canada, asked the Canadian Government to help their father through discreet diplomatic channels. When quiet diplomacy failed, Elia's daughter appealed publicly to the Secretary-General of the United Nations, Kurt Waldheim, asking him to intercede with the Syrian Government. It was all in vain; Elia was never seen alive again.[43]

Based in New York, the American Jewish Committee embarked on a public campaign to alert the world to the plight of Syrian Jews. On 2 January 1972 a headline in the *New York Times* publicised the committee's efforts: 'GROUP SAYS SYRIA PERSECUTES JEWS; American

---

[41] Harold Troper, *The Ransomed of God* (retitled *The Rescuer*, 2007), page 32.
[42] Harold Troper, *The Ransomed of God* (retitled *The Rescuer*, 2007), page 30 and page 242, note 18.
[43] Harold Troper, *The Ransomed of God* (retitled *The Rescuer*, 2007), pages 32-3.

Committee Says Several Are in Prison.' The report had been sent from Paris the previous day. It began: 'Syria is the only Middle East country still persecuting and harassing its Jewish minority and forbidding its emigration, according to a year-end survey by the American Jewish Committee of the situation of Jews in the Moslem world.'[44]

A remarkable effort was undertaken by a Canadian Jewish woman, Judy Feld Carr, to coordinate all the campaigns that had been launched on behalf of the Jews of Syria. Carr had become convinced that it was possible to rescue the Syrian Jews in their entirety. Her twenty-year campaign unfolded against the background of a confrontation between a police State and a frightened people. At no point before the end of the campaign's twenty years did the situation of Syria's Jews improve. Contact between Jews and Muslims was restricted. Muslims who attacked or robbed Jews were seldom brought to justice. Jewish businessmen were obliged to work alongside a Muslim partner, who frequently was able to gain most of the profits. When a Jew died, his or her property was transferred to the Syrian Government, which either sold it or granted it to a Palestinian Arab refugee.[45]

Judy Feld Carr and her husband Rubin Feld managed to make telephone contact with the Chief Rabbi of the Syrian Jewish community, Ibrahim (Abraham) Hamra. Knowing that the Syrian secret police were monitoring their conversations, and were reading their telegrams and letters, the couple's messages to the Rabbi were carefully veiled. Even references to biblical verses were frowned upon by the secret police, as they had made clear to Rabbi Hamra. But in the Jewish New Year of 1973, which began on September 27, Rabbi Hamra sent a telegram of greeting to Judy and Rubin Feld that simply referred them to: 'The Book of Jeremiah, chapter 31, verses 15 to 17.' Judy Feld Carr wept when she found the passage that Rabbi Hamra wanted them to read:

---

[44] Henry Giniger, 'Group Says Syria Persecutes Jews,' *New York Times*, 2 January 1972.
[45] Saul S. Friedman, *Without Future: The Plight of Syrian Jews*, page 30.

Thus said the Lord: A cry is heard in Ramah – wailing, bitter weeping – Rachel weeping for her children. She refuses to be comforted for her children, who are gone.

Thus said the Lord: Refrain your voice from weeping, your eyes from shedding tears; for there is reward for your labour – declares the Lord; they shall return from the enemy's land. And there is hope for your future – declares the Lord: your children shall return to their country.[46]

The situation of Syrian Jewry remained dire. On 4 March 1974, five months after Israel's defeat of the Syrian forces on the Golan Heights, four young Syrian Jewish women were found raped, robbed and murdered in a cave on the Syrian side of the Syrian-Lebanese border. The bodies, which had been mutilated, were returned for burial to their parents in sacks. The *New York Times* reported that the finger of one of the young women had been cut off to remove her ring. The newspaper also reported the Syrian authorities' claim that the four women – obviously intending to escape from Syria – had been travelling with smugglers who were taking them across the border into Lebanon. When the smugglers saw that they had jewellery and other valuables with them, they decided to rob them.

In Damascus, following the funeral of the four women, an estimated one thousand Jewish women mounted an unprecedented protest, marching through the streets, chanting that they and their families must be allowed to leave Syria. These women had previously been in virtual detention in the Jewish Quarter of Damascus since the October War. The demonstration was dispersed by the police, who then accused two prominent male members of the Jewish community of being complicit in the murders.[47]

The Jewish world was indignant at the fate of the four women and at the charges against the two Jewish men. Spurred on by news

---

[46] Jeremiah 31:15-17.
[47] Henry Kamm, 'Syrian Jews Suffering Under Harsh Curbs,' *New York Times*, 14 April 1974.

from Damascus, Israeli operatives smuggled as many Jews as they could out of Syria through Lebanon and Turkey. They worked in the strictest secrecy, because any contact made by Syrian Jews with Israel was regarded as treason. But the number of Jews who could be saved in this way was very small.[48] The route through Lebanon also became impossible during the Lebanese Civil War of 1975–7, when as many as two hundred Lebanese Jews were killed – not as targets of the warring factions but in their crossfire.[49]

In the United States, some 25,000 Jews who had left Syria in the 1920s were living in the New York borough of Brooklyn. The Borough Congressman, Democrat Steven Solarz, travelled to Syria in February 1975 to intercede for the then 5,000 Jews who remained in the country. President Hafez al-Assad told Solarz: 'I cannot let them go because if I let them go how can I stop the Soviet Union sending its Jews to Israel, where they will strengthen my enemy.' For two years Solarz persevered, asking Assad to let two hundred Syrian Jewish women – for whom there were no eligible Jewish men – leave for the United States. After President Jimmy Carter met Assad in Geneva, the Syrian leader finally let the two hundred Jewish women leave Syria. Solarz met them at New York's Kennedy airport in 1977.[50]

As the years passed, reports of the plight of Syrian Jewry continued to reach the West. In February 1979, Judith Cummings wrote in the *New York Times*: 'A Jew who recently escaped from Syria stated that a new wave of repression had been imposed on the Jewish community, signaling a retreat from human rights gains of the last two years (1977-8).' During his meeting with journalists 'the man wore a black mask in order to protect his relatives still in Damascus. He said the Jewish community was subjected to harassment, detention, and torture since several successful escapes by Jews to Israel. Members

---

[48] Harold Troper, 'Campaign on Behalf of Syrian and Soviet Jews,' in Malka Hillel Shulewitz (editor), *The Forgotten Millions: The Modern Jewish Exodus from Arab Lands*, page 55.
[49] Kirsten E. Schulze, 'The Jews of Lebanon,' in Tudor Parfitt (editor), *Israel and Ishmael: Studies in Muslim-Jewish Relations*, page 94.
[50] Steven Solarz, in conversation with the author, 1 March 2009.

of his family were jailed and brutally beaten after the escape of two of his brothers. Syrian Jews have restrictions on internal travel and transfer of property. The word Mussawi (follower of Moses) is stamped in bright ink on the identity card.'[51]

The road forward in the rescue of Syrian Jews – for it was essentially a rescue effort, not an emigration programme – was long and difficult. It involved secret meetings, clandestine payments, international pressure, repeated rebuffs and the combined efforts of the government of Israel, the Tel Aviv–based World Organisation of Jews from Arab Lands (WOJAC) – established in November 1975 – and Jewish organisations in Canada, the United States, Britain and many other countries. Monitored and driven forward by the energy and determination of Judy Feld Carr, these efforts eventually bore fruit. The catalyst was the Madrid Conference of 1991, when Israel and its Arab neighbours began face-to-face talks to resolve the Palestinian Arab problem. Following the conference, the Syrian Government, headed by Hafez al-Assad, agreed to abandon two decades of implacable resistance to Jewish emigration. All 3,886 Jews in Syria were free to leave – for anywhere but Israel.

The mass exodus of Syrian Jews did not alter the anti-Jewish prejudice that persisted within Syria. In 1983 the Syrian Minister of Defence, Mustafa Tlass, wrote and published a book, *The Matzah of Zion*, in which he endorsed the age-old anti-Jewish Blood Libel. In his preface, Tlass wrote of the 1840 Blood Libel: 'Damascus was shaken by a heinous crime, Father Thomas al-Kabushi fell victim to the Jewish community who wanted to extract his blood for the manufacture of festival unleavened bread. . . .' Tlass went on to write of 'the religious beliefs of the Jews and the destructive perversions they contain, which draw their orientation from a dark hate towards all humankind and all religions.' On 8 February 1991 the Syrian representative at the United Nations Human Rights Commission in

---

[51] Judith Cummings, 'Repression of Jews in Syria is Charged,' *New York Times*, 3 February 1979.

Geneva, Mrs. Nabila Chaalan, told the Commission: 'We should like to launch an appeal to all members of this Commission to read this very important work that demonstrates unequivocally the historical reality of Zionist racism.'[52]

On 20 October 1992, when there were still a thousand Jews waiting to leave Syria, the Syrian Government called a halt to the exodus.[53] Judy Feld Carr and her supporters renewed their campaign, helped by the Canadian and American Ambassadors in Damascus. After three months the Syrian Government relented. Of the 3,656 Jews saved by Judy Feld Carr, her supporters and the many international Jewish welfare agencies, 1,262 made their way via the United States and Canada to Israel. A climax of celebration came on 18 October 1994, when the former Chief Rabbi of Syria, Avraham Hamra, landed at Ben-Gurion airport with his wife, his six children, his mother and five of his brothers and sisters. Those watching were delighted when the youngest of the Chief Rabbi's sons, nine-year-old Benjamin, 'flung himself into the arms of an uncle who was waiting on the tarmac.'[54]

Judy Feld Carr had done work of vital importance. In June 1993 the Sephardi Bikur Cholim synagogue in New York, in the presence of many of the Syrian Jews then living in the city, honoured her with an engraved plaque, which recorded the fact that she 'arose while it was "still night"[55] and woke up the world to the plight of our brethren in Syria. Through her efforts lives have been saved, families sustained and loved ones united. She has saved entire worlds and will be blessed by generations to come.'[56]

---

[52] Proceedings of the United Nations Human Rights Commission, Geneva, 8 and 12 February 1991.

[53] Batsheva Tsur, 'Jews in Syria still "hostage,"' *Jerusalem Post*, 10 January 1993.

[54] Jenni Frazer and Geoffrey Paul, 'Clandestine exodus reunites Syrian Jews,' *Jewish Chronicle*, 21 October 1994.

[55] One of the phrases in the description of 'A Woman of Valour' in the Book of Proverbs, 31:10-31, sung or spoken each Friday night at the start of the Jewish Sabbath by the husband in praise of his wife. The phrase begins: 'She riseth also while it is still night, and given food to her household . . .'

[56] Quoted in Harold Troper, *The Ransomed of God* (retitled *The Rescuer*, 2007), page 238.

20

A NEW LIFE IN NEW LANDS

'The exceptional richness of their heritage'

In the four years between 1948 and 1951 a total of 687,739 Jewish refugees reached Israel. Of these about one quarter – some 100,000 – arrived from Europe. About 500,000 – more than three quarters – arrived from Arab and Muslim lands. The number of newcomers in those four years almost exactly doubled the 1947 Jewish population of British Mandate Palestine, an astonishing, and almost certainly unique, increase in population through immigration in modern times. In 1951, Jewish immigrants from Muslim lands made up almost three quarters of that year's immigration.[1]

The immigrants from Europe, almost all of them having spent months, even years, in Displaced Persons' camps (DP camps) in the British and American occupation zones in Germany, were mostly the penniless, exhausted, traumatised remnant of murdered families and communities lost in the Holocaust, fleeing the lands where they and their ancestors had lived and worked for hundreds of years. The immigrants from Arab and Muslim countries were mostly the penniless, exhausted, traumatised expellees who had been made refugees as a result of the sudden, furious reaction to the creation of the State of Israel by the governments and peoples among whom they and their ancestors had lived and worked for 1,400 years.

The task of finding homes and work for these immigrants in Israel was a massive one, as was the task of integrating them into what

---

[1] Ashkenazi immigrants in 1951: 48,197 (27.7 per cent); Oriental immigrants, 125,456 (72.3 per cent).

for many was a foreign country with a language they did not know, and with a way of life they had not experienced before. Israel was a country still recovering from its destructive, costly and traumatic War of Independence. The Jews from Muslim lands – the Sephardi, or Mizrachi ('Oriental') Jews as they were known – came from cultures and backgrounds very different to that of the Ashkenazi or 'Western' Jews among whom they found themselves. They were looked down upon by many of the Ashkenazi, and considered 'primitive,' as the future Israeli Prime Minister, Levi Eshkol, described the Iraqi Jews.[2] They were thought to be fit mainly for manual labour and domestic service.

In a Knesset session in Tel Aviv on 8 March 1949, Eliahu Eliashar, a parliamentary representative of the Sephardi Jews, spoke on behalf of the Jews from Muslim lands. Born in Jerusalem, he had studied medicine at the University of Beirut and law in Cairo. In the First World War he had served as a junior medical officer in the Turkish Army. In his speech, Eliashar described the special problems of the Oriental communities, particularly the degradation of those living in slums. 'Our hope and prayer,' he said, 'is that the Prime Minister's pledge to uproot illiteracy, overcrowding, and illness in the slum neighborhoods will be carried out.'[3]

Immigration to Israel reached its peak in the second year after the country's establishment. In 1949 a total of 239,076 immigrants arrived in Israel, the majority from Arab lands. In 1950, the first full year of peace, there were 169,405 new immigrants and a further 173,901 in 1951. 'Absorption problems,' wrote David Ben-Gurion a quarter of a century later, 'hardly felt during the first year of the State, became almost unbearable in the three years that followed. There were grave shortages of housing, food, and employment. Some 20 percent of the immigrants were unable to work because of their age or the state of their health. There were cripples as well as people suffering from tuberculosis, heart trouble, nervous diseases,

---

[2] Quoted in Shlomo Hillel, *Operation Babylon*, page 265.
[3] David Ben-Gurion, *Israel: A Personal History*, page 354.

and so on. There were also the blind, the aged, and the deaf-mutes.'[4] At the end of 1949, The Joint, in cooperation with the Jewish Agency and the Government of Israel, established an organisation – Malben – to handle all immigrant social cases.[5]

Israeli policy towards the mass of immigrants entering the country from both Europe, and from Arab and Muslim lands was facing a serious challenge. In March 1949 more than 32,000 immigrants reached Israel, the highest number yet recorded for a single month, averaging a thousand a day. In the months ahead there was hardly any diminution of the flow. The Immigration Gate Camp in Haifa, which could house six thousand newcomers with difficulty, sometimes housed as many as eight thousand. On 6 October 1949 the Jewish Agency Executive met in Jerusalem, and, faced by the dire lack of resources with which to house and feed future newcomers, took the decision to limit the number of new immigrants to 35,000 for the coming twelve months.[6] At that very moment, 22,000 Jews were waiting to go to Israel in camps in France, Italy, Aden and Teheran; many more were expected to join them.

An anguished and urgent debate began within the Jewish Agency. Fortunately for the mass of Jews still on the move, it was resolved within a few months by the reduced but considerable allocation for the year 1950 of 80,000 places for European Jews and a further 80,000 for Jews from Arab and Muslim lands.[7] Four years later, speaking to a convention of high school students on 11 June 1954, Ben-Gurion stressed the need to integrate new immigrants, from whatever background, and warned: 'We cannot have two Jewish nations that differ from one another in every aspect of their lives. We are all together in the same boat on a stormy sea, and if we won't row together with equal energy there is the danger that the boat will be wrecked by the waves.'

---

[4] David Ben-Gurion, *Israel: A Personal History*, page 362.
[5] 'Malben' is the Hebrew acronym for 'Organization for the Care of Handicapped Immigrants.'
[6] The Jewish New Year 5710 had begun five days earlier.
[7] Jewish Agency Executive minutes, Central Zionist Archive.

In 'a few short years,' Ben-Gurion pointed out, four hundred new villages had been established in Israel. 'This is mostly the work of the new immigrants and it attests to the creative ability latent in this population. But a barrier still exists between the established community and the new *aliyah* – Emigration. 'It holds social and moral threats and makes integration of the exiles a vital necessity . . . we must not abandon the immigrants of Iraq, Rumania, Yemen, and Poland.'[8]

On 17 August 1949, Ben-Gurion told the Knesset, with stark honesty: 'The challenge of our historic mission in this country awakened the pioneering fervour that was hidden in the hearts of Jewish youth in the little towns of Lithuania, Poland, Galicia, Rumania, and America. The immigrants who will arrive during the coming years will be mostly from the Oriental countries, the lands of Islam, the nations of Asia and Africa. The Jewish communities in these countries did not have the opportunity in recent generations to avail themselves of the cultural treasures of mankind and of the Jews, even to the same degree that this was possible in Europe.' And yet, Ben-Gurion insisted, 'there is no reason to believe the Jews of North Africa, Turkey, Egypt, Iran, or Aden differ basically from the Jews of Lithuania, Galicia, and America. They also have hidden within them the rich springs of pioneering, work, and creativity. If we invest in them only a fraction of the efforts that we invested in the Jewish youth of Europe, we will achieve the desired results.'[9]

While the Israeli leadership strove to support the Jewish refugees from Muslim lands and make them an integral and equal part of Israeli life and society, no Arab nation tried to integrate the Palestinian Arab refugees into their new homelands. Instead, the Palestinian Arabs were kept in refugee camps on independent Arab soil, sustained in their refugee status by a United Nations agency set up – on 8 December 1949 – solely for them, the United Nations Relief and Works Agency for Palestinian Refugees in the Near East (UNRWA). No such agency was set up for the Jewish refugees from Muslim lands,

---

[8] David Ben-Gurion, *Israel: A Personal History*, pages 435-6.
[9] David Ben-Gurion, *Israel: A Personal History*, page 371.

or for the eleven million and more European refugees of the Second
World War – including Jews, Germans and Poles, many of whom were
living in Displaced Persons camps. These refugees were helped by
another United Nations agency, the United Nations Relief and
Rehabilitation Administration (UNRRA), whose purpose was to take
them out of the DP camps, find them new homes and help them
become integral parts of the countries that took them in. In UNRWA
camps, by contrast, the Palestinian Arab refugees, their children and
grandchildren were made to feel by their sovereign Arab 'host' nations
that their one task in life, generation after generation, was to fight,
campaign, organise, agitate, demand and prepare for the return to
what had been their former homes in pre-1948 Israel.

The early days of the mass emigration from Muslim lands were hard in
the extreme for the new immigrants. Tented encampments gave way
only slowly to hutted encampments. These were the *ma'abarot* (transit
camps), which by 1952 were housing a quarter of a million immigrants,
and of which Maurice Roumani, a young Jewish immigrant from Libya,
has written: 'Thousands of people were often crammed into a small
space where shelter consisted of tin huts, tents, shacks made of card-
board or whatever materials were at hand. Often immigrants arriving
at their destination found nothing more than an open field.'[10]

Slowly land was found and the immigrants were sent to settle and
farm it according to their country of origin. In the three years after
their arrival in Israel, Jews from Libya had established twelve cooperative farming communities (known as *moshavim*). Three decades
later they were farming and developing more than twenty-two such
communities.[11]

Initially the Oriental Jews were marginalised, many living in poverty, poorly educated, doing manual labour and working as domestic
help. But slowly and steadily this changed. 'The settlers from Baraq
and Devora' – write two sociologists, Joseph Eaton and David

[10] Maurice M. Roumani, *The Case of the Jews from Arab Countries: A Neglected Issue*,
page 10.
[11] Maurice M. Roumani, *The Jews of Libya*, page 167.

Solomonica, who studied the Moroccan immigrants at two villages in Israel – 'have come a long way since a truck picked them up at the Haifa harbour, as tired immigrants, to deposit them in unfinished cement houses, to whom the label "reluctant pioneers" has been ascribed. Few social planners expected them to become pace setters who would contribute increasingly to the country's viability by regenerating the soil and the development of Jewish farming.' Those who had allocated the Moroccan immigrants to the villages 'expected them to remain dependent clients for a long time with little in common with the already settled European "pioneer" generation' who had come in the 1920s and 1930s. Twenty years after their arrival, the Moroccans who were sent to Devora and Baraq 'have become part of Israel's mainstream.'[12]

In 1953 a Hungarian-born Israeli anthropologist, Raphael Patai, published a comprehensive account of the history, culture and immigration of the Oriental Jews and their integration into Israel. He noted the difficulties facing them on arrival in Israel. At a time when yet more Jewish immigrants from Muslim lands were on their way, he wrote, 'the Oriental Jews are faced with inferior housing conditions in the tents and barracks of the reception camps; they find themselves penniless and subsisting on charity as did beggars in their home communities; the jobs available are poorly paid and only rarely of the kind to which they are used from previous experience.' This situation, Patai added, 'creates dissatisfaction with the present, coupled with a nostalgia for the past.'

Raphael Patai also noted how the attitude of the Ashkenazi Jews in Israel towards the Oriental Jews 'ranges from full sympathy and readiness to go all out to help them in their adaptive process, on the one end of the scale, to scornful derision and an overt wish to prevent their influx into the country, on the other.' What was certain, he wrote, was that the Oriental Jews 'come to Israel with a feeling of homecoming, of returning to the country which is as much theirs as any other Jewish group's. . . . Their loyalty to Israel, its cause and its

---

[12] Joseph W. Eaton and David Solomonica, *The Rurban Village*, pages 13-14.

aims, was sufficiently expressed, they opine, when they chose to come to Israel.' As to legislation that 'aims at Westernizing certain aspects of life in Israel,' the Oriental Jewish immigrants 'fight against it, vociferously and unrestrainedly, for in their eyes the passing of such laws means the imposition of the mores of one part of the Jewish population of Israel upon the whole country.' That was why, 'instead of welcoming common schooling for their children and those of the Ashkenazim, the most numerous Oriental Jewish community' – the Jews from Iraq – 'insists on separate schools for their own children. They know that common schooling means the elimination of their traditions from the lives of their own children.'[13]

Israel wrestled with these dilemmas for three decades. On 3 August 1960, Ami Assaf, the Deputy Minister of Education, told the Knesset in Jerusalem: 'It is estimated that the Oriental community today accounts for half the children and youth and sixty-two percent of all children being born at present. It is true that only twelve percent of children from Oriental communities received first-class marks in Grade 8 Seker (high school entrance) examinations, compared to fifty percent of the children of European descent. The Minister of Education recognizes the need for special measures to accelerate the bridging of the gap between children from different social strata. In the past four years much has been done in various directions that has already begun to bear fruit. . . . We are dealing with a wide gap resulting from a divergence of social backgrounds and communal affiliations. The Ministry now considers the problem mainly a social one and believes that with thorough work over an extended period and sufficient means, gradual improvement and progress among these underprivileged groups can be achieved.'[14]

On 12 September 1964, in another Knesset debate, the Speaker, Yisrael Yeshayahu, a Jew from Yemen who had helped organise Operation Magic Carpet fifteen years earlier, declared: 'I have always felt and still feel that the Asian and African immigrants will

---

[13] Raphael Patai, *Israel between East and West*, pages 284-5 and 297-8.
[14] David Ben-Gurion, *Israel: A Personal History*, page 571.

achieve complete redemption only by their own efforts, by revolutionary educational leadership from within. They generally conduct themselves with a quiet nobility, a sense of rational responsibility, love of the Homeland and the nation of Israel, and it may be assumed they will continue to do so in the future. But it is also true that they need assistance if they are to become equal partners with the advantaged segment of the nation that comes from Europe and America.'

Mordekhai Zar, who had been born in the Persian city of Meshed, and who had reached Israel in 1936, spoke in the Knesset with understanding of the different characteristics of the Ashkenazi and Sephardi Jews in Israel. The problem, he said, was 'how to combine the good in both sectors. From this rostrum I wish to issue a call to the entire nation, a call for greater tolerance between our two sectors who share the same fate.'[15]

Within two decades of these words being spoken, greater tolerance had begun to emerge as the immigrants from Muslim lands found their equal place and their political strength in Israeli society. This levelling and integration was helped from the outset by the Israel Defence Forces (IDF). The IDF, in which three years of military service was compulsory for all male Jewish citizens and two years for Jewish women, introduced programmes during military service that ensured that every young person who left its ranks for the labour force did so with a certificate of elementary education or the equivalent of two years of high school. Jews from Muslim countries were the main beneficiaries of these programmes.[16]

Prejudice took a long time to overcome. In 1972 a British visitor to Israel, Gerald Kaufman, recorded an evening with senior Israeli civil servants: 'There was a buzz of agreement when one of the most eminent bureaucrats present denounced the all-pervasive bureaucracy. Nobody mentioned the absence from the room of a single person whose origin was Iraqi, Moroccan or Yemeni.'[17] But as the years

---

[15] David Ben-Gurion, *Israel: A Personal History*, pages 712-3.
[16] Maurice M. Roumani, *From Immigrant to Citizen*, Chapter VI.
[17] Gerald Kaufman, *To Build the Promised Land*, page 229.

passed, more and more of the immigrants from Muslim lands went through high school and university, became officers in the citizen's army, entered local and then national politics, and made their mark on the highest echelons of Israeli society.

Tel Aviv-born Major-General Moshe Levy – whose parents were immigrants from Iraq, and who in 1950 had been one of the Israeli emissaries imprisoned in Baghdad at the start of the mass emigration – became Chief of Staff of the Israel Defence Forces in 1983. Another of the clandestine Zionist emissaries to Iraq – and their historian – Shlomo Hillel, was Israeli Minister of the Police from 1969 to 1977, was elected Speaker of the Knesset in 1984, and later became President of the Society for Preservation of Israel Heritage Sites. Israel Kessar, who had left Yemen for Palestine as a young boy in 1934, served as the head of Israel's million-strong Trade Union movement (the Histadrut) in the 1980s, and as Minister of Transport from 1992 to 1996. Ten Israeli Supreme Court justices and forty judges on other Israeli courts have been of Iraqi descent. Of the 120 members of the 2009 Knesset, at least ten were born in Muslim lands, among them Damascus-born Israel Hasson, Casablanca-born Eli Aflalo, and Chaim Amsellem, born in Oran.

Cairo-born David Sultan, who for forty years served in the Israeli Foreign Ministry, returned to Egypt in 1992 to serve as Israeli Ambassador in Egypt; he was also Israeli Ambassador to Turkey and Canada. Cairo-born Levana Zamir, some of whose forebears had lived in Egypt since 1750, others for even longer, became the head of the Israeli Business Women's Association and the President of the Israel-Egypt Friendship Association. Under her leadership the first exhibition of Israeli-Egyptian paintings was held in Cairo in 1982, under the auspices of the Egyptian Ministry of Culture.[18]

Israel was enormously enriched by the contribution of Jews from Muslim lands, who came as refugees and brought with them many

---

[18] Ada Aharoni, Aimée Israel-Pelletier, Levana Zamir (editors), *History and Culture of the Jews from Egypt in Modern Times*, pages 348-50.

important talents and skills. Egyptian-born Haim Saban's broadcasting interests became significant in both the United States and Germany. Yitzhak Tshuva, who left Libya at the age of five, built a thriving property business in Israel, and purchased the Plaza Hotel in New York. The army, a great social leveller, was also a fertile field of advancement. Iranian-born Dan Halutz served as Chief of Staff, the highest position in the Israel Defence Forces.

Moroccan-born David Levy was Foreign Minister during the early Israeli-Palestinian talks in 1992. Another Moroccan-born Jew, Shlomo Ben-Ami, who left Tetuan with his parents in 1955, was Foreign Minister of Israel at the time of the Camp David negotiations with the Palestinians in 2000. Moroccan-born Amir Peretz, whose father had been head of the local Jewish community of Boujad, became Mayor of the southern Israeli town of Sderot in 1983, chairman of the Histadrut trade labour union movement in 1995 and leader of the Labour Party a decade later. Had the Labour Party won the election in 2006, Peretz would have become the first non-Ashkenazi Prime Minister in Israel's history. Instead, he became Defence Minister in a coalition government. In 2006, Moroccan-born Meir Sheetrit was Israel's Minister of Construction and Housing.

At the beginning of the Twenty-First Century one Iranian-born Jew, Moshe Katsav, was President of Israel, and another, Shaul Mofaz, was Israeli Minister of Defence. In January 2009, when the shelling of southern Israel by Hamas rockets from the Gaza Strip began to intensify, one of those who protected his community was Aviram Dahari, the Mayor of Kiryat Gat, a refugee from Yemen as a youngster. During the Lebanon war two years earlier, Dahari had given shelter in Kiryat Gat to several hundred Israeli refugees from areas shelled by Hezbollah in the north.[19]

Israel in 2010 still awaited a Prime Minister born under Muslim rule. But in the Cabinet of 2009 were three Jews born in Muslim lands: Tunisian-born Silvan Shalom – who had left the city of Gabès with his parents in 1959 when he was one year old – a former Finance

---

[19] Yehuda Marks, 'Kiryat Gat's First Priorities – Its Citizens,' *Hamodia*, 8 January 2009.

Minister from 2001–3 and Foreign Minister from 2003–5, who became Minister of Regional Cooperation and Minister of the Development of the Negev and Galilee in 2009; Binyamin (Fouad) Ben-Eliezer, also a former Minister, who became Minister of Industry, Trade and Labour; and Moroccan-born Yakov Margi, who became Minister of Religious Services.

Israeli arts and entertainment were also beneficiaries of the immigration from Muslim lands. The Israeli pop and folk singer Rita – Rita Yahan-Farouz – was born in Iran. Leaving Teheran at the age of eight with her parents, she began her musical career as a singer in the Israeli Army during her military service. As of 2008 she had eleven prize-winning albums in Israel. Moroccan-born Smadar Levi was at that time another of Israel's most popular singers – in Arabic, Spanish and Hebrew; in 2007 she sang in San Francisco under the auspices of the Israel Center of the local Jewish Federation.

Some Israelis with origins in Muslim lands spoke at the start of the Twenty-First Century of their sense of Arab identity. One such Israeli was Sasson Somekh, who left Iraq at the age of seventeen, and who became Professor of Literature at Tel Aviv University and a close friend of the Egyptian writer Naguib Mafouz. An Israeli expert on Arabic literature, he served for three years in Egypt as director of the Israeli Academic Centre in Cairo. Professor Somekh explained why he considered himself an 'Arab Jew': 'An Arab Jew is someone who is immersed, or grew up in, Arab culture, with Arabs, and knows the way of the life.' When he learned at school of the Arab defeat of the Byzantines and the Persians in the Seventh Century, he 'would be on their side.' When he learned of Saladin's defeat of the Crusaders he 'was very happy – as an Iraqi, as an Arab.' He added: 'I grew up in Baghdad, and I was the perfect Arab.'[20]

In 2010, Zvi Yehezkeli, an Israeli-born Jew with Kurdish and Iraqi roots, headed the Arab affairs desk of Israel Television Channel 10. 'I am an Arab,' he said, expressing his feeling of being strongly linked to his family past. 'My language is Arabic, I'm a Jew but I'm Arabic.'

---

[20] Quoted in Rachel Shabi, *Not the Enemy: Israel's Jews from Arab Lands*, pages 234-5.

For Yehezkeli, the term 'Arab Jew' was an attitude of mind 'that tilts the Israeli fulcrum from Europe to the Middle East, in language, in culture' and in a link-up with the 'tastes' of the Middle East.[21]

The Jews who fled from Muslim lands after 1948 made their contribution not only to Israel but to all the lands that gave them refuge. The loss to the Arab States that did not want them was considerable in every area of human endeavour. Dhiaa Kasim Kashi, a Muslim Shiite in Iraq, later reflected that from a cultural standpoint, Iraq 'suffered a big shock when the Jews left.' One reason was that 'all of Iraq's famous musicians and composers were Jewish,' as were a large portion of its other artists. In addition, 'Jews were so central to commercial life in Iraq that business across the country used to shut down on Saturdays because it was the Jewish Shabbat. They were the most prominent members of every elite profession – bankers, doctors, lawyers, professors, engineers, etc.'

In Kashi's view, had the Jews stayed, they would have helped 'manage the country far better.' In particular, the Jews would have served as a 'moderating influence' on Iraqi society and as a bulwark against the 'extreme brand of Arab Nationalism' embodied by Saddam Hussein, which ultimately led the country into three devastating wars and economic collapse. Tamar Morad, Dennis Shasha and Robert Shasha, the editors of *Iraq's Last Jews, Stories of Daily Life*, commented on Kashi's remarks: 'If many of the individuals who fled Iraq rose to prominence thereafter, it may be due to the exceptional richness of their heritage. They were thoroughly integrated into the larger community and used Arabic as their main language.'[22]

Britain, France, Italy, the United States and Canada were among the beneficiaries of this mass emigration. Italy gained from the emigration of Jews from Libya, France from the Jews from Morocco, Algeria and Tunisia. Britain gained from the immigration of Egyptian and

---

[21] Quoted in Rachel Shabi, *Not the Enemy: Israel's Jews from Arab Lands*, pages 235-6.
[22] Tamar Morad, Dennis Shasha and Robert Shasha (editors), *Iraq's Last Jews, Stories of Daily Life, Upheaval and Escape from Modern Babylon*, pages 199-206. Some former Iraqi Jews continue to speak Arabic among themselves.

Syrian Jews. In London, some five hundred Jewish families from Aden have also maintained their communal life, centring on the largest of their three synagogues, the Congregation of Aden Jews Synagogue.[23]

Some Jews from Muslim lands found fame and fortune in their new homelands. In the Canadian city of Edmonton, Iranian-born Jacob Ghermezian built the world's first large indoor shopping mall and amusement park, and was a leading patron of Jewish education in the city. Also in Edmonton, Jacob Masliyah, who left oil-rich Iraq in 1960 when he was eighteen, became a pioneer of Oil Sands Engineering in the vast oil sands development in northern Alberta; a distinguished chemical engineer and educator, he was inducted in 2008 as an Officer to the Order of Canada. In Britain, Iranian-born David Alliance built up a clothing empire. His public work included the Prince of Wales' Youth Business Trust, the Council for Industry and Higher Education, and the University of Manchester Foundation. He entered the House of Lords in 2004.

France benefited from the diverse talents of Algerian Jewish immigrants, including the World Bantamweight boxing champions Robert Cohen and Alphonse Halimi, the Nobel Prize-winning physicist Claude Cohen-Tannoudji, and the economist Jacques Attali. Jewish immigrants also rose to prominence in many other places. Ruth Pearl, the mother of American journalist Daniel Pearl – a Jew murdered by Islamic extremists in Pakistan in 2002 – was born in Iraq. Iranian-born Jimmy (Jamshid) Delshad, a member of the large Iranian-Jewish community in Los Angeles, was elected Mayor of Beverly Hills in 2007.[24]

Of the 15,000 Jews in Tangier when the Second World War came to an end in 1945, only four hundred remained in 1991. The rest were to be found as citizens of Israel, Canada, the United States,

---

[23] Leon Jacob and Moshe Samuel (editors), *Aden Jews Congregation* (brochure).
[24] 'Rabbi Haim Ovadia,' *JIMENA Voice*, volume 1, number 8, November 2006. Jews of Iraqi ancestry also found a home in Los Angeles, including Rabbi Haim Ovadia, whose maternal great-grandfather, Hakham Yehuda Fetaya, had left Baghdad for Palestine in 1936, and whose father had left Iraq in 1949 to become one of the founders of the Iraqi Heritage Centre in Israel, in the town of Or Yehuda.

Venezuela and Spain. At the time of writing, the largest Tangierian Jewish community outside Israel was in Toronto, home to five thousand Jews from Tangier. The author of the history of the Jews of Tangier, M. Mitchell Serels, served as their rabbi for three years. A further eight hundred Tangierian Jews settled in Montreal.[25] The unofficial Chief Sephardi Rabbi of Canada, Rabbi Amram Assayag, who was born in Tangier, went to Toronto as a teenager and became an inspiring leader in his community. Jews from Iraq also settled in Toronto; in 2006 they celebrated the thirtieth anniversary of their three-hundred-strong community.[26]

In 1971, during a visit to the Gallipoli peninsula, I crossed the Dardanelles to the Turkish town of Canakkale (Chanak). It was a Saturday, and I decided to go to synagogue. To my surprise, the synagogue was crowded to capacity and the service was being conducted with all the Scrolls of the Law on the pulpit. After the service there was a festive meal, far grander than a normal Sabbath Kiddush. I was told that the entire community was leaving the next day for Israel, together with their prayer books and Scrolls of the Law. Some two hundred Turkish Jews, the descendants of the Spanish Jews who flourished in Ottoman Turkey, were on their final exodus.

Those Jews who left Turkey knew that even in the secular Turkish Republic created in 1924 there had been moments of danger. On the night of 6/7 September 1955, Muslim extremists in Istanbul had carried out a sustained attack against Greek, Jewish and Armenian property. More than four thousand shops and one thousand houses were destroyed. In the aftermath of this night of destruction, 10,000 of Turkey's 36,000 Jews had left the country, mostly for Israel.

In both 1986 and 2003, Islamic militants attacked the Neve Shalom Synagogue in Istanbul with fatal results. In the 1986 attack, which took place during Sabbath services, twenty-two Jewish worshippers were killed when attackers burst into the prayer hall and opened fire. Following that incident the synagogue decided to keep

---

[25] M. Mitchell Serels, *A History of the Jews of Tangier*, pages 175-181.
[26] Frances Kraft, 'Iraqi congregation celebrates 30 years in Toronto,' *Canadian Jewish News*, 30 March 2006.

hard hats under every seat in case of another attack. In 2003 two truck bombs exploded outside both the Neve Shalom and Beth Israel Synagogues, both of which were crowded with Jewish families celebrating the Bar Mitzvahs of their sons. At least twenty Jews were killed and more than three hundred were wounded.

Today, Turkey's remaining 26,000 Jews, almost all of them in Istanbul, are uneasy at the resurgence of Islamic fundamentalism. Yet since 1924, Turkey has been a secular society welcoming to its Jewish community, just as it had been welcoming under Muslim Ottoman rule in previous centuries.[27]

Jews born in Muslim lands, with their experience of being forced to flee their homes, have also made significant contributions towards ameliorating the current Arab-Israeli conflict. One of them is Egyptian-born Sir Ronald Cohen, who was knighted in 2000 for his services to the venture capital industry. In 2003 he founded the Portland Trust, 'committed to promoting peace and stability between Palestinians and Israelis through economic development.'[28] The Portland Trust provides Palestinian Arabs on the West Bank with investment opportunities and affordable housing. Sir Ronald's experiences in Egypt, where he went to a school in which Jews, Christians and Muslims studied together, gave him 'a feeling of empathy with the Palestinians and a belief in future coexistence with the Israelis.'[29] Thus, a Jew who lived among Muslims, and who also saw the harsh side of the conflict, has built an active structure of cooperation from a faith in future Arab-Israeli harmony.

---

[27] In 2009 there were an estimated 24,000 Jews in Istanbul, 2,300 in Izmir, 140 in Bursa and 100 in the capital, Ankara.

[28] Portland Trust mission statement: www.portlandtrust.org.

[29] Sir Ronald Cohen, in conversation with the author, 18 September 2009.

21

THE SEARCH FOR RECOGNITION

'A matter of historic justice'

Jews who have lived under Muslim rule, wherever they live today, are determined to make the international community aware of their sufferings in the aftermath of the 1948–49 Arab-Israeli War. The first recognition of their plight came in 1957, when Auguste Lindt, the United Nations High Commissioner for Refugees, spoke of the Jews who were being expelled from Egypt. 'Another emergency problem is now arising,' he said, 'that of refugees from Egypt. There is no doubt in my mind that those refugees from Egypt who are not able, or not willing to avail themselves of the protection of the Government of their nationality, fall under the mandate of my office.'[1]

In the immediate aftermath of the Six-Day War of 1967, Dr. E. Jahn, a member of the office of the United Nations High Commissioner for Refugees, noted with regard to 'Jews from Middle Eastern and North African countries,' that 'such persons may be considered prima facie within the mandate of this office.'[2] Then on 22 November 1967 the United Nations Security Council also pronounced on the refugee issue, when it voted for Resolution 242 regarding the future borders of Israel. For two days, the Soviet Union had sought to refer to 'Palestinian' refugees, but Britain and the United States wanted the resolution to apply equally to both the Palestinian refugees from

---

[1] Report of the United Nations High Commissioner for Refugees, Geneva, 29 January to 4 February 1957.
[2] United Nations High Commissioner for Refugees, Document No. 7/3/2/Libya, 6 July 1967.

Israel and the Jewish refugees from Muslim lands. Lord Carrington for Britain and Arthur Goldberg for the United States were both emphatic in this wish, and ultimately prevailed. Hence the open wording of the Resolution, which affirms 'the necessity . . . for achieving a just settlement of the refugee problem.'[3]

Following the Six-Day War, the plight of those Jews still living under Muslim rule gained international coverage. On 28 January 1970 a *New York Times* headline declared: '3 ARAB LANDS SAID TO OPPRESS JEWS; Iraq, Syria, Egypt Scored at a Parley in Paris.' The article had been sent from Paris the previous day. It began: 'Delegates from 26 countries appealed to world opinion today to save the handful of Jews remaining in Iraq, Syria and the United Arab Republic.'[4] The United Arab Republic (UAR) was Egypt.

On 10 November 1975 the United Nations' General Assembly in New York adopted Resolution 3379, by a vote of 72 to 35 (with 32 abstentions), stating that 'Zionism is a form of racism and racial discrimination.' Every Arab and Muslim government voted in favour of the resolution, intensifying the harsh anti-Israel stance within the United Nations. The question of compensation for Jews who had been driven out of Arab and Muslim lands was clearly not going to receive meaningful support at the United Nations.[5]

In Paris two weeks later, on 24 November 1975, Jews originally from Arab and Muslim countries came together from Israel, Europe and the Americas to establish the Tel Aviv-based World Organization of Jews from Arab Countries (WOJAC). WOJAC demanded that the remaining Jews in Syria and Iraq be granted their 'elementary human and civil rights, including freedom to emigrate,' and that 'fair compensation' be paid by the Arab States 'for communal and private property which was stolen, frozen or expropriated as well as for

---

[3] United Nations' Security Council Resolution 242: United Nations website, www.un.org/documents/sc/res/1967/scres67.htm.

[4] John L. Hess, '3 Arab Lands Said To Oppress Jews,' *New York Times*, 28 January 1970.

[5] It took sixteen years before the Zionism Is Racism resolution, Resolution 3379 of 10 November 1975, was revoked by Resolution 4686 on 16 December 1991.

injuries suffered by Jews as a result of discrimination or persecution by the responsible Arab countries.'[6]

On 27 October 1977, President Jimmy Carter made the first-ever United States presidential statement on this issue, speaking of Jewish refugees 'who have the same rights as others do.' The Camp David agreements between Israel and Egypt, brokered by the United States, referred specifically to the 'mutual settlement' of all refugee financial claims – those of Jews as well as Arabs.

The saga of Jewish dispossession was not only a matter of history. In 1986 the *New York Times* highlighted the plight that year of Jews in Lebanon. On February 24 a headline read: 'JEWS IN LEBANON URGED TO GET OUT.' The report began: 'Leading French Jews, saying that the Jews of Lebanon are in imminent danger, called on them today to leave for other countries. The appeal at a conference here today came amid a continuing campaign by extremist Moslems against Lebanese Jews.'[7]

What rights did these Lebanese Jewish refugees have? What rights did the hundreds of thousands of Jews have, who had fled before them from so many Muslim lands? In an interview on 27 July 2000, President Bill Clinton brought the issue into the Twenty-First Century, focusing on the dispossessed of 1948. A fund ought to be set up, he said, that 'should compensate the Israelis who were made refugees by the war, which occurred after the birth of the State of Israel.' Israel, he went on to explain, 'is full of people, Jewish people, who lived in predominately Arab countries who came to Israel because they were made refugees in their own land.'[8]

In *Locked Doors: The Seizure of Jewish Property in Arab Countries*, published in 2001, Itamar Levin, an Israeli journalist and expert on

---

[6] 'Resolution Adopted by the Preparatory Convention of WOJAC in Paris on 25.11.1975' (flyer): World Organization of Jews from Arab Countries. A year later, at WOJAC's request, I produced an illustrated booklet, *The Jews of Arab Lands: Their History in Maps* (London: Board of Deputies of British Jews, 1976).

[7] Richard Bernstein, 'Jews in Lebanon Urged to Get Out,' *New York Times*, 24 February 1986.

[8] ABC News transcript: 'Israeli TV Interviews Clinton,' 27 July 2000.

Holocaust victims' assets, called on the Israeli Government to 'risk raising the claims filed by refugees' as part of either Israeli-Palestinian or Israeli-Syrian negotiations. 'Taking this risk,' he wrote, 'would mean some sort of justice for anyone forced to leave their home, against their will, carrying only one suitcase in hand.'[9]

In the Twenty-First Century no year has passed without some indignity being imposed on Jews in Muslim lands. In the first days of 2002, seventy Egyptian Jews and Jewish visitors to Egypt attempted to pray at the graveside of Rabbi Yaakov Abuhatzeira in Alexandria, Egypt, but were refused permission to do so by the Egyptian authorities. It is Jewish custom to visit the gravesite of a righteous man on the anniversary of his death; Rabbi Abuhatzeira was the father of the Baba Sali – Rabbi Yisrael Abuhatzeira – a renowned kabbalist scholar revered by several million Jews from Arab lands in Israel and around the world.[10] Islamic groups in Egypt nonetheless insisted that their Government prohibit Jews from visiting the grave.

In 2002 the major Jewish-American organisations founded Justice for Jews from Arab Countries (JJAC). Launched at a press conference outside the United Nations in New York on 30 September 2002, its mandate was, and remains: 'To ensure that justice for Jews displaced from Arab countries assumes its rightful place on the international political agenda and that their rights be secured as a matter of law and equality.' Ten months later, in July 2003, Stanley Urman, the organisation's Executive Director, and David Matas, a Canadian human rights lawyer, issued a dossier setting out the case for the rights and redress of Jews who had been dispossessed by Arab nations after 1948. Their theme was that in the absence of historical truth and contemporary justice 'there can be no reconciliation, without which there can be no just, lasting peace between and among all peoples of the region.'[11]

---

[9] Itamar Levin, *Locked Doors*, page 235.

[10] 'Jews Denied Permission To Pray At Rabbi's Grave,' Israel Faxx, 4 January 2002, IsraelNationalNews.com.

[11] David Matas and Stanley A. Urman, *Jewish Refugees from Arab Countries: The Case for Rights and Redress* (brochure), page 1.

Also in 2003, David Matas and Stanley Urman, together with Irwin Cotler – soon to be Minister of Justice and Attorney General of Canada – published a detailed report on the confiscation of Jewish property, based on the legal decrees of several Arab governments. 'Figures as to losses vary,' they wrote, noting that the estimate of the World Organization of Jews from Arab Countries (WOJAC) was 'well over $100 billion.' In the Cotler-Matas-Urman report, as in the earlier Urman-Matas dossier, the main focus was not on the monetary aspect, but on justice.[12]

The time had come, many Jews from Muslim lands believed, for their story to be at the forefront of the Jewish narrative. The debate on the issue of restitution and justice was certainly gaining international attention. At the end of October 2003 a bi-partisan resolution submitted to the United States Congress – but never adopted – recognised the 'Dual Middle East Refugee Problem.' It spoke of the forgotten exodus from Arab countries of nine hundred thousand Jews, who 'were forced to flee and in some cases brutally expelled amid coordinated violence and anti-Semitic incitement that amounted to ethnic cleansing.'[13]

As part of a bizarre Libyan exercise in public relations, in April 2004, Saif al-Islam Gaddafi, the son of the Libyan leader, said that all 30,000 Libyan Jews who had earlier fled the country 'were entitled to be compensated by the State for property confiscated before their departure.' Nothing came of this. Those Libyan Jews in Israel, Gaddafi's son added, would be able to return to Libya – 'their country and original homeland' – leaving their homes in Israel to the Palestinian Arabs.[14]

A real breakthrough came one year later. On 3 June 2005 the Canadian Prime Minister, Paul Martin, made the first statement on Jewish refugees by a Western leader outside the United States. He

---

[12] Irwin Cotler, David Matas and Stanley A. Urman, *Jewish Refugees: The Case for Rights and Redress*, 2003.
[13] Washington DC: House of Congress Resolution 311.
[14] Alex Sholem, 'Come Home, Gaddafi's son invites Libyan Jews to return,' *The Jewish News*, 16 April 2004.

declared: 'A refugee is a refugee and the situation of Jewish refugees from Arab lands must be recognized.' Martin added: 'All refugees deserve our consideration as they have lost both physical property and historical connections.'[15]

One problem that confronted all campaigners for redress – and continues to confront them to this day – is that the plight of Palestinian Arab refugees is not only visible, but also perpetuated by the United Nations' annual renewal of their status as refugees. The Jews from Muslim lands, despite having been legally recognised as refugees historically, were not perceived as refugees in recent decades, having been integrated into society in Israel and other countries. Eli Timan, an Iraqi Jew living and working in London, commented: 'The difference is that we got on with our life, worked hard and progressed so that today there is not a single Jewish refugee from Arab lands.'[16] It had been the goal of the Jewish refugees to become citizens, and in this they had succeeded.

On 4 April 2007, the senior Republican on the House Foreign Affairs Committee in the United States, Cuban-born Congresswoman Ileana Ros-Lehinten (Florida), stated at a Congressional Hearing: 'Jews who were born in Arab countries have lost their resources, their homes, their heritage and their heritage sites.'[17] In written evidence to the Congressional Hearing, the Canadian Member of Parliament and former Justice Minister Irwin Cotler set out the legal case for redress, arguing that 'the rights for Jewish refugees from Arab countries have to be a part of any peace process if that peace process is to have any integrity.'[18]

In November 2007, on the eve of the Annapolis Conference, at which Israeli and Palestinian leaders tried – as they had done at Oslo in 1993 – to embark on the path to a lasting agreement, a number of Jews from Muslim lands sought to put their issue – recognition and

---

[15] *Canadian Jewish News*, interview, 3 June 2005.
[16] Eli Timan, letter to the author, 13 December 2007.
[17] 'Justice for Christians, Jews And Other Displaced Minorities,' *The Editors*, 21 July 2007.
[18] Quoted in the *Canadian Jewish News*, 9 August 2007.

redress – on the negotiating table. Baghdadi-born Heskel Haddad, who had fled from Iraq in 1951, gave an interview to the press in which he said that it was 'imperative' to raise the issue at Annapolis. Haddad calculated that the amount of land and property that the Jews had been forced to leave behind in Iraq, Egypt and Morocco totalled 100,000 square kilometres, five times the size of the State of Israel.[19]

On 27 November 2007, at the end of the Annapolis Conference, Israel's Foreign Minister, Tzipi Livni, spoke of the relevance to any future Israeli-Palestinian agreement of the plight of Jewish refugees from Arab countries after 1948. A month later Maurice Shohet, a leader of the Iraqi Jewish community in the United States, joined fourteen other Jews, who had emigrated to the United States from many lands, in a meeting at the White House with President George W. Bush. At this meeting, Shohet asked the President to remember the rights of the Jews from Arab countries whenever the rights of Palestinian Arab refugees were raised in the international arena.

On 16 January 2008 a headline in the *Jerusalem Post* announced: 'OFFICIAL: BUSH AWARE OF JEWISH REFUGEES' PLIGHT.' According to the report, President Bush, at the start of his final year as President of the United States, had raised the issue of Jewish refugees from Muslim countries with the Israeli Prime Minister Ehud Olmert.

On 19 March 2008, Regina Waldman, an executive committee member of Justice for Jews from Arab Countries (JJAC), appeared before the United Nations Human Rights Council in Geneva, where she testified about her family's flight from Libya after the Second World War.[20] At this meeting in Geneva the Executive Director of JJAC, Stanley Urman, submitted to the Human Rights Council the organisation's report, 'Justice for Jewish Refugees from Arab Countries: The Case for Rights and Redress.' It included documents

---

[19] Etgar Lefkovits, 'Expelled Jews hold deeds on Arab lands,' *Jerusalem Post*, 16 November 2007.
[20] Another Jew who spoke at this open forum was Moroccan-born Sylvain Abitbol, an executive committee member of JJAC and a co-President of the Canadian Jewish Congress.

showing a pattern of State-sanctioned oppression that precipitated the mass exodus of Jews from ten Arab countries.

An important development came on 1 April 2008, when the United States Congress unanimously passed House Resolution 185, the first formal recognition by any Government of equal rights for Jewish refugees from Arab countries. The Congress also affirmed that the United States Government should recognise that all victims of the Arab-Israeli conflict must be treated equally. It further urged the President and all United States officials participating in Middle East discussions to ensure that references to Palestinian refugees 'also include a similarly explicit reference to the resolution of the issue of Jewish refugees from Arab countries.'[21]

On 23 June 2008, Justice for Jews from Arab Countries held a meeting in London, attended by fifty delegates from ten countries. On the following day, at a hearing in the British House of Lords, Edwin Shuker, President of JJAC, spoke about his family's flight from Iraq. Eighty-year-old Sarah Fedida described her family's expulsion from Egypt in 1956. Irwin Cotler, the former Canadian Minister of Justice, told the House of Lords: 'The displacement of 850,000 Jews from Arab countries is not just a "Forgotten Exodus" but a "Forced Exodus."'

The issue of redress for Jewish refugees from Muslim lands – and of their equivalence to Palestinian Arab refugees – continued to gain momentum in the international arena. On 21 August 2008, at a meeting with the Foreign Press Association in Israel, the Israeli Foreign Minister, Tzipi Livni, stated: 'Israel is the homeland for the Jewish people and the Palestinian State is the homeland for the Palestinians. Just as Israel gave refuge to Jews who needed to leave – not only Europe after the Holocaust but also Arab States after the creation of the State of Israel' – and were 'absorbed' in Israel.[22]

---

[21] House Resolution 185, 110th Congress, 1st Session, House of Representatives, introduced on 12 February 2007. Fear of such a resolution led, a year later, to the Egyptian authorities cancelling a tourist trip planned by a group of Jews born in Egypt 'due to false rumours that this group was coming to Egypt for property claims.' Information conveyed by Levana Zamir, House of Lords, London, 23-25 June 2008: The International Association of Jews from Egypt: *Annual Report, 2008.*
[22] Israel Foreign Ministry, 21 August 2008.

In the opinion of Irwin Cotler, David Matas and Stanley Urman, three leading experts on the rights of Jews from Muslim lands, 'the plight of the Palestinian refugees will be solved only as part of an overall Middle East peace settlement. But there cannot be an overall peace settlement without also addressing the wrongs done to Jewish refugees from Arab countries. A peace agreement which provided redress for Palestinian refugees without redress for Jewish refugees would be wrong in principle and unworkable in practice.'[23]

Another step forward in the quest for restitution and justice came in January 2009, when the Israeli Ministry of Pensioners' Affairs created a special department to collect claims by Jews who had lost their property when they left Arab countries. In the words of the Director-General of the Ministry, Dr. Avi Bitzur, 'Israel has talked about this on and off for sixty years. Now we are going to deal with it as we should have all along.'[24]

On 3 February 2009, Dr. Bitzur gave details of the new Israeli campaign for compensation of seized property and assets at a panel entitled 'A Matter of Historic Justice: Jewish Refugees from Arab Countries,' held at the Ninth Annual Herzliya Conference in the Israeli coastal town of Herzliya.[25] That compensation would be part of the equation of Arab and Jewish losses after 1948. The key word was 'justice.' What had for many years been seen only as a part of history – the mass exodus of 850,000 Jews, and the loss of their homes, shops, factories, land, synagogues, schools and personal possessions – was being presented as a living, relevant issue in the struggle for the redress of rights for two peoples: Jews from Muslim lands seeking redress and recognition, and Palestinian Arabs seeking redress and statehood.

---

[23] The Hon. Irwin Cotler, David Matas and Stanley A. Urman, *Jewish Refugees from Arab Countries: The Case for Rights and Redress*, page 57.
[24] Haviv Rettig Gur, 'Government to recover assets in Muslim lands,' *Jerusalem Post*, 27 January 2009.
[25] The speakers included Dr. Avi Bitzur, Director-General, Ministry for Pensioners' Affairs (in the chair); Raffi Eitan, Minister for Pensioners' Affairs, in charge of Restitution of Jewish Rights and Assets; and Edwin Shuker, President of Justice for Jews from Arab Countries.

On 9 June 2009, five days after President Barack Obama spoke in Cairo to the Muslim world, calling for American-Muslim reconciliation, the *New York Times* published a letter from André Aciman, a Jew who had left Egypt with his family in 1964. Aciman wrote that 'with all the President's talk of "a new beginning between the United States and Muslims around the world" and shared "principles of justice and progress," neither he nor anyone around him, and certainly no one in the audience, bothered to notice one small detail missing from the speech: he forgot me. The President never said a word about me. Or, for that matter, about any of the other 800,000 or so Jews born in the Middle East who fled the Arab and Muslim world or who were summarily expelled for being Jewish in the 20th century.'[26]

André Aciman's letter reflected a widespread concern that, even though the first decade of the Twenty-First Century was closing with a search for reconciliation and understanding between Christian and Muslim societies, Jews who had lived in Muslim lands would not be remembered, nor their hopes for justice upheld.

On 22 February 2010 the Israeli Knesset approved a law instructing the Israeli Government to protect the rights of Jewish refugees from Arab countries in all forthcoming peace negotiations; the first Israeli law to recognize Jews as coming to Israel not only to fulfil Zionist aspirations, but as refugees. Working to ensure the law's passing were Nissim Ze'ev, the Knesset member who introduced it – whose parents came from Iraq – and a Libyan-born Israeli businessman, Isaac Devash, who mobilised the leadership of Sephardi and other constituencies in Israel to support it. The search for justice had taken a significant leap forward. It was also a search for reconciliation, based on the international fund proposed by President Clinton in 2000, to benefit both Jewish and Palestinian refugees through an equitable resolution of their mutual sixty-year status as refugees.

---

[26] André Aciman, 'The Exodus Obama Forgot to Mention,' *New York Times*, 9 June 2009.

22

JEWS WHO REMAIN IN MUSLIM LANDS

'I don't want my Jewish heritage erased'

At the beginning of the second decade of the Twenty-First Century, Jews still live in ten Muslim lands. Although they are only a fragment of the Jewish communities of even sixty years ago, they nevertheless participate in the life, culture and commerce of the countries in which they live. In Morocco, in a Jewish community of only two thousand, several Jews have held high office and are much respected. In 1991, King Hassan II appointed a Moroccan Jew, André Azoulay, as his court banker. In 2006, King Mohammed VI appointed a Moroccan Jew, Serge Berdugo, who had earlier been Minister of Tourism, as a roving Ambassador to help in the quest for peace in the Middle East. There are Jewish community offices in seven Moroccan cities.[1]

Casablanca-born Sidney Assor, founder and head of the Association of British Jews of Moroccan Origin, writes: 'The current King, Mohammed VI, has shown a path to all Moroccans by opening the doors to equity, reconciliation and generosity in his dealings with the Jewish community.'[2]

In the Moroccan city of Fez, in 2005, Golda Zafer-Smith was with a group of British Jews and Israelis who joined local Jews in the festival of Simchat Torah – Rejoicing in the Law. 'Friendships were formed, speeches of welcome and thanks were made and the Jews of

---

[1] Casablanca, Fez, Marrakech, Essaouira (formerly Mogador), Meknès, Rabat and Tangier.
[2] Sydney S. Assor, 'Jews of Morocco, View from the Diaspora,' *Jewish Renaissance,* April 2006.

Fez made us proud,' she wrote. 'Sadly it is a dwindling community whose children are now living or studying outside Morocco.'[3]

Where once Jews had flourished and multiplied in Morocco, small remnants – in the case of Fez a mere 150 Jews – saw their historic quarter become an object of both national and tourist acclaim. Although when the Twenty-First Century began there were no functioning synagogues in the Jewish Quarter – the *mellah* – several were being restored with UNESCO funds, and a building attached to the cemetery inside the *mellah* became a museum to house Jewish artifacts and memorabilia.[4]

The Jews of Egypt numbered fewer than two hundred at the start of the Twenty-First Century. This small community benefited from the Israeli-Egyptian Peace Treaty negotiated between Menachem Begin and Anwar Sadat in 1979. Until then the Jews of Cairo celebrated Passover in their own homes. When the Israeli Embassy was established in 1980, a new mode of Passover celebration entered the lives of the remaining Cairo Jews. The Embassy booked a hall in one of the hotels, and brought in a rabbi and kosher food from Israel. Successive Israeli Ambassadors invited the Jewish community members, former Egyptian Jews, and Jewish visitors to Cairo who wished to participate.[5] 'It was quite a boon for us who had been left on our own for so long,' recalled one of the Jews still living in Cairo. But a cooling in relations between Israel and Egypt brought an end to the Israeli Embassy Passover, and it was not until 2005 that Rabbi Mark El Fassy from Paris organised a Passover meal in Cairo's Adly Synagogue, establishing a new and popular local tradition.

The United States Ambassador to Egypt, Francis Ricciardoni, attended this Passover meal in 2007, as did the former Canadian

---

[3] Golda Zafer-Smith, 'Simhat Torah in Fez, 2005,' *Jewish Renaissance*, April 2006.
[4] Jewish Virtual Library, 'The Virtual Jewish History Tour, Fez': www.jewishvirtual-library.org/jsource/vjw/Fez.html.
[5] The first Israeli Ambassador to Cairo, Eliyahu Ben-Elissar, was born in Poland. The second Ambassador, Moshe Sasson, was born in Damascus. Two subsequent Ambassadors – Efraim Dubek and David Sultan – were born in Egypt.

Ambassador, Michel de Salaberie. The Egyptian Jewish eyewitness added: 'I want to wish a good Passover to all the Jewish communities around the world and a happy Mouled El Nabi (Prophet Mohammed's birthday) to all the Moslem communities. 2007 is also special because Passover, Mouled al-Nabi and the Easter festivities celebrated by the Christian communities were all within days of each other, as though God was sending us a celestial message by gathering all three religious celebrations in one knot. It is up to all men to keep it so.'[6]

Today, the synagogue in Cairo cannot always get the quorum of ten men required for communal prayers, and depends to a large extent on Jewish tourists from overseas to be able to conduct synagogue services. The local atmosphere is not conducive to their peace of mind; in 2002, during the Muslim holy month of Ramadan, the State-controlled television ran a popular drama series based on the Nineteenth-Century anti-Semitic forgery *The Protocols of the Learned Elders of Zion* – a book that had fanned the flames of anti-Semitism in Christian Europe for more than a hundred years, and in which the author claimed to reveal an international Jewish conspiracy to control the world. A few months later a copy of the *Protocols* was prominently displayed next to a Torah scroll in an exhibition held in the recently opened city library in Alexandria.[7]

In 2006, Alexandria's small Jewish community of twenty women and three men was headed by ninety-year-old Dr. Max Salame, who many years earlier had been Nasser's family dentist. To make up the required minimum of ten men for the Jewish New Year services that year, the American-Jewish Joint Distribution Committee sent a delegation to Alexandria that included some men from the Jewish Community Council of Cairo. The delegation was headed by the Israeli Ambassador to Egypt, Shalom Cohen, and the Israeli Consul-General in Alexandria, Eli Entebi.[8]

---

[6] Report of an Egyptian Jew, 2007. *Bassatine News, A Community Chronicle put out by the Jewish Community Council (JCC) of Cairo*, Issue No. 21, 22 March 2007.
[7] Efraim Karsh, *Islamic Imperialism: A History*, page 184.
[8] Yoav Stern, 'Alexandria's Jews: 20 Women and 3 Men,' *Ha'aretz*, 17 September 2006.

—

On 25 January 2005 the BBC reported the death a week earlier of Ishaq Levin, one of only two Jews still alive in Afghanistan. Levin was eighty years old and had lived in the synagogue compound.[9] The other Jew, some forty years his junior, was Zebulon Simantov. He was interviewed in 2008 for National Public Radio. He was then living alone in a small room next to the crumbling synagogue in Kabul. His wife and two daughters lived in Israel. Simantov often contemplated joining them, but staying in Afghanistan, he explained, was 'the only way to keep the country's Jewish history alive. I don't want my Jewish heritage erased. My father was a rabbi, my grandfather was a rabbi. We were a big, religious family.'

Simantov, the product of an Orthodox Jewish upbringing, spoke proudly of his Jewish heritage, and of receiving packages of matzo for Passover from Afghan Jews living in New York. Sometimes, he said, Jewish foreigners visit his home for the High Holy Days. 'I feel like the lion of Afghanistan,' he added. 'Nobody can touch me.' Just in case he might be wrong, he only wore his skull cap in private, and he was hesitant to take visitors inside the synagogue in the crumbling compound he called home. His caution was born from years of oppression, first by the mujahedeen – Islamist fighters who defeated the Soviets and tried hard to persuade him to convert – and then by Taliban officials. The Taliban stole the carpets he sold for a living, as well as the synagogue's Torah scroll, and put him in prison. He was still under pressure to become a Muslim.

Simantov was not boycotted as a Jew. The business owners on Flower Street, where he lived, greeted him when he passed by. Karmatullah, a Muslim shopkeeper who stored some of his goods at Simantov's house, regularly shared a cup of green tea and banter with his Jewish neighbour. He said of the Jews: 'We can't say they are part of our history. They immigrated here. But it's OK for Jews to be here as long as they don't aim to occupy our country.' That Jewish immigration had taken place at least a thousand years earlier.

---

[9] '"Only one Jew" now in Afghanistan,' BBC News, 25 January 2005.

When Simantov decided to get married in 1993, there were so few Jewish girls left in Afghanistan that he travelled to neighbouring Turkmenistan to find a bride. Fearing for her safety in war-torn Afghanistan, he sent her to Israel with their two daughters. Although he had not seen them in three years, he talked to them every other week over the telephone.[10]

At the beginning of the Twenty-First Century there were six Afghan Jewish communities in Israel and one in the New York borough of Queens. No Jews lived in the Afghan city of Herat, on the borderlands between Iran and Central Asia, but four badly damaged synagogues remained from the once vibrant Jewish community, as did a hundred and fifty gravestones in the Jewish cemetery. The former Jewish public bath, the *haamma-e-yehudiaha*, had become a bath for male Muslim youth.[11]

In September 1991, one of the leading Yemeni Sheikhs, Abdullah al-Ahmar, was visiting London. At the request of the Israeli Government he was approached by a British Labour Member of Parliament, Greville Janner – a former President of the Board of Deputies of British Jews – to see if the Yemeni Government would allow its Jews to leave. There were 1,500 Jews living in Yemen at the time – the remnant of an ancient Jewish community dating back more than two thousand years.

Janner's first meeting took place with the Sheikh's son at the hotel in London where the Sheikh was staying. A meeting with the Sheikh followed a week later. Janner was then invited to visit Yemen; he spent his first Friday night in Sanaa, the Yemeni capital, with the Jews of the Jewish Quarter. Negotiations followed, and then the exodus of more than a thousand Yemeni Jews to Israel. The only ones who did not leave were those who had been persuaded by a New York-based ultra-orthodox Jewish sect, the followers of the Satmar Rebbe, that they would not be allowed to practise their religion in Israel.

---

[10] Soraya Sarhaddi Nelson, 'In Afghanistan, a Jewish Community of One,' broadcast over National Public Radio, 8 December 2008.
[11] 'Saving the Synagogues of Herat,' *JIMENA Voice*, Vol. 1, No. 4, June 2006.

Of the Yemeni Jews whom he met, Janner wrote: 'I salute these remarkable folk and those wise and good Yemeni leaders who quietly and generously allowed them to leave the land of the Queen of Sheba, and to find new lives in the land of King Solomon.' As for the representatives of the Satmar Rebbe, 'who persuaded the sad remnants to remain,' he wrote: 'I despise them deeply.'

When Janner returned to Yemen in 1998 he met some of the 350 Jews who had remained after the exodus seven years earlier. 'We found them sad, poor and totally under the influence and command of the Satmars,' he later recalled. 'We joined them in their Sabbath prayers, but were advised that the hygiene standards in their homes were deplorable and that we should not accept their hospitality.'[12]

In 2002, Danna Harman, a writer for the *Christian Science Monitor*, visited Yemen. In her diary she noted that two or three Jewish families lived in Sadah, a small, remote town near the Saudi Arabian border. She visited Raydah, a village northwest of the capital Sanaa, where 'some fifty Jewish families maintain their age-old traditions and ways of life,' and observed that 'this minority – the only indigenous one in Yemen – remains insular, teaching its children Hebrew, keeping the religious dietary and cleanliness rules, and marrying within the community.'

Having wandered through the dusty paths of Raydah, Danna Harman wrote of that walk: 'One has just to call out "Where are the Jews?" and immediately dozens of Muslim neighbours will stop what they are doing, point out the way, or even accompany you there. "We are all friends. They are Jewish. We are Muslim. So what?" says Abd Malik Qubatee, as he pounds on the tin door of the Jewish school compound and is greeted warmly by the bespectacled watchman within. Inside the dimly lit one-room schoolhouse, two dozen boys, all with traditional sidelocks and head coverings, are squashed together on rickety benches pouring over their Torahs and reciting passages out loud. Their rabbi, Faiz Aljarazi, sits in the corner with

---

[12] Lord Janner of Braunstone, *To Life! The Memoirs of Greville Janner*, pages 276-86.

his eyes half closed, reaching out and whacking the kids with a stick when they miss a word or stumble over a phrase. The boys sway when they read, intent on their studies and only occasionally throwing a petrified glance at the elderly rabbi.'

Danna Harman wrote that the small number of Jews in Yemen, 'despite protestations of well being, continue to live with restrictions. They cannot serve in the army or be elected to political positions. That said, life seems to have settled down into a comfortable pace for this community.' If they had complaints, or felt harassed, they turned to their local Muslim sheikhs, like the rest of the population. During the previous two years, the Yemeni Government had facilitated the reconstruction of a Jewish school that had been destroyed in 1992 by Islamic fundamentalists. In 2000, when the Israeli-Palestinian Peace Process was moving forward, the government allowed a group of former Yemeni Jews then living in Israel to visit their ancestral lands.[13]

The first years of the Twenty-First Century saw no diminution in Shiite Muslim hostility towards the few Jews remaining in Yemen. On 10 January 2007, five years after Danna Harman's visit, the forty-five Jews of Al Haid, in north Yemen, received letters from a Shiite rebel militia accusing them of 'promoting vice.' The letter demanded that they leave the province. According to the *Yemen Observer*, the forty-five Jews were forced to flee their homes in fear of their lives. They were given refuge in a hotel at the expense of a compassionate local sheikh, after which Shiite militants threatened to bomb the hotel.

A copy of the threatening letter had been faxed to the *Yemen Observer*. It read: 'After an accurate surveillance of the Jews who are residing in Al Haid, it has become clear to us that they were doing things which serve mainly Zionism, which seeks to corrupt the people and distance them from their principles, their values, their morals, and their religion, and spread all kinds of vice in the society. Our religion ordered us to fight the corrupt people and expel them.'

---

[13] Danna Harman, Yemen diary: sent to the author, 28 October 2003.

The hand-written letter ended: 'Allah is Greater, Death to America, Death to Israel, Curse to Jews, and Victory to Islam.'

Dawoud Yousef Mousa, one of the displaced Jews, told the *Yemen Observer*: 'We are a total of forty-five Jews . . . we left our houses in Al Haid area to a hotel here in the northern city of Sadah, after we received warnings to leave our country, Yemen, within ten days from the date of the threat letter.' Mousa added that on January 17, a Wednesday, he was with a group of Jews when they were approached by four men, their faces covered, who threatened to kill them if they did not leave by the Friday, January 19. 'They told us, "No one will protect you, Jews, from us, not even Ali Abdullah Saleh"' – the President of Yemen. The Jews were warned that if they did not leave their homes in two days, they would 'only have themselves to blame' for the consequences, which would include abductions and looting.

The Jews appealed to the Governor of Sadah for protection. 'It is not a secret,' they wrote, 'that we are *dhimmis,* we are in the protection of the Prophet Mohammed, and in the protection of President Ali Abdullah Saleh. We are in your protection.' Determined to remain in Yemen, they declared: 'We would rather die than leave our homes.'[14]

Fortunately for the endangered Jews, the Shiite rebels were defeated by Yemeni Government forces. The Jews were thus freed from the threat of Shiite violence and returned to their homes. But the saga did not end there. On 16 December 2008 the *Yemen Observer* reported that the Jews of Yemen had demanded government protection, or else the means to leave the country, after the murder on December 11 of Rabbi Musa (Moshe) Yaish Nahari by a Shiite extremist. Witnesses reported that when the killer stopped Rabbi Nahari in the marketplace, he shouted, 'Jew, accept the message of Islam,' and then opened fire with a Kalashnikov rifle, killing the Rabbi with five shots. Rabbi Nahari, who had studied with the ultra-Orthodox Satmar Hassidic community in New York, left a wife and nine children.[15]

---

[14] Elizabeth Kendal: http://jmm.aaa.net.au/articles/19249.htm.
[15] 'Yemen's Jewish Community in Shock Over Murder,' *Hamodia: The Newspaper of Torah Judaism,* 18 December 2008.

Rabbi Yahya bin Yaish, the brother of the murdered man, told reporters that the authorities had long ignored complaints from the Jewish community about the rising hostility against them. 'Raydah is no longer like the old days,' he said. 'Raydah today is full of monsters.' People had broken his windows and harassed Jews in the streets. 'Some have even raised their guns to our chests and necks, to our women and children's necks.'[16] Rabbi Yahya told the *Yemen Observer*: 'If the State is unable to protect us and secure us in our homeland, the only alternative should be for the state to buy our houses and properties and grant us the money to leave the country.'

On December 13, Yemen's Ministry of Interior announced that it had arrested eight people accused of abusing the Jews. A former pilot in the Yemeni Air Force, Abdul Azeez Hamoud al-Abdi, then confessed to killing Rabbi Nahari, although he showed no repentance for the crime. Official sources said the perpetrator claimed he carried out these actions to 'get closer to Allah,' and insisted that he had warned the Jews in writing one month before his attack. In his letter, he said, he told the Jews: convert to Islam, leave the country, or face the sword.

Relatives of the murdered Rabbi Nahari arrived in Yemen from Israel, the United States and Britain for his funeral.[17] But as they did, on December 15, two firebombs were thrown into the home of a Jewish family in Raydah. The father of the house, Yisrael Chala, reported that no one was hurt in the explosions.[18]

At the end of 2008 the President of Yemen, Ali Abdullah Saleh, offered to relocate all 270 Jews in Raydah to the capital Sanaa, where they could be more easily defended by his security forces. The Jewish community leaders declined the offer, as it did not involve any compensation for their loss of property and jobs.[19] Then came news on 19 February 2009 that all ten members of Yisrael Chala's family, into

---

[16] 'Hostility on the rise in Yemen after murder,' *Jewish Chronicle*, 19 December 2008.

[17] Nasser Arrabyee, 'Yemeni Jews want to emigrate if not protected,' *Yemen Observer*, 16 December 2008.

[18] Israel Radio, reported in *Hamodia: The Newspaper of Torah Judaism*, 18 December 2008.

[19] Anshel Pfeffer, 'Yemeni Jews: relocation offer,' *Jewish Chronicle*, 2 January 2009.

whose courtyard the two firebombs had been thrown two months earlier, had been flown to Israel. Reaching Ben-Gurion Airport, Yisrael Chala's daughter Esther told reporters: 'We just locked up our house and left.'[20]

At the start of 2009 only 280 Jews remained in Yemen: 230 in Raydah and 50 in Sanaa. Theirs was a community on the move. On 18 March 2009 the North American United Jewish Communities (UJC), in cooperation with the State Department in Washington, set funds aside to absorb 110 Yemenite Jews into the United States – more than a third of all Jews remaining in Yemen.[21] The last days of Yemen's ancient Jewish community were fast approaching.

In the oil-rich island kingdom of Bahrain, with its population of one million Arab Muslims, there was a Jewish community of thirty-seven people at the beginning of the Twenty-First Century. A larger number of former Bahraini Jews, forty-five in all, live in Great Britain. In 2008 the King of Bahrain, Hamad bin Isa Al Khalifah, met some of those forty-five Jews when he visited London and reactivated a law that allowed them to hold dual Bahraini-British citizenship. One of the people the King met was Moshe Sweiry, who had left Bahrain at the age of eighteen in 1967. His father had been a senior financial adviser to the King's father.[22]

The Jewish community in Bahrain has a prominent woman member highly regarded in Bahraini society: Houda Nonoo. In 2006 she was appointed by the King to the Upper House of the Bahrain Parliament, and in 2008, at the age of forty-four, she was sent as Bahrain's Ambassador to the United States, becoming the only Jewish person ever to serve as an Ambassador from an Arab or Muslim country. 'It was a way,' she reflected, 'of showing the uniqueness and

---

[20] Abe Selig, 'Yemenite family make aliyah in secret op,' *Jerusalem Post*, 19 February 2009.
[21] Haviv Rettig Gur, 'UJC to pull 110 Jews out of Yemen,' *Jerusalem Post*, 18 March 2009.
[22] Leon Symons, 'The Arab king who's proud of his Jews,' *Jewish Chronicle*, 15 August 2008.

tolerance of my country.' As the Ambassador of an Arab country, Houda Nonoo even attended a meeting of the Arab League.

Houda Nonoo's grandparents had been Jewish immigrants from Iraq. Her father had managed several cinemas in Bahrain. She was educated first by Italian nuns at a convent school in Bahrain, and then at Carmel College, a Jewish boarding school in England. In Bahrain, she notes, 'I never had any discrimination. We kept our religion at home. It was more or less impossible to keep Shabbat because we had school on Saturdays, but whatever we could do we did. Even now, we keep the High Holy Days – Rosh Hashanah, Yom Kippur and Passover – plus Purim and Hanukah, because they're fun.' As to her personal sense of identity: 'At the end of the day, I'm an Arab. I describe myself as an Arab Jew. I'm proud of it. I was asked by someone in England whether I felt Jewish first and Bahraini second. I said I was Bahraini first.'[23]

Houda Nonoo is a unique symbol of what could come to pass if the mutual tolerance between Israelis and Arabs, and between Jews and Muslims – a tolerance that had many precedents in past ages – becomes a universal aspect of the future.

In modern-day Tunisia there are 1,360 Jews and a Jewish Member of Parliament. Almost a thousand of Tunisia's Jews live on Djerba Island, a community that dates back many centuries before Islam. The village of Hara Sghira, on Djerba, is the focal point of the island's Jewish community. At its centre is the Ghriba Synagogue, one of eleven synagogues on Djerba. Each year there is a Jewish festival, El Ghriba, during which the Jews of the island, and many Jewish visitors from overseas, walk from one synagogue to the other.

The relationship between the Jews and the Muslim majority on Djerba is a relaxed one, but the Jews have faced a number of anti-Jewish acts in the past. In 1985 three worshippers were shot dead

---

[23] Simon Round, 'The unlikely envoy,' *Jewish Chronicle*, 5 December 2008.

inside the synagogue.[24] In 2003, Muslim extremists again attacked the synagogue, this time using a truck bomb. Twenty-one visitors, mostly Germans, were killed, as were some Arab workers who were repairing the building.

In May 2007 a leading British parliamentarian, Lord Janner – who had earlier visited Yemen – gave a promising account of Tunisia after visiting the country to attend the El Ghriba festival.[25] He was met in Tunisia by the President of the Djerban Jewish community, Youssef Wazan, and welcomed at the synagogue by its President, Perez Trabelsi. The Jewish community, Janner noted, 'is treated with respect and friendship' by its Muslim neighbours. At the synagogue during the festival 'there were smiling women descending the stairs under the Holy Ark, placing on hidden shelves their hard-boiled eggs, inscribed with messages of hope and prayer.'[26]

In Lebanon, the 1,800 Jews who remained in Beirut after the Six-Day War of 1967 faced the turmoil of the Muslim-Christian Civil War in 1975 and 1976, when many homes, shops and synagogues in the Jewish Quarter were damaged, caught in the crossfire. The community decided to leave, finding new homes and livelihoods in Israel, Canada and Europe. No more than 150 Jews remained in Lebanon at the start of the Twenty-First Century. From time to time, news of them reached the West: in the lead-up to the 7 June 2009 national elections in Lebanon, the Beirut *Daily Star* reported that two Jews were registered to vote in the port city of Sidon: Isaac Elijah Diwan and Jack Samantoubi Zeitouni.[27]

---

[24] 'Looklex, Tunisia,' website: http://i-cias.com/tunisia/hara_kbira.htm. On the walls of the synagogue today, an array of fish and hands, painted in traditional blue, help to stave off the Evil Eye, that much-feared demon since Talmudic times, created by jealousy. Among the causes of such jealousy noted in the Talmud is making money by cutting down beautiful trees, persistently taking the better half of shared items, and acquiring wealth without effort.

[25] In 2005 Janner had co-founded, with Prince Hassan of Jordan, the Muslim-Jewish organisation, The Coexistence Trust.

[26] Greville Janner, 'A visit to Tunisia,' *Jerusalem Post*, 21 May 2007.

[27] Mohammed Zaatari, 'Only Two Lebanese Jews are Registered to Vote in Sidon,' *Daily Star*, 12 May 2009.

In the last week of July 2009, as an initiative of the Lebanese Jewish Community Council, restoration began on the eighty-four-year-old Maghen-Abraham Synagogue in Beirut. The building had been empty since the start of the Lebanese Civil War in 1975. The restoration cost one million U.S. dollars in all; the funding came mostly from Jews of Lebanese descent living in Europe and the Americas; $150,000 came from the Lebanese Prime Minister-elect, Saad Hariri.[28]

In the Syrian city of Kamishli, in 2006, there were just three Jews – the Pinchas family – where once there was a Jewish community of more than five hundred. To buy kosher meat, Musa Pinchas had to drive nine hours – 640 miles – to and from Damascus, where the local Jewish community of a few hundred got their meat each week from a kosher butcher in Turkey. In Kamishli itself, Musa and his parents, David and Simcha, knew when to begin the Jewish Sabbath on Friday evening because it coincided with the muezzin's sunset call for prayer from the minarets of the mosques. On one wall of their house they kept the Ten Commandments in Hebrew; on another wall they kept a portrait of the Syrian President with an Arabic caption.[29]

The few remaining Jews in Baghdad were the beneficiaries in 2003 of a Jewish Agency initiative to help restore the Jewish cemetery in Sadr City. There, behind high walls, 3,200 graves had been slowly disintegrating. In 2004 a British Jew of Iraqi origin, Marina Benjamin, walked through the cemetery while on a visit to the land of her grandparents Regina Sehayek and Elazar Levy. Like so many Jews born in Muslim lands, or descended from those who shared that rich heritage, Marina Benjamin was drawn to the life and culture of a vanished world. 'Of all the places I visited in Baghdad,' she wrote, 'the cemetery was where I felt most at home. I was oddly comforted by the presence of so many dead. It was as if there, at last, I finally felt the pull of my Iraqi ancestry, because there, more than anywhere I had ever been, that ancestry was real. Stranger still, it was not Regina

---

[28] Jahd Khalil, 'Lebanon: Quietly, Jewish Community Begins Synagogue Restoration,' *Los Angeles Times*, 4 August 2009.
[29] Sasha Troy, 'The last three Jews of Qamishli,' *Jerusalem Post*, 9 February 2006.

but Elazar – the grandfather I never knew as opposed to the grand-mother I loved – who seemed to be calling out to me.'[30]

At the start of the second decade of the Twenty-First Century, the larg-est community of Jews in a Muslim land was the 25,000-strong Jewish community of Iran. In 1979 the Shah, Mohammed Reza Pahlavi, who had been a protector of Iran's Jews and had allowed as many as 75,000 to leave the country for wherever they liked, including Israel, was over-thrown and replaced by an Islamic fundamentalist regime. For the Jews of Iran, this revolution heralded a time of danger. In 1994, and again in 1999, the Iranian Government published the Tsarist-era for-gery *The Protocols of the Learned Elders of Zion.*

The new spiritual leader of Iran, Ayatollah Ruhollah Khomeini, who had returned from his exile near Paris after the Shah was over-thrown, was adamant in his denunciation not only of Zionism but of Jews in general. 'We must protest and make the people aware,' Khomeini warned, 'that the Jews and their foreign backers are opposed to the very foundations of Islam and wish to establish Jewish domination throughout the world. Since they are a cunning and resourceful group of people, I fear that – God forbid! – they may one day achieve their goal, and that the apathy shown by some of us may allow a Jew to rule over us one day.'[31]

At least thirteen Jews were executed in Iran in the first thirty years following the Islamic Revolution of 1979. In May 1998 a Jewish businessman, Ruhollah Kakhodah-Zadeh, was hanged in prison without any public charge having been made against him, and with-out any open legal proceedings. His 'crime' was, apparently, that he had helped Iranian Jews to emigrate.[32]

Within a year of the execution of Ruhollah Kakhodah-Zadeh,

---

[30] Marina Benjamin, *Last Days in Babylon,* pages 260-2.
[31] Ayatollah Ruhollah Khomeini, *Islam and Revolution, Writings and Declarations,* quoted in: Efraim Karsh, *Islamic Imperialism: A History,* page 216.
[32] United States Department of State, *2001 Annual Report on International Religious Freedom,* Bureau for Democracy, Human Rights and Labor, Washington, DC, 26 October 2001.

another blow was dealt to the Jewish community of Iran. On 1 April 1999, the eve of Passover, thirteen Iranian Jews from the cities of Shiraz and Isfahan in southern Iran were arrested and accused of spying for both Israel and the United States. Those arrested included a rabbi, a ritual slaughterer and several teachers. It was also announced that eight Muslims had been arrested, but they were never named or shown on television, as were the Jews. Nor were the Muslims ever seen in court. Almost certainly these eight Muslims did not exist, but were 'arrested' in order to give the impression that the proceedings were not wholly anti-Jewish.

After thirteen months in prison, the thirteen Jews were brought to trial on 1 May 2000, in the Revolutionary Court in Shiraz. Under the Iranian Revolutionary Court system, the judge in the case, Sadeq Nurani, also served as investigator and as prosecutor. It was he who visited the defendants in prison, compiled the evidence against them and heard their alleged confessions. According to Iranian law and international legal convention, all defendants have the right to choose their own legal representation. But from the time of their arrest, the thirteen Jews were denied the right to choose their own attorney.

Shortly before the trial began, the Iranian Judiciary announced that eight of the defendants were finally permitted to hire their own lawyers, and that two had been assigned court-appointed lawyers. In fact, none of the defendants were permitted to choose their own lawyer and the defence team was assigned by the Revolutionary Court. The court was closed to all observers, including the defendants' families, leaders of Iran's Jewish community, foreign diplomats and representatives of human rights groups who had travelled to Shiraz as a result of international concern.

No evidence was presented in court against the thirteen men. In the course of the trial, nine of the defendants 'confessed' to spying on behalf of Israel. Within hours of the first two 'confessions' the two defendants, Dani (Hamid) Tefileen and Shahrokh Paknahad, appeared on Iranian television and 'admitted' their activities on behalf of Israel. In the final court hearing, the lead defence attorney, Isma'il Nasseri, a Muslim, courageously highlighted contradictions and inconsistencies in the confessions. Nasseri argued that the prosecution had no evidence that the thirteen Jews had spied for Israel. He also criticised the court's use of the media in broadcasting the two confessions to manipulate national opinion on the trial.

Nasseri told the court that four defendants had recanted their 'confessions' and that cross-examination of the others had highlighted inconsistencies in their confessions and testimony. His efforts were in vain. On 1 July 2000 the judge announced that ten of the defendants were found guilty both of spying for the 'Zionist regime' – Israel – and of 'world arrogance' – a reference to the alleged worldwide Jewish influence. The three defendants who had been on bail since February were acquitted. Jewish groups around the world and human rights groups condemned the verdict and expressed outrage at the lack of due process throughout the trial.

The two heaviest sentences were handed to Dani (Hamid) Tefileen, a twenty-nine-year-old merchant, and Asher Zadmeh, a forty-nine-year-old university English-language instructor. Tefileen was sentenced to thirteen years in prison on charges of 'cooperation with the Zionist regime, membership in the espionage network and gathering classified information.' Zadmeh was also sentenced to thirteen years in prison on charges of 'forming an illegal group and an espionage network and of cooperating with the Zionist regime.'

Also sentenced to between four and eleven years in prison were Naser Levy Hayim, aged forty-six, a Hebrew teacher (sentenced to eleven years); Ramin Farzam, aged thirty-six, a perfume merchant (ten years); Javid Beit Yakov, aged forty-one, a sporting goods merchant (nine years); Farzad Kashi, aged thirty-one, a teacher of religion (eight years); Shahrokh Paknahad, aged twenty-three, also a teacher of religion (eight years): Farhad Saleh, aged thirty-one, a shopkeeper (eight years); Faramarz Kashi, aged thirty-five, a Hebrew teacher (five years); and Ramin Nematizadeh, aged twenty-three, a merchant (four years).[33]

---

[33] 'Backgrounder: The trial of 13 Iranian Jews,' March 2003, ADL, Anti-Defamation League, New York. http://www.adl.org/backgrounders/Iranian_Jews.asp.

Jewish communities around the world incorporated prayers for the imprisoned men into their weekly synagogue services. Within a month of the verdict, the defence team filed an appeal with the court in Shiraz. On September 21, the Appellate Court of Fars Province reduced the sentences of the ten Jewish prisoners but did not over-turn the guilty verdicts or release any of the men.[34] Eight months later, in March 2001, one of the imprisoned Jews, Ramin Nematizadeh, was released after serving half of his four-year term.[35] A second was freed in January 2002. Three more were reportedly pardoned by Iran's Supreme Leader, Ayatollah Ali Khamenei.[36] The world protests had been effective; the longest sentence actually served was three years.

Since August 2005 the Jews of Iran have lived under a regime whose President, Mahmoud Ahmadinejad, has quoted and reaffirmed the Ayatollah Khomeini's statement that 'this regime occupying Jerusalem must vanish from the page of time.' Ahmadinejad cited Ayatollah Khomeini's words while speaking in Teheran on 25 October 2005, during a conference on 'The World without Zionism.' He then commented: 'This statement is very wise.' Iran's official news agency, in reporting Ahmadinejad's speech and the quotation from Ayatollah Khomeini, used the phrase – which was not in the quota-tion – that Israel must be 'wiped off the map.'[37]

The Jews of Iran remain free to practise their religion. Every Friday in Teheran there are Jewish religious classes conducted by the Orthodox Otzar ha-Torah organisation. There are also three Jewish schools in Teheran, where Jews form a majority of the pupils. In 2005 an Iranian-Dutch filmmaker, Teheran-born Ramin Farahani, made a documentary film about the Jews of Iran. In Isfahan he filmed the Iranian Jewish artist Soleiman Sassoon, whose work was strongly

---

[34] Howard Schneider, 'Iran Court Reduces Penalties for Jews,' *Washington Post*, 22 September 2000.
[35] Richard Ferrer, 'First Iran Jew is Released,' *London Jewish News*, 9 March 2001.
[36] *Jerusalem Post*, 16 January 2002.
[37] Islamic Republic News Agency (IRNA), quoted by the BBC, *Time* magazine and the Al-Jazeera television station.

influenced by both Iranian art and Islamic architecture. Pointing to his paintings, Sassoon explained that he naturally blends Jewish religious motifs such as the Ten Commandments and David's Psalms with a traditional style of Iranian art.[38]

On 22 September 2006, before the start of the Jewish New Year, the BBC carried a broadcast from Frances Harrison in Teheran that painted a vivid picture of how Iran's 25,000 Jews had adapted to conditions under the fundamentalist regime. The Jews who live in Iran, Harrison reported, were 'as proud of their Iranian culture as of their Jewish roots.' At dawn that day, inside the Yusufabad Synagogue in Teheran, Jewish worshippers were bringing out the Torah to read before going to work. Unees Hammami, the leader of the Jewish community, told Frances Harrison: 'Because of our long history here we are tolerated.' He went on to recall that the father of Iran's revolution, Ayatollah Khomeini, had recognised Jews as a religious minority that should be protected. As a result, Jews have one representative in the Iranian Parliament.[39]

Yet because of Iran's hostility to the State of Israel, the government-controlled media frequently fan the flames of anti-Jewish feeling. As Unees Hammami has commented, Iranian State-run television regularly confuses Zionism and Judaism so that 'ordinary people may think that whatever the Israelis do is supported by all Jews.' During the fighting in Lebanon in 2006 the weekly Iranian newspaper, *Yalesarat*, published on its front page two photographs of synagogues full of people waving Israeli flags celebrating Israel's independence day. The paper falsely claimed that the synagogues were in Iran – even describing one of them as the Yusufabad Synagogue in Teheran and locating another in Shiraz. In the words of Maurice Motamed, from 2000 to 2008 the one Jewish member of

---

[38] Shohreh Jandaghain, *First Documentary Film about Persian-Jews in Iran*, 2006. Digital Journal Online (quoted in nationmaster.com: Encyclopaedia>Jews of Iran). See also Ramin Farahani's website: www.raminfarahani.com.

[39] Ahmadinejad's office has even donated money for Teheran's Jewish hospital, founded fifty years ago. It is a charity hospital where most of the patients and staff are Muslims. The director, Ciamak Moresathegh, is a Jew, and since 2008 the Jewish member in the Iranian Parliament.

the Iranian Parliament, 'this provoked a number of opportunists in Shiraz, and there was an assault on two synagogues.'[40]

The Jews of Iran are also subjected to aspects of age-old *dhimmi* discrimination. Jews cannot become army officers, and if one member of a Jewish family converts to Islam he can inherit the entire family's property. The headmasters of the Jewish schools in Teheran are all Muslim, even though there is no law that says this should be so. The greatest vulnerability confronting Iranian Jews, however, is their connection to the State of Israel, where many of them have relatives. In 2001 a group of Jews in Shiraz was arrested and accused of spying for Israel. It was only after protests by Jews worldwide that they were released. In November 2008 an Iranian Jewish businessman, Ali Ashtari, was not so fortunate. He was executed after being accused of spying for Israel; he had been held in prison for two years before his execution.[41]

The Jews of Iran still speak out when they feel they must. When President Ahmadinejad questions the number of Jews killed in the Holocaust, Maurice Motamed was outspoken in his condemnation of the President's views. 'It's very regrettable to see a horrible tragedy so far reaching as the Holocaust being denied. It was a very big insult to Jews all around the world.' Motamed has also publicly condemned an exhibition of cartoons about the Holocaust organised by an Iranian newspaper owned by the Teheran municipality.

The 25,000 Jews who remain in Iran have made a conscious decision to stay there. The Jewish hospital director Ciamak Morsathegh has commented: 'We are Iranian and we have been living in Iran for more than three thousand years.'[42]

Will the 50,000 Jews who still live in Muslim lands be able to achieve a secure Jewish life that was often denied them in the past? There are

---

[40] The attack was brought to a halt by the Iranian security forces, who explained to the perpetrators that the news was not true.

[41] Leon Symons, 'Iranian "Mossad" ring broken,' *Jewish Chronicle*, 28 November 2008.

[42] Frances Harrison, BBC Radio Broadcast, 22 September 2006.

good precedents and bad. For Jews living in Muslim lands, times of suffering and danger have alternated with times of achievement and fulfilment. Some of the most productive Jewish experiences have been in Muslim lands, as have some of the most distressing. Jews have been respected, admired and emulated; they have also been persecuted, robbed and killed.

In the course of 1,400 years, Jews living under Muslim rule made their mark in many ways: as converts to Islam; as privileged members of the courts and administrations of Caliphs and Sultans; as *dhimmis*, with all the restrictions that status entailed; and as fellow-citizens in modern, independent Muslim nations. Throughout those 1,400 years, Jews made enormous contributions to the well-being and continuity of the *umma* – the worldwide community of Muslims. They have had no desire to convert Muslims to Judaism, nor in any way to subvert the Muslim religion.

From the time of Mohammed until today, Jews have often found greater opportunities, respect and recognition under Islam than under Christianity. They have also been subjected to the worst excesses of hostility, hatred and persecution. It is my hope that this book will encourage a better understanding of the past, and help to make possible a future that emulates only the best aspects of the past.

The Jews who left Muslim lands – and their descendants – can feel pride at what they and their forebears achieved in so many Muslim lands, over so many centuries, and can also feel justified in their sense of belonging within the Muslim world. The exodus and dispersal after 1947 of 850,000 of the Jews living in Muslim lands was a cruel interruption to a 1,400-year story of remarkable perseverance and considerable achievement.

MAPS

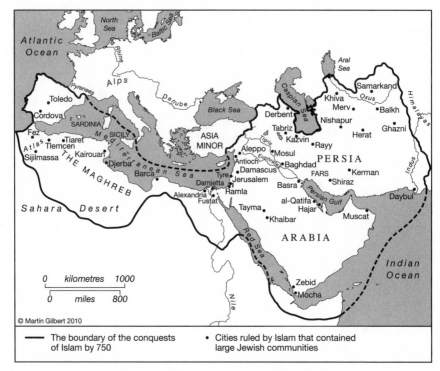

The boundary of the conquests
of Islam by 750

• Cities ruled by Islam that contained
large Jewish communities

1.   The conquests of Islam by 750, and towns with large Jewish communities.

2. Jewish communities in the Arabian Peninsula at the time of
   Mohammed.

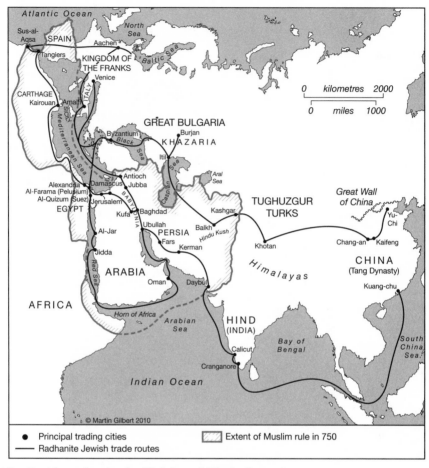

3.   Jewish traders in the Eighth and Ninth Centuries.

4. Jewish communities in Spain during Muslim rule, 711–1236.

5. Jews seeking refuge in Muslim lands from Christian persecution,
    1012–1540.

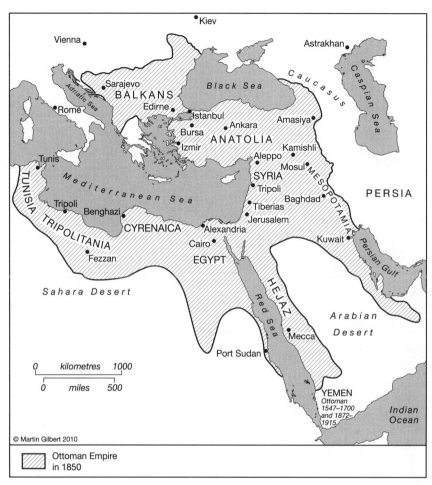

6. The Ottoman Empire in 1850.

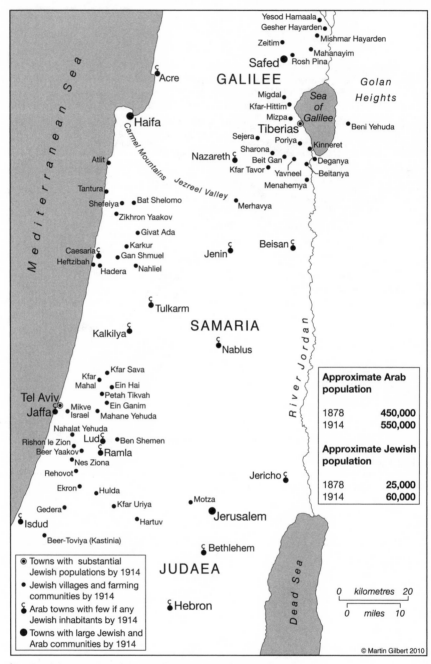

7. Jewish communities in Ottoman Palestine by 1914.

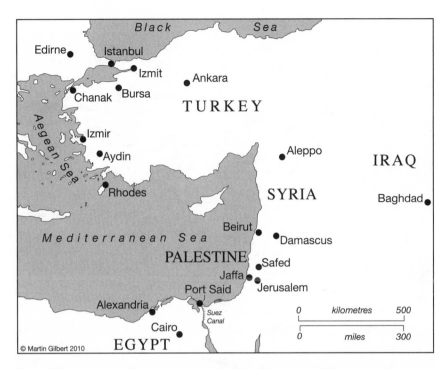

8. Birthplaces of Jews born in Muslim lands, deported to their deaths from France, 1942–1944.

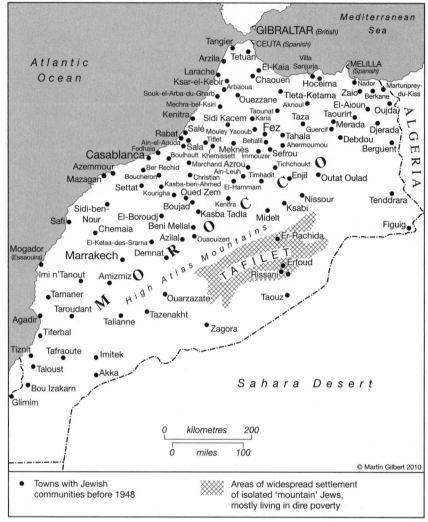

9. Former Jewish communities in Morocco.

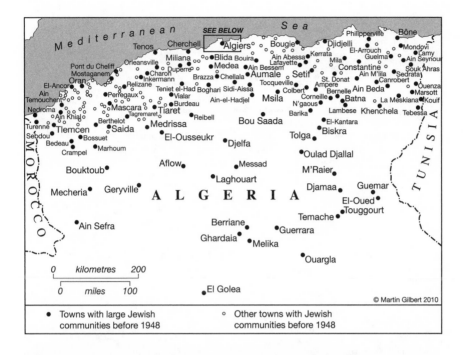

Towns with large Jewish communities before 1948

○ Other towns with Jewish communities before 1948

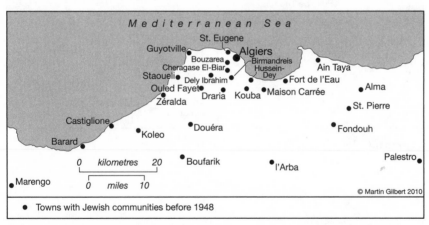

Towns with Jewish communities before 1948

10. Former Jewish communities in Algeria and the area around Algiers.

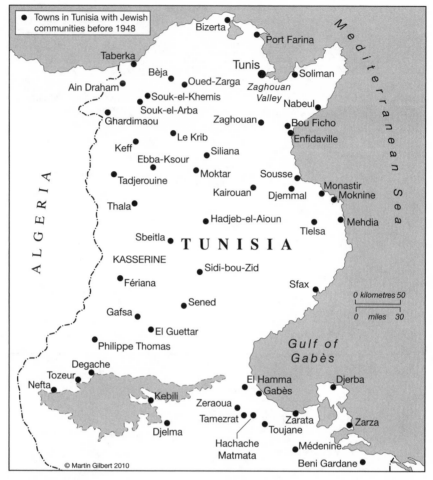

11. Former Jewish communities in Tunisia.

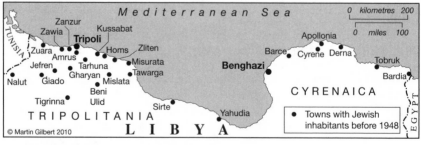

12. Former Jewish communities in Libya.

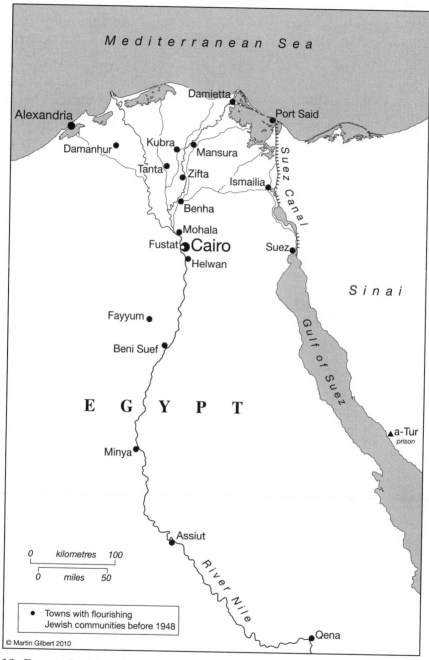

13. Former Jewish communities in Egypt.

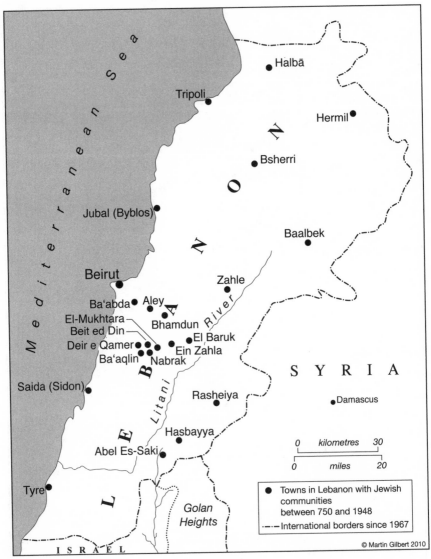

14. Former Jewish communities in Lebanon.

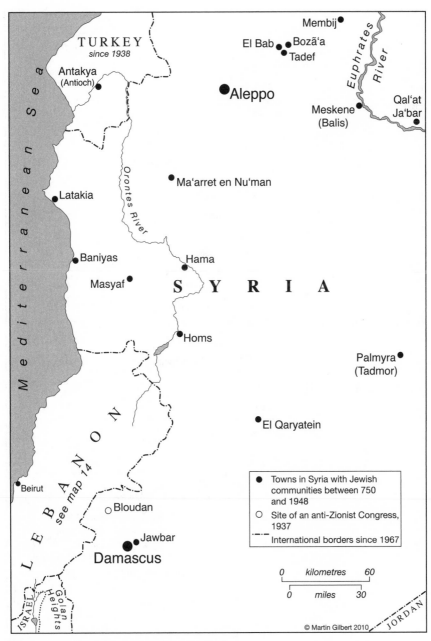

15. Former Jewish communities in Syria.

16. Former Jewish communities in Iraq.

17. Former Jewish communities in Iran.

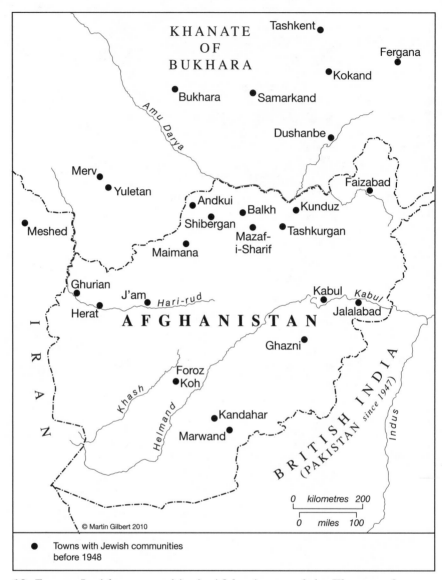

18. Former Jewish communities in Afghanistan and the Khanate of Bukhara.

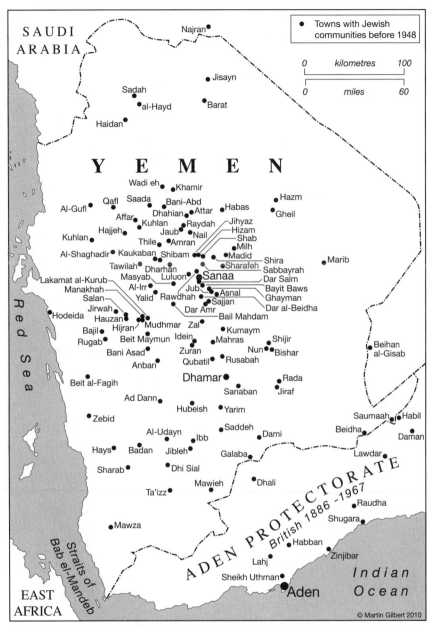

SAUDI
ARABIA

Najran

● Towns with Jewish
communities before 1948

0   kilometres   100

0   miles   60

● Jisayn

Sadah

al-Hayd   ● Barat

Haidan

Y E M E N

Wadi eh   ● Khamir

Qafl   Saada   ● Hazm
Al-Gufl   Bani-Abd
Dhahian   ● Attar   Habas
Affar   Kuhlan   ● Gheil
Hajjeh   Raydah   Jihyaz
Kuhlan   Jaub   Nail   Hizam
Thile   Amran   Shab
Al-Shaghadir   Kaukaban   Shibam   Milh
Tawilah   Dharhan   Madid   ● Marib
Lakamat al-Kurub   Masyab   Luluon   Shira
Manakhah   Al-Irr   Sanaa   Sabbayrah
Salan   Yalid   Rawdhah   Dar Salm
Jirwah   Jub   Asnal   Bayit Baws
Hodeida   Hauzan   Sajjan   Ghayman
Bajil   Hijran   Mudhmar   Dar Amr   Dar al-Beidha
Rugab   Beit Maymun   Idein   Bail Mahdam
Bani Asad   Zal   Kumaym
Anban   Zuran   Mahras   Shijir   ● Beihan
Beit al-Fagih   Qubatil   Rusabah   Nun   Bishar   al-Gisab

Dhamar   ● Rada
Ad Dann   Sanaban   Jiraf
● Zebid   Hubeish   ● Yarim
Al-Udayn   Saddeh   Saumaah   Habil
Hays   Badan   Ibb   Dami   Beidha   Daman
Sharab   Jibleh   Galaba   Lawdar
Dhi Sial
Mawieh   Dhali   A D E N   P R O T E C T O R A T E
Ta'izz   *British 1886 -1967*   Raudha
● Mawza   Shugara
Habban
Lahj   Zinjibar
Sheikh Uthman   *I n d i a n*
EAST   ●Aden   *O c e a n*
AFRICA   © Martin Gilbert 2010

R e d   S e a

Straits of Bab el-Mandeb

19. Former Jewish communities in Yemen.

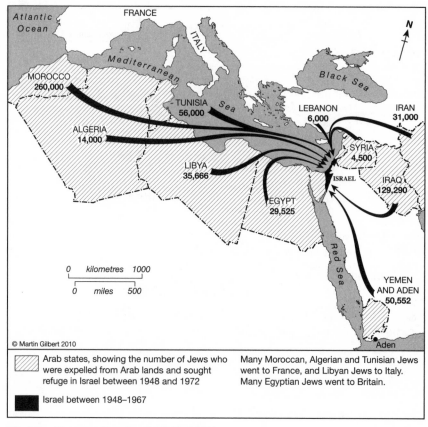

20. The 'Second Exodus,' 1947–1957.

GLOSSARY

of Arabic and Hebrew words cited

ARABIC:

abaya: a Muslim woman's overgarment (also known as a *hijab*), usually
   black, that covers the whole body except the eyes, feet and hands.
ahl al-dhimma: the condition of a *dhimmi* (see below).
al-Alam al-Arabi: 'The Arab World' (a newspaper).
al Andalus: Andalucia, southern Spain.
al-Aqsa: 'The Farthest' (the main mosque in Jerusalem).
al-Ayyam: 'Days' (a newspaper).
al-Faruq: 'He who can distinguish truth from falsehood.'
Al-Futuwwa: 'chivalry' (youth brigades).
al-Hajar-ul-Aswad: 'The Black Stone' (The Ka'bah, Mecca).
al-Haram al-Sharif: 'The Noble Sanctuary' (The Temple Mount,
   Jerusalem).
al-Ilah (*Allah*): God: the Arabic word for God is *Ilah*. The word *Allah*
   is a conjunction of the two words *al-* and *Ilah*; The God.
al-Mowahhidun: 'Unitarians' (the Almohad ruling dynasty).
al-Sahafi al-Ta'ih: 'The Wandering Journalist' (Newspaper).
aman: in Islamic religious law, a safe conduct or pledge of security
   by which a non-Muslim living in the Domain of War who enters
   Muslim territory becomes protected, in his life and property, by
   the sanctions of the law for a limited period.
Ashura: Shiite day of mourning and self-flagellation.
Awfa min al-Samaw'al: 'More loyal than Samuel' (high praise).
Bab al-Radhana: the Gate of the Radhanites (in Kairouan, Tunisia).
Dar al-Harb: 'The Domain of War.'

Dar al-Islam: 'The Domain of Islam.'

Dar al-Yahud: 'The abode of the Jews': the Jewish Quarter; also (in Persia) the Jewish community.

dhimmi: a non-Muslim enjoying the protection of Islam and the Koran, while at the same time subject to disadvantages and humiliation as prescribed in the Covenant of Omar (Pact of Omar), which degraded both the individual and the community.

farhud: pogrom, or violent dispossession (refers to the pogrom in Baghdad in 1941).

fatwa: a legal pronouncement issued by a Muslim religious authority.

fellah (fallah): a peasant, farmer or agricultural labourer, from the Arabic word for a ploughman.

Fi 'l-Jima': 'On Sexual Intercourse' (a treatise by Maimonides).

fitra: innate human nature, innate disposition; the belief that every child is born a Muslim.

Hadith: narrations originating from the words and deeds of Mohammed. *Hadith* are regarded by traditional Muslim schools of jurisprudence as important for understanding the Koran, and in matters of jurisprudence.

hajj: the annual Muslim pilgrimage to Mecca.

halal: allowed, permitted (usually refers to meat permitted to be eaten).

Harakat al'Muqawama al-Islamiyya: Islamic Resistance Movement (Hamas).

hareth el-yahood: 'The Quarter of Dirt' (a name sometimes given to the Jewish Quarter in Muslim towns).

hijra: Mohammed's emigration from Mecca to Medina.

ibn: son of.

Idhbah Al Yahud!: 'Murder the Jews!'

Isra'iliyyat: Jewish lore incorporated into Muslim tradition.

izar: a veil; a large piece of material with which Muslim women are obliged to cover themselves when leaving their houses.

Jadid al-Islam: New Muslims (converts in Persia who practised their Judaism in secret).

jihad: holy war (*al-jihad fi sabil Allah:* 'striving in the way of Allah').

jizya: poll tax (head tax).

Ka'bah: the 'Happiest Stone,' a focal point of the Muslim pilgrimage to Mecca.

kafir: an unbeliever, someone who does not believe in Allah.

Katayib al-Shabab: 'The Youth Regiments' or 'The Youth Battalions' (youth group).

Khalifat Allah: Successor of God (the Caliph).

Khalifat Rasul Allah: 'Successor to the Messenger of God' (the Caliph).

Kitab al-Aghdhiya: 'Book of Foods.'

Madinat al-Nabi: 'The City of the Prophet,' Medina, previously Yathrib.

Mal el Yahud – Halal!: Sanction to 'rob the Jews!'

millet (Turkish) from the Arab *millah*: a religion-based community (any religion).

mellah: the saline area, i.e salt (the Jewish Quarter in Fez).

muezzin: the caller to prayer.

Muharram: the first month of the Muslim year.

musta'min: a person who has received an *aman* (protection, safe conduct).

muwashshah: song form, or ode.

najas: ritual uncleanliness under Islamic law.

qasida: epic poem.

qibla: the direction a Muslim prays (towards Mecca).

Qubbat as-Sakhrah: Dome of the Rock, Jerusalem.

Rais al-Yahud: 'Chief of the Jews,' the head of the Jewish community in a town.

rashidun: 'rightly guided' (the first Caliphs).

Sani al-Dawla: 'The Noble of the State' (a title of distinction).

Sayyid: a Muslim dignitary; also, an honorific title given to male descendants of Mohammed through his grandsons, Hasan ibn 'Ali and Husayn ibn 'Ali.

Sharia: Islamic religious law.

Shia (Shiite): a Muslim sect, followers of 'Ali ibn Abi Talib.

Sirat Rasul Allah: 'Life of God's Messenger' (by Ibn Ishaq).

Sunni: adherent of the Sunna, the largest denomination of Islam.

sura: a chapter of the Koran.

tabiun 'Followers': the generation of Muslims that came after Mohammed's 'Companions.'

Tarbush: a tall, brimless, usually red felt cap with a silk tassel, worn either by itself or as the base of a turban.

ulama, also spelled *ulema*: a community of legal scholars of Islam; those who possess the quality of *ilm* (learning).

umma: the worldwide community of Muslim believers.

Wadi al-Yahud: the Valley of the Jews.

Wakf: a Muslim religious foundation; the granting or dedication of property in trust for a pious purpose, for some object that tends to the good of mankind.

wazir (Arabic); *vizier* (Persian): the adviser, often the senior Minister, of a Muslim ruler.

Yahud Khaibar: the Jews of Khaibar, a name given to a Jewish tribe in Yemen.

yehudi wasikh: filthy Jew.

HEBREW:

aliyah: emigration (to Israel).

Aliyah Bet: 'Immigration B' (organized illegal immigration of Jews to British Mandate Palestine, 1936–1948.)

anusim: those converted by force ('forced ones').

ben: son of.

galut: the Jewish diaspora.

Genizah (from the Hebrew word *Ganoz*, to put aside): religious and other writings in Hebrew, kept in safe storage when no longer needed, to avoid destroying holy books.

Ha-Dover: 'The Speaker' – a newspaper.

Kol Yisrael Khaverim: 'All Israel are Comrades.'

Kosher: food and its preparation as prescribed by Jewish law.

ma'abarah (plural *ma'abarot*): temporary accommodation for new immigrants.

moshav (plural *moshavim*): a cooperative agricultural community of individual farmers, in Israel.

Nagid: governor.

Nasi: prince.

oleh: a new immigrant (to Israel).

perutah: the coin of the smallest value in Talmudic times; the weight of one half grain of barley in pure silver.

Sefer ha-Kabbalah: 'Book of Tradition.'

Sepharad: Spain; the Jewish Sephardi tradition.

yad vashem: 'a place and a name.'

Yishuv: the Jewish community in Ottoman and British Mandate Palestine.

yom nes: 'a day of miracle.'

BIBLIOGRAPHY

of books cited

TEXTS AND COLLECTIONS OF DOCUMENTS

The Quran: The Eternal Revelation vouchsafed to Muhammad The Seal of the Prophets. London and Dublin: Curzon Press, 1971. English text by Muhammad Zafrulla Khan.

A. Asher (editor and translator), *The Itinerary of Rabbi Benjamin of Tudela.* New York: Hakesheth Publishing Co., 2 volumes, 1840.

Andrew G. Bostom (editor), *The Legacy of Islamic Antisemitism: From Sacred Texts to Solemn History.* Amherst, New York: Prometheus Books, 2008.

Andrew G. Bostom (editor), *The Legacy of Jihad: Islamic Holy War and the Fate of Non-Muslims.* Amherst, New York: Prometheus Books, 2005.

Uriel Heyd (translator), *Ottoman Documents on Palestine, 1552-1615.* London: Oxford University Press, 1960.

Albert M. Hyamson, *The British Consulate in Jerusalem in relation to the Jews of Palestine, 1838-1914* (two parts). London: Edward Goldston, 1941.

Ali ibn Abi Bakr Marghinian, *The Hedaya, or Guide – A Commentary on the Mussulman Laws* (Charles Hamilton, translator), 2 volumes. New Delhi: 1982.

Norman A. Stillman, *The Jews of Arab Lands: A History and a Source Book.* Philadelphia: Jewish Publication Society, 1979.

Norman A. Stillman, *Jews of Arab Lands in Modern Times.* Philadelphia: Jewish Publication Society, 1991.

2001 Annual Report on International Religious Freedom. United States Department of State.

Annual Report, 1945. British Military Administration, Tripolitania.

The Complete Artscroll Siddur. New York: Mesorah Publishers, 1984.

Encyclopaedia Judaica. Jerusalem: Keter, 1972.

The Iraq Directory, 1936. Baghdad: Dangoor's Printing and Publishing House, 1936.

Jewish Encyclopedia. New York: Funk and Wagnalls, 1901-1906.

Letters of Maimonides. New York: Philipp Feldheim Publishers, 1982.

Palestine: Statement of Policy by His Majesty's Government in the United Kingdom, Command Paper 3692 of 1930. London: His Majesty's Stationery Office, 1930.

Report on the Commission of Enquiry into the Disturbances in Aden in December, 1947, (Harry Trusted, Commissioner), Colonial No. 233. London: His Majesty's Stationery Office, 1948.

Report of the Commission on the Palestine Disturbances of August, 1929 (Sir Walter Shaw, Chairman), Command Paper 3530 of 1930. London: His Majesty's Stationery Office.

Statement of British Policy on Palestine, Command Paper 1700 of 1922. London: His Majesty's Stationery Office, 1922.

BOOKS

Michel Abitbol, *The Jews of North Africa During the Second World War.* Detroit: Wayne State University Press, 1989.

André Aciman, *Out of Egypt: A Memoir.* New York: Picador, 1994.

Ada Aharoni, *Not in Vain: An Extraordinary Life* (the biography of Thea Woolf). San Carlos, California: Ladybug Press, 1998.

Ada Aharoni, Aimée Israel-Pelletier, Levana Zamir (editors), *History and Culture of the Jews from Egypt in Modern Times.* Tel Aviv: Keness Hafakot, 2008.

Reuben Ahroni, *Yemenite Jewry: Origins, Culture, and Literature.* Bloomington, Indiana University Press, 1986.

Marc D. Angel, *The Jews of Rhodes: The History of a Sephardic Community.* New York: Sepher-Hermon Press, 1998.

Karen Armstrong, *Muhammad: A Biography of the Prophet.* London: Victor Gollancz, 1991.

Eliyahu Ashtor, *The Jews of Moslem Spain.* Philadelphia: Jewish Publication Society, 2 volumes, 1973.

Irene Awret, *Days of Honey: The Tunisian Boyhood of Rafael Uzan.* New York: Schocken Books, 1984.

Bat Ye'or, *The Decline of Eastern Christianity Under Islam: From Jihad to Dhimmitude: Seventh - Twentieth Century.* Cranbury, New Jersey: Associated University Presses, 1996.

Bat Ye'or, *The Dhimmi: Jews and Christians under Islam.* Cranbury, New Jersey: Associated University Presses, 1985.

Bat Ye'or, *Islam and Dhimmitude: Where Civilizations Collide*. Cranbury, New Jersey: Associated University Presses, 2002.

Gourji C. Bekhor, *Fascinating Life and Sensational Death: The Conditions in Iraq Before and After the Six-Day War*. Tel Aviv: Peli Printing Works, 1990.

Charles Belgrave, *Personal Column: A History of Bahrein*. Beirut: Librairie du Liban, 1960.

David Ben-Gurion, *Israel: A Personal History*. Tel Aviv: American Israel Publishing Company, 1971.

E. Ben Hanan, *Elie Cohn, Our Man in Damascus, Israel's Greatest Spy*. Tel Aviv: ADM Publishing House, 1967.

Israel Joseph Benjamin, *Eight Years in Asia and Africa, From 1846-1855*. Hanover: published by the author, 1859.

Marina Benjamin, *Last Days in Babylon, The Story of the Jews of Baghdad; the History of a Family, the Collapse of a Nation*. New York: Free Press, 2006; London: Bloomsbury, 2007.

Mordechai Ben-Porat, *To Baghdad and Back: The Miraculous 2,000 Year Homecoming of the Iraqi Jews*. Jerusalem: Gefen Publishing House, 1998.

Norman Bentwich, *Palestine of the Jews: Past, Present, and Future*. London: Kegan Paul, Trench, Trubner, 1919.

Itzhak Ben-Zvi, *The Exiled and the Redeemed: The Strange Jewish 'Tribes' of the Orient*. London: Vallentine, Mitchell, 1958.

Walter Besant and E.H. Palmer, *Jerusalem, The City of Herod and Saladin*. London: Richard Bentley and Son, 1871.

Ken Blady, *The Jews of Habban, South Yemen, Jewish Communities in Exotic Places*. Northvale, New Jersey, and Jerusalem: Jason Aronson, 2000.

Carl Brockelmann, *History of the Islamic Peoples*. New York: Capricorn Books, 1960. Translated from the German 1939 edition by Moshe Perlmann.

François-René Viscount de Chateaubriand, *Itinéraire de Paris à Jérusalem*. Paris: Le Normant Fils, 1811.

André Chouraqui, *Between East and West: A History of the Jews in North Africa*. Philadelphia: Jewish Publication Society, 1968.

Hayyim J. Cohen, *The Jews of the Middle East, 1860-1972*. New York, Toronto and Jerusalem: Wiley and Keter, 1973.

Mark R. Cohen, *Under Crescent and Cross: The Jews in the Middle Ages*. Princeton, New Jersey: Princeton University Press, 1994.

Joan Comay, *The Diaspora Story: The Epic of the Jewish People among the Nations*. London: Weidenfeld and Nicolson, 1981.

The Hon. Irwin Cotler, David Matas and Stanley A. Urman, *Jewish Refugees from Arab Countries: The Case for Rights and Redress*. New York: Justice for Jews from Arab Countries, 5 November 2007.

Robert Curzon, *Visits to Monasteries in the Levant*. London: Humphrey Milford, 1916.

Jacob d'Ancona, *The City of Light*. London: Little, Brown, 1997 (translated by David Selbourne).

Renzo De Felice, *Jews in an Arab Land: Libya, 1835-1970*. Austin: University of Texas Press, 1985.

Ellis Douek, *A Middle Eastern Affair*. London: Peter Halban, 2004.

Joseph W. Eaton and David Solomonica, *The Rurban Village*. Rehovot, Israel: Settlement Study Centre, 1978.

Walter J. Fischel, *Jews in the Economic and Political Life of Medieval Islam*. London: Royal Asiatic Society, 1937.

Jonathan Frankel, *The Damascus Affair: 'Ritual Murder', Politics, and the Jews in 1840*. Cambridge: Cambridge University Press, 1977.

Daniel M. Friedenberg, *Jewish Minters & Medalists*. Philadelphia: Jewish Publication Society, 1976.

Harry Friedenwald, *The Jews and Medicine: Essays*. New York: Ktav Publishing House, 1944.

Saul S. Friedman, *Without Future: The Plight of Syrian Jewry*. New York: Praeger, 1989.

Solomon Gaon and M. Mitchell Serels (editors), *Sephardim and the Holocaust*. New York: Jacob E. Safra Institute of Sephardic Studies, Yeshiva University, 1978.

Moshe Gat, *The Jewish Exodus from Iraq, 1948-1951*. London: Frank Cass, 1997.

Jane S. Gerber, *The Jews of Spain: A History of the Sephardic Experience*. New York: Free Press, 1992.

Martin Gilbert, *Atlas of the Holocaust*. London: fourth edition, Routledge, 2009.

Martin Gilbert, *From the Ends of the Earth: The Jews in the Twentieth Century*. London: Cassell, 2001.

Martin Gilbert, *The Jews of Arab Lands, Their history in maps*. London: Board of Deputies of British Jews, 1976.

Martin Gilbert, *Letters to Auntie Fori: The 5,000-Year History of the Jewish People and Their Faith*. London: Weidenfeld and Nicolson, 2002.

Martin Gilbert, *The Story of Israel*. London: Carlton Books, second, enlarged edition, 2007.

Martin Gilbert, *Historical Atlas of Jerusalem*. London: fourth edition, Routledge, 2008.

M.J. de Goeje and other (editors), *Tabari's History of the Prophets and Kings*. Leiden: Brill, three series, fifteen volumes, 1879-1901.

S.D. Goitein, *A Mediterranean Society: The Jewish Communities in the Arab World as Portrayed in the Documents of the Cairo Geniza, Volume II, The Community*. Berkeley: University of California Press, 1971.

S.D. Goitein, *Jews and Arabs: Their Contacts through the Ages*. Third, revised edition. New York: Schocken Books, 1974.

Morris S. Goodblatt, *Jewish Life in Turkey in the XVIth Century: As Reflected in the Legal Writings of Samuel de Medina*. New York: Jewish Theological Seminary of America, 1952.

David Goldstein (editor), *Hebrew Poets from Spain*. London: Routledge & Kegan Paul, 1965.

Solomon Grayzel, *A History of the Jews from the Babylonian Exile to the Present*. Philadelphia: Jewish Publication Society, 1968.

Yehoshafat Harkabi, *Arab Attitudes to Israel*. Jerusalem: Israel Universities Press, 1972.

Frederick Hasselquist, *Voyages and Travels in the Levant in the Years 1749, 50, 51, 52*. London: Charles Linnaeus, 1766.

Frank Heynick, *Jews and Medicine: An Epic Saga*. Hoboken, New Jersey: Ktav Publishing House, 2002.

Shlomo Hillel, *Operation Babylon: Jewish Clandestine Activity in the Middle East, 1946-51*. London: William Collins, 1988.

H.Z. (J.W.) Hirschberg, *A History of the Jews in North Africa*. Leiden: Two Volumes, E.J. Brill, 1974.

Lukasz Hirszowicz, *The Third Reich and the Arab East*. London: Routledge & Kegan Paul, 1966.

Philip K. Hitti, *History of the Arabs, From The Earliest Times to the Present*. London: Macmillan, 1961.

Albert Hourani, *A History of the Arab Peoples*. London: Faber and Faber, 1991.

Ibn Ishak, 'Sirat Rasul Allah,' published as *The Life of Mohammed*. London: Oxford University Press, 1955 (translated by Alfred Guillaume).

Leon Jacob and Moshe Samuel (editors), *Aden Jews Congregation* (brochure), 2006.

Lord Janner of Braunstone, *To Life! The Memoirs of Greville Janner*. Stroud, Gloucestershire: Sutton Publishing, 2006.

Philip Jordan, *Jordan's Tunis Diary*. London: Collins, 1943.

Josephus, *The Jewish War*. London: Penguin Books edition, 1959. Translator, G.A. Williamson.

Esther Juhasz (editor), *Sephardi Jews in the Ottoman Empire: Aspects of Material Culture*. Jerusalem: The Israel Museum, 1990.

Efraim Karsh, *Islamic Imperialism: A History.* Newhaven and London: Yale University Press, 2006.

Gerald Kaufman, *To Build the Promised Land.* London: Weidenfeld and Nicolson, 1973.

Nissim Kazzaz, *The End of a Diaspora: The Jews in Iraq during the Twentieth Century.* Jerusalem: Ben-Zvi Institute, 1991.

Elie Kedourie, *Democracy and Arab Political Culture.* Washington, D.C.: The Washington Institute for Near East Policy, 1992.

Hugh Kennedy, *The Court of the Caliphs: The Rise and Fall of Islam's Greatest Dynasty* (the Abbasids). London: Weidenfeld and Nicolson, 2004.

Hugh Kennedy, *The Great Arab Conquests: How the Spread of Islam Changed the World We Live In.* London: Weidenfeld and Nicolson, 2007.

Nancy Elly Khedouri, *From Our Beginning To Present Day.* Bahrain: Al-Manar Press, 2007.

Sir Alec Kirkbride, *From the Wings: Amman Memoirs, 1947-1951.* London: Frank Cass, 1976.

Serge Klarsfeld, *Memorial to the Jews Deported from France, 1942-1944.* Paris: Beate Klarsfeld Foundation, 1978.

Teddy Kollek and Moshe Pearlman, *Jerusalem: A History of Forty Centuries.* New York: Random House, 1968.

Edward Kossoy and Abraham Ohry, *The Feldshers.* Jerusalem: The Magnes Press, 1992.

Lucette Lagnado, *The Man in the White Sharkskin Suit: A Jewish Family's Exodus from Old Cairo to the New World.* New York: HarperCollins, 2007.

Jacob M. Landau, *Jews in Nineteenth-Century Egypt.* New York and London: New York University Press, 1969.

Siegfried Landshut, *Jewish Communities in the Muslim Countries of the Middle East.* London: Jewish Chronicle Publications, 1950.

Edward William Lane, *An Account of the Manners and Customs of the Modern Egyptians written in Egypt during the years 1833-35.* London: Library of Entertaining Knowledge, 1837.

Stanley Lane-Poole, *Egypt.* London: Sampson Low, Marston, Searle and Rivington, 1881.

Michael M. Laskier, *The Jews of Egypt, 1920-1970.* New York: New York University Press, 1991.

Sultana Latifa (Suzy Vidal), *The Jasmine Necklace.* Verviers (Belgium): Imprim'Express, 2002.

Itamar Levin, *Locked Doors: The Seizure of Jewish Property in Arab Countries.* Westport, Connecticut: Greenwood Publishing, 2001. Translated by Rachel Neiman.

Bernard Lewis, *The Jews of Islam*. Princeton: Princeton University Press, 1984.

Bernard Lewis, *The Middle East: 2,000 Years of History from the Rise of Christianity to the Present Day*. London: Weidenfeld and Nicolson, 1995.

Bernard Lewis, *Semites and Anti-Semites*. London: Phoenix, 1997.

David Levering Lewis, *God's Crucible: Islam and the Making of Europe, 570 to 1215*. New York: W.W. Norton, 2008.

Sonia and V.D. Lipman (editors), *The Century of Moses Montefiore*. London: The Littman Library of Jewish Civilization, 1985.

Stephen Longrigg, *Iraq, 1900-1950: a Political, Social and Economic History*. London: Oxford University Press, 1953.

Perceval Barton Lord, *Algiers, with notices of the neighbouring States of Barbary*. London: Whittaker, two volumes, 1835.

John Lowthian, *A Narrative of a Visit to Jerusalem and Several Parts of Palestine in 1843-4: Extracted from the Journal of Mr. John Lowthian of Carleton House, Near Carlisle*. London: 1845.

Liora Lukitz, *Iraq: Quest for National Identity*. London: Frank Cass, 1995.

Robert Lyman, *Iraq 1941: The battles for Basra, Habbaniya, Fallujah and Baghdad*. Botley, Oxford: Osprey Publishing, 2006.

Klaus-Michael Mallman and Martin Cueppers, *Halbmond und Hakenkreuz: Das 'Dritte Reich,' die Araber und Palästina*. Darmstadt: Wissenschaftlichen Buchgesellschaft (WBG), 2006. (*The Crescent and the Swastika: The 'Third Reich,' The Arabs and Palestine*.)

Neville J. Mandel, *The Arabs and Zionism before World War I*. Berkeley: University of California Press, 1976.

David Matas and Stanley A. Urman, *Jewish Refugees from Arab Countries: The Case for Rights and Redress* (brochure). Tel Aviv: Justice for Jews from Arab Countries, 2003.

Gavin Maxwell, *Lords of the Atlas: The Rise and Fall of the House of Glaoua*. London: Longmans, 1966.

Ora Melamed (editor), *Annals of Iraqi Jewry: A Collection of Articles and Reviews*. Jerusalem: Eliner Library, 1995.

Tamar Morad, Dennis Shasha and Robert Shasha (editors), *Iraq's Last Jews: Stories of Daily Life, Upheaval, and Escape from Modern Babylon*. London: Palgrave Macmillan, 2008.

Ester Muchawsky-Schnapper, *The Jews of Yemen: Highlights of the Israel Museum Collection*, Jerusalem: Israel Museum, 1994.

Ester Muchawsky-Schnapper: *The Yemenites. Two Thousand Years of Jewish Culture*. Jerusalem: Israel Museum, 2000.

Götz Nordbruch, *Nazism in Syria and Lebanon: The ambivalence of the German option, 1933-1945*. Routledge: London, 2009.

Sherwin B. Nuland, *Maimonides*. New York: Schocken, 2005.

Tudor Parfitt (editor), *Israel and Ishmael: Studies in Muslim-Jewish Relations*. Richmond, Surrey: Curzon Press, 2000.

Tudor Parfitt, *The Jews in Palestine, 1800-1882*. London: Royal Historical Society, 1987.

Tudor Parfitt, *The Road to Redemption: The Jews of the Yemen, 1900-1950*. Leiden: E.J. Brill, 1996.

Raphael Patai, *Israel between East and West: A study in human relations*. Philadelphia: Jewish Publication Society, 1953.

Joan Peters, *From Time Immemorial: The Origins of the Arab-Jewish Conflict Over Palestine*. New York: Harper and Row, 1984.

Ermete Pierotti, *Customs and Traditions of Palestine, Illustrating the Manners of Ancient Hebrews*. Cambridge: Deighton, Bell, 1864.

Tome Pires, *Suma Oriental (1512-1515)*. London: Bell and Daldy, 1944.

William R. Polk, *The Opening of South Lebanon, 1788-1840*. Cambridge, Massachusetts: Harvard University Press, 1963.

Y. Porath, *The Emergence of the Palestinian-Arab National Movement, 1918-1929*. London: Frank Cass, 1974.

Terence Prittie and Bernard Dineen, *The Double Exodus: A Study of Arab and Jewish Refugees in the Middle East*. London: Goodhart Press, 1972.

Samir Raafat, *Cairo, The Glory Years: Who built what, when, why and for whom.* . . . Alexandria, Egypt: Harpocrates Publishing, 2003.

Samir W. Raafat, *Maadi, 1904-1962: Society & History in a Cairo Suburb*. Cairo: The Palm Press, 1994.

Chaim Raphael, *The Road from Babylon: The Story of Sephardi and Oriental Jews*. London: Weidenfeld and Nicolson, 1985.

Claudia Roden, *The Book of Jewish Food: An Odyssey from Samarkand and Vilna to the Present Day*. New York: Alfred A. Knopf, 1996.

Cecil Roth, *The House of Nasi: The Duke of Naxos*. Philadelphia: Jewish Publication Society, 1948.

Maurice M. Roumani, *The Case of the Jews from Arab Countries: A Neglected Issue*. Tel Aviv: World Organization of Jews from Arab Countries (WOJAC), 1977.

Maurice M. Roumani, *From Immigrant to Citizen: The Contribution of the Army to National Integration in Israel*. The Hague: Foundation for the Study of Plural Societies, 1979.

Maurice M. Roumani, *The Jews of Libya: Coexistence, Persecution, Rehabilitation.* Brighton: Sussex Academic Press, 2007.

Barry Rubin, *The Arab States and the Palestine Conflict.* Syracuse, New York: Syracuse University Press, 1981.

Tova Murad Sadka, *No Way Back* (a novel). Pompano Beach: Exposition Press of Florida, 1984.

George Sandys, *A Relation of A Journey Begun in An. Dom. 1610.* London: W. Barrett, 1615: Bodleian Library collection.

Victor D. Sanua, *Egyptian Jewry: A Guide to Egyptian Jewry in the Mid–Twentieth Century, The beginning of the demise of a vibrant Jewish community.* New York: International Association of Jews from Egypt, 2nd edition, 2006.

Houman Sarshar (editor), *Esther's Children: A Portrait of Iranian Jews.* Beverly Hills, California: Centre for Iranian Jewish Oral History, 2002.

David Solomon Sassoon, *A History of the Jews in Baghdad.* Letchworth: Solomon D. Sassoon, 1949.

Robert Satloff, *Among the Righteous: Lost Stories from the Holocaust's Long Reach into Arab Lands.* New York: Public Affairs, 2006.

Joseph B. Schechtman, *On Wings of Eagles: The Plight, Exodus, and Homecoming of Oriental Jewry.* New York and London: Thomas Yoseloff, 1961.

Vivianne M. Schinasi-Silver, *42 Keys to the Second Exodus: Memoir of a life, the seeds of which were planted in Egypt and flourished in Canada.* Ste-Anne-de-Bellevue, Quebec: Shoreline, 2007.

Gershom G. Scholem, *Sabbetai Sevi: The Mystical Messiah (1626-1676).* Princeton: Littman Library of Jewish Civilization, 1973.

Daniel Schroeter, *The Sultan's Jew: Morocco and the Sephardi World.* Stanford, California: Stanford University Press, 2002.

M. Mitchell Serels, *A History of the Jews of Tangier in the Nineteenth and Twentieth Centuries.* New York: Sepher-Hermon Press, 1991.

Rachel Shabi, *Not the Enemy: Israel's Jews from Arab Lands.* New Haven and London: Yale University Press, 2009.

Violette Shamash, *Memories of Eden: A Journey Through Jewish Baghdad.* Virginia Water, Surrey: Forum Books, 2008.

Stanford J. Shaw, *The Jews of the Ottoman Empire and the Turkish Republic.* New York: New York University Press, 1991.

Shlomo Sheena, Yaacov Elazar, and Emmanuel Nahtomi, *A Short History of The Zionist Underground Movement in Iraq.* Tel Aviv: Research Institute of the Zionist-Pioneer Underground Movement in Iraq, 2004.

Nir Shohet, *The Story of an Exile: A Short History of the Jews of Iraq.* Tel Aviv:

Association for the Promotion of Research, Literature and Art (founded in Israel by Jews from Iraq), 1982.

Malka Hillel Shulewitz (editor), *The Forgotten Millions: The Modern Jewish Exodus from Arab Lands.* London: Cassell, 1999.

Reeva Spector Simon, Michael Menachem Laskier and Sara Reguer (editors), *The Jews of the Middle East and North Africa in Modern Times.* New York: Columbia University Press, 2003.

Rabbi David Sutton, *Aleppo: City of Scholars.* New York: Artscroll Sephardic Heritage Series, 2005.

Lieutenant-Colonel P.M. Sykes, *A History of Persia.* London: Macmillan, 2 Volumes, 1915.

Tad Szulc, *The Secret Alliance: The Extraordinary Story of the Rescue of the Jews Since World War II.* London: Macmillan, 1992.

Charles C. Torrey, *The Jewish Foundation of Islam.* New York: Jewish Institute of Religion, 1933.

Harold Troper, *The Ransomed of God: The Remarkable Story of One Woman's Role in the Rescue of Syrian Jews.* Toronto: Malcolm Lester Books, 1999.

Arminius Vámbéry, *Travels in Central Asia: Being the Account of a Journey from Teheran Across the Turkoman Desert on the Eastern Shore of the Caspian to Khiva, Bokhara and Samarkand Performed in the Year 1863.* London: John Murray, 1864.

Suzy Vidal-Pirotte, *Extaday: a Childhood in Cairo, 1939-1949.* Verviers, Belgium: Express, 2004.

Edwin Sherman Wallace, *Jerusalem the Holy.* Edinburgh and London: Oliphant, Anderson & Ferrier, 1898.

Peter Wien, *Iraqi Arab Nationalism: Authoritarian, totalitarian, and pro-fascist inclinations, 1932-1941.* London: Routledge, 2006.

Charles James Wills, *Persia as It Is: Being Sketches of Modern Life and Character.* London: Sampson Low, Marston, Searle and Rivington, 1886.

Reverend Joseph Wolff, *Narrative of a Mission to Bokhara in the Years 1843-1845.* London: John W. Parker, 1846.

C. Wyman Bury, *Arabia Infelix, or the Turks in Yamen.* London, Macmillan, 1915.

Mona Yahia, *When the Grey Beetles Took Over Baghdad.* London: Peter Halban, 2000.

Israel Zinberg, *A History of Jewish Literature, Volume Four, The Jewish Center of Culture in the Ottoman Empire.* New York: Hebrew Union College Press, Ktav Publishers, 1974.

ARTICLES

Michel Abitbol, 'Zionist Activity in the Maghreb,' *Jerusalem Quarterly*, Issue 21, Autumn 1981.

André Aciman, 'The Exodus Obama Forgot to Mention,' *New York Times*, 9 June 2009.

Frank S. Adams, 'Arabs and Zionists Warn of Fighting: In Final Appeals to UN, Each Pledges War to Finish if Turned Down on Palestine,' *New York Times*, 25 November 1947.

Nasser Arrabyee, 'Yemeni Jews want to emigrate if not protected,' *Yemen Observer*, 16 December 2008.

Eliyahu Ashtor, 'Abu al-Munajja Solomon ben Shaya,' *Encyclopaedia Judaica*, Volume 2, column 180. Jerusalem: Keter, 1972.

Eliyahu Ashtor and Haïm Z'ew Hirschberg, 'Jerusalem, "Arab Period,"' *Encyclopaedia Judaica*, Volume 9, column 1411. Jerusalem: Keter, 1972.

Simhah Assaf, *British Journal of the Palestine Exploration Society*, Issue VII, from page 22.

Simhah Assaf, 'Bustanai ben Haninai,' *Encyclopaedia Judaica*, Volume 4, column 1537. Jerusalem: Keter, 1972.

Sydney S. Assor, 'Jews of Morocco, View from the Diaspora,' *Jewish Renaissance*, April 2006.

Ron Barkai, 'Jewish Medical Treatises in the Middle Ages,' in Natalia Berger (editor), *Jews and Medicine: Religion, Culture, Science*. Philadelphia: Jewish Publication Society, 1997.

Eliezer Bashan (Sternberg), 'Omar, Covenant of,' *Encyclopaedia Judaica*, Volume 12, column 1378-82. Jerusalem: Keter, 1972.

Eliezer Bashan (Sternberg), 'Omar ibn al-Khattab,' *Encyclopaedia Judaica*, Volume 12, column 1382. Jerusalem: Keter, 1972.

Eliezer Bashan (Sternberg), 'Solomon ben Judah (d. 1051),' *Encyclopaedia Judaica*, Volume 15, columns 122-4. Jerusalem: Keter, 1972.

Meir Basri, 'Prominent Iraqi Jews of recent times,' *The Scribe*, Issue 76, Spring 2003.

Bat Ye'or, 'Islam and the Dhimmis,' *Jerusalem Quarterly*, Issue 42, Spring 1987.

C.H. Becker, 'Ibn Killis, Fatimid vizier,' *Encyclopaedia of Islam*, Volume Two.

Haim Beinart, 'Córdoba (Cordova, also Corduba),' *Encyclopaedia Judaica*, Volume 5, columns 963-6. Jerusalem: Keter, 1972.

Avi Beker, 'The Forgotten Narrative: Jewish Refugees from Arab Countries,' *Jewish Political Studies Review*, 17: 3-4, Fall 2005.

Gourji C. Bekhor, 'The Baghdad Hangings,' *The Scribe*, Issue 9, Volume 2, January-February 1973.

Abraham Ben-Jacob, 'Babylonian Jews in Israel,' *The Scribe*, Issue 5, Volume 1, May-June 1972.

Abraham Ben-Jacob, 'Kurdistan,' *Encyclopaedia Judaica*, Volume 10, pages 1295-1301. Jerusalem: Keter, 1972.

Mordechai Ben-Porat, 'Jamil Shemtov' (obituary), *Nehardea: Journal of the Babylonian Heritage Centre*, No. 16, Spring 2008.

Abraham Ben-Yaacob, 'Baghdad, Early and Early Modern History,' *Encyclopaedia Judaica*, Volume 4, columns 86-7. Jerusalem: Keter, 1972.

Richard Bernstein, 'Jews in Lebanon Urged to Get Out,' *New York Times*, 24 February 1986.

Joshua Blau, 'Ibn Quraysh, Judah (second half of the Ninth Century),' *Encyclopaedia Judaica*, Volume 8, columns 1193-4. Jerusalem: Keter, 1972.

Benjamin Bright, 'The Exodus revisited,' *Jerusalem Post*, 24 April 2006.

Mallory Browne, 'Jews in Grave Danger in all Moslem Lands: Nine Hundred Thousand in Africa and Asia Face Wrath of Their Foes,' *New York Times*, 16 May 1948.

Hugh Chisholm, 'Ismail Pasha,' *Encyclopaedia Britannica*, Thirteenth Edition, page 875. London: Encyclopaedia Britannica Company. 1926.

Martin Chulov, 'The Plot to Blast Bali – The Verdict,' *The Australian*, 8 August 2003.

Hayyim J. Cohen, 'Afghanistan,' *Encyclopaedia Judaica*, Volume 2, column 328. Jerusalem: Keter. 1972.

Hayyim J. Cohen, 'Aleppo,' *Encyclopaedia Judaica*, Volume 2, columns 562-5. Jerusalem: Keter, 1972.

Hayyim J. Cohen, 'Iran,' *Jewish Encyclopedia*, Volume 8, columns 1439-1443. Jerusalem: Keter, 1972

Mark R. Cohen, 'Islam and the Jews: Counter-Myth, History,' *Jerusalem Quarterly*, Issue 38, Spring 1986.

Mark R. Cohen, 'What Was the Pact of 'Umar? A Literary-Historical Study,' *Jerusalem Studies in Arabic and Islam*, Number 23: Magnes Press, The Hewbrew University, Jerusalem, 1999.

David Corcos, 'Almohads,' *Encyclopaedia Judaica*, Volume 2, columns 662-3. Jerusalem: Keter, 1972.

David Corcos, 'Benoliel, Moroccan family,' *Encyclopaedia Judaica*, Volume 4, column 544. Jerusalem: Keter, 1972.

David Corcos, 'Fez,' *Encyclopaedia Judaica*, Volume 6, columns 1255-8. Jerusalem: Keter, 1972.

Xavier Cornut, 'The Moroccan Connection,' *Jerusalem Post*, 23 June 2009.

Barbara Crossette, 'Malaysia Tightens Secrecy on Official Documents,' *New York Times*, 8 December 1986.

Judith Cummings, 'Repression of Jews in Syria is Charged,' *New York Times*, 3 February 1979.

Clifton Daniel, '74 Tripolitanian Jews Slain in Arab Riots,' *New York Times*, 8 November 1945.

Clifton Daniel, 'Tripoli Riots are Laid to Poverty; Looting Stirred Many Arab Attacks, At Height of Attacks on Jews, Some Slayings were Result of Lust for Blood, British Seek Sources of False Rumors,' *New York Times*, 14 November 1945.

Abraham Danon, *Revue des Etudes Juives (R.E.J.)*, Volume XL, 1900, page 207 (The Jews of Salonika).

Ben-Zion Dinaburg (Benzion Dinur), *Zion* (Jewish Historical Quarterly), Issue III, 1929.

Encyclopaedia Hebraica, 'Jerusalem, Crusader Period,' *Encyclopaedia Judaica*, Volume 9, column 1415. Jerusalem: Keter, 1972.

'Exilarch,' '1,000 years ago Sepharad Ransoms a Babylonian Rabbi,' *The Scribe*, Issue 6, Volume 1, July-August 1972.

Richard Ferrer, 'First Iran Jew is Released,' *London Jewish News* (London, Ontario), 9 March 2001.

Eric Fingerhut, 'Forgotten refugees, Effort under way to focus on Jews of Arab lands,' *Washington Jewish Week*, 26 July 2007.

W.J. Fischel, 'Abbas I,' *Encyclopaedia Judaica*, Volume 2, columns 38-9. Jerusalem: Keter, 1972.

W.J. Fischel, 'Afghanistan,' *Encyclopaedia Judaica*, Volume 2, columns 326-7. Jerusalem: Keter, 1972.

W.J. Fischel, 'Bahrein,' *Encyclopaedia Judaica*, Volume 4, columns 101-2. Jerusalem: Keter, 1972.

W.J. Fischel, 'The Jews in Medieval Iran from the 16th to the 18th Centuries: Political, Economic and Communal Aspects,' *Irano-Judaica*, Jerusalem, 1982.

Jenni Frazer and Geoffrey Paul, 'Clandestine Exodus Reunites Syrian Jews,' *Jewish Chronicle*, 21 October 1994.

Baruch Gilead, 'Iran,' *Encyclopaedia Judaica*, volume 8, columns 1439-43. Jerusalem: Keter, 1972.

S.D. Goitein, 'Evidence on the Muslim Poll tax from Non-Muslim Sources,' *Journal of the Economic History of the Orient*, Issue Six, 1963.

Shlomo D. Goitein, 'Jerusalem in the Arab Period,' Lee I. Levine (editor), *The Jerusalem Cathedra*, Yad Izhak Ben-Zvi Institute, Jerusalem, and Wayne State University Press, Detroit, 1982.

R. Gottheil, 'An Answer to the Dhimmis,' *Journal of the American Oriental Society*, New York, Issue 41, 1921.

Elliott A. Green, 'The Forgotten Oppression of Jews Under Islam and in the Land of Israel,' *Midstream*, September/October 2008.

Haviv Rettig Gur, 'Government to recover assets in Muslim lands,' *Jerusalem Post*, 27 January 2009.

Haviv Rettig Gur, 'UJC to pull 110 Jews out of Yemen,' *Jerusalem Post*, 18 March 2009.

Abraham Meir Habermann, 'Soncino, family . . .' *Encyclopaedia Judaica*, Volume 15, columns 140-2. Jerusalem: Keter, 1972.

Heskel M. Haddad, 'Shavuot in Baghdad in 1941 (The Farhod),' *Midstream*, May/June 2006.

Abraham Haim, 'Amasiya,' *Encyclopaedia Judaica*, Volume 2, columns 794-5. Jerusalem: Keter, 1972.

John L. Hess, '3 Arab Lands Said To Oppress Jews,' *New York Times*, 28 January 1970.

H.Z. Hirschberg, 'Arabia,' *Encyclopaedia Judaica*, Volume 3, columns 232-6. Jerusalem: Keter, 1972.

H.Z. Hirschberg, 'Ka'b al'Ahbar,' *Encyclopaedia Judaica*, Volume 10, column 488. Jerusalem: Keter, 1972.

Greville Janner, 'A visit to Tunisia,' *Jerusalem Post*, 21 May 2007.

Jewish Chronicle Foreign Staff, 'Many Jews murdered in Arab countries,' *Jewish Chronicle*, 16 June 1967.

Joseph Kaplan, 'Nahmanides,' *Encyclopaedia Judaica*, Volume 12, columns 774-7. Jerusalem: Keter, 1972.

Reuben Kashani, 'The Jews of Afghanistan,' *Ariel: The Israeli Review of Arts and Letters*, No. 113, Jerusalem, 2002.

Simha Katz, 'Baku,' *Encyclopaedia Judaica*, Volume 4, column 119. Jerusalem: Keter, 1972.

Dr. Hermann Kellenbenz, 'Bankers and Banking,' *Encyclopaedia Judaica*, Volume 4, column 167. Jerusalem: Keter, 1972.

Robert F. Kennedy, 'Jews Make Up for Lack of Arms with Undying Spirit, Unparalleled Courage,' *Boston Globe*, 3 June 1948.

Jahd Khalil, 'Lebanon: Quietly, Jewish Community begins synagogue restoration,' *Los Angeles Times*, 4 August 2009.

M.J. Kister, 'The Massacre of Banu Qurayza: A Re-examination of a Tradition,' *Jerusalem Studies in Arabic and Islam*, Issue 8: Magnes Press, The Hebrew University, Jerusalem, 1986.

Israel Klausner, 'Charles Netter,' *Encyclopaedia Judaica*, Volume 12, column 1001-2. Jerusalem: Keter, 1972.

J.L. Kraemer, 'War, Conquest and the Treatment of Religious Minorities in Medieval Islam,' in S.W. Baron and G.S. Wise (editors), *Violence and Defense in the Jewish Experience*. Philadelphia: Jewish Publication Society, 1977.

Frances Kraft, 'Iraqi congregation celebrates 30 years in Toronto,' *Canadian Jewish News*, 30 March 2006.

Gideon M. Kressel, 'What actually happened at Khaybar?' in A. Paul Hare and Gideon M. Kressel, *Israel As Centre Stage: A Setting for Social and Religious Enactments*. Westport, Connecticut: Bergin and Garvey, 2001.

Jacob Landau and Mim Kemal Oke, 'Ottoman Perspectives on American Interests in the Holy Land': Moshe Davis (editor), *With Eyes Towards Zion*. Boulder, Colorado: Greenwood Publishing Group, 1986.

M. Lecker, 'Wadi 'l-Kura,' *The Encyclopaedia of Islam*, New Edition, Volume 11, pages 18-19.

Etgar Lefkovits, 'Expelled Jews hold deeds on Arab lands,' *Jerusalem Post*, 16 November 2007.

David Littman, 'Jews under Muslim Rule in the late Nineteenth Century,' *Wiener Library Bulletin*, Issue Number 28, London, 1975.

David Littman, 'Jews under Muslim Rule: the Case of Persia,' *Wiener Library Bulletin*, Issue Number 32. London, 1979.

David Littman, 'Mission to Morocco (1863-1864),' in Sonia and V.D. Lipman (editors), *The Century of Moses Montefiore*. London: Oxford University Press, 1985.

Simon Marcus, 'Hamon, family . . .' *Encyclopaedia Judaica*, Volume 7, columns 1248. Jerusalem: Keter, 1972.

Simon Marcus, 'Ibn Verga, Joseph (d.c. 1559),' *Encyclopaedia Judaica*, Volume 8, columns 1202-3. Jerusalem: Keter, 1972.

Yehuda Marks, 'Kiryat Gat's First Priorities – Its Citizens,' *Hamodia*, 8 January 2009.

Karl Marx, 'Declaration of War: on the History of the Eastern Question,' *New York Daily Tribune*. New York, 15 April 1854.

Julian Louis Meltzer, '. . . 14 DIE IN CAIRO EXPLOSION 10 Jews Included in Toll . . .' *New York Times*, 23 September 1945.

Shmuel Moreh, 'Ibrahim ibn Sahl al-Andalusi al-Isra'ili (Abu Ishaq, 1208–1260?),' *Encyclopaedia Judaica*, Volume 8, columns 1213-4. Jerusalem: Keter, 1972.

Shmuel Moreh, 'Samuel ibn Adiya,' *Encyclopaedia Judaica*, Volume 14, column 819. Jerusalem: Keter, 1972.

Aviva Müller-Lancet, 'Bukhara,' *Encyclopaedia Judaica*, Volume 4, column 1473. Jerusalem: Keter, 1972.

Efraim Orni, 'Caesaria: Modern Times,' *Encyclopaedia Judaica*, Volume 5, column 13. Jerusalem: Keter, 1972.

Efraim Orni, 'Gederah,' *Encyclopaedia Judaica*, Volume 7, column 354. Jerusalem: Keter, 1972.

Mordecai Paldiel, 'A righteous Arab,' *Jerusalem Post*, 3 April 2009.

Moshe Perlmann, 'Eleventh-Century Andalucian Authors on the Jews of Granada,' *Proceedings of the American Academy for Jewish Research*, Issue 18, 1948-49.

Moshe Perlmann, 'Ibn Kammuna, S'ad Ibn Mansur (c.1215-1285),' *Encyclopaedia Judaica*, Volume 8, columns 1186-7. Jerusalem: Keter, 1972.

Anshel Pfeffer, 'Yemeni Jews: relocation offer,' *Jewish Chronicle*, 2 January 2009.

Samir Raafat, 'Dynasty: The House of Yacoub Cattaui,' *Egyptian Mail*, 2 April 1994.

Yehuda Ratzaby, 'Abyad, Yihya ben Shalom (1873-1935)': *Encyclopaedia Judaica*, Volume 2, column 198. Jerusalem: Keter, 1972.

Yehuda Ratzaby, 'Baruch Ben Samuel (d.1834),' *Encyclopaedia Judaica*, Volume 4, columns 279-80. Jerusalem: Keter, 1972.

Yehuda Ratzaby, 'Lawani, Da'ud (Levfi, David),' *Encyclopaedia Judaica*, Volume 10, columns 1484-5. Jerusalem: Keter, 1972.

Simon Round, 'The unlikely envoy,' *Jewish Chronicle*, 5 December 2008.

Herman Rosenthal and J.G. Lipman, 'Daghestan,' *Jewish Encyclopedia*, Volume 4, page 411. New York: Funk and Wagnall, 1902.

Miriam Russo-Katz, 'Jewellery,' in Esther Juhasz (editor), *Sephardi Jews in The Ottoman Empire: Aspects of Material Culture*. Jerusalem: the Israel Museum, 1990.

Victor D. Sanua, 'The Contributions of Sephardic Jews To The Economic And Industrial Development of Egypt,' *Image Magazine*, March 1998.

Victor D. Sanua, '"Egypt for the Egyptians": The Story of Abu Naddara (James Sanua) 1839-1912, A Jewish Egyptian Patriot,' *Image Magazine*, September 1997.

Victor D. Sanua, 'Haim Nahoum Effendi (1872-1960),' *Image Magazine*, February 1998.

Howard Schneider, 'Iran Court Reduces Penalties for Jews,' *Washington Post*, 22 September 2000.

Simon R. Schwarzfuchs, 'Alliance Israélite Universelle' ('All Israel are comrades'), *Encyclopaedia Judaica*, Volume 2, columns 648-54. Jerusalem: Keter, 1972.

Abe Selig, 'Yemenite family make aliyah in secret op,' *Jerusalem Post*, 19 February 2009.

Rabbi M. Mitchell Serels, 'Moroccan Jews on the Road to Auschwitz,' in Solomon Gaon and M. Mitchell Serels (editors), *Sephardim and the Holocaust*. New York: Yeshiva University, 1987.

Professor Yehouda Shenhav, 'The Truth About Jewish Assets in Iraq,' *The Scribe*, Issue 70, October 1998.

Aryeh Shmuelevitz, 'Bursa,' *Encyclopaedia Judaica*, Volume 4, column 1531. Jerusalem: Keter, 1972.

Aryeh Shmuelevitz, 'Zionism, Jews and the Ottoman Empire as reflected in the weekly *Hamevasser*,' in Tudor Parfitt with Yulia Egorova, *Jews, Muslims and Mass Media: Mediating the 'Other.'* London: Routledge, 2004.

Alex Sholem, 'Come Home, Gaddafi's son invites Libyan Jews to return,' *Jewish News*, 16 April 2004.

Leon H. Spotts, 'Benider, Moroccan family,' *Encyclopaedia Judaica*, Volume 4, column 520. Jerusalem: Keter, 1972.

J.H. Steinschneider, 'Ibn Ezra, Isaac (12th century),' *Encyclopaedia Judaica*, Volume 8, column 1170. Jerusalem: Keter, 1972.

Yoav Stern, 'Alexandria's Jews: 20 women and 3 men,' *Ha'aretz*, 17 September 2006.

Leon Symons, 'The Arab king who's proud of his Jews,' *Jewish Chronicle*, 15 August 2008.

Leon Symons, 'Iranian "Mossad" ring broken,' *Jewish Chronicle*, 28 November 2008.

Sasha Troy, 'The last three Jews of Qamishli,' *Jerusalem Post*, 9 February 2006.

Batsheva Tsur, 'Jews in Syria Still "hostage,"' *Jerusalem Post*, 10 January 1993.

Regina Waldman, 'A Jewish Woman from Muslim Society Reflects on Life in Islamic Lands,' *JIMENA* (Jews Indigenous to the Middle East and North Africa), 2006.

Avraham Yaari, 'Baghdad, Hebrew Printing,' *Encyclopaedia Judaica*, Volume 4, column 93. Jerusalem: Keter, 1972.

Mohammed Zaatari, 'Only Two Lebanese Jews are Registered to Vote in Sidon,' *Daily Star* (Beirut), 12 May 2009.

Golda Zafer-Smith, 'Simhat Torah in Fez, 2005,' *Jewish Renaissance*, April 2006.

WEBSITES

'Alex Cinema, Cinematographers': http://www.bibalex.org/AlexCinema/cinematographers/Togo_Mizrahi.html.

'Haim El Muallim' Farhi (1740-1818)': www.farhi.org/history.htm.

Jewish Virtual Library, 'The Virtual Jewish History Tour, Fez': www.jewish-virtuallibrary.org/jsource/vjw/Fez.html.

'Joint Statement: Pakistani Taliban's treatment of Sikhs,' 2 May 2009: www.indianmuslims.in.

Sarah Szymkowicz, 'The Virtual Jewish History Tour, Yemen': http://www.jewishvirtuallibrary.org/jsource/vjw/Yemen.html.

MANUSCRIPTS

Samuel J. Cohen, 'My Exodus from Egypt,' Tel Aviv, 10 May 2009.

Bertha Fattal, 'Bertha's Memoirs,' 2008.

Danna Harman, Yemen diary, 2002.

Marc Khedr (Moura Amin Khedr), 'This is my life: my internment at Abu Zaabal and Tora concentrations camps,' written August 2002, revised October 2004.

Soraya Sarhaddi Nelson, 'In Afghanistan, a Jewish Community of One.' National Public Radio, 8 December 2008.

Ovadia Yerushalmy, 'The Longest Five Minutes in My Life,' Tel Aviv, 10 May 2009.

NEWSPAPERS AND MAGAZINES

Al-Ahram (Cairo)

Annual Report (International Association of Jews from Egypt)

Bassatine News, A Community Chronicle put out by the Jewish Community Council (JCC) of Cairo

Boston Globe

Canadian Jewish News

Daily Star (Beirut)

Egyptian Official Gazette

Gazette, Government of Iraq, Baghdad

Ha'aretz

Hamodia: The Newspaper of Torah Judaism

Hansard, Parliamentary Debates, House of Commons, London

IAJE Newsletter (International Association of Jews from Egypt)

Jerusalem Post

Jerusalem Report

Jewish Chronicle (London)

JIMENA Voice (Jews Indigenous to the Middle East and North Africa)

Le Monde
Le Soir Echos (Rabat)
London Jewish News (Ontario, Canada)
Los Angeles Times
Manchester Guardian
New York Times
Revue des Etudes Juives (R.E.J.)
Revue egyptienne de droit international
The Jerusalem Quarterly
The Scribe: Journal of Descendants of Babylonian Jewry. London, 1971-2002
    (75 issues)
Washington Jewish Week

ARCHIVES

Beth Hatefutsoth Photo Archive (Tel Aviv)
Central Zionist Archives (Jerusalem)
HIAS (Hebrew Immigrant Aid Society) Archive (Baltimore)
Israel Foreign Ministry Archive (Jerusalem)
National Archives (Kew)
National Archives (Washington)
Weizmann Archive (Rehovot)
World Jewish Congress Archive (New York)

INDEX

Compiled by the author